PAINTING · COLOR · HISTORY

COLLECTION PLANNED AND DIRECTED BY
ALBERT SKIRA

Modern Painting

Text by Maurice Raynal

SKIRA

We wish to extend our sincere and grateful thanks to the Curators and Directors of Museums and to the many private collectors who, with unfailing kindness, gave us access to the works of art in their keeping.

TRANSLATED BY STUART GILBERT

★

The Planning of this Book:
How and Why

WE WOULD begin by mentioning that the present work is completely different from our three-volume History of Modern Painting published some years ago. The method we have followed in the planning of this book is an entirely new departure, and no less new the treatment and arrangement of our subject-matter. It is undeniable that art today presents such a bewildering multiplicity of styles and tendencies that even the best-informed art lover is often at a loss to get his bearings. Here he will find, we believe, what in other fields would be called a precision instrument; a means both to just evaluation and an accurate understanding of the subject.

At first sight the art of the first half of this century strikes us as a complex of conflicting trends. No sooner have the Fauves made good than the Cubists take arms against them; Futurism challenges Neo-Plasticism, the champions of Dada make war on the Expressionists—and so on all along the line. Yet, despite their seeming antagonisms, these movements interlock in a coherent sequence, and in fact when there is talk of "Modern Painting," we have a good idea of what is meant.

A good idea, but—let us admit—a somewhat vague one. For a real understanding of Modern Painting we need to study the various movements in their chronological order and to ascertain how they reacted on each other. Also we need to follow the evolution of individual artists who, though in the first instance stemming from one or other of these groups, struck out on lines of their own, in isolation, and found their own solutions to art's eternal problems. Thus several lines of development, of individuals and groups, run parallel, and for an appreciation of their significance have to be examined concurrently, in the light of their exchanges and cross-currents, and also in the context of certain great exhibitions, landmarks in the history of 20th-century art.

Obviously an entirely new method of presentation of the subject was called for, if we were both to bring before our readers' eyes the vast and infinitely varied achievements of Modern Art and at the same time to provide a clear and searching analysis of their significance. Two duties fall to the historian: that of setting forth the facts, and that of explaining them; we believe that the lay-out of this book meets both requirements.

(1) Each page is dated and the reader is thus enabled to follow, year by year, the course of events and assign each work its place in the chronology of art.

(2) In order to combine the historical method—a study of the evolution of the various movements as a continuous process—with the comparative method—the collation of outstanding works produced during a given period—we include a number of folded pages which, when extended, give a synoptic view of the most significant works, placed side by side. Thus, according as these pages are left folded or opened out, the reader can follow the historical evolution of the various movements, or pause to compare and appraise their several achievements at a given point of time.

This system of presentation has seemed to us at once the most logical and the most revealing and we venture to hope that these innovations will throw new light on one of the most fertile and in some ways most bewildering periods in art's long history.

The Genesis of Modern Painting

From Goya to Seurat

ASKED to sum up his impressions of the 19th century, an art-historian might describe it as pre-eminently an age of discovery. The inquiring spirit of the French Encyclopaedists and Romanticism had made good; the study both of nature and of man preoccupied the thinkers of the day. And, thanks to the forceful personalities of great artists, painting underwent drastic and far-reaching changes during the 19th century. Such was the eagerness to explore new fields that a taste for research developed which had had no equivalent in the previous centuries, for the good reason that the basic concepts of painting had hardly changed at all since the Quattrocento. Thus it has seemed desirable to begin this work with a survey of this legacy of the recent past which our modern painters have taken over and transformed in the light of their own discoveries.

As a result of the replacement of the collective spirit of the past by individualism, we find, to begin with, a cult of the Ego carried to remarkable lengths. Thus the objectivity of classical art was done away with; the painter spoke of expressing his subject "as he felt it," not as it intrinsically was. In fact his aim was now to "find himself," that is to discover and define his own personality. Even in speaking of his Cubist Period, when objective veracity was held to be the artist's chief concern, Picasso himself has said: "When we invented Cubism, it was not just to make cubist paintings but to express what was within ourselves." In other words the Cubists envisaged a new kind of objectivity, in terms of which each artist created his private world. Painting was no longer a means of celebrating religion, affairs of state, or any popular ideal, nor yet of depicting the human figure for some practical purpose (the function of photography). Rather, painting was progressing towards that autonomy and freedom from representational service which has culminated in abstract art, in which the picture is a product of the artist's sheer physical urge to paint, and nothing more.

Obviously such a program, if it was to be carried out successfully, called for new artistic means and a methodical approach. Doubtless it answered to that general desire for knowledge which the scientific discoveries of the age had stimulated, and which, viewed from the angle of Romanticism, seemed to authorize not only the exploration of the Ego but a surrender to its demands, indeed a cult of them. For the host of new, amazing inventions due to the advance of science seemed to sponsor, if indirectly, the claims of the imagination, hitherto regarded as an unsafe guide, and, by the same token, undermined the authority of the reasoning faculty, whose conclusions now seemed too mechanical and anyhow unfruitful. Common sense, too, came under fire and, with it, the mandate of "good taste." Intuition took the place of observation, that short-cut to the picture. And, finally, now that human personality was in the ascendant, some artists took to investigating the significance of dreams and that mysterious underworld of the subconscious in which so many sensational discoveries had recently been made. This partly accounts for the curious effect produced by those modern paintings divested of any reference to reality which are known as abstract art. This, too, is why our 20th-century painting, as regards its more drastic innovations, has ceased to be inspired exclusively by the strict impersonality of classical art. The modern artist is as indefatigable as the scientist in seeking out new fields to conquer, not out of idle curiosity but with a desire to extend the range of his technical means. To this end he studies all art-forms, ancient or modern, familiar or little known, and investigates the art of prehistoric ages, lesser known works of classical antiquity, primitive art of all periods and climes, folk art, the art of children and even that of madmen. On the scientific side he favors the more esoteric sciences; similarly he prefers experimental types of literature and philosophy, non-Euclidean geometry, new inventions, and shows an interest in machinery (from which artists like Fernand Léger evolved a whole aesthetic). In these retrospects and explorations the artist's aim is not to discover, like the fashion-designer, motifs to imitate or to modernize, but to elicit the intrinsic significance of certain procedures, the trade secrets so to say of the great creators; all in fact that might facilitate his own "experiments."

Briefly, then, all the classical conceptions of art were cast into the melting-pot, from the prerogative of Reason to the data of sensory experience (now suspected of being both untrustworthy and inhibitive). Paradoxically enough, the observation of nature herself became more fruitful, now that the eye was no longer regarded as an automatic registering apparatus like the camera but as a living organ whose operations were largely conditioned by the mind. These new conceptions were not so to speak spontaneously generated in the minds of our 20th-century painters; rather, they stemmed from those of their immediate predecessors, whose tendencies and aspirations they carried a stage, or several stages, further.

It was Goya whose profound resentment of authority and skeptical turn of mind led him instinctively to question the classical conception of the "divine right" of Reason in the realm of art. Indeed he allowed himself a revolutionary, anarchic freedom such as no artist before him had dared to arrogate. Nor was he merely a destructive force; while making a clean sweep of time-honored traditions, he also built up in his imagination a new world of his own, a fantastic world peopled with the visions welling up from the depths of his subconscious self. Moreover, in saying "My brush has no right to see better than I" he was the first to voice that mistrust of the retinal image and reliance on the mind which were to be basic to 20th-century art. He adumbrated, too, the drastic changes in pictorial technique that have taken place in the present century when he said "color does not exist in nature any more than line," and "only advancing and receding planes exist." These remarks lie at the origin of a procedure that became generalized: the definition of forms by means of volumes.

The romantic revival which took place in the 19th century assumed an interesting form in the work of Ingres, for he attempted to subject to classical discipline the promptings of his sensual temperament and an instinctive desire for freedom of expression. He set much store on spontaneity and the example he gave in this respect had a remarkable and salutary influence on 19th-century art. While, to his thinking, Raphael stood for absolute perfection Ingres took good care not to copy him, and felt more drawn to the Fontainebleau School and Primaticcio, the more human qualities of whose art appealed to him. He spoke appreciatively about the "early gropings of certain arts" more perfect in his eyes than many masterpieces. In Ingres' art we can discern a constant struggle between the reasoning mind and instinct. It was with reference to the occasions when the latter got the upper hand that Ingres' classical-minded pupil Amaury-Duval spoke of his master's "insouciance." As a matter of fact "insouciance" of this kind was, as we shall see, the keynote of the new art of the 20th century. By the same token comments were often made on certain alleged mistakes in Ingres' work—mistakes that his successors came to regard as so many demonstrations of the creative freedom of the artist.

So much for Ingres' "insouciance." Another word that soon came into favor was "impression," and Corot was the first to use it in connection with painting. He aimed at bodying forth the emotions he experienced when gazing at scenes of nature; and this insistence on the artist's direct emotive responses—his impression—pointed the way towards Impressionism. "To be oneself," he added, "is the only way of moving the beholder."

Courbet was more than a magnificent technician whose craftsmanship has never been excelled. He also introduced into painting a note of generous indignation with the injustices of the social order, and this new conception of the artist as a man with a mission has been taken over by not a few 20th-century artists. But Courbet's greatest service to art was of a more purely painterly order. True, as a realist he was in the long lineage of French painters that extends from the makers of the mediaeval frescos to Le Nain and Chardin. But he also devised new methods of rendering volumes, procedures that Cézanne was to develop and amplify, and which were carried still farther by the vanguard 20th-century painters.

This view of painting as a law unto itself, and its corollaries, stimulated painters thoroughly to overhaul the technique of their art. Under the auspices of that individualism which, as a result of the romantic movement, had been endorsed and practiced by artists of the

19th century, the 20th-century artist could safely ignore the personal reactions of his predecessors. He had his own temperament and it largely sufficed him. So it was not their personalities, but the artistic means of his great forerunners that he studied with close attention. In the case of Delacroix, for instance, he was struck by the analogies between painting and music that Delacroix had discovered. In pursuance of the theory expounded by Baudelaire of "correspondences" (between the arts), both the methods and the terminology of music were taken over. Delacroix's vivid, eye-filling colors were described as "resonant," his translucent, vibrant brushstrokes as creating "discords," "harmonies," or "polyphonies" as the case might be, and the term "color orchestration" came into vogue. Moreover the counterpoint of primaries and complementaries so brilliantly exploited by Delacroix directly pointed the way to the so-called rainbow palette of the Impressionists.

These influences took effect under varied aspects. The starting-off point of Impressionism was the artists' "discovery" of nature, the love of which had been inculcated by novelists and poets of the romantic age. And it was this love of nature that gave the Impressionists the idea of studying, with an observant eye, the changes perpetually taking place in the appearances of the natural world. By a quite logical process Corot's idea of *emotion* as the source of the creative impulse was given a wider application, or, rather, included in *sensation*— a purely painterly sensation necessitating the discovery of a technique for expressing it. One of the new means was a pictorial element hitherto unnoticed, that of *atmosphere*. Now that artists, whether deliberately or unconsciously, were sponsoring painting's claim to autonomy vis-à-vis the subject, many other discoveries were made by the Impressionists, and a whole technique was evolved for recording on canvas the most fleeting aspects of nature. Later on a similar technique was used for subjects of a wholly permanent, unchanging character. But henceforth every form of intellectualism and by the same token every academic influence was superseded by a tendency towards expression of the artist's sensory response to visual data. And though there have been reactions against this tendency it has persisted throughout 20th-century art. Indeed we can be practically sure of finding traces of Impressionism when we examine the work of any 20th-century painter, and this despite the fact that the concept of Space has replaced that of atmosphere—though not so drastically that the latter is absolutely excluded in all cases. Moreover, though for many years Monet's heroic ventures were under a cloud, they are now seen to possess (if not from the strictly impressionist viewpoint, from that of his wonderful handling of what is practically abstract "atmospheric" color) an almost startling modernism.

Cézanne, again, had opened new horizons with his handling of the "sensation." Hitherto it had seemed enough to give a plain, faithful record of its impact on the sensibility. But while to understand and to say what one has understood is one thing, to create by means of the intelligence is another. Cézanne had not been content merely with possessing sensory responses more active and alert than those of ordinary people, and instead of expending his "little thrill" (as he called it) solely on the depiction of the object, he used it for reconstructing its basic form in terms of a new, architecturally ordered composition. And our 20th-century painters' great esteem of Cézanne is largely due to the fact that this aesthetic was arrived at by him intuitively and instinctively, without recourse to the deductive reasoning employed by the great masters of the classical epoch.

If this book begins under the aegis of Seurat it is because, of all the experimentalists of the last century, Seurat was the most perspicacious. By a fusion of expert knowledge with far-ranging imagination, he created that new kind of space which, replacing the concept of "atmospheric ambiance," has become the chief concern of the leading 20th-century painters. It was he, too, who, starting out from the empirical Cézannesque handling of optical sensation, demonstrated most lucidly the principles of that two-dimensional perspective which has been basic to the greatest works produced during the first half of the present century.

1884-1906

FROM THE SALON DES INDÉPENDANTS TO FAUVISM

1884   A new art group, "Les Vingt," is founded at Brussels by Octave Maus (January) • Founding of the Société des Indépendants in Paris: Seurat, Signac, Cross, Redon, Angrand, Dubois-Pillet. Seurat exhibits his **Baignade à Asnières** (Tate Gallery, London). Divisionism • Launching of **La Revue Indépendante** (edited by Félix Fénéon) • Birth of Modigliani, Schmidt-Rottluff, Beckmann, Brusselmans.

1885   Pissarro meets Theo Van Gogh, then Signac and Seurat; falls under the spell of the pointillist technique • Birth of Delaunay and La Fresnaye.

1886   Eighth and Last Group Exhibition of the Impressionists (May 15—June 15, 17 participants), Rue Laffitte, Paris • Seurat at Honfleur. Exhibits **La Grande Jatte** (Art Institute, Chicago) at the second Salon des Indépendants • Fénéon publishes **Les Impressionnistes en 1886**; and Zola, **L'Œuvre** • Gauguin's first stay at Pont-Aven in Brittany, at the Pension Gloanec (June-November) • Vincent Van Gogh arrives in Paris (March); meets Lautrec, Pissarro, Degas, Gauguin, Seurat • The Douanier Rousseau exhibits for the first time at the Indépendants, showing four pictures • Moréas publishes his **Manifesto** and launches a review, **Le Symboliste**, with Gustave Kahn • Publication of Rimbaud's **Illuminations** • Munch joins the group known as "The Bohemians of Christiania," whose leading figure is the poet Hans Jäger • Birth of Kokoschka and Permeke.

1887   Antoine founds the Théâtre Libre in Paris • Exhibition of "Les Vingt" at Brussels • Toulouse-Lautrec paints his first scenes of Montmartre life • Birth of Juan Gris, Marcel Duchamp, Marc Chagall, Hans Arp, Kurt Schwitters • Death of Jules Laforgue • Mallarmé publishes his **Poésies complètes**.

1888   Gauguin's second stay at Pont-Aven. Renewed contact with Emile Bernard: Cloisonnism, Synthetism. Sérusier paints **The Talisman** • Bonnard, Vuillard, Maurice Denis, Ranson and Sérusier meet at the Académie Julian, Paris • Seurat at Port-en-Bessin. Exhibits **Les Poseuses** (Barnes Foundation, Merion, Pa.) and **La Parade** (Stephen C. Clark Collection, New York) • At Ostend James Ensor paints his large-scale work: **The Entrance of Christ into Brussels** • Birth of Chirico and Schlemmer.

1889   Paris World's Fair. The Palace of Machinery. The Eiffel Tower • Exhibition of the Impressionist and Synthetist Group at the Café Volpini; the Nabis are much impressed • First number of **La Plume** appears • Verlaine publishes **Parallèlement**; Bergson, **Les Données immédiates de la Conscience** • Lautrec's first appearance at the Indépendants: **Au bal du Moulin de la Galette** (Art Institute, Chicago).

1890   Founding of La Société Nationale des Beaux-Arts by Puvis de Chavannes, Rodin, Carrière • Paul Fort founds the Théâtre d'Art; Alfred Vallette launches **Le Mercure de France** • Seurat at Gravelines. Exhibits **Le Chahut** (Kröller-Müller Museum, Otterlo) • Gauguin makes a long stay at Le Pouldu with Séguin, Filiger, Meyer de Haan. Returns to Paris in December • Munch visits Paris, sees pictures by Pissarro, Seurat, Lautrec and, at Theo Van Gogh's gallery, by Gauguin and Vincent Van Gogh • Death of Van Gogh (July 29) • Birth of Morandi.

1891   Retrospective Van Gogh Exhibition at the Indépendants • Death of Seurat (March 26) • Gauguin auction sale at the Hôtel Drouot (February 23). He leaves for Tahiti (April 4) • Rouault enrolls at the Ecole des Beaux-Arts in Elie Delaunay's class; this teacher is soon succeeded by Gustave Moreau • Launching of **La Revue Blanche** by the Natanson brothers • Drawings by Steinlen in the **Gil Blas** illustrated magazine • Gatherings of Symbolist poets at the Café Voltaire • Aurier's Manifesto of Symbolist Painting in **Le Mercure de France** • Bonnard shows for the first time at the Indépendants • Lautrec's first poster for the Moulin Rouge • Birth of Max Ernst.

1892   Lautrec's first color lithographs. Posters for Le Divan japonais and Les Ambassadeurs • Seurat Retrospective Exhibition at **La Revue Blanche** • First Salon de la Rose-Croix at Durand-Ruel's • The Douanier Rousseau paints **Bonne Fête** and **Le Centenaire de l'Indépendance** • Matisse comes to Paris, enrolls at the Académie Julian • Munch sends 55 pictures to the exhibition of the Berlin Artists' Association, where they are sharply criticized and withdrawn after one week • Rejected at the Salon du Champ-de-Mars, H. de Groux's **Christ Scorned** is exhibited at the Palais des Arts libéraux, Paris. Warmly praised by Puvis de Chavannes, Redon, Degas, Carrière, Mallarmé, Mirbeau, Geffroy and others • Birth of Gromaire.

1893   Lugné-Poe founds the Théâtre de l'Œuvre. Sets and programs by Vuillard and his friends • Matisse enrolls at the Ecole des Beaux-Arts, meets Rouault in Gustave Moreau's class. Rouault paints **Samson tournant sa meule** • Opening of the Vollard Gallery • Gauguin returns from Tahiti, exhibits 40 pictures at Durand-Ruel's (November) • First exhibition of the Munich Secession: Böcklin, Corot, Courbet, Liebermann, Millet • Exhibition in Berlin of pictures rejected for the "Great Exhibition." Munch is a committee-member and shows his works • Birth of Miro.

1894 Uproar over the Caillebotte bequest to the Luxembourg Museum, Paris (executor of the will is Renoir) • First murals by Vuillard • Appearance of **Le Rire** and **L'Ymagier** (R. de Gourmont, A. Jarry) • Odilon Redon Exhibition at the Durand-Ruel Gallery (April) • Vuillard makes sets for Ibsen's **Master Builder** at the Théâtre de l'Œuvre. Birth of Soutine.

1895 Cézanne Exhibition at the Vollard Gallery (November-December, over 100 pictures) • Lautrec visits London. Sets for La Goulue's booth at the Foire du Trône • Salon de la Nationale: stained-glass windows by Tiffany after designs by Lautrec, Bonnard, Vuillard, Sérusier, Vallotton • Vollard publishes **Quelques aspects de la vie de Paris**. Lithographs by Lautrec, Bonnard, Vallotton • Gauguin's second auction sale at the Hôtel Drouot. He leaves again for Tahiti • Publication of Rimbaud's **Poésies complètes** with a preface by Verlaine • Munch's first lithographs printed at A. Clot's in Paris • Launching in Berlin of the magazine **Pan**. Editors are Bierbaum and Meier-Graefe; among the contributors are Munch, Lautrec, Vallotton, Signac • Rouault fails to win the Prix de Rome at the Ecole des Beaux-Arts; Gustave Moreau advises him to leave the school. Rouault exhibits at the Salon des Artistes Français • Picasso enters the School of Fine Arts at Barcelona • Birth of Moholy-Nagy and André Beaudin.

1896 Bonnard's first one-man show at Durand-Ruel's (49 paintings, posters, lithographs) • Lautrec travels in Spain • **Ubu Roi** performed at the Théâtre de l'Œuvre (December 10) • Death of Verlaine and E. de Goncourt • Marcel Proust publishes **Les Plaisirs et les Jours** • First Exhibition of the "Libre Esthétique" Group at Brussels • S. Bing opens the Art Nouveau Gallery, Rue de Provence, Paris. Munch Exhibition. Munch frequents the circle of Mallarmé and of the Mercure de France • The magazine **Die Jugend** launched at Munich (January) • Kandinsky and Jawlensky arrive at Munich from Russia. • Lautrec does the program-cover for Oscar Wilde's **Salome** • Picasso enters the School of Fine Arts in Madrid • Birth of André Masson.

1897 **La Revue Blanche** publishes Gauguin's manuscript **Noa-Noa** • In Tahiti Gauguin paints his vast work: **Whence come we? What are we? Whither go we?** • The Douanier Rousseau exhibits **La Bohémienne endormie** at the Indépendants • Founding of the Vienna Secession, with Gustav Klimt as chairman • The cabaret "Els 4 Gats" is started at Barcelona in a neo-Gothic setting designed by Puig y Cadalfach. Picasso holds his first exhibition there • Rouault paints a series of fantastic landscapes on sacred and profane themes • Munch's **Frieze of Life** is exhibited at the Salon des Indépendants.

1898 Mellerio publishes **La Lithographie originale en couleurs** • Bonnard illustrates Peter Nansen's **Marie**; Lautrec, Jules Renard's **Histoires naturelles**. Lautrec Exhibition in London • Death of Stéphane Mallarmé (September 9) • Matisse exhibits **La Desserte** at the Salon de la Nationale. Stays in Corsica and at Toulouse • Marquet works at Arcueil and in the Luxembourg Gardens, Paris • Friesz enrolls at the Ecole des Beaux-Arts, Paris, in Bonnat's class, where Dufy joins him in 1900 • Robert Delaunay shows a precocious talent for painting at the Lycée Michelet, at Vanves, on the outskirts of Paris; among his schoolmates are Robert Rey, Maurice Raynal, Eugène Marsan. Their drawing teacher is Emile Schuffenecker, the painter and friend of Gauguin • Rodin's statue of **Balzac** is refused by the Société des Gens de Lettres • Vienna: First issue of the Secession periodical **Ver Sacrum** in January. First Secession exhibition is a great success. On November 12, opening of the second exhibition and dedication of the House of the Secession, built by Josef M. Olbrich • Paul Klee studies at Knirr's in Munich • Death of Gustave Moreau. Rouault becomes curator of the Moreau Museum • Birth of Magritte.

1899 Group Exhibition of the Nabis at Durand-Ruel's. **Homage to Odilon Redon** • Second Cézanne Exhibition at Vollard's • Chocquet auction sale at the Hôtel Drouot • Matisse, Derain, Jean Puy, Laprade meet at the Académie Carrière, Paris • Signac publishes his study: **D'Eugène Delacroix au Néo-Impressionnisme** • Special issue of the review **La Plume** devoted to James Ensor • Death of Sisley • Derain and Vlaminck meet at Chatou • Nolde comes to Paris and enrolls at the Académie Julian • Birth of Tamayo • Salon des Cent held at 31, Rue Bonaparte, Paris. Posters for the show are done by Ibels, Jossot, Boutet, Lautrec, Berthon, Bonnard, Ensor and others • Salon de la Rose-Croix at the Durand-Ruel Gallery • The Catalan painter Nonell exhibits at Vollard's • Berlin: Founding of the Berlin Secession, with Max Liebermann as chairman. First exhibition opens on May 20. Launching of the magazine **Die Insel** • Vienna: First issue of the magazine **Die Fackel**, edited by Karl Kraus.

1900 Gaudi constructs the labyrinth of the **Parque Grüell** at Barcelona • Paris World's Fair. Centennial Exhibition of French art at the Champ-de-Mars • Félix Fénéon organizes a Retrospective Seurat Exhibition at La Revue Blanche • Bonnard illustrates Verlaine's **Parallèlement** for Vollard (109 color lithographs) • Picasso's first stay in Paris • Birth of Yves Tanguy • Dufy comes to Paris, enrolls at the Ecole des Beaux-Arts in Bonnat's class • Munich: Kandinsky, Klee and Marc study at the Academy; no personal contact between them as yet. The "Phalanx" group of artists is formed • Paula Modersohn comes to Paris, studies at the Académie Colarossi. Much impressed by a showing of Cézanne's works at Vollard's. Meeting with Emil Nolde • Weimar: Max Beckmann attends the Art School.

1901 Friesz meets Pissarro. Guillaume Apollinaire comes to Paris. Redon Exhibition at Vollard's. Van Gogh Exhibition at the Bernheim-Jeune Gallery. Derain introduces Vlaminck to Matisse during a visit to the Van Gogh Exhibition. Matisse goes to see Derain and Vlaminck at Chatou • Dresden: Kirchner and Bleyl study architecture at the Technical Institute • Madrid: Picasso launches a short-lived review called **Arte Joven**. Exhibits pastels in Barcelona. Second trip to Paris. First Paris exhibition at Vollard's with Iturrino. Meeting with Max Jacob. Beginning of the Blue Period • Death of Toulouse-Lautrec.

1902 Matisse and Picasso exhibit at Berthe Weill's. Picasso returns to Spain • Lautrec Memorial Exhibition at the Salon des Indépendants. Lautrec Exhibition at Durand-Ruel's. Vollard publishes **Daphnis et Chloé** with lithographs by Bonnard • Munich: Kandinsky opens his own art school and becomes chairman of the "Phalanx" • Picasso returns to Paris, shares a room with Max Jacob (October) • Berlin: Shown in the Secession Exhibition are 28 pictures by Munch (including the **Frieze of Life**), 3 pictures by Kandinsky and Hodler's **William Tell** • Picasso paints a **Blue Landscape** whose composition and lay-out foreshadow the Cubist architecture to come • The exhibition of 15th- and 16th-century Flemish painting at Bruges much impresses Georges Minne (1866-1941), Gustave van de Woestyne (1881-1947) and Valerius de Saedeleer (1867-1941), leaders of a group of artists working in the small village of Laethem-Saint-Martin. A second group, made up of Permeke (1886-1952), de Smet (1887-1943) and Van den Berghe (1883-1939), works in the same village until 1914 • Dresden: Impressionist Exhibition at the Arnold Gallery. Heckel, Kirchner and Bleyl work together.

1903 Acting on Rambosson's initiative, Desvallières, Rouault and Piot found the Salon d'Automne, seconded by Matisse, Marquet and Bonnard • Picasso settles in Paris at 13, Rue Ravignan, in the "Bateau Lavoir." Meets Jarry, Raynal, Salmon, Cremnitz • Deaths of Gauguin, Pissarro and Whistler • La Revue Blanche ceases publication • Matisse, Marquet, Dufy, Friesz exhibit at Salon des Indépendants • Matisse, Marquet, Puy, Manguin exhibit at Berthe Weill's • Gauguin Exhibitions at Vollard's and Salon d'Automne • Berlin: Works by Cézanne, Gauguin, Van Gogh, Bonnard and Munch exhibited at the Secession. Launching of the magazine **Kunst und Künstler**, published by Cassirer • Vienna: Secession Exhibition of Impressionist and Neo-Impressionist Painting (Seurat's **La Grande Jatte**) • Kandinsky travels to Tunis and Kairwan • Marc visits Paris for the first time • In Bern, Klee begins his series of grotesque etchings • Founding of the "Wiener Werkstätte" (Vienna Workshop).

1904 Matisse at Saint-Tropez with Signac. First exhibition at Vollard's (preface by Roger Marx) • Braque comes to Paris. Enrolls at the Ecole des Beaux-Arts, then at the Académie Humbert • Kandinsky exhibits at the Salon d'Automne and at the Exposition Nationale des Beaux-Arts, Paris • Cézanne exhibits at the Salon d'Automne (42 pictures) and in Berlin at Cassirer's • Picasso paints **Woman Ironing** • Utrillo paints at Montmagny, near Paris • The sculptor Brancusi and the writer Wilhelm Uhde arrive in Paris • Matisse tries his hand at Pointillism • Marquet paints the **Portrait of André Rouveyre** • Derain studies at the Académie Julian • Arp makes his first stay in Paris • Birth of Salvador Dali at Figueras, near Barcelona • Kirchner discovers Negro art and carvings by the Palau islanders at the Ethnological Museum in Dresden • August Macke enters the School of Applied Art and the Academy, at Düsseldorf • Munch completes the second **Frieze of Life** for Linde, at Lübeck • Neo-Impressionist Exhibition of the "Phalanx" at Munich. Cézanne, Gauguin and Van Gogh Exhibition at the Munich Art Association. Founding and first exhibition of the **Deutscher Künstlerbund**, an alliance of artists and groups with modern tendencies • Kokoschka studies at the School of Arts and Crafts in Vienna • Hodler Exhibition (91 pictures) at the Vienna Secession.

1905 Seurat (40 works) and Van Gogh Exhibitions at Salon des Indépendants • Picasso meets Apollinaire, who publishes an illustrated article on the painter in **La Plume**, issue of May 15. Picasso travels to Holland. Enters on his Pink Period. Etches a series of **Saltimbanques**. Paints **Les trois Hollandaises** • Pascin arrives in Paris • At Montmartre Vlaminck meets Van Dongen, Picasso, Max Jacob and Apollinaire. Exhibits at the Indépendants • At the Salon d'Automne: Vlaminck, Derain, Matisse, Manguin, Marquet, Van Dongen, Puy, Valtat. The critic Louis Vauxcelles singles out several exhibitors as "fauves" (wild beasts); the term catches on; hence the name "Fauvism" • Derain joins Matisse at Collioure, where the latter begins **Luxe, Calme et Volupté** • Rouault exhibits at the Salon d'Automne—not, however, in the Fauve gallery • Vollard buys some 30 pictures from Picasso for 2000 francs • Paula Modersohn studies at the Académie Julian under Cottet, whose work greatly influences her • Fernand Léger settles in "La Ruche," Rue de Dantzig, Paris • John Marin and Max Weber come to Paris • Jawlensky paints in Brittany and Provence • Formation of the "Die Brücke" group in Dresden (Heckel, Kirchner, Schmidt-Rottluff, Bleyl) • Nolde does the **Phantasien** etchings in Berlin • The "Stylists" grouped around Gustav Klimt leave the Vienna Secession.

1906 Gris, Modigliani and Severini come to Paris • Braque exhibits at the Indépendants • Gauguin Exhibition at the Salon d'Automne • Matisse buys Negro statuettes from Sauvage, a curio-dealer in the Rue de Rennes, Paris • Picasso and Matisse meet at Gertrude Stein's • Matisse exhibits 55 pictures at the Druet Gallery. Leaves his studio at 19, Quai Saint-Michel, moving first to the former Couvent des Oiseaux in the Rue de Sèvres, then to the former Couvent du Sacré-Cœur • Vollard buys up all the pictures in Vlaminck's studio • At the Salon des Indépendants, grouping 5500 works this year, Matisse exhibits **Le Bonheur de vivre** • Picasso takes an interest in archaic, Iberian and Negro art. Begins work on **Les Demoiselles d'Avignon** • The Douanier Rousseau meets Apollinaire, Delaunay, Picasso, Vlaminck and others • Fernand Léger paints in Corsica under the influence of Matisse. Together with Arcos, Duhamel, Mercereau and Vildrac, Albert Gleizes founds the "Abbaye de Créteil" • Pascin makes drawings for the German magazine **Simplicissimus** • Kandinsky works at Sèvres, near Paris, and exhibits at the Salon d'Automne • Death of Cézanne at Aix-en-Provence • Alfred Stieglitz opens the Photo-Secession Gallery, 291 Fifth Avenue, New York • In Berlin Munch does sets for Max Reinhardt's production of Ibsen's **Ghosts**. Munch paints the third **Frieze of Life** for the foyer of the Berlin Kammerspiele • With **Free Spirit** Nolde begins his series of grotesque and religious works. Nolde, Pechstein, and later Cuno Amiet and Axel Gallén become members of "Die Brücke," in Dresden. First Die Brücke album with original engravings comes out. In the autumn Die Brücke stages its first exhibition at Dresden-Löbtau; in the winter, a second exhibition includes works of graphic art. Neo-Impressionist Exhibition at the Arnold Gallery, Dresden, including works by Signac, Seurat, Gauguin and Van Gogh.

Literary and Artistic Life in Paris

★

If we wish to understand the art of Lautrec and that of the great painters during the last decades of the 19th century, we need to have some idea of the atmosphere of Paris at the time, the night life in Montmartre, the ever closer connection between literary and art movements, the great strides made in the technique of illustration, the increasing number of reviews, cabarets, theaters and shows of every imaginable kind, the part played by color lithographs, woodcuts, posters, illustrated books, the first appearance of the cinema—in short the complete change in the décor of Parisian life, and the new way of seeing the world it called for. One of the consequences of this change was the development of a lively interest in art not only amongst the intelligentsia but amongst the general public. Many, however, had an impression that with the declining years of the century a great age was dying and a period of decadence setting in. Thus, like the English artists and poets of the 'nineties, the French Symbolist poets, brilliantly original though they were, were often saddled with the opprobrious epithet of "decadent."

REVIEWS AND MAGAZINES

A great many small reviews and periodicals made their appearance from 1885 onwards, and did much to disseminate the avant-garde theories of the day. Thus in 1886 there appeared successively La Pléiade *(March 1),* Le Décadent *(April 10), and* La Vogue *(April 11), the last-named edited by Léo d'Orfer (then from May 13 by Gustave Kahn, assisted by Fénéon), in which were published Rimbaud's* Illuminations, *Verlaine's* Poètes maudits *and Fénéon's study of Seurat and the Neo-Impressionists. Other magazines launched in this year were* Le Symboliste *(G. Kahn, Moréas, Paul Adam), the "new series" of the* Revue Indépendante, *which proclaimed as its ideal "the union of all the arts in a common effort to refashion modern life," and G. Lecomte's* La Cravache. *In 1889 came* Le Moderniste, *sponsored by Albert Aurier, Gauguin's exponent and Symbolism's chief theorist; and, lastly, Léon Deschamps'* La Plume, *destined to remain until 1904 (as Ernest Raynaud put it) "the most faithful mirror of contemporary aesthetic life." The last-named periodical organized at its office (in the Rue Bonaparte) a permanent exhibition of painters in sympathy with the aims of the review. The "Salon des Cent" published at modest prices color posters, lithographs, reproductions of works in the museums, and devoted special issues not only to poets (Verlaine and Moréas) but also to painters, amongst them Redon and Ensor. January 1890 saw the first issue of the* Mercure de France, *whose program was to give "a complete panorama of the new movement in literature and art." In October 1891 the famous* Revue Blanche *was launched by the Natanson brothers; it brought together all whose names were coming to the fore in literature and art, and championed notably Lautrec and the Nabis. In 1894 came Arsène Alexandre's* Le Rire *and Alfred Jarry's and Remy de Gourmont's* L'Ymagier *which, with masterpieces of ancient* imagerie, *included Gauguin's woodcuts. All these reviews contained illustrations by modern artists, organized exhibitions and devoted much of their space to art movements, while their premises were used for making contacts and the exchange of views on art. Turning to the dailies and weeklies, we must not overlook* Le Gil Blas Illustré *(with Steinlen's drawings) and* Le Figaro *(with Forain's).*

THE THEATERS

This period was remarkable for the number of "art theaters" that now sprang up, and not only were the best symbolist and foreign plays performed in them but, for the first time, young painters were regularly commissioned to design scenery, costumes and programs.

In 1887 Antoine's Théâtre Libre *started its run of uncompromisingly realistic plays. In 1890 Paul Fort founded the* Théâtre d'Art, *seconded by Mallarmé, Verlaine, Verhaeren and Maeterlinck, and Fort recruited Sérusier and Gauguin as designers. A benefit performance for the latter was given on the eve of his sailing for Tahiti. In May 1893 Lugné-Poë founded the* Théâtre de l'Œuvre, *enthusiastically backed by his friends Vuillard, Maurice Denis and Ranson, who played an active part on the production side and employed the new procedures of color lithography and tempera painting for the sets and programs. The Œuvre opened with a production of Ibsen's* Rosmersholm, *with sets by Vuillard, who was, according to Lugné-Poë, "the most interested in the stage and the best art adviser" of the group. The most sensational production was that of* Ubu Roi *on December 10, 1896. Lugné-Poë also employed foreign artists, Burne-Jones and Munch; the latter designed the program of* Peer Gynt. *Nor must we forget the* Théâtre des Pantins *launched in 1897 with Bonnard's puppets, and the famous* Théâtre du Grand-Guignol.

THE CIRCUS, FAIRS, DANCE-HALLS

From the days of Renoir's Clown Musician *and* Circus Girls *(1868) and Degas'* Miss Lola *(1879), scenes of circus life had never lost their appeal for painters. And Toulouse-Lautrec, Seurat, Bonnard and Forain as well as many minor artists continued to explore this rich field of visual adventure.*
Parisians had then the choice of four establishments of this order: the Hippodrome, the Cirque Médrano (which still exists), the Cirque Fernando (now the Cirque d'Hiver) and the Nouveau Cirque (no longer in existence) built in 1866 on the site of the Bal Valentino in the Faubourg Saint-Honoré. The exploits of acrobats, lion-tamers, clowns and circus-riders, no less than the striking color effects of a vast yellow arena ringed round by red-plush tiers of seats in the crude glare of gaslight (the lighting arrangements were still somewhat primitive) fascinated the painters, who found in the circus a host of promising subjects, and often struck up friendships with the performers. Before becoming the mother of Utrillo and herself a great painter, Suzanne Valadon was a circus acrobat. Loie Fuller, Footit and Chocolat, and Monsieur Loyal also provided the artists with subjects for some justly celebrated works.
The periodical Fairs at Neuilly and Le Trône, with their merry-go-rounds and their booths—two panels for the exterior of La Goulue's booth were painted by Lautrec—likewise supplied artists with many exciting themes. Nor must we forget the popular dance-halls, such as the Moulin Rouge, Bullier's and the Moulin de la Galette, which contributed to give this period of Paris life its memorable gaiety and glamour.

MONTMARTRE

In the early days of Impressionism Montmartre was still almost a country village. From 1886 onwards (at the time when Lautrec decided to live there and get its atmosphere on to canvas) it became more and more the center of Paris night-life and, by the same token, the resort of artists, writers and Bohemians in general. There was a spate of shows and entertainments on the famous Butte, and though its somewhat feverish jollity often seemed artificial, this was in keeping with the mores of the period. This was also the heyday of the café-concert, the music-hall and the "cabaret artistique"; two such cabarets, especially, made Parisian history, Rodolphe de Salis' Chat Noir *(with its shadow-plays) and Aristide Bruant's* Le Mirliton.

SPORT

Artists cast an observant eye on the beginnings of the craze for sporting events—athletic contests of all kinds, tennis, foot-races and especially bicycle-racing (round about 1885). The long-distance cycle-races, such as that from Paris to Brest (in which figured such champions as Terront and Corre), as well as track-racing (with Zimmermann, the American), furnished artists with striking themes, in which the hunched-up attitudes of the racing cyclists struck a new note. In January 1885 the Georges Petit Gallery ran an exhibition on the theme "Sport in Art." In 1895 Tristan Bernard, sporting editor of the Revue Blanche, spent most of his time at the Buffalo cycling track, where Lautrec often joined him.

LITHOGRAPHY, POSTERS, ILLUSTRATED BOOKS

Fin-de-siècle *art is characterized by its decorative trend and its exploitation of subsidiary techniques. Thus etching, neglected by all the Impressionists except Pissarro, came into high favor after 1890, Gauguin and Munch revived the woodcut, and the lithograph especially became popular with artists and public. Print-shops opened everywhere in Paris, Munich and Vienna, the centenary of lithography was celebrated in 1895, and specialist periodicals began to appear: in 1895* L'Estampe Originale, *and in 1897* L'Estampe Moderne *and* L'Estampe et l'Affiche. *The coming of color lithography led to a new treatment of the illustrated book; the first venture was that of Maurice Denis, who illustrated Gide's* Voyage d'Urien *in 1893, and the first real success, Bonnard's illustrated* Parallèlement, *appeared in 1900. These led the way to the triumph of poster-art, perhaps the most significant form of expression of this period. It was, in fact, a symbol of the correlation between such diverse arts as book-illustration, the art of the theater and that of the music-hall, to the new developments of which it drew attention. The first color poster was Chéret's, for the Bal Valentino, in 1869; then came Bonnard's France-Champagne poster in 1889; then Lautrec's posters for the Moulin Rouge, beginning in 1891. The historical importance of the poster is great not only because Lautrec put the best of his genius into it, but also because it formed the most direct link between art and life under all its aspects, completely changed the look of the streets, and effectively conditioned the visual responses of the Parisian public to the new trends of art.*

Seurat's Experiments and Theories

From Impressionism to a Color Architecture

FOUNDED in 1884, the *Société des Artistes Indépendants* included some four hundred artists, amongst them Cross, Signac, Dubois-Pillet, Luce, Angrand and Seurat. Their first exhibition took place in May in a temporary shed set up in the Cours des Tuileries, Seurat's *Baignade* figuring in the canteen. It shared the fate of the First Impressionist Exhibition, being furiously attacked by press and public alike.

In 1886 the Impressionists made plans for an Eighth Impressionist Exhibition, to open on May 15 at a gallery in the Rue Laffitte. But the announcement that Seurat and Signac were to take part in it met with a hostile reception. Monet, Renoir, Sisley and Caillebotte withdrew. One of the organizers, Eugène Manet, brother of Edouard Manet who had died in 1883, also objected to the inclusion of Signac and Seurat. As for Degas, he was non-committal; however, he insisted on the deletion of the word "impressionist" from the exhibition poster. Finally Degas, Berthe Morisot, Guillaumin, Pissarro, Schuffenecker, Redon, Signac, Gauguin and Seurat figured in it and the last-named showed his *Sunday Afternoon on the Island of the Grande Jatte*, which was attacked and championed with equal fervor.

Of the art critics only Félix Fénéon had the foresight and courage to speak well of the newly founded "Salon des Indépendants." He became the spokesman of the group soon to be organized by Seurat and Signac and shortly after published a pamphlet, *Les Impressionnistes en 1886*. In this he set forth the theories behind the movement which, originally given the name of Neo-Impressionism, was subsequently called Divisionism, then Pointillism—pending the day when Gauguin derisively named it "Ripipoint" (which might be freely rendered as the "dot-and-carry-one style").

The ideas behind the new movement might well have stemmed from a famous saying of Cézanne: "I have tried to make of Impressionism something solid and abiding like the art of the old masters." For the object of these young artists was to convert the fugitive impressions of Impressionism into something stable, architecturally ordered.

Round about 1884 science was "in the air," and Seurat, like other young painters, took to reading scientific works which, though they had no bearing on aesthetics in the strict sense of the term, dealt with the phenomena of color: N.O. Rood's *The Scientific Theory of Color*, Chevreul's *Principles of Harmony and Contrast of Colors*, and David Sutter's *Phenomena of Sight*.

The conclusion drawn by Seurat from these works might be summed up as follows: the painter's task is not merely to represent light but to make the picture itself a source of light. He painted in pure colors, those of the spectrum, which viewed from the right distance blended automatically in the eye. From a "law" of Chevreul relating to "simultaneous contrasts" of color was deduced the following corollary: "When two objects of different colors are placed side by side, neither keeps its own color and each acquires a new tint due to the influence of the color of the other object." Pissarro, who was much attracted by the new technique, gave a lucid definition of it: "The idea is to substitute optical mixture for the mixture of pigments, and, with this in view, to break up tones into their constituent elements. For optical mixture produces far intenser luminosities than those of pigments mixed on the palette." This was, in short, the program of "Divisionism."

The problem of rendering depth has intrigued artists of all epochs. The Egyptians, Primitives, and mediaeval fresco-painters who were unacquainted with, or deliberately ignored, linear perspective as practiced by the Greeks, gave the impression of employing what came to be known as "flat perspective"—that is to say effects of distance produced by color alone and far more poetic in quality than classical perspective, which was merely imitation of the retinal image. To Seurat's thinking, Divisionism was not enough, the problem of the third dimension had to be faced up to and solved. "Painting," he said, "is the art of hollowing a surface."

GEORGES SEURAT (1859-1891). MODEL STANDING, STUDY FOR "LES POSEUSES," 1887. (10⅛ × 6¾") LOUVRE, PARIS.

GEORGES SEURAT (1859-1891). COURBEVOIE BRIDGE, 1886-1887. (18⅛ × 21 ¾ ")
COURTAULD INSTITUTE, LONDON.

He envisaged a new kind of Space, enabling him to give plastic values to the light-effects he
was trying to secure in terms of his responses to visual experience. This was a repudiation
of impressionist theory, and Seurat's attempt to organize his composition in terms of plasticity
was, for the times, quite a new departure. His naturally classical turn of mind served him
in good stead. The problem he set himself as regards the structure of the picture could be
very simply stated; the artist had to insert three dimensions on a surface that had only two
—obviously without literally boring a hole in it. And to get this effect of "hollowness," or
recession, Seurat had recourse to the classical method of contrasts and analogies, but also
to an interplay of horizontal and vertical lines, of curves and arabesques.

Such in brief are the lines on which Seurat and the other Divisionists initiated a new way
of seeing the world. There is no question that it was in Seurat's own work that these new
methods of "organizing plastic space" were most coherently and logically applied and that he
made a very real contribution to modern art. But the fallacy inherent in this plan of transforming impressionist glimpses of the fleeting into something durable and static led in many
cases to productions that seemed contrived and frigid. Indeed it was only Seurat who used
Pointillism as a constructive, not an analytic element in his composition.

Signac, Cross and even Gauguin, Van Gogh and Pissarro took something from Pointillism,
but each adjusted it, more or less provisionally, to his personal taste, taking as his point
of departure the theories which Seurat himself, who was nothing if not methodical, had
formulated in a sort of code (though reserving for himself the right to modify or add to it at

the prompting of his creative imagination). In a letter dated August 28, 1890, to his friend Maurice Beaubourg, the novelist, he set forth the laws of his aesthetic with almost Aristotelian precision, as follows:

AESTHETIC. Art is harmony. Harmony implies an analogy of contraries and also an analogy of similarities, of tone, hue and line, disposed in relation to their dominants and under the influence of light, in gay, calm or sad combinations.
The contraries are:

For tone, a more $\begin{Bmatrix} \text{luminous} \\ \text{bright} \end{Bmatrix}$ tone as against a darker.

For the hue, the complementaries; as when a certain hue of red is opposed to its complementary color (e.g. red-green; orange-blue; yellow-violet).
For line, lines forming a right angle.
Gaiety of tone is given by the luminous dominant; of hue, by its warm dominant; of line, by lines ascending from the horizontal.
Calm of tone is equality of dark and light; of hue, equality of warm and cool; of line, the horizontal line.
Sadness of tone is given by the dark dominant; of hue, by the cold dominant; of line, by lines descending from the horizontal.

TECHNIQUE. In view of the phenomenon of the duration of a light-impression on the retina, a synthesis necessarily ensues. The means of expression is the optical mixture of the tones and hues (local color and that resulting from illumination, by the sun, by an oil-lamp, by gas and so forth); that is to say, of light elements and their reactions (shadows), according to the laws of contrast, gradation, and irradiation.
The frame should be in a harmony opposed to that of the tones, tints and lines of the picture.

Signac shared honors with Seurat in working out the theories behind the pointillist technique. His *Portrieux* is an experimental work repaying study of the way in which the disciplines of a deliberately provocative geometry correct the fluidity and tremulous light of moribund Impressionism.

PAUL SIGNAC (1863-1935). PORTRIEUX, 1888. (17⅝ × 25⅛") RIJKSMUSEUM KRÖLLER-MÜLLER, OTTERLO.

Vincent Van Gogh

From Seurat's Discoveries to the Expression of Emotion through Color

ABRUPTLY in February 1886 Van Gogh decided to quit Antwerp and move to Paris. His brother Theo gave him a warm welcome and a home at 54 Rue Lepic. He began by enrolling at Cormon's art school; at that time there was little choice. However, it was there he met Lautrec, who became one of his warmest admirers, even on one occasion going so far as to challenge Henri de Groux to a duel for speaking slightingly of Van Gogh at a dinner-party. Visits to the Louvre to begin with, then a study of Impressionism, influenced both his technique and his aesthetic. Also he made friends with Pissarro, Degas, Gauguin, Signac and with Seurat whose large works he particularly liked. He was sometimes to be seen in Père Tanguy's shop and also at the Cabaret du Tambourin. In 1887 he worked at Asnières with Emile Bernard, who became one of his most intimate friends.

What most attracted him was Pointillism. Getting rid of the somber browns of his Dutch Period he gradually took to using brighter colors. Thanks to his amazing proficiency in handling paint, he quickly mastered the secrets of the "dot." During his two years' stay in Paris he

Van Gogh met Seurat in 1887 and came under the spell of Pointillism. "It's a marvelous discovery," he wrote to his brother. "But I already foresee that neither this technique nor any other will become a universally accepted dogma."

VINCENT VAN GOGH (1853-1890). THE RESTAURANT, PARIS. SUMMER 1887. $(17\frac{5}{8} \times 21\frac{1}{8}'')$
RIJKSMUSEUM KRÖLLER-MÜLLER, OTTERLO.

VINCENT VAN GOGH (1853-1890). THE FOURTEENTH OF JULY IN PARIS, 1886-1887. (17¼ × 15¼″)
HAHNLOSER COLLECTION, WINTERTHUR.

It was above all Van Gogh who ushered in that liberation of color from representational service which the Fauves subsequently carried to the extreme limit, constructing solely with color in its purest, most elementary state. A brilliantly original picture, dashed off sketchwise, this *Fourteenth of July* reflects perhaps better than any other that trance-like state in which Van Gogh composed so many of his works. We may be sure that the rapturous delight in color so obvious here was not lost on the Fauves, and may well have been at the source of their most daring experiments.

VINCENT VAN GOGH (1853-1890). OUTDOOR CAFÉ AT NIGHT, ARLES 1888. (31 × 24¾")
RIJKSMUSEUM KRÖLLER-MÜLLER, OTTERLO.

That great visionary of modern painting Van Gogh was haunted by the apocalyptic vastness of the night-sky and painted the stars as madmen and children paint them, as palely gleaming blurs of light which, however, he always integrates into the color orchestration of the picture.

produced no less than 200 canvases, many of them views of Montmartre and the Paris suburbs, which rank among his most significant works. This was his Paris Period. Early in 1888, at Lautrec's instance, he moved south to Arles, where he announced that he proposed to found "the Studio of the Future."

If, in Cézanne's words, Monet was "only an eye—but what an eye!" the Dutchman Van Gogh was only a soul—but what a soul! That of an utterly honest man in quest of an Absolute which he found only in a self-given death. But before reaching this tragic solution, he struggled unremittingly to implement a superhuman dream. And, in the course of the struggle, he assigned to painting an end that was, perhaps, not wholly new, but which he stamped with the mark of his passionate, cruelly frustrated personality. With Van Gogh showing the way, painters were soon to switch their interest over from pure painting and technique to what was called "character." For he was quick to note the marks of suffering and privation on the faces of poor folk and portrayed them with sympathetic understanding.

Impressionism aimed solely at the expression of visual sensations; Van Gogh aimed at the expression of emotional experience. Amongst his favorite painters were Rembrandt, Delacroix, Millet and Daumier. He was all nerves, susceptibility, exaltation, and for him quite trivial incidents had a vast, almost transcendental significance. For a while he worked as a missionary in a mining district, but without success. What he really sought in painting was a kind of self-analysis, but in this too he failed. He found in art a therapeutic treatment of his ever smoldering unrest, but it could not avert the final, desperate catastrophe.

Unstable, physically unfit, an erotomaniac, a heavy drinker, Van Gogh had all the ills that flesh is heir to. Hence his nerve-racking uncertainties as to his true capacities and his vocation. Was he destined to be a preacher, a painter, or something else—or just one of life's misfits? He never solved these problems to his satisfaction. Always he was the victim of a temperament at the mercy of every passing impulse, unsure of its ends. Thus his career was one long, almost aimless pilgrimage. His consciousness of his infirmities drew him towards the moral and physical outcasts of a social order with whom he felt a kinship. And his lack of self-confidence prevented him from finding within himself the will-power and energy needed to overcome his "inferiority complex." This perhaps is why he sought deliverance in closely scrutinizing the world around him and trying to perfect his art. He, too, was not to paint "as a bird sings." He haunted the studio of his fellow countryman Mauve and took counsel from the Great Masters—in the same spirit as he took up theology courses; less to find arguments for a faith he lacked than anyhow to know the dogmas. Soon he had amassed considerable knowledge: all but that of his own genius; for he never shook off the idea of his incompetence. At that time he was still in Holland. On his father's death he resolved to travel, but, having no program, merely drifted to the nearest city. This was Antwerp, where he found a quite new atmosphere, and one which led him to go back on many of his old ideas and question the merits of his "reformative" zeal. For one thing, he discovered Rubens, who swept him off his feet. After a while he moved to Paris where new discoveries awaited him: Impressionism, Pointillism, Japanese art. And suddenly his palette grew brighter. He took to using brilliantly pure tones and painting nudes, sunflowers, *japonaiseries* and such pictures as his *Fourteenth of July*. He wrote to his brother that he now was painting "in the impressionist style." He was trying to assign a new function to color and make it a derivative of his moods, calm or agitated as the case might be. And color now became not only a way of escape from his tormented self, but a sort of alcohol, in which he sought to find a counter-irritant. Certain physical effects of color had already been observed: that blue calms, red excites, and so on. Van Gogh was to press these discoveries to an extreme. Thus figures, landscapes and interiors, often the same ones, are treated by him quite differently according to his physical or mental state at the time of painting. He saw yellow, for instance, not as the product of some mathematical equation (the pointillist view), but as signifying love or friendship. "How lovely yellow is!" he once exclaimed, and though all his life long he got nothing but rebuffs from women, yellow—love's emblem to his mind—was always his favorite color. "With red and green I have tried to depict those terrible things, men's passions," was another of his remarks. After painting a café interior he explained, "I have tried to convey that a café is a place where a man can ruin himself, go crazy, commit a crime."

Thus Van Gogh's conception of painting was essentially a sort of color symbolism, not without analogies with the symbolism of Christian art, which not only prescribed certain attitudes for the figures in religious pictures, but also fixed the color appropriate to each; thus blue was assigned to the Virgin, violet to martyrs, red to the devil and so forth. "Color in itself expresses something," Van Gogh said, "never mind the subject."

Under his influence painting was to acquire a new significance and to be regarded as a sort of visual poetry. Van Gogh, and Gauguin too, sponsored the intervention of the mind in the use of color, which each employed in terms of a private symbolism. Thus a new language of color arose, comparable in its way with the familiar "language of flowers." Color was in fact on the way to acquiring a prestige it had never hitherto enjoyed and taking its revenge on line, fetish of the past.

James Ensor

Color built up by Light

As a rule Expressionists are gloomy people who rarely smile, and then only with an effort. Ensor, however, was a jovial Expressionist and refused to take even death too seriously. His art reminds us of those sumptuous still lifes painted by his Flemish forerunners, in which upon a table piled with tempting fare, one sees a skull (hence the name *Vanitas* for a picture of this kind). Death, too, it seemed, had overlooked Ensor until his ninetieth year, when, almost as an afterthought, it carried him quietly off. During the First World War, in fact, his death was falsely announced on no less than three occasions, and it was with vast amusement that he read his obituary notices in the newspapers.

James Ensor was born in 1860 at Ostend, and there he lived uninterruptedly to the end of his life in an atmosphere of tranquil domesticity, surrounded by the motley bric-à-brac and souvenirs—iridescent sea-shells, fishing nets, glass floats of many colors, *chinoiseries*—whose company he liked best, though he pretended to look upon them with an indulgent smile. He watched the scenes of life with an ironic detachment and had much of the verbal fantasy of the author of *Finnegans Wake*. "Towards a Land of Mockbelieve," he wrote, "and thrills galore I set sail in a dream-ship beflagged with inky flames."

Ensor took his art seriously, though for him painting was not the handmaid of any utopian vision. He used it for gently scolding a world whose imperfections he discerned, but of which he never quite despaired. Whereas Redon thought up a private and peculiar wonderland, Ensor remained under the lifelong spell of the dreamworld of his own childhood, which, fortunately perhaps, had for him no spurious glamour. No doubt it was peopled by the most attractive fairies, but there were also spiders, ogres, even macabre stuffed Chinamen. In short the fairyland through which he leads us is frankly realistic; a familiar of its denizens, he looked upon them with a twinkle in his eye throughout his long life.

Following a Flemish tradition, he invests his satire with a lively humor deriving more from Hieronymus Bosch, from Huys and Brueghel (in the *Proverbs*) than from caricaturists such as Hogarth, Rowlandson or Gillray. Unlike the eerie, lunar visions of Redon, his own are wholly classical in conception and full of the pictured comments of a born observer, shrewd but only faintly cynical. The idea of death recurs persistently, but he bedecks his skeletons with masks, wings and gaudy finery, makes them strike quaint and ludicrous attitudes. He was never in the least afraid of death, however much he thought of it, and his art has also a happy, carefree side. Thus in his *Garden of Love* and his celebrated *Entrance of Christ into Brussels*, we see on all sides merry, smiling faces, fantastically radiant like those in some jovial old picture-book. But Ensor also has a curious reserve, leading him often to hide the features of his characters under inexpressive masks. These manikin-like entities, living a wholly fictitious life, make his works seem like a phantasmagoria of nacreous shells, phosphorescent fishes, and shining, puffed-out faces in which his boyishly mischievous handling of color has its fling, and sweeps all before it. Indeed many of his pictures produce the paradoxical impression of still lifes that have somehow come alive.

But there was one theme by which Ensor was frankly overawed, forgetting Belgian *Zwanze* and for once feeling no wish to smile—and this is when he painted the sea. He was born within sight of the sea, and never forsook it even for a day.

It was indeed his vital element. Even when writing about it, he used a poet's pen: "Wondrous sea of Ostend, all in pearls and opals, virgin sea I love—alas, that the coarse brush of the painter should dare to sully your divine lineaments and smirch your garment woven of rainbow glints and silken white!" Naïve and quaintly phrased perhaps, but spoken from the heart. Here Ensor, the humorist, has for once laid irony aside. And humbly in his art he extolled the grandeur of sky and sea, paying them homage with a simple fervor that it never occurred to him to mask with his habitual irony.

JAMES ENSOR (1860-1949). THE ENTRANCE OF CHRIST INTO BRUSSELS (DETAIL), 1888. CASINO, OSTEND.

The Entrance of Christ into Brussels is Ensor's greatest work, not only for its dimensions—it covers over ten square yards of canvas—but also for the magnificent painting that has gone to the making of this fantastic scene. The idea of picturing how his contemporaries would react if Christ came to Brussels was for Ensor a splendid opportunity for giving free rein to his imagination. Like Victor Hugo in his description of the "Mysteries" in *Notre-Dame de Paris,* the artist depicts a huge concourse of all types of humanity. Here the Flemish genius for narration, a keen sense of satire, and the skill of a great craftsman and colorist implement a pageantry at once grandiose and burlesque. We see Christ riding on an ass in the midst of a motley crowd whose excitement is whipped up by the drums and trumpets of the "Belgian Bigots' Band." A streamer proclaiming "Up with the Socialist State!" is slung across the street. Another welcomes Christ with the words "Long live Jesus, King of Brussels!" With what gusto Ensor caricatures these worthy people who today are singing Hosannas and tomorrow will be shouting "Crucify Him!" To vent his scorn he replaces their faces with grotesque masks, for their true expression is the leer, in which stupidity, vulgarity and greed, and all the other ills the heart of man is heir to, are plain to see. Ten years later Ensor transposed this picture into an etching, in which some new streamers and slogans bring the scene up to date and, crowning glory, is a poster vaunting Colman's Mustard.

PAUL GAUGUIN (1848-1903). DECORATIVE LANDSCAPE, 1888. (33¾ × 22⅜″)
NATIONALMUSEUM, STOCKHOLM.

Paul Gauguin

Renewed Prestige of Color - Abstraction and Symbolism

GAUGUIN found in painting something he had hardly dared hope for: a means of synthesizing (to use a word he greatly favored) the conflicting impulses of his peculiarly unstable temperament, and integrating them into an harmonious whole. All his pictures, whether the scene be Brittany or the South Seas, reveal distinctive color rhythms, their tone and form alike imbued with a deep but never desperate melancholy. His brilliantly original palette is remarkable for its rich, resonant harmonies, and though his colors are often high-keyed, they are muted, recalling—a legitimate analogy since Gauguin often associated painting with music—the effect of muted trumpets in jazz bands.

After a brief trial of Impressionism, he found that the meticulous attention which its tiny juxtaposed touches necessitated cramped his style. Also he reproached the movement with concentrating on purely optical phenomena at the expense of "the mysterious processes of the mind." Thus we soon find him repudiating most of the methods of his impressionist friends, painting in broad planes of color and refusing to linger over details. A need for spaciousness, for an ever larger freedom, made itself felt in his art as in his private life, where it took the form of an urge to travel. That he developed so keen an interest in Japanese prints may be partly due to this cult of the exotic and remote. Then a new idea waylaid him—he was always having new ideas. Living was cheap in Brittany and life was hard in Paris; so he migrated (in 1886) to Pont-Aven. Here he found Schuffenecker, an old friend, and made Emile Bernard's acquaintance. They spent much time discussing art and the burning topic of the day, the recently published Symbolist Manifesto, which declared that the whole duty of the artist was "to clothe the idea in perceptible form." Here was a theory after Gauguin's own heart; it justified his replacing the prevailing semi-anecdotal art by the ideology that meant so much to him. Needless to say, he affected to disdain Symbolism, but he stood by its principles none the less. Thus in his South Sea pictures we find him attempting "to clothe in a perceptible form" the ideas behind his *Tahitian Eve* and *The Enigma lurking in the Depths of her Eyes*. Likewise he championed "Synthetism," as a counterblast to the analytic methods of Impressionism, though this did not prevent his ridiculing it when he saw fellow artists making a fetish of its theories. His fondness for Japanese art, for stained-glass windows, and even for the gaudy picture-sheets so popular in the last century—all of which seemed to fit in with his conception of Synthetism—led him on to what was known as Cloisonnism, which consists in binding areas of color with heavy contour-lines. It was during this phase that he painted that amazing *Vision after the Sermon*. By now his true personality was asserting itself. "There are noble lines," he said, "and deceptive lines; the straight line gives infinity, the curve restricts creation." He wanted "to get as far away as possible from whatever gives the illusion of an object." Japanese art had taught him much; he now wished to eliminate and refine, to suggest form by pure color. This is the key to his telling simplifications and the fine spareness of his close-knit forms. "Art," he said, "is an abstraction." He no longer contemplated nature with an eye to reproducing it, but "meditated" his picture beforehand. Of his *Christ in the Garden of Olives,* he remarked: "It is imbued with an abstract sadness, and sadness is my vocation." Another of his sayings was: "What wonderful thoughts can be evoked by form and color!" His obsession with "thought" never left him, and it led him to give such titles to his canvases as: *When are you getting married ?, Why are you angry ?, The Spirit of the Dead keeps Vigil*, and his famous *Whence come we ? What are we ? Whither go we ?* Fortunately his preoccupation with ideas did not inhibit his discoveries in the field of pure painting, whose value lies precisely in the fact that they stem from the Unconscious—to which, as it happened, Odilon Redon was also proclaiming his indebtedness at this time. The dreams he dreamt in Brittany became realities in the South Seas, indeed his Tahitian technique bears out that fine remark he

PAUL GAUGUIN (1848-1903). THE VISION AFTER THE SERMON, OR JACOB WRESTLING WITH THE ANGEL, 1888. (28⅝ × 36⅛") NATIONAL GALLERY OF SCOTLAND, EDINBURGH.

One of the first paintings made by Gauguin at Pont-Aven, on his return from Martinique, in accordance with the new theories of Synthetism and Cloisonnism. Albert Aurier published an enthusiastic description of it in *Le Mercure de France* (February 1891), using it to illustrate his famous definition of the work of art as "ideological, symbolistic, synthetic, subjective, decorative."

made in earlier days: "Whenever my clogs strike this iron soil of Brittany, I hear that dull, muffled yet mighty resonance which I seek for in my painting." Here we have one of those "correspondences," as Baudelaire named them, which rise to the mind when different stimuli produce the same sensation. Already Delacroix had drawn attention to the close similarity between the effects of music and painting on the sensibility. And to Gauguin's thinking the harmonious effects of musical chords and combinations of primary colors with their complementaries were almost literally identical, giving the same satisfaction to the ear and eye respectively. Packed with emotive allusions, his art constantly aspired towards a pictorial equivalent of states of mind. His influence, however, on the Nabis, on Sérusier (who became the exponent of Gauguin's aesthetic theories), on Bonnard, Vuillard, Vallotton and Maurice Denis, was largely due to his genius for the decorative and to his wonderful handling of color at its most intense. "How do you see this tree?" he asked Sérusier. "It's green, you say? Well then, put on green, the richest green on your palette." None the less Gauguin greatly admired both Ingres and Delacroix, and even declared that there was nothing that could not be expressed by drawing. "Line *is* color," he once said categorically. Two decades later the Fauves and Cubists, though rejecting the ideological content of Gauguin's aesthetic, showed much interest in his technique and adopted his practice of binding flat planes of color with dark, expressive contour-lines.

Odilon Redon

Color, Vehicle of the Unconscious Mind

Mᴏʀᴇ́ᴀs declared in his Manifesto published on September 18, 1886, that Symbolism was the only mode of expression "capable of logically conveying the contemporary tendencies of the creative spirit in art." Amongst the literary reviews, *La Plume, Le Mercure de France* and *La Pléiade* championed the new theory as applied to literature. It was Albert Aurier, in an article on "Symbolism in Painting" in the *Mercure de France* (1891), who first pointed out its possible application to pictorial art and he acclaimed Gauguin leader of the Symbolist art movement.

The aim of this school was "to clothe the idea in a form perceptible to the senses." Nature was to be observed "by way of the dream," and all primitive, archaic and exotic forms of art into which symbolic allusions could be read were to be turned to account. The work of art was to be "ideological, symbolistic, synthetic, subjective, decorative." Paul Sérusier now became the painter-theorist of the new school. It was Odilon Redon, however, who was the real forerunner of Symbolism in painting. Though there was only a year's difference of age between him and Monet, Renoir, Cézanne and Sisley, he never shared in the impressionist venture. Indeed he went so far as to say that "painting is not the mere representation of three-dimensional form, but human beauty crowned with the prestige of thought." And though here again the word "thought" is used in connection with painting, Redon gave it a meaning quite different from that which Courbet or Gauguin gave it; for him it was synonymous with poetic feeling. It was, in fact, with a long tradition sponsored by the work of Bosch, Arcimboldo, Dürer, Hogarth, Goya, Blake, Fuseli and de Grandville that Redon linked up his theories, a tradition he set out to renew and amplify, and Surrealism was to carry on.

In the solitude of his provincial home, near Bordeaux, young Redon (like so many youngsters) discovered that, by looking long enough, he could find quaint little shapes and scenes in lace curtains, in wallpaper, on misted windows, in drifting clouds. We must picture a small boy, precocious and living in a dreamworld of his own, having few of the traits of childhood, but already many of the mental kinks of grown-ups. For him the least object became a microcosm of fascinating secrets. To our wondering eyes his art discloses a strange cosmogony, but one of such precision that we are almost convinced of its reality. All his life Redon preferred the company of poets to that of painters; he was an intimate friend of Mallarmé, Valéry and Francis Jammes. To his mind, what was true to life was not necessarily lifelike and his aim was "to bring improbable things to life, under a probable form." He wrote much, moreover, and always with discernment. In his dream of opening "magic casements" by grace of the poet's vision, he tried as it were to psychoanalyze animal, vegetable and even mineral entities, so as to make them yield their secrets; and these he utilized for building up his private universe. He made no secret of the source of his inspiration. "Everything takes form when we lay ourselves open to the uprush of the Unconscious." His sole concern was to discover that element of the magical or fabulous which lies at the heart of all things seen, their immanent quintessence, and to express it. Indeed all life was like a fairy-tale to him, a fairy-tale whose truth he ever sought to demonstrate. And when he called on color alone to implement his vision, he endowed it with a special significance, lifting it above the plane of reality by glints of sharp, metallic tones, like electric sparks. The living things he pictures, whether butterflies or monsters, seem like creatures prisoned in the eerie silence of glass globes or frozen into the disquieting immobility of waxworks.

When thought intrudes on painting there is always a danger that the latter will be given a literary turn, and tend towards illustration. But in the case of Redon, is it painting that "illustrates" the poetry or vice versa? It would seem that his art owes all to imagination, and "image" is implicit in the word "imagination." The truth is that, with Redon, "thought" found in painting its appropriate medium, its native tongue.

PAUL SÉRUSIER (1863-1927). THE TALISMAN.
(10½ × 8⅜″) MADAME BOULET-DENIS
COLLECTION, CLERMONT-D'OISE.

Sérusier gave the name of *The Talisman* to this famous picture, which he painted under Gauguin's direction at Pont-Aven. Prescribing as it did the use of color at its brightest, most intense, Gauguin's doctrine had a revolutionary effect on the young Nabis. After a while, however, the Nabis, having extracted what they wanted from his theories, proceeded to discard them. Much as they admired Gauguin, they never regarded him as a heaven-sent teacher. Sérusier made this clear when, speaking of the Pont-Aven group, he wrote: "It was not a school with a master and a group of disciples sitting at his feet. All were independent artists who pooled their several discoveries and loathed the official curriculum." *The Talisman* was shown by Sérusier to his fellow students at the Académie Julian; in it the influence of Gauguin's aesthetic is manifest. A close friend of the Master, Sérusier acquainted his friends with the new ideas that Gauguin sponsored, and in particular his fondness for legendary lore and allegories. Pont-Aven is in Brittany, and to that homeland of the fairy folk, and to the Forest of Broceliande, abode of Merlin, Gauguin may have owed this lifelong predilection.

1888

The Nabis had subscribed amongst themselves to purchase a picture by Gauguin, the idea being that each in turn was to have the temporary use and enjoyment of it. Thadée Natanson informs us that Bonnard often forgot his turn. The small, but beautifully composed picture shown here was made at the time when Bonnard was doing his military service, a full year after the famous exhibition of the "Impressionist and Synthetist Group" (held early in 1889 at the Café Volpini in the grounds of the Paris World's Fair), in which Gauguin had figured so prominently. In *The Review* the influence of Gauguin is unmistakable: in the large, flat surfaces, bound with heavy contour-lines, and the subdued, skillfully contrasted colors. All the same his sense of humor kept the upper hand and prevented the young painter from taking the Master's theories and homilies over-seriously. Indeed there was never anything of the doctrinaire in Bonnard's attitude to art.

PIERRE BONNARD (1867-1947). THE REVIEW (8⅝ × 11¾″) PRIVATE COLLECTION, SWITZERLAND.

1890

The Nabis

From Gauguin's Influence to the Lautrec Spirit

FEW GROUPS of artists hold together long, the time soon comes when the members part company, each following the lead of his own temperament; the cohesion of the Nabis, however, evidenced in their very first exhibition (1891), proved relatively long-lasting. In the mid-nineties great confusion reigned in the world of art. In a book entitled *The Idealist Movement in Painting* (1896), André Mellerio sought to reconcile the various art currents of the day, and rather arbitrarily lumped together such artists as Seurat, Signac, Luce, Angrand, Lucien Pissarro, Van Rysselberghe, Schuffenecker, Lautrec, Ibels, Anquetin, Guillaumin, Maufra, Verkade, Maurice Denis, Emile Bernard, Filiger, Sérusier, Vuillard, Roussel, Vallotton, Ranson, Bonnard and others. Mellerio began by assigning the members of this impressive galaxy to five categories: Neo-Impressionists, Synthetists, Neo-Traditionalists, Mystics and "Chromo-luminarists." He then sought to unite these groups under a common standard, that of a "symbolist idealism," highly literary in tone, which invited modern painters to let the Idea prescribe the form and to achieve expression by means of signs—signs that the artist created and in themselves sufficient to communicate impressions. But if it was simply a matter of conveying impressions, why go about it in this roundabout way? Could not the same result be secured by purely pictorial methods? This was what the Nabis aspired to do.

The name "Nabis"—from a Hebrew word meaning prophets or *illuminati*—was given them by the poet Cazalis. Among the adherents to the newly formed group were Sérusier, Ranson, Vuillard, Maurice Denis, Roussel, Ibels, Bonnard, Piot, Verkade, Vallotton and Maillol. Denis organized group dinners at the *Os à Moelle* restaurant, and though arguments ran fast and furious, high good humor invariably reigned at these reunions. Nicknames were handed out right and left; thus Bonnard became the "Japanese Nabi," Verkade—a giant of a man —the "obeliskal Nabi," and Vuillard the "Zouave." And soon the *Revue Blanche* office became another rallying center.

Needless to say, writers swarmed at the office of that famous magazine, but the Nabis fought shy of literary incursions into painting, Vuillard, Bonnard, Roussel and Vallotton being among the first to point out how badly painting had fared at the hands of men of letters. For they had not forgotten the regrettable articles written by men like Zola, Huysmans and so many others, proving, it seemed, that novelists, and even poets, were impervious to the lyrical appeal of painting pure and simple.

Fresh in their minds were the pointers given by Gauguin to Sérusier when the two were painting together in Brittany. "How do you see this tree?" asked Gauguin. "It's green, you say? Well then, put on green, the richest green on your palette. And that shadow? Rather blue? Then don't scruple to paint it in ultramarine straight from the tube." Here was the dawn of an era of painting in pure, unbroken color, and of juxtapositions of colors of an unprecedented boldness. Thus imagination now was given the leading role and the painter was no longer expected to abide by the data of the retinal sensation; hence the charge leveled by Albert Aurier against Impressionism that it was "no more than the representation of surface appearances," whereas (according to him) art should be "the materialization of what is loftiest and divinest in the world—the Idea." Here we have the earliest declaration of that supremacy of the thinking mind which Matisse championed in his conversation and his art, and the Cubists affirmed still more emphatically, and which was to dominate all the painting of the first half of the 20th century.

However, this cult of the "Idea" had not the same appeal for everyone. Gauguin, Sérusier and Maurice Denis, particularly the last two named, inveterate intellectuals, subscribed to it, though in different ways. Not so Bonnard, Roussel, Vallotton and Vuillard, and it was they who set the tone of the Nabi movement, by taking as their themes everyday incidents, intimate scenes of family life, which in their hands became the vehicles of ingenious experiments in color and composition. And though well aware of Gauguin's advice to Sérusier, they avoided strident tones, preferring finer shades of color, provided these were handled not in terms of such classical techniques as modeling and chiaroscuro, but adjusted to a two-dimensional conception of space—a procedure which, when all is said and done, was their sole tribute to "Ideism."

For them the symbolist adventure was by now ancient history. Worse, it tended to bring back academic disciplines under an insidious form. Bonnard was determined to safeguard that precious impulse towards freedom which was enlarging his vision of things, while Vuillard found in his own sensibility all he needed for giving his work solid architectural form. Even the names they gave their pictures were calculated to vex their symbolist friends. Thus Bonnard was responsible for *Grandmother with her Hens, The Cup of Coffee, The Cat, The Wine Shop*, and Vuillard for *The Pickle Jar, Still Life with Cabbages*, and *The Wild Rabbit*. Obviously such homely themes were anathema to the "Ideists." Meanwhile the leading art critics of the day, men like Roger Marx, Gustave Geffroy and Albert Aurier, expressed a lively interest in the new ventures. The possibilities of painting on cardboard were explored; the painters mixed turpentine into their pigment and this, combined with the absorbent quality of the cardboard, gave wonderfully "mat" effects. Another device was to leave the cardboard bare in places; and another to apply cool tones upon an undercoat of warm. In short, the Nabis relied on technique alone to put across their impressions.

It was at Pont-Aven in 1888, at the prompting of Gauguin, that Sérusier produced his famous *Talisman*. Painted on the lid of an old cigar-box, this picture was a revelation to his friends at the Académie Julian in Paris, the Nabis-to-be, who were then still dallying with Impressionism. Adept and commentator of the works of Plotinus and Father Didier's "Holy Proportions," Sérusier imparted to the group something of his own respect for order, restraint, style and well-knit composition. He became their leading spokesman, and his authority made itself felt, at least for a time. In addition to easel pictures, he made a number of large-scale decorations in the tempera technique. The excellence of his work is beyond question, though it lacks the appealing intimacy, the spontaneous charm and the high painterly ability we find in that of such artists as Vuillard and Bonnard.

The Nabis had another advocate in Maurice Denis, an accomplished writer to whom we owe some enlightening treatises on art. He had a gift for putting into words the theories and aspirations of the new generation of artists. In one often quoted phrase he summed up the guiding principle of contemporary painting: "We must never forget that a picture, before being a warhorse, a nude woman, an anecdote or whatnot, is essentially a flat surface covered with colors arranged in a certain order." This provocative statement, hotly attacked at the time, is still challenged today by the champions of an art aiming above all at psychological expression. Then again, describing his reactions to a work by Gauguin, Denis wrote: "Thus we came to realize that every work of art was a transposition, the emotive equivalent of an experienced sensation." Denis always insisted on the absolute necessity of the *organization* of the picture on the lines laid down by Seurat, and in this respect his views have had much effect on the painting of our time. As for his own work as a painter, Denis began by conforming to the Symbolist program, in, for example, his *Minuet of the Princess Maleine* and his pictures of young girls in long, flowing dresses whose arabesques inaugurated what came to be called the "Modern Style." After a stay in Italy (to which we owe his fascinating *Souvenirs*), where he had frankly surrendered to the charm of Florentine and Sienese art, he encouraged painters to follow in the steps of the Primitives, whose spontaneity he said "smelt so sweetly of life." Under the influence of a Dominican, Father Janvier, who was friendly with the Nabis, Denis gave his art a religious turn and, conjointly with Georges Desvallières, founded in 1919 the "Studios of Sacred Art" with the aim of promoting a revival of religious painting.

Expert though he was in all the technicalities of art, Denis had a regrettable tendency to let his very real talent be submerged by an excess of knowledge and this, in fact, hindered him from practicing the spontaneity he so strongly advocated for others.

MAURICE DENIS (1870-1943). APRIL, 1892. (14½×23½″) RIJKSMUSEUM KRÖLLER-MÜLLER, OTTERLO.

Both these pictures illustrate a tendency that made its first appearance in the work of the Nabis and in 1896 went by the name of Jugendstil in Munich and "Modern Style" in France. Characteristic of this technique is its use of swirling arabesques having little relevance to the plastic organization of the picture. There are traces of this in the work by Denis, whereas Vuillard's arabesques play a structural part in a composition at once witty and architecturally ordered.

EDOUARD VUILLARD (1868-1940). IN BED, 1891. (29×36⅛″) MUSÉE D'ART MODERNE, PARIS.

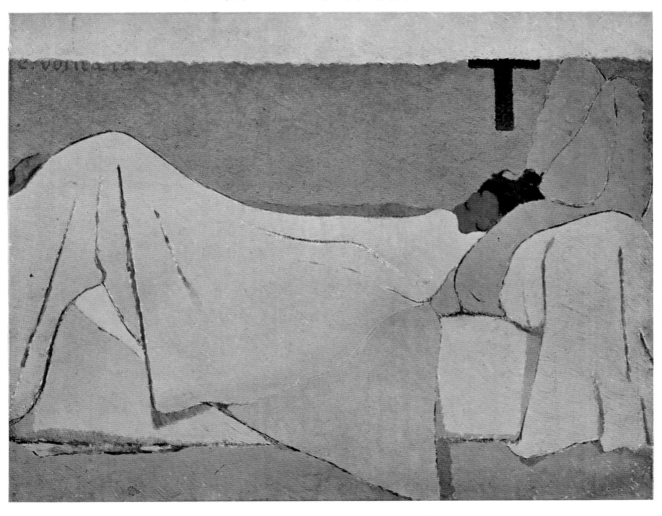

The Lautrec Spirit

Towards the Turn of the Century

LIKE RAPHAEL, Toulouse-Lautrec died at the age of thirty-seven. A few days before his
death he was heard to murmur: "And life's a fine thing, they say!"
In the wistful irony of this remark we have the key to all his work. His keen intelligence prompted him to laugh, if a little wryly, at an existence which, despite successes in the field of art,
was full of sadness. And his marvelous powers of observation, his brilliant summings-up of
forms and faces—never failing in the smiling tolerance that comes of good breeding—confess
the disillusionment of a man of taste confronted by life's seamier aspects.

Born in 1864 at Albi, Henri de Toulouse-Lautrec-Monfa came of an old and renowned family,
that of the Counts of Toulouse. A delicate child—this was due, perhaps, to the fact that
he came of a very old stock weakened by inbreeding—, he had two bad falls when he was
fourteen, breaking first one thigh and then the other. This checked the natural growth of
his limbs and gave him a grotesque, top-heavy stature, his legs remaining too short for his
body. His whole career was influenced by this disablement; he was deterred from indulging
in the normal recreations of a country gentleman, riding, hunting, dancing and the like. His
father lost interest in the boy, but fortunately his mother did her best to make life easy
for him. Unable to play an active part, and condemned to being a looker-on throughout
his adolescence, he used his eyes to good effect and sharpened his wits on what he saw. With
something of a child's delight in "making pictures" for his own pleasure, he made sketches
in which we already find a feeling for essentials, a competence and intensity which he was
never to surpass.

The horses he could not ride, the animals he could not hunt, the birds whose airy freedom
mocked the relative immobility to which he was condemned—these furnished themes that
whiled away the long hours spent seated in his chair. Thus his whole activity centered on
what was for him, to begin with, only a pastime, something to make him forget his troubles;
indeed he drew without a thought of "art," like a man idly tracing arabesques on a café
table. Impressed by his talent, his parents had him take lessons from Princeteau, a sporting
painter. Next he entered the Ecole des Beaux-Arts in Paris, where he studied under Bonnat
and Cormon. But he soon cut short his training and took to haunting Montmartre, then
the center of artistic activity in Paris. Gradually, under the joint influences of Manet, Degas,
Van Gogh and Japanese art, the mere amateur blossomed out into an artist taking his craft
with high seriousness. But, still mindful of the numbing effect of the teaching of the Schools,
he would not let his spontaneity be trammelled by rules, and found even Degas, whom he
greatly admired, too theory-bound for his taste. Already he was thinking less of the picture
to be painted than of the idea to express. Montmartre, for him, was merely a hunting-ground
and his interest in its denizens was not that of a chronicler of mores; he found there a queer
sampling of humanity, just what he needed to whet his imagination.

While the moral implications underlying Van Gogh's work, his sense of a mission and in
particular his vast compassion for suffering humanity, had no direct influence on his contemporaries and it was only his technique that moved them to emulation, it was quite otherwise
with Toulouse-Lautrec. If Lautrec applied himself to depicting scenes of the life around
him, this was due not only to personal inclination but also to the "climate" of his time.
Writers of the day, from Maupassant to Tristan Bernard, were attracted to such subjects, and
Parisians in general, including the artists, developed a great liking for circuses, cabarets, café-
concerts, athletic meetings and the theater. Thus, much as the Impressionists had turned to
Nature for their inspiration, so the painters of this period drew theirs from the Parisian scene.
But what appealed particularly to the young men of the Nabi and Cubist generations was what
we may call "the Lautrec spirit," meaning an intellectual approach to life on the artist's part.
It took the form in Lautrec's case of a vast disillusionment with things in general, but a

good-humored disillusionment, untouched with bitterness. For though none better realized the basic absurdity of life, he did not take it tragically but turned it into a smile. He had, indeed, something of the Voltairian belief that, however dark the present, "everything comes right in the end."

The "Lautrec spirit" played a considerable part in shaping the mentality of the artists of what was to be looked back to as a sort of golden age, when life was relatively carefree. But Lautrec's influence made itself felt on his successors not merely by way of an attitude to life, but in the field of practical achievement and especially with regard to his consummate draftsmanship. His drawing has the happy unconstraint of a *grand seigneur* used to being obeyed, and compared with his, that of Ingres and even Degas seems heavy, too carefully thought out, somewhat pretentious, not to say pontifical. Indeed one often gets the impression Lautrec was amusing himself when he made those vivid sketches of people and incidents, truer to life than life itself, most of them concerned with such dynamic spectacles as dancing, riding, sports, in which his physical infirmity debarred him from participating otherwise than as a keen-eyed, fascinated onlooker. Basic to his drawing is a fine economy of means, a balance adroitly struck between extreme boldness and the saving grace of measure. He had the gift of expressing *everything* in a few brief strokes, light or emphatic, playful or savage as the case may be. He never shrinks from taking risks, and always his amazing sureness of hand saves him in the nick of time. To describe his technical resources one is tempted to fall back on the terminology of the grammarian and speak of telling elisions, bold ellipses, skillfully run-on or truncated lines. There can be little doubt that Lautrec enlarged the possibilities of draftsmanship as practiced in his day and that his successors turned his discoveries and

HENRI DE TOULOUSE-LAUTREC (1864-1901). THE MOULIN ROUGE, 1890. (45 ¼ × 59″)
HENRY P. MCILHENNY COLLECTION, PHILADELPHIA.

HENRI DE TOULOUSE-LAUTREC (1864-1901).
LA GOULUE ENTERING THE MOULIN ROUGE, 1892. (31 ⅝ × 23 ½ ")
G. BERNHEIM DE VILLERS COLLECTION, PARIS.

inventions to good account. Indeed it would not be going too far to say that thanks to Lautrec the art of drawing was rejuvenated, endowed with a new creative energy.

True, Lautrec once said: "I've tried simply to tell the truth, not to idealize," and, coming from any other artist, such a remark might suggest mere copying of what the eye perceives. But for Lautrec "the true" always signified "the living"—and life is always "true" in this sense. In his quest of truth, Lautrec was led inevitably to seek out new means. This breaking of new ground can be seen to wonderful effect in the linear inventions of his posters, those posters which, so we are told, Braque and Picasso used to strip off the walls where they were fixed, while the paste was still wet, and carry them off triumphantly to their studios (the same has been done in our time with theirs).

Lautrec's painting had by and large the same quality as his drawing: an air of being done on the spur of the moment, thanks to which it has the special charm of the sketch. All in light yet telling touches, it reveals that *fa presto* execution which, never overdoing its effects, makes each point with ease and elegance, and combines vigor with intimacy. Even in his colors Lautrec was careful to avoid any sort of lushness; he had a fondness for painting on cardboard whose neutral ground appealed to him and which lent itself to rapid, sketch-like execution, while absorbing any garishness in the pigment and readily producing those effects of broken tones and soft, warm, expressive color in which he excelled and which the Nabis admiringly took over from him.

Plain to see in this canvas by Vuillard as in Lautrec's facing it, is the influence of Japanese art: the use of flat planes, whether somber or completely black, with contrasts and patches of color to indicate the play of light on surfaces.

EDOUARD VUILLARD (1868-1940). TWO WOMEN BY LAMPLIGHT, 1892. (13 × 16⅛")
G. GRAMMONT COLLECTION, PARIS.

Edouard Vuillard

★

APPARENT in his art, Vuillard's natural modesty is one of his most attractive traits. He knew his limitations and never sought to overstep them or to embark on ventures that were, so to say, beyond his means. Nor was he haunted like so many modern artists by any longing for "undiscovered countries." Yet, true to instincts that had never played him false, he always respected those of others; indeed none showed a friendlier understanding than he of the audacities of the younger men. Thanks to his exquisite feeling for color and the rich intensity of his palette, no less than to the stability of his architecturally ordered composition, Vuillard enjoyed the rare privilege of enlisting the admiration of all the painters of his day, whatever their aesthetic bias. There were many reasons for this, chief being the "classical" and wholly admirable humility of a great painter towards an art which he never put to the service of personal ambition or self-display.

Vuillard's art had a unity, a singleness of aim, hard to come by at a time when so many different theories and movements were clamoring for attention. Symbolism, for instance, whose influence on painting was so vacillating and short-lived, appealed for the most part to artists whose lack of real gifts could be masked by the strict application of ready-made aesthetic rules. Though Vuillard has been assigned to this school, his sensibility ranged far beyond it. Then, again, Japanese art must have delighted Vuillard, with its simplicity, its quaint patterning, its cunning arabesques; yet it is equally certain that this art had nothing new to teach him. All its distinctive virtues—and many others—were already his, and the most he found in it was an endorsement of the similar direction in which his instinct led him. He reminds us, too, of Verlaine with whom he had a good deal in common both temperamentally and in his artistic methods. The affinities between the poet and the artist become evident when we recall the impression produced on the reader by Verlaine's *Fêtes galantes* and *Chansons grises*, by the gossamer lightness of their texture, all in delicate touches, bold elisions, beautifully thought-out verbal arabesques, and the vistas they open to the imagination: *Où l'indécis au précis se joint.*

A precise indecision! Whereas in Bonnard's more spectacular vision, indecision is allowed to exercise all its compelling, if precarious charm, Vuillard, while remaining thoroughly impressionist, puts into practice—quite instinctively—Cézanne's famous injunction: to make of Impressionism "something solid and abiding." Despite certain similarities of color, there is a basic difference between the techniques of the two artists; Bonnard being more concerned with the atmospheric content of the picture, effects of tremulous light and air, and Vuillard with its architectural structure. Their resemblances may be partly due to the fact that both were fond of neutral colors and of painting on cardboard, an absorbent ground. We find much the same divergencies between the work of Picasso and Braque respectively during the period of Analytic Cubism.

Vuillard had been considerably impressed by the teachings of the Pont-Aven School. Led on by his friends Denis and Roussel, he plunged into the fray, even joined in the dinners in the Passage Brady, and did posters, programs and publicity pictures in oils, or oftener in the then fashionable tempera technique, on canvas or cardboard, for the Théâtre de l'Œuvre. Vuillard's "Intimism" found an outlet in his quest of simplification; thus he eliminated from his drawing all but essentials, using bold, expressive, often distorting, yet sober and invariably constructive lines. That feeling for precision, which was to make him the most accomplished of the Nabis, was coming to the fore. His brush is lightly charged with pigment, tones are warm but devoid of brilliancy, for the most part variations on neutral tints, whites and browns especially, the monastic hues we associate with Dominicans and Benedictines. When, on rare occasions, he indulges in bright colors, he takes care to mute them, and gets effects of a deep sonority more telling than his friends' exaggerated use of the "loud pedal."

EDOUARD VUILLARD (1868-1940). OLD LADY EXAMINING HER NEEDLEWORK, 1893. (11⅜ × 10½")
PRIVATE COLLECTION, PARIS.

One of Vuillard's masterpieces. The subtlety of the tones and the refinement of the composition recall a Vermeer, but
a Vermeer more spontaneous, more "alive."

In fact his work reminds us of a murmurous, spellbinding chamber music, all the more compelling for its serene restraint. If ever there was an art for professionals, it is Vuillard's; few
are the artists who have not been fascinated by it.

Nevertheless it is inimitable. Like Renoir, Vuillard has had no disciples, doubtless because
his art is not the outcome of any theory, but the reflection of a unique personality. In his
highest achievements, lying as they do between the decorative fantasy of his early days and
the naturalistic academicism of 1920, Vuillard achieves a balance so miraculously perfect
that we might say that in his qualities there are no defects.

Revival of Book Illustration

★

THE PRACTICE of employing great artists for the illustration of books is no new one; from the days of the Carolingian illuminators it has continued, by way of Fouquet, Holbein, Fragonard and Boucher up to our time, with Dufy and Matisse. Not uninterruptedly however; after the French Revolution the illustrated book went out of favor with the public for nearly a hundred years. Delacroix's lithographs for *Faust* brought him in a paltry hundred francs, he had to publish his *Hamlet* at his own expense, and Chassériau found few buyers for his *Othello*. During this period publishers preferred to employ professional illustrators, and, with a few laudable exceptions, the result was hackwork. Moreover engraving was coming to be regarded more and more as merely a means of reproducing pictures.

However, it was to have a new lease of life, and a brilliant one. It is always hard to say just when a revival begins, and this is no exception. Should it be dated to 1862 (foundation of the Society of Etchers), or to 1875 when Manet illustrated Poe's *The Raven* and Mallarmé's *L'Après-midi d'un Faune*? Or to 1888 when Redon began illustrating Flaubert? These were but premonitory signs; five years had yet to pass before it was seen that Bracquemond had been justified in writing: "The original creators and pioneers of the art of engraving were invariably painters; the professionals whom we have in mind today when speaking of engravers have merely made technical improvements in the processes those painters had discovered." So now artists were once again to renovate the arts of illustration and engraving, as they were renovating stage decoration and tapestry design.

The last great painter-illustrated work, Delacroix's *Faust*, had shown how lithography and typography could be integrated into an organic whole. The new era began with a book of lithographs, Gide's *Voyage d'Urien* (1893), illustrated by Maurice Denis. From 1836 onward the art of color lithography had been practiced widely in France and before the end of the century had some magnificent successes to its credit; notably the lithographs produced by Lautrec, Chéret and Bonnard. It was chiefly Lautrec who brought this technique into high favor with the younger generation of artists. Among his outstanding achievements in this genre were the album devoted to Yvette Guilbert (who, after objecting to Lautrec's posters of her, consented to the publication of this set of sixteen lithographs), his illustrations of Clemenceau's *Au pied du Sinaï* (1898) and of Jules Renard's *Histoires naturelles* (1899). Bonnard, after illustrating Peter Nansen's *Marie* in 1898, made lithographs for *Parallèlement* in 1900 and for *Daphnis et Chloé* in 1902. Now that Lautrec and the Nabis had pointed the way, painters were called in to illustrate all the leading books of the day. The woodcut had been brought back into favor prior to 1914 by Dufy and Derain. Matisse and Picasso produced big illustrated books and the Surrealists made a point of illustrating theirs; in short, painters and poets now joined forces, as partners in the quest of beauty.

How is this sudden change to be explained? Millet, Corot, Jongkind and Degas (to name but a few of many artists) were perfectly familiar with the technique. Renoir, Pissarro, Sisley, Guillaumin, Berthe Morisot and most of the Impressionists had made engravings, but they kept them stored away in portfolios. None of them had illustrated books—with the exception of Manet and Gauguin. The truth was that their ventures had little or nothing in common with those of the writers of the day. It was not until the launching in 1891 of the *Revue Blanche*, a forum for the vague anarcho-socialist leanings of the contemporary intellectuals, that painters and poets recognized their solidarity and joined forces. Their aesthetic tendencies were in accord; Mirbeau and Jules Renard, Félix Fénéon and Natanson put their pens at the service of the Nabis. As a consequence of these contacts and shared ideals there arose a collaboration which has lasted till our time and to which are due some of the handsomest books the world has seen. Baudelaire's foresight had, once again, proved unerring when he wrote that "in the years to come painter and poet more than ever will march shoulder to shoulder."

Vogue of Posters and Lithography

★

WITH THE vogue of lithographs in black-and-white or color and with that of the poster, which set in round about 1890, the art of the day became accessible to a much wider public than ever before.

Indeed this new form of art had a success as sudden as it was widespread. To Jules Chéret with his "Saxoléine" (which appeared in 1886) goes the credit of being the inventor of the poster in colors, but his methods were rapidly improved on by others.

Lautrec was much taken with this new means of expression; his early efforts, it is said, owed much to Bonnard's advice and encouragement. The two artists executed their first posters in the Imprimerie Ancourt; soon after, they transferred the scene of their activities to Auguste Clot's, another printing-house. Lautrec's first poster (1891), made for the Moulin Rouge, features La Goulue and Valentin-le-Désossé. In 1895 Messrs Boussod and Valadon organized a competition for a publicity print for Sloane's "Napoleon"; among the twenty-five competitors, Lautrec was given the fourth place. This may be accounted for by the fact that the selection committee included men like Detaille, Gérôme and Vibert; anyhow the first prize (1000 francs) went to Métivot, who enjoyed some renown as a humorist in the 'nineties but is quite forgotten today; the second and third prizes to Chartier and Dupray. Already Lautrec had decided that the lithographic methods of the time were out of date and stereotyped, and was trying out new procedures. He took infinite pains over his proofs, haggled over the quality of the paper and insisted on mixing the inks himself. Moreover he left nothing to the inspiration of the moment, and transferred not merely general designs but fully worked-out paintings on to the stone. In his posters he aimed at the effect of murals, eschewed modeling, gave little heed to "values," and employed flat tones.

Each artist made technical discoveries of his own but never thought of keeping them to himself and pooled them with his friends'. Thus Lautrec found a way of obtaining striking effects by having dark greens put on *after* the black, or again by the rather tricky process of simultaneous inking, i.e. printing off several colors at one passage through the press.

Bonnard's earliest lithographs were made between 1889 and 1895. It was the success of his first poster, "France-Champagne" (1889), for which he was paid a hundred francs, that decided him to make painting his vocation. This poster, we are told, created quite a sensation when it made its appearance on the walls of Paris. He did the pictures for Terrasse's *Solfège illustré* and illustrated some books for Vollard, notably Verlaine's *Parallèlement*. Many commissions for posters came his way; amongst others for the Figaro, the Club des Cent, the Painter-Engravers Exhibition, and for the *Revue Blanche*. The last-mentioned poster scored a great success owing to the unsymmetrical arrangement of the letters forming the name of the magazine and for its eye-catching repetition on the poster.

Vuillard, too, was greatly attracted by lithography, and from 1891 on was much commended for his skillful handling of contrasts in black and white, his subtle modulations and the curious effects of vibrancy and translucency in which he excelled. He designed programs and made posters for the Théâtre de l'Œuvre (notably for Ibsen's *Rosmersholm, The Master Builder, An Enemy of the People*), and, needless to say, for the *Revue Blanche*.

As a rule the subjects of the lithograph were of an everyday order: café-concerts and music-halls, street-scenes, glimpses of family life and so forth. In fact, in their directness of approach, spontaneity and fidelity to life, they might almost seem to have prefigured the snapshot of today. The horse traffic in the Paris streets, florists, children, puppies, cyclists—all alike were pretexts for piquant little compositions, sparkling with life. Lautrec, Bonnard and Vuillard were not the only pioneers in this field; we must not overlook the work of Vallotton, Sérusier, Ranson, Denis, Steinlen and even Alfred Jarry, who did so much, by way of lithographic illustrations, to further the art of the modern book.

LA REVUE A PARAIT CHAQUE MOIS EN LIVRAISONS DE 100 PAGES le n° 1 fr. BUREAUX 1 r. Laffitte EN VENTE PARTOUT

Imp. Edw. Ancourt PARIS

PIERRE BONNARD (1867-1947).
LA REVUE BLANCHE, 1894.
($31\frac{3}{8} \times 24\frac{1}{4}$") POSTER.

Poster art calls for spontaneity and, above all, brilliant color. In his canvases of this period Bonnard was using discreet, delicately emotive neutral tones; here he brings off the remarkable feat of imparting vividness to tones reputedly the coldest. This poster has a wit and a sophisticated charm that well convey the atmosphere of the 'nineties. All his life long Bonnard loved to roam the streets of Paris; the title of Guillaume Apollinaire's *Le flâneur des deux rives* was after his own heart. For he, too, never wearied of exploring the Parisian scene in that golden age of fifty years ago when no one seemed in a hurry, you could linger on the sidewalks without being jostled, and in the streets the traffic still moved at a decorous speed set by the horse cabs and buses. Bonnard was fascinated by the languid grace of women in dark dresses outlined against the greyish walls of the old houses; by glimpses of white petticoats when they daintily lifted their skirts to cross the street; by the sight of a ragged street-urchin bustling a pompous citizen, or even a mongrel going about its canine business. He rendered these scenes in what seems the simplest possible way, in neutral tones, with playful, piquant touches, accents so apt and seemingly inevitable that one hardly realizes the cunning and consummate artistry behind them.

It was Bonnard's *France-Champagne* poster that inspired Lautrec to try his hand at this form of art. The two men became close friends and often met at the Ancourt printing works where the prints were pulled by "Le Père Cotelle," whom Lautrec has immortalized by a likeness on the cover of *L'Estampe Originale*. Both Lautrec and Bonnard were greatly drawn to lithography. The seeming ease of Lautrec's line was not wholly spontaneous. It is said that when he was making large posters, he would lie flat on the stone and make change after change in the design, multiplying *pentimenti*, in a tireless quest of the significant, absolutely right line. It was at the music-hall named *Le Jardin de Paris* that Lautrec got the subject of this poster. The sight of the members of the orchestra displaying such prodigious energy while remaining seated may have gratified vicariously his craving for the violent activity from which his infirmity debarred him. Lautrec always sat in the front row of the stalls, and the "Jane Avril" composition was built up from this viewpoint. Here Lautrec brilliantly emancipated 20th-century drawing from the classical realism of the 19th. The prolongation of the neck of the bass fiddle so as to frame the dancer in an endless arabesque, the witty arrangement of the sheet of music, the fantastic treatment of the player's head—all have a boldness exceptional for the epoch.

HENRI DE TOULOUSE-LAUTREC (1864-1901).
JANE AVRIL AT THE JARDIN DE PARIS, 1893.
($21\frac{3}{8} \times 15\frac{3}{4}$") POSTER.

Pierre Bonnard

★

BONNARD was born on October 13, 1867, at Fontenay-aux-Roses. The charming name of this Paris suburb, suggesting as it does visions of flowers and colorful retreats, seems particularly appropriate for the birthplace of a great painter whose art is all in delicate nuances, fine shades of feeling. And having touched on names, we may follow up with those of some of Bonnard's pictures, which give a good general idea of his favorite motifs: *Daphnis and Chloe, The Little Fauns, The Cabhorse, Paradise, Leaving the Moulin Rouge, The Three Graces, Woman Undressing, The Panorama, The Boulevard de Clichy, The Dining-Room, The Cock and Hen, In a Southern Garden, Boating on the Seine.*

As is well known, many great artists have made heavy weather of their careers; Bonnard's life was relatively plain sailing. He did well at school, in classics, and then entered an attorney's office, hoping in time to qualify as a magistrate. Then one day in 1889, having taken out a drawing from the office file, which he was using as a hiding-place for such things, he succeeded in selling it for a hundred francs. It was a sketch for a poster advertising a well-known brand of champagne. This was enough to make him promptly throw up his law studies, and we can imagine him echoing Gauguin's cry of liberation: "From now on I paint every day!"

The work of the great exile of Tahiti has always impressed young artists, and Bonnard was no exception. One of Gauguin's sayings, "There are only two kinds of artist—imitators and revolutionaries," was an obvious enjoinder to choose freedom. But this was not so easy as it sounded. For Gauguin himself had opened up so many and such various new paths, whose names were not, like Impressionism, coined by ironical critics, but assigned them by the painters themselves, that (since youth is always eager to be in the *avant-garde*) the younger artists were hard put to it to decide which to choose—Cloisonnism, Symbolism, Synthetism or Ideism, not to mention Neo-Traditionalism, the very latest of the -isms.

But, by way of Gauguin, it was Japanese art that most influenced Bonnard. After carefully studying Japanese prints, he tested for himself the efficacy of flat planes, modeling reduced to a minimum, two-dimensional composition, lines intersecting in such a way as to create a new kind of depth. The "Japanese Nabi" (as his friends called him) also experimented in the use of drawing alone for synthesizing form, in a somewhat decorative manner. In his painting he kept to flat tints and soft colors, all the softer because applied to an absorbent ground (cardboard), and heavily diluted with turpentine. In this early phase, however, Bonnard concentrated mostly on drawing, poster-designing and lithography, perfecting his black-and-white technique and his handling of the arabesque. In any case his palette was still very subdued, in accordance with the anti-impressionist trend of the day, and he made much use of blacks and greys.

Though involved in the sometimes chaotic debates for which the *Revue Blanche* office served as a friendly forum, Bonnard managed to retain the youthful spontaneity that was to be the lifelong charm of his personality. Given his impulsive temperament, these discussions, which usually took an esoteric or scientific turn, must have gone against the grain; and in fact he reacted against this intellectualization of art, and little by little moved in the direction of a greater freedom.

The truth is (and in fact he made no secret of it) that Bonnard was a born Impressionist, and for this reason symbolist or "ideist" theories could never hold him long. All he asked of painting was for it to embody the impressions given him by what he saw, and his whole life was a long, observant, fascinated contemplation of the infinite variety of things. Thus, once he had escaped from the literary atmosphere of the *Revue Blanche*, he rid his palette of all constraint and gave rein to that creative joy in light and color which enabled him to transform even the humblest domestic object into something rare and wonderful, glowing with all the colors of the rainbow. The basic principle of Bonnard's art can be summed up

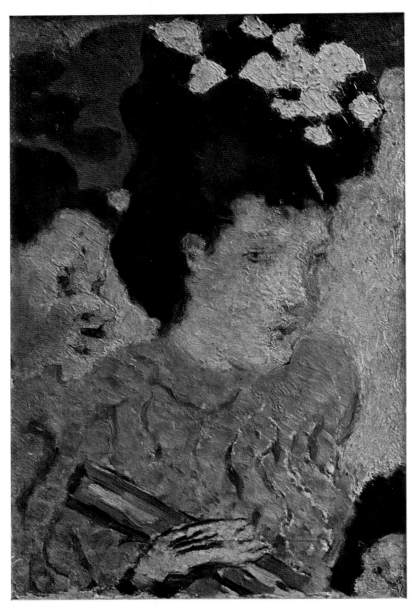

PIERRE BONNARD (1867-1947).
WOMAN'S HEAD, CA. 1892. (10⅝ × 7″)
PRIVATE COLLECTION, WINTERTHUR.

It was probably this exquisitely harmonious color-scheme that led Maurice Denis to remark on Bonnard's "felicitous handling of dark tones and greys."

in three words: freedom of imagination. Guided entirely by his natural impulses, he indulged in the boldest, most surprising dissonances, and those "grace notes" of which he alone had the secret; also those frequent—but how delightful!—"blunders" for which critics so often upbraided him. When he painted, the colors seemed to flow from his brush like the many-hued ribbons from a conjuror's sleeve. And lo and behold, a new Space had emerged, created by the warmest, rarest color-schemes, but an accommodating Space in which the eye feels happily at ease! It is easy to see why Bonnard was not cut out for an official career. He had no gift for figures or routine-work. Punctuality and punctiliousness would have gone against the grain of a young man who

loved to linger on the way to observe a passing cloud, the glimmer of a street-lamp, the quivering of a leaf or a blade of grass, the flutter of a woman's dress. We can picture him gazing fixedly at the object, his eyes wide with wonder, until he forgets all about it, lost in a day-dream; then later, when he stands in front of his canvas, the image floats up again, resummoned by some law governing the persistence of visual impressions.

In rendering sensations Bonnard went further than all the Impressionists, including Cézanne and Renoir. With him painting reached a pitch of abstraction never yet attained in the quest of "pure painting." He painted —to use Monet's simile—"as a bird sings," but in his case it was like the nightingale which never quite recaptures its first refrain, and indulges in endless variations until its voice dies out among the trees. Thus it was with Bonnard's great mural compositions; they do not always "hold the wall together" according to the rules of decoration, but seem magically to extend it to infinity, like the vast skies in Tiepolo's domes. Defenders of Academicism have thought to belittle certain tendencies of modern art by saying it is merely decorative. They use the word "decoration" in an invidious sense, meaning what is added by way of ornament to please the eye. Actually, great painters have never fought shy of what decoration implies, far from it, and Bonnard was not the first to give it so large a place in art, nor will he be the last. For him the problem was not to embellish a wall, but to organize it as a picture-surface—which was, in fact, the classical ideal. When he spoke of Intimism and Decoration, Bonnard was elucidating two aspects of his art: that of the easel-painter intent on expressing emotional experience, whose concentration within a restricted space intensifies it; and that of the decorator, whose vision calls for large surfaces over which the imagination can freely range, uncramped by spatial restrictions.

PIERRE BONNARD (1867-1947). THE TERRASSE FAMILY, 1892. (12⅛ × 10¼")
MOLYNEUX COLLECTION, PARIS.

Bonnard's sister, Andrée, married Claude Terrasse, the composer, and they had several children. One of Bonnard's masterpieces, this canvas boldly develops the Japanese technique of composition in flat planes. It has something of the fresco and of the decorative sweep of the artist's next phase. With the variety and spontaneity of its drawing and Bonnard's choice of delicate, infrequently used colors, this canvas marks another step towards the liberation of painting from illusionist imitation which culminated in the art of the 20th century.

Félix Vallotton

★

BORN in Switzerland, at Lausanne, Vallotton went to Paris when he was sixteen and studied at the Académie Julian. There he was severely disciplined, his teacher being Jules Lefèbvre who had made his name with *Truth arising from the Well*, once the pride of the Luxembourg Museum, but now relegated to the attics. Young Vallotton, to begin with, was all for his master's uncompromising academicism. The change came in the early 'nineties when he met the Nabis and, burning his old idols, developed an enthusiasm for decoration, poster-art and lithography. After exhibiting at the Salon des Indépendants (he had abandoned the official Salon in which his portrait *M. Jasinsky* had undergone violent attacks from a certain section of the public) he joined the *Revue Blanche* group and did some portraits of artists and writers. On the technical side he indulged in a freedom in keeping with the poetic imaginings of a highly strung temperament.

The spontaneity of his work of this period surprises, when we recall the rigorous precision, not to say bleakness, of his later art. At this stage he painted seaside and street scenes and his ebullient technique found all it needed for its display in the most everyday objects—hats, shoes, dogs and cats—which he depicted with remarkable liveliness and wit. The dynamic effervescence of this relatively brief phase in his career makes a singular contrast with the staid and static composition characteristic of his later manner.

Most of the Nabis took their mission—of "prophets" or "illuminati"—with high seriousness, but Vallotton's light touch and gentle irony soon won him many supporters among the group. He became extremely popular and sought after. Maurice Denis included him in his picture *Homage to Cézanne*, and we see him again in one of Lautrec's lithographs, alongside Vuillard, Thadée Natanson and Missia, his wife. Vuillard painted a delightful portrait of him and Missia together. Natanson has referred to Vallotton's "sarcastic, devastating remarks whose terseness and acuteness matched those of his woodcuts." This—the woodcut—was the medium he employed for the famous portraits which, first exhibited at the 1893 Salon des Indépendants, illustrated Remy de Gourmont's *Livre des Masques*. The masks in question were mostly the faces of Vallotton's contemporaries and friends. He brought to his art a spirit of lively invention which many years later (in 1921) made him the target of Surrealist attacks. The Surrealists accused him of having completely overlooked the "enigmatic" side of Lautréamont when making his portrait. Vallotton's riposte had all the adroitness one would expect of him. "That portrait was pure invention, done out of my head; I had nothing to go on, as nobody, not even de Gourmont, could tell me anything about the man. But I knew what I was getting at. Though this portrait was the fruit of my imagination, it has made good in the event and most people think it lifelike." The neatness of the retort lay in its being so much in line with the Surrealists' own ideas.

But it was with his adoption of a new, highly personal aesthetic that Vallotton's true temperament emerged. Henceforth he painted nudes and portraits that aim above all at the expression of character, and always with a cruelly precise technique whose studied coldness, often carried to an excess that disconcerts us, suggests the presence of some repressed anxiety or fixed idea. Vallotton's drawing was now reduced to bare essentials, but he seemed to practice this austerity less with a view to giving his line any specific quality than with a deliberate intent to discard every trace of the superfluous. One suspects that this was a counterblast to the happy spontaneity of his friends Vuillard and Bonnard, which he lacked—and envied. "The smooth perfection of the egg" delighted him, so he said. Thus his figures have a frozen immobility, a truth truer than life and oddly disquieting for the observer.

We find in Vallotton's work what might be described as a new objectivity. Indeed the *Neue Sachlichkeit* movement may well have been inspired by the intriguing, hermetic, thought-provoking art of Félix Vallotton.

The Redon Exhibition

at Durand-Ruel's in 1894

LITTLE has been written about Redon, the somewhat esoteric nature and inaccessibility of whose art have limited the number of his admirers. It was his friend André Mellerio who did most, though with little success, to interest the general public in his work, and we quote a passage from his Introduction to the Catalogue of the Redon Exhibition *in extenso*. Written in the florid style of the period, it may disconcert the modern reader, but Mellerio's fervor and discernment carry conviction.

"Ignorance, bestiality, perversity, sublimity—in all these Redon discerns as it were a common basis, and that is suffering. In some of the faces he depicts there is an intensity of expression so potent that it both lures us like a magnet and inspires us with a panic fear—fear of the abyss we glimpse across the limpid pupils of those dilated eyes. Redon shows us embryonic Nature, ridiculous or horrifying in her first fumbling essays; and then he shows the culmination of her work in the refinement of the human face, with its intimations of a soul that quivers on the brink of winging to still greater heights. This amazing comprehension of the depths and heights of the human situation reminds us of Pascal's *Pensées*, in which one of the greatest thinkers of all time has analyzed the dual aspect of man's being and sought to plumb at once the mystery of his base origin and that of his exalted destiny.

"In bodying forth the inner world of homo sapiens the artist has proved himself equal to his ambitious task. For Redon has succeeded in forging out a style at once supple, grave and vibrant with emotion. With a mere charcoal sketch he achieves a grandiose vision; with black

and white he creates real darkness, real light. Moreover by an adroit technique that is the wonder of experts in that field, he has given the seemingly defunct art of the lithograph new, amazing life. If some future historian seeks in the arts a mirror of the troubled period we are living in, torn between the rival claims of science and mysticism, unable to ignore the discoveries of the scientist or to restrain the soaring aspirations of the immortal soul, will he not turn to the work of Odilon Redon, and to its pregnant synthesis of the Symbol and Expression?"

ODILON REDON (1840-1916).
LITHOGRAPH ILLUSTRATION
FOR "LA TENTATION DE
SAINT ANTOINE" BY FLAUBERT.

PAUL GAUGUIN (1848-1903). WOMAN WITH A FLOWER, 1891. (28¾ × 18½") PRIVATE COLLECTION, COPENHAGEN.

PAUL GAUGUIN (1848-1903). LANDSCAPE AT LE POULDU, 1890. (28¾ × 36⅛")
PAUL FIERENS COLLECTION, BRUSSELS.

From October 1889 to November 1890 Gauguin stayed in Brittany, first at Pont-Aven, then with his friend Meyer de Haan at Le Pouldu. In a letter to Emile Bernard he wrote : "The only outcome of a strenuous year's work is a storm of abuse emanating from Paris that, I must confess, discourages me. So much so that I can hardly bear to paint now. Still I do make a few studies, if you can call them that—just daubs that please the eye. But my heart isn't in it."

The Gauguin Exhibition

at Durand-Ruel's in 1893

Gauguin organized, in November 1893, a large one-man show in Paris of the works he had brought back from his first trip to Tahiti, forty-nine paintings and two pieces of sculpture. In June of the previous year he had written to his wife: "I have eleven months of active work behind me, representing forty-four rather large canvases, which ought to bring in at least 15,000 francs for the year, provided the public is willing to buy." But buyers were few and far between. After two years in the South Seas (June 1891-July 1893) Gauguin had landed at Marseilles with four francs in his pocket. A windfall in the form of a small inheritance (due to the timely demise of an uncle) enabled him to defray the cost of the exhibition, which, financially, was a complete fiasco.

The public's reactions were mixed, but generally speaking no one took his pictures seriously. While a number of writers and poets were loud in admiration of his work, the painters of the older generation—Renoir, Monet and Pissarro among them—made no secret of their distaste for it. Degas, on the other hand, staunchly championed Gauguin, and the younger men, rallying behind the Nabis, showed the keenest interest. In his preface to the catalogue Charles Morice declaimed against "that tradition of nature imitation which is the greatest bane of painting." While the exhibition was still on, Morice and Gauguin conceived the idea of working up a book together on the basis of the latter's Tahitian impressions. The result was that extraordinary book Noa-Noa.

FÉLIX VALLOTTON (1865-1925). AT THE MUSIC HALL, 1895. (20⅝ × 13″)
TROESTER COLLECTION, GENEVA.

In this curious composition we have one of those spontaneous records of visual experience, like snapshots, that characterized Vallotton's first manner. There is also here a playfulness, indeed a verve, somewhat astonishing in Vallotton's
case, and even reminiscent of the work of certain naïve or "Sunday" painters.

A New Romanticism

Expressionism

THE GERMAN inventors of the term "Expressionismus" had in mind one of the root meanings of the word "expression": the exteriorization of emotion. Diderot had observed that "expression comes first to the artist; mastery of design and execution, later," and we need not be surprised that fifty years ago the German critics applied this word Expressionismus to painting in general, though in particular to that kind of painting in which the vivid rendering of human emotion ranks above the solution of purely plastic problems. And it is common knowledge that art in Germany seems always to have been relatively indifferent to problems of an aesthetic order, and above all concerned with the manifestation of emotion. The Expressionist, as a rule, does not aim at treating his picture objectively, in terms of the rules of art and as an end in itself; he uses it as a recipient for his emotional outpourings. Thus he rejects the classical conception of the painter as a servant of his art, and makes art the servant of his feelings; this is, in fact, a return to the Romantic ideal in its most impassioned form. At the turn of the century these two diametrically opposed ideals, Classical and Romantic, joined vigorous issue, and each in turn could claim successes to its credit.

Unlike the Impressionists, who regarded a purely objective rendering of the retinal image and the interplay of forms and colors as sufficient for the composition of the picture, the Expressionists—amongst whom art critics ranked indiscriminately Van Gogh, Gauguin, Lautrec, Munch, Ensor and their successors Rouault, Picasso (during his Blue Period), the Germans Nolde and Kirchner, the Austrian Kokoschka and, later, Soutine—followed in the footsteps of Daumier, Millet and Courbet, and stressed the function of the "mind" in the making of a work of art: a function first advocated by Courbet, then by Van Gogh, Gauguin and Redon. Thus painting was no longer regarded as an end in itself, but as a means of bodying forth the artist's states of mind, his personal feelings, his soul-searchings, his philosophical, metaphysical or social theories, or, on occasion, visions of the universe viewed from an ultra-individualist angle. This explains why the great Expressionists came to be regarded, and to regard themselves, as the votaries, or victims, of an heroic isolation. In pursuance of this thoroughgoing solipsism, the Expressionist rebelled against all set rules, the disciplines involved in the technique of painting, all demands of a plastic order, and even against the use of technical procedures that did not make the expression of emotion their only aim.

Obviously such views differed *toto caelo* from the purely visual conceptions of art sponsored by Cézanne, Renoir, Seurat, Matisse and the Fauves. True, we shall have occasion to point out that, in a later phase of modern art, these two extremes tended to come together and sometimes even coalesced, notably when under the shock of some violent personal emotion an artist was forced out of his studied objectivity. For the present we may sum up the Expressionist position as follows. The leaders of the movement were usually men endowed— or afflicted—with a fiercely egocentric, not to say morbid sensitivity making them indifferent to social contacts, and even "enemies of society." In painting they sought to find an outlet for, and an escape from, their physical or psychical afflictions, since it provided them with a means of exteriorizing these and—as is so often the secret wish of the egocentrist—"unloading" them on the community at large.

We shall see in the course of this survey of the currents and cross-currents of painting during the first half of the 20th century, how Expressionism, after a temporary setback, while the Nabis, Fauves, Cubists and other experimentalists were in the ascendant, came to the fore again with a new access of vigor. This was to a large extent the result of social upheavals, revolutions and wars that led the artists, anyhow for a while, to divert their attention from purely plastic researches—as being too remote from life and savoring of "ivory tower" exclusiveness—towards the problems and perplexities of what Malraux has named *La Condition Humaine* ("Man's Fate").

PAUL CÉZANNE (1839-1906). L'ESTAQUE: THE VILLAGE AND THE SEA, 1878-1883.
(20⅜ × 25⅛") PRIVATE COLLECTION, LUCERNE.

Cézanne lived at L'Estaque, near Marseilles, for many years and never wearied of painting it under its varied aspects (chiefly in 1878 and 1883-1885). Noteworthy here is the highly personal treatment of the subject, in slanting, parallel, still somewhat impressionist brushstrokes, and the rhythmic disposition of the factory chimneys.

The Cézanne Exhibition

at Vollard's in 1895

A long overdue homage to Cézanne's genius, this large-scale exhibition took place at Vollard's gallery in 1895, some thirty-five years, that is, after the artist had begun his career and only eleven before his death.

Referring to it fondly as his "little thrill," Cézanne stressed the part played by sensation in the creative act, but gave it a new directive. For he no longer merely recorded what the eye perceived, as the Impressionists had been content with doing when they exploited a purely physical emotion which, when all was said and done, hardly rose above the level of the satisfactions of the gourmet. Cézanne went further; after accumulating all that his visual experience provided in the way of raw material, he proceeded to filter this through the mesh of his creative mind. He was not interested in imitating sensations, but worked over them much as a mason chips and hews the stones with which he means to build a house.

Thus Cézanne raised the retinal sensation, regarded by the Impressionists as sufficient in itself, from the purely physical plane to that of an ideal content, and used it merely as a starting-off point, a means to the realization of an over-all architectural concept. Hence his highly individual ideas of rhythm, style and constructive distortion, justified by geometrical referents that determined not only planes, lines and volumes, but every brushstroke in the composition. Thus he took part in the creation of a new classicism "remaking Poussin after nature."

PAUL CÉZANNE (1839-1906). THE BOY IN A RED WAISTCOAT, 1890-1895. (36⅛ × 25⅝")
PRIVATE COLLECTION, ZURICH.

The four portraits Cézanne made of this young Italian model are amongst the works that had most influence on the new generation of artists. In 1895 Gustave Geffroy wrote of this picture that "it can bear comparison with the finest figure pieces ever made." Noteworthy is the deliberately expressive distortion of the arm.

PIERRE BONNARD (1867-1947). AMBROISE VOLLARD'S PICTURE-SHOP.
From a pen-and-ink drawing reproduced in Charles Terrasse's monograph on Bonnard.

Ambroise Vollard's Picture-Shop

★

WHEN THAT remarkable man, Ambroise Vollard, first arrived in Paris from Reunion Island, his sole assets were a Creole accent and a burning ambition to make good. Starting in a small way as junior clerk to a Parisian picture-dealer, he quickly learned the ropes and by 1890 had set up a shop of his own.

His famous "cellar" in the Rue Laffitte became the most thriving picture market of the day. Degas, Pissarro and Renoir dropped in regularly; other *habitués* were Cézanne, Emile Bernard, Vuillard, Bonnard and, later on, Rouault, Matisse, Picasso and Chagall. Known for his caustic wit, Vollard was no less distinguished as an amateur chef and at the famous dinners in the basement his curry-and-rice was the high spot of the evening.

Not content with dealing in pictures, he branched out into art publishing, and even did some writing himself. His name, however, is inseparable from his gallery, which looked like an old curiosity shop, perpetually cluttered up, yet somehow fascinating in its colorful disorder, and was the scene of many famous exhibitions. The first was the great Cézanne Exhibition of 1895, at which one hundred canvases were somehow crowded on to the walls. The same year saw Vollard's publication of Bonnard's first lithographs, and in 1897 he held a Nabi Exhibition. He sponsored Picasso's first Paris exhibition in 1901, showed works by Gauguin in 1903, and by Matisse in 1904. The following year Vollard bought up all the works in Picasso's studio (Pink Period), and in 1906 all those in Vlaminck's. In 1907 he encouraged Rouault to take to ceramics. In 1917 he fitted out a studio for him in his own home, commissioning him at the same time to illustrate *Les Réincarnations du Père Ubu*, which he had just written. In 1927 he commissioned Chagall to illustrate La Fontaine's *Fables*. Vollard was ceaselessly active both as a dealer and as a publisher until his death in 1939.

Edvard Munch

Painter of the Nordic Soul, its Problems and Perplexities

APART from its intrinsic value the work of Edvard Munch has a special importance in modern art, as being typical of a period when the normal preoccupations of the artist were so often allied with psychological aberrations or with that intense concern for ethical and social problems which went with what was known as the *mal du siècle*, prevalent at the time in the Scandinavian countries, in Holland and especially in Germany. The art of Munch not only had a widespread influence on art in general but also formulated what came to be known as Expressionism, a term used often in a rather disparaging sense, to describe the cult of self-expression carried to its highest pitch.

On a general survey of Munch's output what first strikes us is its lack of uniformity; one has the impression that all his life the artist was uncertain of his path, was feeling out in all directions and using all the technical expedients available, with a view to expressing sensations and emotions devoid of any unity of inspiration. Moreover he seems to have been the victim of vague, intractable obsessions and was never much inclined to cultivate those formal or coloristic qualities which characterize the work of the "pure" artist.

Indeed Munch rarely troubled his head about purely painterly problems. An entry in his diary reveals his attitude to art: "No more painting of interiors with women knitting and men reading! I want to show people who breathe, feel, love and suffer. I want to bring home to the spectator the sacred element in all human beings, so that he takes off his hat before them as he would in church." This is a far cry from impressionist serenity, for which in fact he had a hearty detestation, as one of his friends, that charming painter Edvard Diriks, told me in 1905. Diriks, by the way, was far from sharing his friend's ideas, though both of them had studied neo-impressionist art. During his first stay in Paris (in 1885, when he was twenty-two) Munch was greatly drawn to Van Gogh, Gauguin and Lautrec. But he associated more with writers than with painters. While in his twenties he was studying painting at the School of Arts and Crafts in Oslo and taking lessons from Christian Krohg the painter, he was a member of the club known as "The Bohemians of Christiania," whose leading figure was a poet, Hans Jäger. In this group the subjects of discussion were almost always social, ethical, religious, psychological or sexual problems—never painting. Munch played an active part at these gatherings, and all were impressed by his innate nobility of mind, his passionate defense of his ideals.

Munch was certainly not a psychopath like Van Gogh, but his nerves were always on the stretch; as the result of a nervous breakdown in 1908 he had to enter a clinic at Copenhagen. His neurotic temperament may have been partly due to the circumstances of his childhood; his father was a harsh, sour-tempered man and his early years were darkened by the death of his mother and two sisters. This explains, no doubt, his obsession with death, his dread of it and the great care he took of his physical health—not labor lost, since he lived to the age of eighty-one. Mentally it was another matter; Munch had recurrent phobias, when he was seized by a violent antipathy for women or crowds, for water or for flowers (these last because he associated them with disease and death). His high-strung, easily exasperated sensibility may explain his predilection as an artist for rather gruesome subjects: women embracing skeletons, funerals, burials and especially hospital scenes—scenes his father, a doctor who had devoted himself to ministering to the poor, had forced him as a boy to witness. Munch's earliest large works tell us something about the man himself; in 1886 he painted *The Sick Girl, Puberty* and *Men of Letters*. Some years later he conceived the idea of his *Frieze of Life*, a vast picture sequence illustrating all the aspects of the human predicament, man's griefs and joys, anxieties and yearnings, and on this he worked nearly all his life. In the *Dance of Life*, reproduced here, we see how Munch manages to work a note of sadness into even a would-be joyous scene. Though he detested women on principle, he had several

EDVARD MUNCH (1863-1944). THE DANCE OF LIFE, 1899-1900. (49⅛ × 74¾")
NATIONAL GALLERY, OSLO.

love-affairs and suffered horribly from jealousy. On one occasion, in the course of a quarrel, a woman fired on him with a revolver, wounding his hand. It was perhaps to escape from these troubles and from himself that (in 1916) he bought an estate at Ekely, on the Oslo fiord.

Though in painting Munch found a solace, a brief liberation from his anxieties and frustrations, he took no interest in plastic problems; what gives his work its power is that it so poignantly reflects his personal emotions. Of the sincerity of these emotions, and of the loftiness, indeed nobility, of his ideals there is no doubt, and to this is due his feeling for the monumental. It is interesting to note the attitudes of the figures in his large-scale compositions, their air of utter weariness, despairing gestures, drooping arms. In other works, on the contrary, the line is jagged, syncopated, ravaged with *pentimenti*; we feel that the artist is hoping for a respite, in the exhaustion that may follow this outburst of pent-up emotion. Indeed a sense of lassitude may account in part for those long languid lines, those weaving arabesques which in other works betray the influence of Jugendstil, though here Munch gives them a real, not merely decorative, significance and expressive values.

In his lithographs and woodcuts, however, he gives utterance to a feeling of revolt; the vigorous contrasts of whites and blacks without the use of intermediate tones tell of a fighting spirit, not a mood of resignation to his lot. Skeletons, harpies, vampires, skulls, intensely dramatic scenes—always of a symbolical order—are hacked out on the woodblock in a sort of frenzy and he dispenses with the use of color, always enervating, to his thinking. In his woodcuts he links up with the rugged force of the old German masters of that medium, even when (as, however, rarely happens) the subject is a cabaret scene. It is perhaps in this field that we see his very real originality at its best, and his drawing, always rather "precious" in his paintings, has an admirable force and spontaneity.

In short, along with Van Gogh, and perhaps Goya too, he may be regarded as the most radical exponent of what Germans mean by "Expressionismus"—not that as a painter he is comparable to the great Dutchman but because of the deep sincerity with which he expresses a temperament limited perhaps in scope, but typical of a contemporary *Weltanschauung*.

Jugendstil and "Modern Style"

★

THE TERM Jugendstil, derived from the name of a famous magazine *Die Jugend* (Youth) which made its appearance in 1896 at Munich, was applied to a new type of art which quickly gained ground all over Europe. In Vienna it went under the name of "Die Sezession" and in England, where its figurehead was Aubrey Beardsley, it was sometimes known as the *fin-de-siècle* or "Yellow Book" style. In Spain it was enthusiastically welcomed at Barcelona, whereas in France the so-called "modern style" was never taken very seriously.

Stemming from a revolt in Germany against academic art, Jugendstil launched a movement marked by a rather cheap romanticism. The themes it favored, in paintings and engravings, were taken from mediaeval legends or classical mythology and were often treated with an inexpertness verging on the uncouth, while on the decorative side, by way of posters, ceramics, wrought iron, sculpture and architecture, it promoted a tropical luxuriance of arabesques, a swirl of meaningless curves and convolutions.

The claim of the practitioners of this style, that it was bringing "a new freedom" to art, had little or no justification, one reason being that they absolutely vetoed the use of the straight line (doubtless because of the disciplines it calls for). In any case, after a brief hour of rather tawdry glory, the New Art disappeared almost as rapidly as it had emerged.

Here Munch has symbolized the destiny of man and woman, subject even in death to the dominion of love. During 1896 and 1897 Munch had frequented symbolist circles in Paris.

EDVARD MUNCH (1863-1944). MEETING IN INFINITY, 1899. (7 × 9¾")
NATIONAL GALLERY, OSLO.

PIERRE BONNARD (1867-1947). THE CIRCUS, CA. 1900. (21⅛ × 25½"). PRIVATE COLLECTION, PARIS.

Towards the 20th Century

★

THE 1900 Paris World's Fair, which had just begun, was destined to make history and, within limits, to launch a "style"; but of that style there is no trace in contemporary painting, anyhow the painting that matters. Though it is obvious how much the art of Munch, as regards its form, owed to the brief phase of Jugendstil (see above), neither Bonnard nor Picasso in that year 1900 yielded to the lures of *l'Art nouveau*. In the work of neither do we find reminiscences of the "faraway and long ago," or symbolic-sentimental evocations. As in the days of Manet, Renoir and Degas, artists continued to show a taste for scenes of circus life, dance-halls, race-courses and theaters. It was not the anecdotal element that attracted them, but the possibilities these offered for experiments of a plastic—and dynamic—order, in which the recent technical discoveries could be played off against each other. By annexing elements from Synthetism, Divisionism and Lautrec's vivid draftsmanship, these painters sought to revitalize the message of Impressionism. But theirs was a short-lived eclecticism, and in fact *fin-de-siècle* decadence was at hand.

PABLO PICASSO. WOMAN'S HEAD   ⟶

On his second visit to Paris in 1901, Picasso saw Lautrec's paintings and was enchanted by his draftsmanship, his at once impressionist and pointillist palette, but not yet by his uncompromising, almost brutal treatment of his personages.

GEORGES ROUAULT (1871).
PROSTITUTES, 1903.
(10¼ × 7⅜") HAHNLOSER
COLLECTION, WINTERTHUR.

At the Salon d'Automne, breaking for the first time with his "brown" manner, for which even the most favorably disposed critics of the time had severely castigated him, Rouault took to using reds, greens and blues. Though he did not indulge in the ultra-violent color effects favored by the Fauves, the intensity of his palette led him to be assimilated to them for a while. Here color is stepped up to a virulence exceptional with Rouault, by his use of deep black lines emphasizing clashes. This is in keeping with the tendency he here shows to distortion of a caricatural rather than an aesthetic order. Rouault's new manner reveals a pessimistic outlook on life ; he chooses his subjects from a world of prostitutes, procuresses or clowns, stressing the pathos of their lot, but with an undertone of reprobation.

The Salon d'Automne

★

PRESIDED over by the architect Frantz Jourdain, with Matisse, Marquet and Bonnard as its "star attractions," this new Salon—whose creation was largely due to the enterprise of Rambosson, Desvallières and Rouault—opened its doors in October 1903, in the Petit Palais on the Champs-Elysées. Not, however, in the lofty halls of that august building, but in the basement; for thus its conservator, H. Lapauze (who resented this intrusion of the ultra-modern) had decreed. Among the artists showing were Gauguin, Redon, Matisse, Desvallières, Guérin, Laprade, Marquet and Rouault. However it was not particularly successful, and Lapauze made this a pretext for refusing to let his Petit Palais be used for next year's Salon d'Automne. Thanks to the good offices of Henry Marcel, Director of the Beaux-Arts, this second exhibition was held in the Grand Palais des Champs-Elysées and, chiefly owing to the inclusion of a large Cézanne retrospective, was a success.

But now the members of the Institute banded together to have the Salon d'Automne expelled from the Grand Palais, which they claimed should be reserved for the Salon des Artistes Français. However, Eugène Carrière championed the new Salon in the teeth of a ruthless press campaign, and it was allowed to stay. The 1905 exhibition, which included Matisse, Marquet, Van Dongen, Derain, Vlaminck, Manguin, Rouault, Friesz, Puy and Valtat, was fiercely attacked both by academic reactionaries and by the old guard of Impressionism. But to no avail; the tide had turned, Fauvism had made good and the Salon d'Automne become an institution.

VINCENT VAN GOGH (1853-1890). WHEAT FIELD WITH CYPRESSES, 1889. (28½ × 36″)
BY COURTESY OF THE TRUSTEES, TATE GALLERY, LONDON.

The role assigned to technique in painting was now by way of acquiring new significance. Line and color were evaluated in terms of their impact not only on the eye but on "the thinking mind," as Van Gogh and Gauguin rather pompously described it, and they were called upon to interpret feelings that words fall short of expressing. A new symbolism of line and color came into being, in which the sources of both Fauvism and Expressionism are discernible.

The Van Gogh Exhibition

at Bernheim-Jeune's in 1901

If the Fauves-to-be sought honorable precedents for their passionate cult of color, they could certainly find these in the art of Monet, Renoir and Seurat. Nevertheless it was the epoch-making revelation in 1901 of Van Gogh's genius that touched off the train of events which led Matisse, Vlaminck and Derain to embark on a complete overhaul of all previous conceptions of the use of color. Vlaminck's remark on this occasion has often been quoted: "That day I felt I loved Van Gogh more than my own father." He expressed himself more seriously and better conveyed the impression produced by Van Gogh on him and his friends when he wrote: "Until then I hadn't known Van Gogh. He struck me as having brought off all that could possibly be done, but the mere fact of the unreserved admiration I felt for the man and his work made me somehow rebel against him. I was delighted with the reassurances he gave me, but it had been a nasty blow! In his work I found some of my own aspirations. The same Nordic affinities perhaps? And also a revolutionary urge and an almost religious feeling for the interpretation of nature."

Anyhow the three young artists were swept off their feet by this riot of pure color verging on the paroxysmal which, combined with a use of black that Impressionism had vetoed, seemed to "electrify" the picture-surface and to conjure up new worlds. They were particularly impressed by The Fourteenth of July *and its rhythmic orchestration of long, resonant brushstrokes and short dabs of vivid color implementing a wholly new perspective. Moreover Van Gogh's work provided an example of an art whose complete unity was admirable, if hard to come by. The young Fauves got from him an impression of utter sincerity and sureness of aim that dispelled any qualms they might have had about an artistry so different in many ways from theirs. Thus they sensed that Van Gogh had a message for them; he was not a* malade imaginaire *like Munch, his mental trouble was all too real, as was proved by his tragic end. But our Fauves, on the contrary, were healthy, robust young men and could hardly be expected to understand the so to speak fatality behind Van Gogh's technique. This is, perhaps, why the Fauve venture was short-lived and such influence as it had was in the long run attributed to the lesson of Van Gogh. The fact that one of them could say ironically of another Fauve, "He's a lion who pretends to like raw meat but feeds on grass!" suggests that, with all their enthusiasm for Van Gogh, the Fauves could really appreciate only one of the qualities of his painting, its seeming truculence. Perhaps, too, the willful savagery, the dazzle and reckless prodigality of their palette were in the last analysis somewhat superficial; though they spoke loudly, at bottom they had not much to say. Meanwhile they tried to adapt a frankly expressionist technique to a purely plastic way of seeing, and set to organizing color symphonies whose structure, they fondly hoped, possessed that "solid and abiding" quality aimed at by Cézanne.*

In this connection it is interesting to note how the expressionist revival now in progress in contemporary painting has brought Van Gogh into unique prominence. A generous enthusiasm whose object is less Van Gogh the artist than "poor Vincent," the man with whom fate dealt so unkindly, is making of him a sort of legendary hero. In fact he is by way of becoming one of those super-artists whom it is sacrilege to criticize.

This is one of the last pictures painted by the artist at Saint-Rémy. Here he gives free rein to his tumultuous emotions; it is not only the violence of the "mistral" driving across the Alpines that inspires this vision of wheat fields, cypresses, clouds and mountains caught up in some elemental carnival of form and color.

VINCENT VAN GOGH (1853-1890). ON THE EDGE OF THE ALPINES, SAINT-RÉMY, MAY 1890. (22⅜ × 27⅝") RIJKSMUSEUM KRÖLLER-MÜLLER, OTTERLO.

PABLO PICASSO (1881). WOMAN'S HEAD, 1901. (20⅜ × 13″) RIJKSMUSEUM KRÖLLER-MÜLLER, OTTERLO.

Almost every writer on aesthetics who has dealt with Matisse's work admits that no great master's art is harder to analyze and describe. The truth is that there is something fundamentally mysterious about his dynamic handling of light and color. In this connection we may recall that three of the very greatest colorists of the previous generation, Pissarro, Degas and Monet, ended up by being almost blind. Now Matisse was short-sighted from his earliest days. And it may be that the secret of the amazing alchemy of color peculiarly his lay midway, so to speak, between his spectacles and his imagination. Handicapped as he seemed to be, Matisse had the keenest, most penetrating, most ruthlessly acute vision one can imagine, and indeed invented some new shades of color.

Apart from this amazing gift, whose only explanation is summed up in the word "genius," there is nothing in Matisse's life to gratify the curiosity of those who like building up myths around the eminent, and making the great artist into a tragic hero. As a matter of fact this bold innovator, pioneer in so many fields, always led a quiet life and enjoyed robust good health. This may not tally with the romantic portrait one might hope to draw of a "revolutionary" artist, remembering the lives of such men as Delacroix, Courbet, Jongkind, Gauguin and Van Gogh; but facts are facts, and we must recognize that Matisse's life was quite different, indeed sedate—like, we might add, his physical appearance.

Taine's determinist theories seem to break down when we consider the prosaic facts of Henri Matisse's early youth. For though his mother had a charming talent for painting flowers on chinaware, the artist himself, born at Le Cateau in the north of France in 1869, was intended by his father to enter the magistracy and he duly studied law, without (as we are so often told of artists) making sketches in his notebooks when he should have been studying.

We may perhaps begin by recalling what Matisse himself once said: "The work of art should be, for the tired businessman no less than for the literary dilettante, a cerebral sedative, rather like a comfortable armchair." Now (and this is a well-established fact) it was in the course of a slow recovery from appendicitis that Matisse, then just under twenty, was advised by a friend to try his hand at painting, as a suitable pastime for a convalescent. Accordingly his mother supplied him with a box of paints, a gift frowned on by Matisse senior who would have preferred to see his son engaged in serious work. However, the combined effect of copying some colorprints and reading Goupil's *How to Paint* was enough, not merely to take his mind off his physical discomfort, but to give him a feeling of well-being, almost of bliss, such as he had never known before. "I felt transported," he writes, "into a sort of paradise in which I felt gloriously free, at ease, on my own, whereas before I'd been bored and rather worried by the hosts of things people seemed to expect of me."

Thus the origins of Matisse's vocation can be traced to that craving for freedom, for escape, which has never left him. And this desire to strike out his own path testified to an individualism already strongly marked, but which, owing to his youth, had so far failed to hold its own against outside pressure. It is clear that, even then, he chafed at the feeling that a social order in which he never felt at home was trying to foist on him its habits and conventions. From the start Matisse displayed a quite amazing talent for art. Picasso knew what he was talking about when he said: "At bottom it depends entirely on oneself. It's like a radiant sun in one's belly. Nothing else matters, really. That's the reason why, for instance, Matisse is Matisse. It's because he has a sun in his belly." In point of fact, nothing we know about his upbringing throws light on that gift for color which Matisse was to develop to an incomparable perfection. Let us simply say that he was a born colorist, as others are born singers, and that, for some mysterious reason, color was for him like the sap of a tree, something present in his lifeblood and conditioning his growth. One has, then, the impression that Matisse's cult of color was not, as in the case of many great artists, a by-product of his temperament; it was, rather, a vital necessity, ineluctable, innate. This may explain why he fostered this rare gift so sedulously and developed it to the utmost, feeling (half unconsciously perhaps) that it was the keystone of his art. Another distinctive trait is his exceptional level-headedness and circumspection. From earliest youth Matisse had not only a natural sense of balance and proportion, but a habit of self-criticism somewhat unusual in artists, who are generally prone

VINCENT VAN GOGH (1853-1890). PORTRAIT OF DR GACHET, AUVERS, JUNE 1890.
(26¾ × 22½″) BEQUEST OF DR P. GACHET, LOUVRE, PARIS.

Dr Gachet, who was quite a "character" and a familiar figure at the Café Guerbois in Paris, was one of the earliest patrons and friends of the Impressionists, who often came to visit him at Auvers. On leaving the Saint-Rémy asylum in May 1890, Van Gogh came to stay with him and painted his portrait. The first version is in the Frankfort Museum; this slightly different version, which he gave Dr Gachet, has been presented by his children to the Louvre. In a letter to his brother Van Gogh wrote: "I'm working on his portrait, a white cap on his head, his hair very blond and fair, his hands in light flesh-tints, and a cobalt-blue background. His dress-coat is blue and he's resting his elbow on a red table with a yellow book beside him ... Monsieur Gachet is absolutely *crazy* about this portrait."

VINCENT VAN GOGH (1853-1890). SUNFLOWERS, 1888. (37¼ × 28¾″)
V. W. VAN GOGH COLLECTION, LAREN (HOLLAND).

Message of Matisse

The Triumph of Color

DESTINED to be the chief concern of 20th-century art, the liberation of painting from representational service was carried a stage further, about 1900, by Matisse. He often used the word "expression," but always with reference to the picture *qua* picture and not to its psychological implications; indeed he went out of his way to avoid suggesting the inner life of the figures he painted. For what he meant by "expression" had nothing to do with what the Expressionists meant by that word; in fact he might have echoed a remark of Corot's which at the time it was made sounded outrageous: "I paint a woman's breast just as I'd paint an ordinary milk-can." Magician of the palette that he was, Matisse could depend on color alone to convey the message of his art, a message stated exclusively in terms of painting. Thus now for the first time the subject of the picture ceased to matter, and the way lay open to every manner of abstraction. The painter was invited to build up forms solely by combinations of various colors, all the colors of the spectrum. In other words, as we see in the picture reproduced below, Matisse entirely re-created the subject, and it was now that the term "creative art," soon to become the keyword of modern art, acquired a meaning concrete enough to cover and define the vast technical and stylistic innovations that were to revolutionize the whole art of painting in the opening years of the 20th century.

For the first time Matisse allows his penchant for color to get the upper hand. Here the theory, already envisaged by him, of substituting an imaginary reality for seen reality is put into practice. His earlier concern for depth is waning, and color is on the way to becoming self-sufficient. In short, we are nearing Fauvism. Matisse here went in for color in its purest state, banishing any hint of values in favor of "the fieriest, simultaneous clashes of colors," to which, at the same time, he succeeded in imparting a luminosity never before attained.

HENRI MATISSE (1869-1954). TOULOUSE LANDSCAPE, 1898-1899. (8⅝ × 13⅜")
PRIVATE COLLECTION, PARIS.

Fauvism

★

NOTEWORTHY in the history of art is a constant "swing of the pendulum," each generation reacting strongly against the tendencies of its immediate predecessors. Thus round about 1900 there was a swing-back towards the use of a fuller palette, and this was all the more emphatic because of the eclipse, brief though it was, that color had undergone.

For in the 'nineties the discreet, domesticated lamplight favored by the Nabis had replaced the flooding sunlight of the Impressionists and their followers. The tumultuous color lyricism of Van Gogh, the areas of broad, flat, even tones used by Gauguin in his evocations of exotic scenes, the all-pervading sheen of Redon's compositions and Seurat's lustrous, architecturally ordered structures—all these had been abolished in the languorous art of the Nabis, with its glimmering interiors, muted hues and tender nuances. For not only did they paint on cardboard, an absorbent ground, but they usually chose for their subjects scenes of bourgeois life, replete with carpets, drapes and cosy armchairs, bathed in a tenuous light filtering through curtained windows.

Thus the time was ripe for a reaction, a return to sunlight and the open spaces, the textural excitements of unbridled color, and when this reaction came, it brought about an upheaval in the world of painting whose effects are still apparent in contemporary art.

The circumstances under which the artists who came to be known as the Fauves (literally, the wild animals) acquired this name were typical of the way such names are coined. At the Salon d'Automne, where a special room had been set apart for the works of the new group, such epithets as "crazy," "phony," "preposterous" were freely applied to the brilliant, utterly sincere, if greatly daring innovations of the young artists. Louis Vauxcelles the critic, noticing a small child's head of Florentine inspiration (it was a work by Marque, the sculptor), exclaimed: "Look! There's a little Donatello cowering in this wild beasts' cage!" The term caught on and gave birth to a new -ism, "Fauvism." Thus, once again, a casual jest supplied art history with the name of a new movement.

As a result of a series of coincidences which might almost seem purposeful, were not such encounters so frequent in the annals of art, the Académie Julian and the Ecole des Beaux-Arts, where the teachers were Bouguereau, Ferrier, Gérôme, Bonnat and Gustave Moreau, counted amongst their students Matisse, Marquet, Rouault, Camoin, Manguin, Friesz, Dufy and Braque; while amongst those at Carrière's school were Matisse (who studied there almost a year), Puy, Derain, Laprade and Chabaud—to mention only the outstanding figures.

But it was unquestionably Henri Matisse who, with his sheer delight in color and in the physical properties of the medium, launched the new movement, and it was he who still continued exploring its latent possibilities at the time when his earliest associates were reverting more and more to traditionalist procedures. In any case Matisse's vast influence on his own generation and the next, both in France and in other countries, owed less to his position as leader of the school than to the universal appeal of the new, amazing type of art, peculiarly his, which went far beyond the premises of what was known as Fauvism.

Under the leadership of Matisse, whose *La Desserte* (1897), *View of Toulouse* (1898-99) and *Notre-Dame* (1901) had already set the tone of the movement—and also strongly influenced by Van Gogh—, Vlaminck, Friesz, Derain and Manguin now joined forces in an almost frenzied cult of the dynamic possibilities of color stepped up to its highest intensity. None the less, aware of the perilous fragility of color and purely coloristic art, they resolutely turned their back on Impressionism, whose shortcomings they detected (as Cézanne, Renoir, Gauguin and Seurat had detected them): its lack of solidity and that durability which only architecturally ordered composition can achieve. Thus the Fauves sought to discover a reality more valid than that of mere appearance, a reality that could be built up by the use of pure, unbroken colors. They had in mind those emotive "shocks," as Matisse called them, flashes of visual

to follow their "inspirations" quite uncritically—indeed they would judge it almost sacrilegious to subject them to intellectual control. Time and again Matisse spoke of "organizing his brain"—a curious and characteristic expression. So we need not be surprised if he always mistrusted the promptings of instinct. Hence his set purpose from his earliest days never to play the "self-taught" artist, his assiduous frequenting of schools, academies and museums, and also his patient study of both contemporary works and the masterpieces of the past. Thus it is that what seem to be his most brilliantly spontaneous works, products of a sudden flash of inspiration, are actually the most carefully thought out and meticulously executed.

It is seldom profitable to linger over the earliest works of a great master. Inevitably they are a mixture of borrowings, hesitations, precocious skill, efforts that often miss their mark yet promise high achievement. Only early influences need be taken into account. Thus it is interesting to note that in 1890 Matisse drew inspiration from Chardin *(Still Life with Books)*. Logic and intuition skillfully and sensitively blended—all Matisse is in this work.

By 1897, with his famous *La Desserte*, Matisse was trying out Impressionism. He had broken loose from the Ecole des Beaux-Arts and, temporarily, from the thrall of Classicism, of which his teachers had somewhat sickened him. In his *Still Life with a Stone Jug* (1897) we find him already indulging in extraordinarily vivid colors. The doctrines of Fauvism were, in fact, taking form. In 1898 and 1899 he painted monumental male nudes in aggressively bold blues and greens. From 1898 on *(View of Toulouse)* his fervid imagination evoked visions so intense that even the absolute purity of the colors he employed could hardly cope with them. Yet by now Matisse was trying to bridle his sensations (which perhaps scared him a little), and to master the secrets of a composition that he wished to be at once architecturally ordered and unconstrained. Now, too, feeling surer of his means, he harked back to color (1904). And the use of flat planes, thick impasto, the pointillist system of dots—all were tested by him in this early phase.

Nevertheless, Matisse's desire to "organize his brain" was not due solely to his feeling for order and proportion. He was too well aware of the fragility of an art—Impressionism, for example—which depends too much on the artist's sensibility. Having studied law and philosophy, he could appreciate the maxim that "the senses deform, the mind forms." But it was chiefly in studying the great masters that Matisse perceived the virtues of balance, just proportion and economy of means.

It may seem paradoxical that an artist whose watchword was caution should, by launching Fauvism, have revolutionized the art of his day. Matisse, who in his youth had resented "having to do what was expected of him," gave proof of a temperament all the more exceptional in that, rebel though he was, he made a point of subjecting his art to strict control. The liberty he claims is that of the pioneer, a creative liberty, and stems from that unique, unqualified self-reliance which is one of the characteristics of his highly original genius. What, indeed, could be more disconcerting than this revolutionary who, instead of bringing the house tumbling down about our ears, pushes forward a comfortable armchair and amiably invites our assent to the most unorthodox conceptions? Fully alive to the risks he courts, Matisse makes no secret of his inconsistencies, the curiously perverted logic of his solutions, and conscious of sometimes skating on thin ice, admits the fact quite frankly. Thus when creating visual effects planned out exclusively in his "organized brain," and at the same time professing to justify them by natural appearances, he brings off victories that may be of a Pyrrhic order—but are none the less effective and eye-satisfying.

In conclusion, we may point out that Matisse's art is never static, but continually evolving through a series of actions and reactions; sometimes brutally direct, sometimes all grace and charm; now good-humored, now imperious; now crystal-clear, now hermetic; now sensuous, now cerebral. In the same way, according to the artist's whim, his art is now the mistress and now the servant of color (or perhaps both at once). The result is that, though its professed aim is merely to help us relax, a Matisse exhibition is a series of visual adventures, at once exciting and inexplicable, which compel our wonder and delight.

intuition, like the images that surge up before the mind's eye of a poet. Vague as this may sound, the Fauve aesthetic was actually based on a well-defined program: downright rejection of the nuances and sophistications of the impressionist palette, pictorial architecture on the grand scale, avoidance of all realistic renderings of nature, and, above all, experiments in new permutations and combinations of colors. Thus they conjured up strange visions of green skies, vermilion rivers, lemon-colored trees and emerald-green faces, and converted the orderly, harmonious language of traditional art into rapturous, exciting orgies of colors.

For they resolutely did away with classical perspective and its corollaries: depth, the rendering of volumes, illusionist chiaroscuro, modeling and the rest. If authority were needed, they referred their critics back to the Primitives and the Gothic artists; to Rubens, El Greco, popular colorprints, the stained-glass window and Negro art.

Yet a day soon came when, despite their name, the Fauves took thought for order and moderation, for they had realized the perils of indiscipline, and when, as now, they cast a backward glance at Cézanne, it was at Cézanne the architect. Taking heroic measures, they sought to assign to color the function of creating its own discipline. The subject of the picture was envisaged solely from the angle of its plastic possibilities, and henceforth varying intensities of tones, relative dimensions of the painted surfaces, suitably placed whites, arrangements

Here the joyousness pervading all Matisse's work seems almost uncontrollable, flooding through the solid architecture of the composition. Here, too, Matisse employs a special procedure, known as the "transposition of tones" (the color of a tree-trunk changing in its ascent) which both Fauves and Cubists were to turn brilliantly to account. Suavely flowing arabesques and restful colors conjure up some lost Arcadia, as a classical artist might have pictured it.

HENRI MATISSE (1869-1954). PASTORAL, 1905. (18 × 21⅝″) PRIVATE COLLECTION, PARIS.

Here we have the Fauve palette at its most virulent, a riot, but a paradoxically disciplined riot of pure colors. Matisse
eschewed the rather brutal dynamism Vlaminck and Derain rejoiced in, and depended on contrasts and clashes of discrepant
tones to create that equivalent of depth which the Fauves were aiming at.

HENRI MATISSE (1869-1954). WOMAN READING, 1906. (28⅝×23½″) PRIVATE COLLECTION, PARIS.

HENRI MATISSE (1869-1954). INTERIOR AT COLLIOURE, 1905. (23 ½ × 28 ⅝″)
PRIVATE COLLECTION, ASCONA (SWITZERLAND).

Here we see color triumphant, playing havoc with tradition. Objects are placed with a fine disregard for any function they may serve. In fact the artist seems unaware of the extreme temerity of his venture and the transmutation which, an alchemist of color, he here is making. This work marks the birth of Fauvism.

of thick, expressive contour-lines, happily contrived arabesques—all these were called on to provide the cohesion and balance necessary to the formal organization of the picture. And under cover of a ceaseless flow of metaphors, allusions, reticences, the immemorial problem of suggesting depth and space was solved by the relative intensity and judicious distribution of tones. Light was no longer a source of illumination, but one of intensity. All irrelevancies were eliminated in favor of essentials, and this simplification was held to justify a multiplicity of colors. In short, a new pictorial syntax was devised, flexible enough for formulation in terms of the artist's personal conceptions. True, as before, the Fauves still sought to body forth the initial "shock" of the visual sensation and, so far as possible, to allow instinct to take its course in their renderings of it, but they now were careful not to jeopardize their chances of creating work whose appeal was at once instantaneous and durable. This spectacular movement lasted only some five years, long enough, however, to give the world some noble works, superbly lyrical and gorgeously colorful. The rapid disruption of the group, and the modifications brought to the theories they set out from, prove that the venture was never pressed to a logical conclusion. Was this prudence or lack of conviction ? There is certainly a gulf between what the Fauves set out to be and what they ultimately became. Towards 1911 Matisse foresaw where Fauvism would lead if pushed to the limit; he preferred

HENRI MATISSE (1869-1954). PORTRAIT WITH THE GREEN STRIPE, 1905. (15 ¾ × 12 ½ ")
J. RUMP COLLECTION, ROYAL MUSEUM OF FINE ARTS, COPENHAGEN.

Matisse freely confessed that what interested him most was not landscape or the still life, but the human face. With a self-restraint contrasting with the unabashed enthusiasm of Fauvism for the shrillest tones, Matisse, when evoking a woman's face, showed a tendency towards abstractionism. He disincarnated or spiritualized it, so as to distill the secrets of its plastic qualities. Put on in broad tracts of faintly sub-acid color, the tones yield an equivalent of depth. Once more, almost effortlessly it would seem, Matisse contrived to reconcile the most strident tonalities.

to go no farther, not wanting to break with that traditional respect of natural reality to which he always clung, precariously maybe at times. And in the end, Fauvism made good more as a technique than as an aesthetic.

"I never set foot inside a museum. The very smell of such places makes me sick, no less than their pedantry and boredom. I loathe the word 'classical.' And science sets my teeth on edge." These remarks, made by Maurice Vlaminck to Derain during one of their meetings at Chatou, give a good idea of the artist's temperament. Vlaminck was born in the heart of Paris, near Les Halles. Both his parents were musicians, and are reputed to have led a completely Bohemian life, giving little thought to the education of their son. From early childhood to the present day, Vlaminck has always lived in the country, working the land. Indeed he regards himself as primarily a farmer and rather dislikes being called an artist. He taught himself to paint, and this may explain why he has always had a fondness for types of art that appeal to the peasantry, such as the gaudy colorprints that are so popular in rural France. From them he got his taste for bright colors, sharp clashes of tones, and the licence he allows that spontaneous flow of fancy one of whose by-products is the pleasant little poems he has given us—for nothing if not versatile, Vlaminck is a poet, too, besides being a talented violinist. His feeling for nature is quite in the country-dweller's vein; he loves to evoke the joys of Sunday outings in the woodlands, even if sometimes a passing storm throws the facile contrast of its shadows on the colorful group of merrymakers. Nature, in his art, wears romantic trappings, rather like those of the colorprints he copied as a boy.

Though he ended up by transmuting his interpretations of the visible world, purely painterly to begin with, into dramatic, emotional visions of scenes and objects, Vlaminck was the Fauve who, of all the group, best deserved that name. In fact, if it had depended on him alone to keep the flag flying, Fauvism would not have beaten its premature retreat.

Even when Fauvism was at its tempestuous height (1905) Derain felt that building with color called for more than the exclusive use of ultra-vivid tones. He realized that ochres and browns as well were needed to set them off, if he was to get the full effect that he was aiming at.

ANDRÉ DERAIN (1880-1954). FIGURES IN A MEADOW, 1906. (15 × 21 5/8") PRIVATE COLLECTION, PARIS.

MAURICE VLAMINCK (1876). THE BOAT WASH-HOUSES, 1906. (19⅝ × 28⅝")
PRIVATE COLLECTION, PARIS.

What attracted Vlaminck in the boat wash-houses on the Seine was the interplay of parallel lines, those of their walls and roofs and the river-bank, and the well-defined rectangular blocks of color enabling him to dispense with curves.

In his art the use of vivid colors is not conditioned solely by a desire to stress concordances or clashes; it also serves to demonstrate the power of color in itself, treated as a constructive element. "The most authentically 'painter' of us all," Derain once said of him. The truth is that, far more than the novels he wrote for a while, more even than music (which he taught to earn a living), painting satisfies his craving to give expression to his sensual impulses. Hence his aversion for abstractions, subtle effects, and any scientific theories of art. Vlaminck is above all a rebel or, rather, naturally unruly. Thus there is nothing surprising in the headstrong violence of his early work, offset, however, by the sureness of his eye, the resourcefulness of his drawing, and the sheer beauty of his heavily charged, flowing brushstrokes. What is certain is that, though affecting "toughness," and in fact self-willed, Vlaminck is always ready to be disarmed by a child's smile or a penny bunch of flowers. Derain's first contribution to Fauvist art testified to an acceptance of the principle that the artist's task is to organize a kind of super-space functional to and determined by the picture-surface alone. Yet from the start his work betrayed a certain hesitation, due at once to his painterly instincts and to his general culture, or rather to a conflict between these two sides of his personality. This may have been aggravated by the fact that in Matisse, with his scholarly caution, and in Vlaminck, with his blind faith in instinct, he saw living embodiments of the tendencies at war within himself. He may tell us that, in the early days of Fauvism, he often felt so despondent that but for Matisse's encouragement he would have lost heart altogether, but his work of the period belies this. He already had a forceful brushstroke, complete mastery of his means, a gift of ranging from the most delicate nuances to the most brilliant colors with easy virtuosity, while in his draftsmanship he displayed a boldness, a sweep and

MAURICE VLAMINCK (1876).
HOUSE IN THE COUNTRY, 1906.
(24¼ × 25½")
PRIVATE COLLECTION, PARIS.

"Only the whole gamut of colors on the palette," Vlaminck has declared, "orchestrated to the utmost limit of their expressive power and resonance, can convey the color-emotions produced by landscape." And as if to prove his point, the artist has here brought into play all the resources of the rainbow palette with happy ease and an almost reckless lavishness. This was the heyday of Fauvism, with caution thrown gaily to the winds and discretion in abeyance. Stepped up to its highest pitch, color surges across the canvas, building up its own "orchestration," and pivoted on the solid, upstanding mass of the house, fans out in wild and forceful rhythms.

a self-confidence that many an older artist might have envied. Thus his work bore the stamp of a sensual temperament combined with a genuine passion for art. This latter found expression to begin with in an exuberance of color carried to a point that startled even Vlaminck. Yet, surprisingly enough for a Fauve, he was always guided by a desire to create harmonies rather than the bold clashes of color to which Matisse and Vlaminck constantly and successfully aspired. For though he used the shrillest, warmest colors, he made a point of tempering them with subdued tones and curbing their violence with almost classical restraint. Derain was perhaps the first to discover that though Fauve technique could "construct," it could not really "build" a picture in the architectural sense—which was what he always aimed at. For adventurous-minded though he was, he also had a saving prudence, as indeed became evident when, at a later stage, he accepted the disciplines of Cubism and a whole system of controls at which his instinct chafed, but which his calmer, intellectual self bade him respect. Having said in his youth, "What's gained by lacking culture?" he went so far as to say

A kind of latent Impressionism and an innate, indeed an infallible sense of order and restraint held Braque back from the thoroughgoing Fauvism practiced with such untrammelled gusto by Vlaminck. This picture is built up entirely in terms of one or two dominant colors, the keynotes of the composition; these consolidate the pictorial architecture and implement an harmonic richness all the more forceful for its pent-up energy. For here the driving force of color is strongly held in leash. Thus we have no explosive clashes of tones, but a satisfying over-all harmony of colors somewhat reminiscent of the sheen of watered silk, charming the eye, caressing the senses and exquisitely modulated.

GEORGES BRAQUE (1882).
THE HARBOR AT LA CIOTAT,
1906. OWNED BY THE ARTIST.

ANDRÉ DERAIN (1880-1954). LE FAUBOURG, COLLIOURE, 1905. (23 ½ × 28 ⅝") PRIVATE COLLECTION, PARIS.

Matisse and Derain met at Collioure in 1905, and under the radiant southern sun the Fauve program took form, but not without setbacks. Derain has said, "Sometimes I felt quite despondent, but Matisse always cheered me up." This work, so rich in happily inspired passages, and as sparkling as a Byzantine mosaic, splendidly belies his apprehensions.

(much later in life): "Art's greatest danger is an excess of culture!" Doubtless he then realized that there are two sorts of culture: one well assimilated and constructive, the other a mere perfection of the mind. This is a dilemma which he never quite resolved and it accounts for the curious ambivalence we sometimes find in his work. But though it may have cramped the full development of his personality, it also contributed to dazzling successes, notably in the works of his Fauve period, when he had not yet stifled his juvenile vivacity under effects which, for all their fascination, seem studied rather than inspired.

Coming to Paris from Bordeaux in 1890, Marquet at once struck up a friendship with Matisse, whom he met in Gustave Moreau's studio. The two young men shared hard times together when they were employed by a decorator named Jambon and for a mere pittance spent their days painting tawdry stage-sets for Paris theaters. There is a well-authenticated story that, at the same miserable rate of pay, they also made the floral decorations which adorn—if the term be permitted—the tops of the galleries at the "Grand Palais des Champs-Elysées" in Paris. This early friendship lasted unbroken until Marquet's death in 1947.

While Matisse had no great liking for the much-vaunted "movement that displaces lines," Marquet, in the heyday of Fauvism, was, so to speak, dynamism incarnate. Nothing delighted him more than the clashes of strident colors and masses in movement dear to the Fauves. But very soon (and the same was true of Derain and Friesz) we find him showing a preference for discreeter tonal harmonies as against color orchestration on the grand scale. Marquet was famous for his sparkling wit, which, though caustic, even cruel on occasion, was never spiteful; the truth was that he had a keen eye for the imperfections of the world around him, even

ALBERT MARQUET (1875-1947). BEACH CARNIVAL, 1906. (19⅝ × 23⅝″) PRIVATE COLLECTION, PARIS.

Marquet's Fauvism lies more in an intensity of movement than in one of color. Looking down from his balcony the artist has transformed a rather drab peasant masquerade into a wonderfully picturesque scene, vibrant with life and gaiety, somewhat in the manner of the Nabis.

those of Nature herself, and was always wanting to amend them. A superb draftsman, he had Lautrec's gift for conveying in a single line the essentials of a face, but he was equally capable of transforming a decrepit cabhorse into a mettlesome Pegasus, though he was the first to smile at the animal's ridiculous capers—and his own. We find in Marquet a ceaseless tug-of-war between the promptings of his volcanic southern temperament and his distaste for any uncalled-for exuberance. What makes his work so attractive is not that he has reconciled these two conflicting tendencies, but that each is given its run, in turn. A man of high intelligence and exquisite taste, Marquet had the gift of pressing the lyrical (not to say caricatural) bravura of his brushwork and drawing to just that danger-point where the accuracy he aims at is imperiled—but no further. Yet for all his sophistication and his ironic turn of mind, he had a very real love of Nature and his landscapes are glowing tributes to her beauty.

Marquet was certainly a Fauve in the exact meaning of the term, but a Fauve who sometimes flung himself against the bars of the famous "cage" described by Vauxcelles; yet sometimes, too, retired to a corner of it to dream serenely of his native forest.

Birthplace of Boudin and always a favorite resort of the Impressionists, Le Havre was also the hometown of Friesz and Dufy, and Braque, too, spent his childhood and adolescence there. The art of these three Fauves, with its bright colors and clean-cut forms, certainly owed much to the surroundings of their youth: the brilliant, sea-mirrored light and the colorful life of a busy harbor.

Although Braque's dalliance with Fauvism was brief before he moved on to Cubism, he left his mark on the movement in a very personal manner. We may note how subtly he

GEORGES BRAQUE (1882). LA CIOTAT, 1906. (21⅛ × 26¼″) PRIVATE COLLECTION, PARIS.

It was at La Ciotat that Braque first felt the call of the Mediterranean. Here he still keeps to some of Cézanne's methods, which indeed he never wholly abandoned. He avoids the use of over-strident tones, and aims at harmonies rather then clashes of strongly opposed colors.

wedded the arabesque to color, on equal terms, so as to contain and to exalt form simultaneously. He also employed those Cézannesque contrasts which tend to counteract the aggressive crudity of pure, unmixed color. While still a Fauve, Braque actually brought off some compositions in, practically, a single color, thus going beyond the premises of the movement and anticipating the monochrome canvases of his early cubist period. It is not unlikely that these works, though few in number, both speeded up the evolution of Fauvism and suggested the principles of the new aesthetic in which he was to play a leading part.

Fauvism was hardly more than a passing phase for Friesz. He had never had a blind faith in the efficacy of color as enough in itself for constructing form. Thus he soon reverted to the classical method of rendering depth by modeling and, contenting himself with the master's practices, never attempted to outdo Cézanne, as did most of his Fauve friends. From this time on Friesz gave proof of an unrivaled technical ability, and soon developed into one of the ablest, most sought-after art teachers of the day.

His work on the whole has a thoroughly refreshing, full-blooded vigor, which, however, he never allows to break out into baroque extravagance. His world is an Arcadia in which the vegetation is lush, the nymphs are buxom. There are many curves (signs of quiet strength) as against very few angles (signs of impatience or excitability). Noteworthy, too, is Friesz's handling of volumes, and his care never to let their dynamic properties get out of hand. He later said: "We, the creators of Fauvism, were the first to immolate it."

Dufy had the good fortune to meet Matisse soon after coming to Paris in 1901. He owned to being intimidated by the Louvre, and to feeling more at home with the Impressionists

OTHON FRIESZ (1879-1949).
LA CIOTAT, 1905.
(14½ × 14½") PRIVATE
COLLECTION, PARIS.

"A study of complementaries and contrasts of color has led me to this conclusion : that one should seek to create an equivalent of solar light by a technique based on color orchestration and a transference of sensory emotions, the originative emotion being one's response to nature. For the discovery of the best way to effect this transposition and its basic principles, fervent research and much enthusiasm will be required." Later on Friesz developed an excessive interest in technique and neo-classical order. But in the early days of Fauvism he achieved a balanced compromise between his instinctive dynamism and his technical virtuosity, and the brilliant, well-knit compositions of this period may justly be regarded as his best work.

(at Durand-Ruel's), with Cézanne and Van Gogh. Also he found in the naïvely colorful fantasies of folk art and old colorprints a confirmation of his natural bent. From the Fauves he took over the method of constructing in height and using the strongest colors; of all the Fauves Dufy kept longest to the use of pure, unblended colors, and these he juxtaposed without recourse to neutral zones between them. For he liked effects of violent contrasts; when a dark tone adjoins a bright one, he circumscribes the latter with some darker lines so as to enhance its resonance. Such indeed was his passion for pure color that he wholly

Luxe, Calme et Volupté came as a revelation to Dufy and indeed proved to be a landmark in his artistic career. "No sooner had I set eyes on Matisse's picture than I grasped the new *raison d'être* of painting, and impressionist realism lost all its charms for me when I saw this miracle of the creative imagination at play, in drawing and in color." In the heyday of Fauvism Dufy preserved a characteristic liveliness and lightness of touch differentiating his work from that of his friends, in which these qualities were all too often conspicuous by their absence.

RAOUL DUFY (1877-1953).
COUNTRY BALL AT FALAISE,
1906. (18 × 21½")
PRIVATE
COLLECTION, PARIS.

disregarded natural appearance, and gave free rein to his imagination. He shunned direct emotions, that is to say never let himself be subjugated by the raw material presented to his eye. Dufy's art lays no claim to power; it often reminds us of that series of "arrested falls" as which the process of walking has been defined. More than in any other Fauve we find in Dufy that brevity which is the soul of wit, and a quickness in the uptake enabling him to record the briefest flicker of imagined beauty. And his fondness for cool tones does much to enhance that impression of amazing lightness which so much charms us in his work.

Luxe, Calme et Volupté came as a revelation to Dufy—but not only as a revelation of the genius of Matisse; by the same token it revealed to him his own temperament and reassured him as to tendencies he had felt chary of encouraging. He realized that the creative imagination was now to supersede the nature-imitation that had hitherto dominated painting. Later on, when he had discovered his appointed path, Dufy once remarked: "The thing is to create the world of things one does *not* see." And with this in mind he gave less thought to eliciting (like Matisse and Derain) the essential type-forms of objects than to building up an entirely new vision of the world which reflected his impulsive, dynamic yet exquisitely refined temperament and owed far more to imagination than to direct observation.

The 1905 Salon d'Automne included work by various artists who had obviously adhered, in varying degrees, to the Fauve aesthetic; amongst them Louis Valtat, Henri Manguin, Jean Puy, Charles Camoin and Kees Van Dongen.

Louis Valtat shared the "honors" of that famous special number of *L'Illustration* in which a number of Fauve pictures were reproduced with more or less fidelity and the artists themselves were wantonly attacked, often for the stupidest reasons. His contribution to Fauvism was an exceptionally brilliant palette which he put less to the service of the architecture of the picture than to a dazzling play of colors. Valtat was one of the first to take up ceramics and his intensely colorful productions in this medium had something of the "fierceness" which gave the Fauves their name.

Henri Manguin, another outstanding figure at the Salon d'Automne, also displayed much zest for colors stepped up to their maximum intensity; but, a true lover of Nature, he served her rather than forced her into his service as did the true Fauves. He circumscribed his figures with strongly indicated boundary lines which gave them a certain stiffness. Ultimately he disowned these works as being mere youthful follies.

Charles Camoin, friend of Cézanne and fervent propagandist of his work, was a devotee of light and applied himself to mastering its secrets. The effects he thus achieved were often strikingly original. His blithesome art is at its best in his Mediterranean landscapes.

Jean Puy met Matisse at Carrière's school and, like the others named above, exhibited at the 1905 Salon d'Automne. He, too, did not wholeheartedly accept the theories of Matisse, Vlaminck and Derain. Puy had a well-balanced mind, a desire for simplification of both form and color, and these prevented him from indulging in the extravagances of his friends, but also from bringing off their brilliant feats. He reproached Matisse with dehumanizing his figures by an excessive use of pure color and employed greyish tones like the Nabis'.

Van Dongen brought to the new movement an unbridled enthusiasm for color contrasts. He was more interested in decorative, ornamental effects than in the structure of the picture. Thanks to his gift for figure painting, he soon became immensely popular with that section of fashionable society which always patronizes modern art not so much for its genuinely creative as for its startling qualities. He did many portraits of actresses and dancers; also of prominent statesmen such as Barthou and Painlevé and of famous men of letters, amongst them Anatole France. He adapted Fauve technique to a style of portraiture whose aim was much more that of rendering likeness than a constructive metamorphosis.

We conclude by naming some of the artists of this generation who, while highly gifted, tended to "academicize" the Fauve methods by introducing elements of traditional chiaroscuro and perspective. They were Pierre Laprade (1875-1931), Henri Lebasque (1865-1937) and Jacqueline Marval (1866-1932), not to mention others who, though drawn towards a more architectonic art, were haunted by memories of the Nabis.

84

RAOUL DUFY (1877-1953). THE FOURTEENTH OF JULY, 1907. (31¾ × 19⅝″) PRIVATE COLLECTION, PARIS.

Bright sunlight, gay bunting and festoons were a heaven-sent pretext for a lavish use of all the colors of the rainbow.
Here Dufy indulged in an exuberant color orchestration of a scope and violence exceptional with him.

ERNST LUDWIG KIRCHNER (1880-1938). WOMAN ON A BLUE DIVAN, 1907. (31⅜×35⅜")
KIRCHNER ESTATE, BASEL.

Kirchner's draftsmanship had much influence on German painting. His reduction of three-dimensional form to flat planes and his use of a restricted range of colors applied in well-demarcated areas owe something to the technique of the color woodcut. Moreover certain characteristics of the woodcut can also be seen in the harsh drawing of the head and the broken, angular lines binding the tracts of color.

Die Brücke ★ The Bridge

Painting in Germany at the Beginning of the Century

A T DRESDEN in 1905 Ernst Ludwig Kirchner, Erich Heckel, Karl Schmidt-Rottluff and Fritz Bleyl founded a group they called Die Brücke (The Bridge), this name being meant to symbolize the aspiration shared by these artists of linking together all the vanguard art movements then on foot in Germany. Next year Emil Nolde and the Swiss painter Cuno Amiet joined them, followed at intervals by Max Pechstein, Axel Gallén, Otto Müller and, surprisingly enough, Van Dongen. After a checkered career the group finally broke up, as a result of internal dissensions, in 1913.

There is no doubt that the artistic climate then prevailing in Germany was unpropitious for young artists who wished to keep abreast of the new tendencies and the ideals taking form in Western art. Memories of the bogus, pre-Raphaelite classicism of the "Nazarenes" were still fresh in their minds, and equally antipathetic was the anecdotal, eye-flattering art of the "little romantics" working in the Biedermeyer style. Nor were they much impressed by the procedures of the belated Impressionism sponsored by Liebermann and, despite a somewhat new approach, by Corinth. The sheer dullness, the lack of vitality in all these forms of expression drove the young painters almost to despair, and, to make things worse, they had to reckon with the artistic backwardness of the general public, little disposed to welcome new endeavors. The storm of abuse that had befallen the 1892 Munch Exhibition in Berlin and the attacks of the art critics on Paula Modersohn when she gave an exhibition in 1899 at Bremen had not been forgotten, nor the rejection of Nolde's first large-scale picture *Die Bergriesen* (The Mountain Giants) in 1896 at Munich. Conditions in fact were so bad that Kirchner, Schmidt-Rottluff and Heckel had to turn to architecture to earn a living.

Before long that feeling of despair which we have mentioned gave place to a spirit of revolt. Inveterate romantics that they were, these German artists tended more and more to use painting as a means of expressing the artist's private soul-searchings, and it was Munch who gave the lead to this type of Expressionism.

Meanwhile—and this, too, fell in line with their revolt against their immediate predecessors, whose total lack of interest in the problems of "pure" art, and notably in the new ventures of contemporary French painting, they so much resented—the Die Brücke artists harked back to a form of art that had been practiced in Germany as far back as the 15th century: the woodcut. It was in 1476 that the first book entirely illustrated with woodcuts, *Der Spiegel menschlicher Behältnisse*, came out at Cologne (and simultaneously at Basel). The harsh, angular design, hacked out laboriously with the graving-knife in the woodblock, evidenced that will to dramatic, almost uncouth effect typical of the German Primitive. In their woodcuts the young artists kept to these traditional procedures, showing a curious bluntness, not to say brutality, both in their linework and in their choice of subjects. For most of the Die Brücke group were temperamentally unstable, morose and introspective, and moreover had a habit of tormenting themselves with problems of religion, sex, morality and politics. That sense of "guilt," of which we hear so much nowadays, took in their art the form of a ruthless analysis of the thing seen, an avoidance of smoothly flowing curves and, in general, of all the more amiable aspects of reality.

As regards painting, expression through color now became the chief concern of the artists of the "Bridge." Matisse had just given (in 1907) an exhibition at the Cassirer Gallery in Berlin, and his work had met with an enthusiastic reception. Also they had now "discovered" Negro art and were devoting much attention to the Primitives of the Rhineland. Thus before long purely painterly considerations began to take precedence of the expression of emotions, and even the subjects of their pictures underwent a change. Alongside religious compositions, Nolde sometimes indulged in flower pieces; Schmidt-Rottluff produced near-abstract works. Kirchner, too, had a morbid sensitivity, which was exacerbated by the course of events in Germany following the First World War. His early efforts at drawing and painting had been encouraged by his father, and, when in Dresden, he studied the theories of color expounded by Goethe and Helmholtz. One of his aims was a synthesis of Fauvism and Cubism, no easy matter. Indeed he was always torn between conflicting tendencies which he vainly tried to reconcile, nor could he ever evolve a technique that wholly satisfied him. But he was an indefatigable searcher, though his goal eluded him. Suffering from an incurable disease and horrified by the political and intellectual conceptions then prevailing in Germany, he committed suicide in 1938.

In a general way all the Die Brücke group drew inspiration from the Fauves, their palettes grew brighter, they employed the strongest, most brilliant colors. As for their drawing, it kept to the jagged, angular forms dear to the old German Masters.

Indeed what we have here is nothing short of a renaissance of German art, all the more effective for deriving from a thirst for freedom, but a well-considered freedom, based on collective effort and a revolt against the narrow-mindedness of "bourgeois morality."

1907-1914

1907   Purrmann, Bruce and Leo Stein form a group of artists who study under Matisse's guidance • Rouàult does ceramics • At Vitebsk, his native city, Chagall paints his first pictures, then moves to St. Petersburg and studies at the Imperial School of Fine Arts • Commemorative Cézanne Exhibition at Salon d'Automne • Apollinaire introduces Braque to Picasso, who is just finishing **Les Demoiselles d'Avignon.** Beginnings of Cubism • Die Brücke Exhibition at the Richter Gallery, Dresden. Second Die Brücke Album comes out. Nolde leaves the group • Kandinsky Exhibition at the Katharinenhof Gallery, Frankfort.

1908   With two exceptions, the jury of the Salon d'Automne rejects all the canvases that Braque has brought back from L'Estaque; he withdraws them all and shows them at Kahnweiler's Gallery, opened the year before. In **Gil Blas** (November 14) Louis Vauxcelles speaks derogatively of painting in " little cubes " • Picasso gives a banquet in his studio in honor of the Douanier Rousseau • Matisse publishes his **Notes of a Painter** in **La Grande Revue** and paints **Harmony in Red** and **Harmony in Blue** • At the first "Wiener Kunstschau" Kokoschka's work is violently attacked by public and critics alike.

1909   Diaghilev presents the Russian Ballet at the Châtelet Theater, Paris • Marinetti sends the **Futurist Manifesto** to Paris where Severini has it published in **Le Figaro** (February 22). Boccioni, Carrà and Russolo meet in Marinetti's studio • In Moscow Larionov paints works "dominated solely by the laws of light" (Rayonnism) • With Jawlensky, Kandinsky founds the New Association of Munich Artists and is elected president • Braque exhibits at Salon des Indépendants. • Modigliani meets Brancusi and turns to sculpture • Derain does woodcuts to illustrate Apollinaire's **L'Enchanteur pourrissant** • Kupka moves towards ever greater abstraction.

1910   At Florence Chirico paints his first canvases of deserted towns • In Milan Balla, Boccioni, Carrà, Russolo and Severini sign the **Manifesto of Futurist Painting** (published February 11) • Marc's first one-man show at the Brakl Gallery, Munich • John Marin's first one-man show at the 291 Gallery, New York • Picasso spends the summer at Cadaquès (Catalonia) with Derain • At Salon des Indépendants Delaunay exhibits **The Eiffel Tower,** painted at Nantua; Léger exhibits **Nudes in the Forest,** and Rousseau **The Dream** (bought by Vollard) • Death of the Douanier Rousseau (his epitaph was written by Apollinaire) • Mondrian and Chagall come to Paris • Klee exhibits 55 drawings and other graphic works in Zurich • The Berlin Secession selection committee refuses the work of 27 artists, including Nolde. The New Secession and the New Association of Munich Artists are founded. The magazine **Der Sturm** is launched on March 3 • Meeting of Macke and Marc at Munich • Kandinsky's first abstract drawings and watercolors; he writes **The Art of Spiritual Harmony** • Rouault Exhibition at Druet's, Paris.

1911   On December 18, Kandinsky and Marc open the first exhibition of **Der Blaue Reiter** at the Thannhauser Gallery, Munich, with works by Burljuk, Delaunay, Kandinsky, Macke, Marc, Münter, Henri Rousseau, Arnold Schönberg and others. Kandinsky and Marc collaborate on a book, **Der Blaue Reiter** (The Blue Rider), published at Munich in 1912 • Braque and Picasso introduce letters of the alphabet into their canvases • Cubist rooms at the Indépendants (Delaunay, Gleizes, Le Fauconnier, Léger, Gris, Metzinger) and at Salon d'Automne (the same painters, with the addition of Duchamp and Villon, but without Picasso or Braque) • Brancusi's **The New-born Babe,** an egg-shaped sculpture • Launching of the magazine **Soirées de Paris** • Commemorative Rousseau Exhibition at the Indépendants • Chagall: **Myself and the Village, Dedicated to my Fiancée** • Chirico comes to Paris • Marcoussis meets Braque, Picasso, Apollinaire • Dufy does woodcuts for Apollinaire's **Le Bestiaire.**

1912   Blue Rider Exhibition at Der Sturm Gallery, Berlin • Second Blue Rider Exhibition at Munich • Section d'Or Exhibition, Paris: Jacques Villon, Marcel Duchamp, Duchamp-Villon, Gleizes, Metzinger, Delaunay, Gris and La Fresnaye. Lecture by Maurice Raynal on Cubism. For the first time Kupka exhibits entirely abstract compositions. First number of the review **Section d'Or** • Publication of **Du Cubisme,** by Gleizes and Metzinger • At Salon des Indépendants Delaunay shows **Simultaneous Windows** (which led Apollinaire to coin the name "Orphism") and Juan Gris, **Homage to Picasso** • First **Papiers collés** by Braque and Picasso, who spend the summer together at Sorgues • Marcel Duchamp paints **Nude descending a Staircase** (which he calls a "chrono-photograph") • Klee, Macke and Marc come to Paris for the first time, where they meet Delaunay, Apollinaire, Picasso and Uhde • Léger's first one-man show at Kahnweiler's • The Tenth Salon d'Automne, at which the Cubists turn out in full force, provokes a wave of indignation.

1913   In Moscow Malevitch exhibits a plain black square on a white ground as the only subject of a painting (Suprematism). Larionov publishes the **Rayonnist Manifesto,** dated 1912. Tatlin's Constructivism • Canudo launches the magazine **Montjoie** • Picasso, Braque and Gris spend the summer with Max Jacob at Céret, the "Barbizon of Cubism" • Delaunay paints **Simultaneous Disks,** and La Fresnaye, **The Conquest of the Air** • Utrillo's first one-man show at Blot's, preface by Libaude • The Armory Show in New York: international exhibition of modern art with 1100 works by over 300 artists • Apollinaire publishes **Les Peintres cubistes.**

1914   Chagall's first one-man show at Der Sturm Gallery, Berlin, preface by Apollinaire • In London Wyndham Lewis launches the Vorticist review **Blast** • In Paris Marcel Duchamp paints **Nine Malic Molds** and does his first "ready-mades" • In April Klee, Macke and Moillet travel to Tunisia (Kairwan) • Upon the outbreak of war most of the young French artists are mobilized • Picasso is at Avignon, then in Paris. • Gris is at Céret and later at Collioure with Matisse and Marquet • Delaunay is in Spain and Portugal • Carl Hofer a prisoner of war in France • Villon at the front • Permeke wounded at Antwerp • Erich Heckel serves in a German hospital unit in Belgium • Macke killed in action • Chagall and Kandinsky return to Russia • Pevsner and Gabo in Norway, Pascin in New York • Mondrian, back in Holland, paints his first pictures entirely in horizontals and verticals (e.g. **Pier and Ocean**) • Jawlensky takes refuge in Switzerland, where he remains until 1921.

Towards Cubism

★

Picasso's *Two Female Nudes* is a landmark in his career, since in it two of his "periods" are combined: Cézannesque Cubism and Cubism in the full sense of the term. During his Blue Period (1901) Picasso sought above all to express his tragic sense of life and brought to this a seriousness, a feeling of responsibility very different from the lighthearted spontaneity of the colorful pictures he had painted when he first came to Paris. He now asked himself, "What am I after in my painting?" and sought to clarify his attitude to life. Thus in his Blue Period he gave expression to that generous compassion for the underdog which has never left him throughout his long career, and clothed it in a poignant, richly poetic form. In the conditions of circus life he found a symbol of the hand-to-mouth existence to which so many are condemned and of the pathetic instability of their lot. Yet this was only a passing phase in his art, which he soon abandoned. For in the technique of his Blue Period we find a curious dichotomy between the harshness of the drawing in certain passages and elsewhere the fragile grace of rippling curves; moreover, color is kept down to a monochrome, from which all touches of brighter hues, however trivial, are excluded.

In his Pink Period (1905) Picasso departed from the austerity of this earlier phase and indulged in a plastic lyricism, an interest in concrete form. The expressionist tendencies derived from Van Gogh and Lautrec were replaced by a concern for pure plasticity; faces are no longer portraits but "heads," the concept of the universal overrules that of the personal, and the individual is sublimated into the type. Thus operations of the mind gradually supersede visual responses, the permanent is substituted for the incidental. And by the same token Picasso alters his technique in terms of the preponderance he now assigns to the purely painterly imagination. His pictures are no longer colored drawings as they were in the Blue Period; planes of color locked up in a graphic framework. His treatment of the figures of the *Two Female Nudes* shows that he is aiming at effects of weight, stability, serenity. No longer does he treat the subject as a vehicle for his emotions; on the contrary, the imperturbability of these two figures has all the studied aloofness of the classical approach. The one exception to this general rule is Picasso's determination to infuse the breath of life, of actuality, into his picture, as is clearly indicated by one of the two figures.

For when we carefully compare the two women we see at once a very great difference between them. The taller woman (on the right) symbolizes as it were Picasso's first move towards a plastic realism still in accordance with classical conceptions—those of Poussin, Corot, Daumier, Courbet and Cézanne, for example. So far this move is merely tentative, for there are traces in her face of the technique and emotionalism of the Blue Period figures; but we now find a look of cheerfulness, serenity and physical well-being that was far to seek in the unhappy, half-starved vagrants of the earlier period.

On the other hand the girl on the left has the enigmatic quality of a symbolic figure. But more important still, while in the face on the right Picasso keeps to the classical technique which has given the world so many noble renderings of the human visage, that on the left already shows a tendency towards geometric organization, an abstract architectural concept of pictorial construction. The face is divided up by straight lines, particularly noticeable being the cleavage of the forehead into two zones of light, an imaginary, not a "natural" light. And this procedure pointed the way to that flat-plane construction which was soon to become characteristic. (See, for example, the *Seated Woman* of 1909.)

Finally, the inconsistency we find in *Two Female Nudes* reappears in the famous *Demoiselles d'Avignon* (1907): here, too, there is a curious difference between the treatment of the figures on the right and those on the left. This latter picture, however, marked the close of the period in which the artist was wavering between two conceptions, pending his definite adoption of the principles of Cubism.

For an understanding of the circumstances which led up to the Cubist "revolution"—for it was nothing short of that—we need to know something of the ideas and aspirations of the young artists who were twenty or thereabouts at the turn of the century, and of the social conditions of the period.

Social Conditions. These had much less effect than might have been expected on the course of the new developments in art. Though this was far from being the "golden age" for artists that some have thought it, conditions of existence were not so hard as to incite them to take an active part in the social agitation of the period. Indeed in those days politics never exercised any great influence on the freedom of artistic expression. Governments left young artists perfectly free to indulge in any adventures that they chose, and in return the artists neither expected nor demanded anything from the powers-that-be. The pundits of official art turned a blind eye to the work of Cézanne, Renoir, Gauguin and Van Gogh (as being "outside the pale," as one of them, Chabas, described it) and, when Cubism made its appearance, merely professed a bland indifference, tinctured with amusement. In fact, aware no doubt of their inability to stem the rising tide, they took the line of least resistance. Round about 1900, there was a violent anti-religious campaign; under the Combes and Waldeck-Rousseau governments the separation of Church and State had been enacted, and laws were passed against the French religious orders, followed by their eviction from the monasteries. The artists of the day displayed no interest in these events; not that they had leanings to atheism but because such controversies struck them as survivals from a bygone age. None of us—I use the personal pronoun since I was one of the group—had the least inkling of the danger threatening from beyond the Rhine; we declined to take the Kaiser's sabre-rattlings seriously. As for the rise of socialism, the growing social unrest, the political scandals—none of these ever diverted the young artists' attention from the problems of their art.

In short we all lived in a little world apart, on the outskirts of a social order that we treated with indifference, if not disdain, and which obligingly ignored our existence. None of our group tried to get in contact even with the masters we admired, as do our young contemporaries. Though sometimes from the windows of the studios in the "Bateau Lavoir" we watched Degas or Renoir coming up or going down the steps that led to it, the idea of getting to know them personally never crossed our minds. It was enough to be acquainted with their art, and anyhow what chance was there that the Masters would show any great interest in the new ventures? Had not Degas, paying an unconscious tribute to them, remarked: "It seems to me that the young folk are trying to do something more difficult than painting?" And as for Renoir, did he not shortly after this discourage Paul Rosenberg the dealer from taking up Picasso? When all is said and done, the aloofness of the young painters was not due at all to vanity, but rather, to a certain shyness; great as were their ambitions, and determined as they were to make a clean sweep of all the traditional conceptions of painting, they were not quite sure of themselves as yet.

Imagination and Poetic Vision. Basic to the cubist aesthetic was the leading role assigned to the imagination, at the expense of observation and the retinal image; these were now relegated to secondary parts. In the early days of Cubism poets and painters—certain painters and certain poets that is to say—joined forces. The fact was that psychological realism had been carried to its extreme limit and the prosaic, if vaguely sentimental, observations of the Parisian scene which had meant so much to the previous generation had begun to pall on the younger men. Enough to lead one's daily life, without making pictures of it! Some lines of an old Indian poet had opened new horizons: "O poet, do not talk to us of rain, but make the rain come down!" Nor had these young men forgotten the strange enchantments of the child's vision of the world; years of often rather haphazard study had never quite effaced these. Thus in their dutiful explorations of the classics they had culled from them not the wisdom of the ages but their most picturesque, unusual, not to say exciting details. Jarry, who was so greatly to influence the outlook of his contemporaries, had already spoken of "the law that governs exceptions." And when they took stock, cursorily perhaps and almost at random, of the accumulated knowledge of the past, it was the spirit, not the letter of it

PABLO PICASSO (1881). TWO FEMALE NUDES, 1906. (59⅜ × 39¼″) PRIVATE COLLECTION, SWITZERLAND.

His Pink Period released Picasso from his obsession with the sadder side of life. He now concerned himself with purely painterly problems. The analytical treatment of the face of the girl on the left prefigures the technique of *Les Demoiselles d'Avignon*, and, at the next remove, of Cubism.

91

PABLO PICASSO (1881). FRUIT AND WINEGLASS, 1908. (10½ × 8½″)
PRIVATE COLLECTION, PARIS.

that interested them; poetry, prose literature, philosophy and science—all were eagerly ransacked, but with an eye not to their factual achievement but to their secret implications. It was poetry above all that fired their imagination; Picasso, Braque, Léger, Gris and Delaunay were constantly to be seen in the company of Guillaume Apollinaire, Max Jacob, Blaise Cendrars, André Salmon, Pierre Reverdy and Jean Cocteau, and the poets, ancient or modern, they most admired were always those who had proved themselves the greatest inventors of new images, new rhythms. Those of the 16th and 17th centuries were not overlooked and their favorites were men like Gongora, closely followed by Baudelaire, Rimbaud and Mallarmé. Indeed it was to the influence of poetry that, as we shall see, these painters largely owed their rediscovery of ancient arts akin to theirs.

Another of Alfred Jarry's remarks had a bearing on the program of the new generation of artists. The author of *Ubu Roi* once spoke of "unfolding a universe that supplements our own." This is in fact a key to the cubist aesthetic, for one of its main objects was the presentation of a world no longer based on visual experience, but wholly built up by the creative imagination. Yet new as was the conception, there was nothing against using conventional means for its accomplishment; after all was not one convention as good as another, provided only it were logical? Thus, pending the discovery of a more suitable "syntax," classical means could serve the artist's turn. Hypotheses, assumptions of a found solution, arguments *per absurdum*—all the procedures of the sciences and metaphysics—played their parts, when called for, in sponsoring the primacy of the thinking mind in the operations, no longer purely visual, of the creative process. It was largely as a result of the obvious flimsiness of Impressionist art, tending as it did to confirm the philosophical dictum that "the senses deform, the mind forms," that our young painters came to question the reliability of sensory impressions and the concept of an intuitively apprehended reality. There was nothing fanciful or anarchic in all this. After all, did not activities of the imagination and the intellect play a large part in other forms of art? Indeed it was plain to see how little there was in common between the psychological portrait, the conventional still life or landscape and the frankly anti-realistic inspiration of a poem, opera, ballet, fugue or tragedy, or even a cathedral.

Then again, a craving for a return to that primordial source of inspiration, the imaginings of childhood, ever the painter's dream, led the young painters to explore the wonderlands of folk art, to feed their fancy on old travelers' tales, novels of adventure, fantasies of humorists, from Mark Twain to Alphonse Allais, by way of Swift.

But, meanwhile, science was not neglected. Ancient works on the architectonics of picture-making were rescued from oblivion and in this connection the methods of Piero della Francesca, Paolo Uccello and Luca Pacioli came under careful scrutiny. Amongst recent writers on art Sérusier came in for attention, and there was much discussion of the "Golden Section," "Divine Proportion" and Father Didier's "Holy Measures." If, as I have said, science was a favored subject, this was not due to any special interest in new inventions—which I have heard Picasso describe as "silly gadgets"—but rather to the emphasis laid on the mysterious operations of Chance and all that these implied. Villiers de l'Isle-Adam was applauded for his remark that it is simpletons who make discoveries and scientists merely perfect them (granted that the "simpletons" he had in mind were children and poets). True, one heard talk about the fourth dimension, non-Euclidean geometry, the theory of numbers and so forth; not that any of us knew much about mathematics, but because these conceptions seemed to sponsor ventures on the artist's part into strange lands beyond the frontiers of conventional art, and to encourage creation rather than the "imitation" specified in Aristotle's famous, but (to us) obnoxious definition of art—the revolt against which in fact was largely responsible for the cubist revolution.

Creation, then, at all costs. The term sounded, perhaps, pretentious, but there was none other available. Actually the Cubists-to-be never imagined themselves capable of making something out of nothing; on the contrary they never lost sight of concrete reality, and indeed one of the best definitions of cubist aesthetic was Juan Gris' remark: "Our aim is to create new combinations of known elements."

The desire to create a new representation of man and the world is as old as humanity itself. All the Primitives felt this need and sought to satisfy it. But usually they drew on old material and merely re-arranged it. This holds good for the Cubists, too, and the precedents they invoked, and in particular their borrowings from Antiquity, were numerous; here we propose to sort them out and classify them.

In a general way, it was to Primitives of all periods that these artists instinctively harked back, charmed by their fervor and freshness of imagination. Ingres, too, had confessed his wistful admiration for "the perfection of the early gropings of certain arts," while David had advised his students to try to view nature "through the eyes of an untutored child." And Cézanne liked to describe himself as "the primitive of the path he had opened up." The Cubists began by rejecting the time-honored instruction of the Schools, and deliberately applied themselves to building up a self-taught art. Thus it was that, leaving the beaten tracks to others, they began with a study of the Primitives in whose work they discerned an imaginative form of expression which, far from copying the outward aspects of things, sponsored a world of intensely poetic yet plastically satisfying visions. In the pre-classical art of ancient Greece they discovered a wealth of symbols and simplifications ranging from the representation of a couple by two posts linked by a cross-bar to flat idols synthetically rendered in queer shapes like violoncellos (in the Cyclades). In Egyptian art they found syntheses of the human figure, a profile and a full-face view being combined in a single head, and a novel kind of space suggested by recessive planes of flat color—procedures after their own heart. Byzantine mosaics taught them that abstract space could be suggested by a plain gold ground, and form broken up analytically by the use of "tesserae."

In the art of the Italian Primitives they lit on procedures of another order. These artists, children of the Christian dispensation, had ways of thinking and emotions nearer our own—though, we need hardly add, it was not the religious faith behind their work that appealed to the Cubists, and they studied the Italian Primitives from a coolly objective viewpoint. They had eyes for technique alone, and for one procedure in particular: the "unnatural" disproportion between the objects represented in so many Primitive compositions. Take for example the archer, the saint and the warriors in one old work; the warriors are taller than the tower occupied by the archer and the angels hovering round the saint, and out of scale with the bridge they are crossing. True proportions are rejected in favor of dimensions of the mind, so to speak, based on the greater or lesser significance assigned to certain objects and figures. This systematic disproportion is basic to cubist art, in which the "true" proportions of familiar objects are deliberately sacrificed to an abstract architectural concept and a compositional scheme in which the normal "balance" of the various elements is disregarded. Unlike that of the Primitives, however, this new vision of the world owed nothing to religious faith, and derived from purely painterly considerations; but for both alike the artists' creative imagination supplied the driving force.

Other primitive arts were found to confirm this new approach to visual experience: those of the Scytho-Siberians, the Hittites, the Iberian races; but it was above all the marvelous achievements of Negro art that fascinated the Cubists. Little interested in its magical implications, the Cubists turned to Negro statuary for the unique lesson it offered of boldly expressive rhythms keyed to intellectual referents.

The geometrical bias of Cubism was not due to Cézanne alone. From the rediscovery of perspective up to Poussin and his famous triangles, geometry may be said to have played a leading part in the stylistic evolution of European art. In fact most of the Italian masters were professional geometers in a stricter sense than was Cézanne, whose conformity with the law of the "Golden Section" was intuitive, like that of the many artisans, such as cabinet-makers, who instinctively employ it. The Cubists approached these problems from a logical, analytical angle, and sought to establish the lay-out of the picture in terms of straight-forward rules—which, however, on occasion they might break, indulging in "poetic license"—and the forms taken by these rules may be likened to those of musical composition (counter-point, harmony, the fugue).

PABLO PICASSO (1881). SKETCH FOR "LES DEMOISELLES D'AVIGNON," 1906-1907. (46⅞ × 36⅝")
CARLO FRUA DE ANGELI COLLECTION, MILAN.

HENRI MATISSE (1869-1954). LUXE, CALME ET VOLUPTÉ. COLLIOURE 1907. (82 ½ × 54 ¼″)
J. RUMP COLLECTION, ROYAL MUSEUM OF FINE ARTS, COPENHAGEN.

Here we have the final, consummate version of this picture. The hesitations of the sketch have vanished, the arabesque is clearly defined, its drawing fuller, more assured. Matisse's aesthetic has come into its own; the color patch is firmed up by the line, and volumes are created by broadly opposed planes. Matisse told an amusing story about this work. Noticing that the right foot of the woman on the left had only four toes, he wondered if in simple justice to her he should not add a fifth. But that would have meant destroying the well-knit organization of the picture-surface, so he decided against it. It was too late to make any change. In the preliminary sketch, however, there still were realistic touches: the academic drawing of the shoulders and the symmetry of the breasts. In the final version of the work these have disappeared.

TWO GREAT PICTURES, TWO MEMORABLE EXHIBITIONS

To THE YEARS 1907 and 1906-07 are dated respectively Matisse's *Luxe, Calme et Volupté* and Picasso's *Les Demoiselles d'Avignon*. These epoch-making pictures gave the initial impetus to the two movements, Fauve and Cubist, which were to dominate the painting of the first half of the 20th century.

Matisse said, "It is through color I get sensations," and like the Impressionists he always remained dependent on nature and the model. And, with him, color alone builds form. Hence Fauvism.

Picasso, on the other hand, does not need nature or a model to inspire him; he builds up the world he paints wholly in his imagination. The color-design association is worked out on a purely mental level. Hence Cubism.

PABLO PICASSO (1881). LES DEMOISELLES D'AVIGNON, 1906-1907. (96 × 92″)
MUSEUM OF MODERN ART, NEW YORK.

Cubism

Aesthetic and Technique

THE GROWTH and flowering of cubist aesthetic took place between 1907 and 1914. The second date coincides with the outbreak of the First World War and it is possible that the dispersal of the artists due to this event had much to do with the cessation of new developments on strictly cubist lines. In any case we find that after 1914 the new aesthetic seems to have spent its driving force and the Cubists tended to strike out in new directions towards a certain stylization, though without abandoning their faith in the supremacy of the mind and the imagination.

The year 1908 is memorable not only because it witnessed, together with the collaboration of Picasso and Braque, the first group demonstration of Cubism, but also because Matisse's famous *La Desserte (Harmonie rouge)* bears this date, and it was in this year he published his epoch-making articles in *La Grande Revue*. Thus the leaders of those two great movements, Fauve and Cubist, met together and exchanged ideas, and also took stock of their differences. It could not be denied that by 1908 Fauvism was tending to repeat itself somewhat monotonously, or else to drift away from its original conceptions. Matisse on the other hand kept to the methods of his first *Desserte* (1897) and of the works he had exhibited at the 1900 Salon des Indépendants. He had frankly abandoned classical perspective, and replaced it by variations in the intensity of his colors. This procedure attracted the attention of the Cubists. Thus it was Matisse who, by way of Braque and Derain, taught Cubism to think; for the Cubists did not fail to see that there was applied logic, as well as sensuous expression, in his handling of color. Indeed Matisse was following a strictly logical course when he no longer asked of light that it should model forms or directly illuminate the object, as it does in nature. Lighting with him is indirect; so as to suggest form it is transmuted into color. The Fauves, furthermore, had definitely rejected three-dimensional composition, and this was another of the doctrines that Cubism took over from them. It also took a lead from the procedure described by Matisse when he said: "Suppose I am to paint a woman's body; I condense the significance of the body by concentrating on its essential lines." The Cubists were following this principle when they set out faces and bodies on the surface of the canvas in terms of their constituent parts, while adding some of that creative inventiveness which Matisse had in mind. The difference between the two tendencies can be summed up in two simple statements; whereas Matisse says, "I am going to paint a woman's body," Picasso would say, "I am out to paint a picture."

Having embarked on the perilous adventure involved in their new conception of the visible world, the Cubists at first proceeded cautiously. We have noted the emphasis they laid on geometrical precision. Their methods of approach were nothing if not methodical, and the words "correct" and "certitude" were often used. I remember hearing them employed by Braque and Juan Gris in our conversations at the "Bateau Lavoir," indeed I often used them myself. None of us, however, always clearly grasped what Picasso was after. "It looks as if you're asking us to eat cotton waste and drink kerosene!" was one of Braque's comments, and in fact Picasso's program struck us all as rather startling, to say the least of it.

In a general way the pioneers of Cubism were trying, as we now can see, to create a new kind of perspective and to replace the idea of "atmosphere" paramount in earlier painting by that of mathematically organized Space; which was logical enough since the artist's duty was to *construct*. But this had to be gone about with circumspection; the artist had, as Braque said, to begin by limiting his means, lest, running wild, they should foster the symptoms of decadence that were perceptible in most post-impressionist art. Color, needless to say, which they regarded as the chief offender, was given short shrift. Thus, by common consent they took to painting in monochrome, a bold innovation justified by their belief in the utmost economy of means. As a matter of fact it had some excellent precedents; thus Uccello, who held that color obscured forms, had freely employed terra verde, Raphael had observed that once the drawing done, a picture was complete, and Corot had candidly admitted, "With me, color is always an afterthought."

We shall see what became of these rather over-simplified ideas some years later. But in 1910 the architecture of the picture was all that seemed to matter. Actually the problem was not so simple as it seemed. Cézanne had talked of "cylinders, cones and spheres." This was not only a valuable pointer for the future but invited attention to some Italian 15th- and 16th-century Masters who were at once painters and geometricians. The Cubists, however, at this early stage were not quite clear in their minds as to the application of Cézanne's injunction. The name "Cubism" was launched by the critic Louis Vauxcelles who, unkindly but not wholly unjustly, thus baptized the earliest efforts of the group; these were, in fact, based on groupings of geometrically precise facets, which frankly "cubified" form. Cézanne's famous remark had been applied too literally, the result being an over-all structure of a purely conceptual order, which, however, created rich, tapestry-like patterns whose "analytic" elements were rendered in earthy and ochreous hues, all the more effective for being so few in number and chromatically so closely allied. It was these compositions that were described as "cobwebs" by that fervent colorist Delaunay who, like La Fresnaye, Lhote and Villon, was trying to give a sort of impressionist atmosphere to his version of Cubism. In this phase the picture was disintegrated into formal, colored elements, each structural and coloristic motif being subjected to a close analysis (Analytic Cubism). For the organization of the proposed new perspective another procedure was employed: the device of showing objects under all their aspects simultaneously and integrally as seen from different angles, that is to say in terms of the *ideas* we have of them. Here we have the beginnings of an *imagined* perspective. It may have owed something to children's drawings, in which both eyes are sometimes shown in a face seen from the side; to the Egyptian portrait in which a profile and full-face view are combined; and to the high reliefs in some cathedrals. This method, which was described by the Cubists as "a folding-back of planes," was also applied to color. Under the rather curious pretext that when we see an object its color catches our eye before its form, form and color were disassembled and merely juxtaposed. Another innovation, which led to striking effects, was the use of a sort of X-ray transparency, enabling new elements to be seen through objects locally opaque. Planes were superimposed with a view to suggesting depth and solving the painter's age-old problem of inserting depth in a two-dimensional surface. There was in fact a whole flowering of plastic devices having a certain resemblance to the grammarian's figures of speech: metaphor, ellipsis, antithesis, catachresis (the use of a word in a sense usually reserved for another), metonymy (the use of one word for another that it suggests) and the rest of it. Moreover, certain new ideas then in the air, "a transvaluation of values," "the will to constant metamorphosis," influenced more or less directly these young painters. Yet, as we have seen, the Cubists' innovations, daring as they were, had a logical basis and seemed to satisfy their desire for certainties and an ever-increasing control of their technical means. But, besides the rules of syntax, they also applied those of geometry, obviously more directly applicable to the architectonics of picture-making. Such esoteric phrases as "The Gate of Harmony," "The Holy Proportion," "The Golden Section" had fired the imagination of the artists of the day, the last-named being particularly cherished by Seurat and Sérusier. They employed the Golden Section according to the definition given by Vitruvius (the easiest to grasp), which laid down that to get a perfectly proportioned layout there should be the same relationship between the larger and the smaller parts of an ensemble as between the larger and the whole. Some, like Picasso, lit on this formula instinctively; others, Juan Gris for instance, deliberately. And it is Gris whose work provides the clearest demonstration of the cubist aesthetic ideal and who summed it up most appositely: "Cézanne goes towards architecture, I start out from it."

This brief résumé of cubist theory will suffice, we hope, to make it clear that most of the *means* sponsored by the new aesthetic are directly opposed to the emphasis on *appearance* characteristic of classical art, and that only the spirit of the latter was retained.

One of the works submitted to the 1908 Salon d'Automne, this picture led the selection committee, who rejected it, to speak of "cubes"; hence Cubism. The part played by geometry in cubist art has been misunderstood. True, Voltaire said there was a "secret geometry" behind all works of art, though few artists were aware of this. Braque, however, knew it, for, beginning from his earliest cubist period, he always imposed an architectural structure on his compositions. But he did not make geometry his starting point; he merely used it as a check, no more than that. Hence the easy flow and seething vitality of this landscape.

GEORGES BRAQUE (1882). L'ESTAQUE, 1908. ($28\frac{5}{8} \times 23\frac{1}{2}$") HERMANN RUPF COLLECTION, BERN.

RAOUL DUFY (1877-1953). L'ESTAQUE, 1908. (22 × 18″) RAOUL DUFY ESTATE.

As can be clearly seen in Dufy's *L'Estaque* and in the companion piece by Braque which we reproduce on the opposite page, though Cubism had by now acquired its name, its aesthetic had not as yet been fully worked out, anyhow as far as these two artists were concerned. It was still a matter of reshaping forms on geometric lines and building up the picture according to the principles laid down by Cézanne. That parallelism of the "force lines" of the composition, which we so often find in Cézanne's canvases, is plain to see in both of these works, and their plastic orchestration is also very similar, consisting as it does of the forms of nature reduced to "cylinders, cones and spheres." For some time yet the advice given by Cézanne was to be interpreted on different lines by the various Cubists-to-be. Cubism came later to be regarded by Picasso, Braque and Gris as a complete, autonomous aesthetic, the be-all and the end-all of artistic practice. Others regarded it rather as a set of rules intended merely to impose a certain order and discipline on the work of painters like themselves who aimed chiefly at expressing their responses to nature. Common to both these pictures is that conception of two-dimensional perspective which was subsequently to be amplified and organized.

Picasso

★

RECENTLY one of the big Paris dailies addressed an intriguing query to some eminent personalities: "Should we adore, or burn, Picasso?" The results were enlightening. Though they felt they could not decently refrain from doing homage to the greatness of Picasso, most of those who answered the question took good care to qualify their admiration. At a loss for better reasons quite a number professed, in all seriousness, to regard him as a sort of evil genius, little short of an incarnation of the devil! As a matter of fact this conception of Picasso as the bugaboo of art is frequently voiced by a certain school of critics, who find it a convenient starting-off point for disquisitions on the trend of modern art in general. Yet this conception is highly dubious to say the least of it. The truth perhaps is that, before deciding whether to burn or to adore him, they would have been well-advised to try to *know* him (as was obviously not the case with several of his critics) and above all to evaluate the profoundly human side of his genius.

Exactly fifty years have passed since I made the acquaintance of Picasso at that famous nest of studios named "Le Bateau Lavoir," to which Max Jacob had escorted me. Picasso had just arrived in Paris and it struck me at once how typically Spanish he was. One felt that he observed the world with an inquisitorial eye, severely, but not without a touch of pity for its follies. He had the fiery ardor of the Spanish temperament and its proud, somewhat disdainful aloofness. Though his father was an art-teacher, he never gave his son, so far as I could gather, much encouragement; and it must be admitted that the pictures the boy had taken to painting at the age of twelve were hardly such as a Spanish, or for that matter any art-teacher could approve of. Naturally enough young Pablo's early efforts had a certain clumsiness, but there were also indications of natural gifts of no mean order and that instinctive understanding of the medium à propos of which Picasso once remarked with characteristic forthrightness, "Technique can't be taught." At the same time he showed already that sense of the pathetic side of life which is never absent from his work, even when he is experimenting with new modes of pictorial representation of the most abstruse kind. No sooner had he come to Paris than he started frequenting public dance-halls and circuses, where he found subjects like those he had come across in Spain, and whose amusing or touching aspects have always had an appeal for him. The precocious imagination shown in his youthful drawings, their graphic audacities and verve were far removed indeed from the painstaking procedures of classical draftsmanship, as exemplified in the work of men like Ingres and Degas, whom his father held up to him as models. He was too impulsive, too spontaneous to have recourse to that stand-by of the conscientious student, his india-rubber, though he had not as yet lit on the device he afterwards adopted, of never erasing a line that dissatisfied him but using it as a pointer to a new one. Moreover he never could bring himself to drawing "from the model." Whenever I saw him at his easel, drawing or painting, he was always working from memory, though this description is not quite accurate in his case, since it is never a question with Picasso of remembering, but of re-creating motifs in his own mind. Obviously it is an easy matter for his enemies to talk of conjuror's tricks or diabolism in connection with this astounding gift of his—of which I confess I have never seen another instance, anyhow carried to such a pitch of perfection. The absence of a model has also the advantage of enabling him to eliminate, when he so desires, all that is accidental from his painting and thus to give it an absolute significance, that of life in its purest state.

1901-1904. The rejection of non-essentials is characteristic of his Blue Period, when his subjects were usually circus figures, pathetic harlequins, undernourished children, cripples; these he did not depict in the Lautrec manner as "characters," but stressed their universal, human qualities. For this, he had little need of color, with the result that the pictures of this period are to all intents and purposes in monochrome. Sooner or later, he knew, he would have to tackle the problems of color in the wider sense, but meanwhile they could wait. Usually, too, in this phase the picture is little more than a colored drawing; he blocks out contour-lines, then inserts color in the areas thus demarcated. This was, in fact, an ancient classical procedure that Manet, Gauguin and Lautrec had revived. It should be noted that, also in this Blue Period, Picasso painted some architecturally ordered landscapes (in 1903) which show affinities with pre-Renaissance Italian art. Perhaps we may see here an anticipation of the architectural concepts of Cubism. Picasso's art in this phase has several specifically Spanish traits, notably an addiction to what the Spanish academic school describes as the *estilo monstruoso*, meaning that emphasis on the grotesque which we find in the Burgos artist Vigarni, the Granadan Diego de Siloe and Berruguete the sculptor, and which culminated in Goya. Another typically Spanish trait is Picasso's habit of including discrepant styles, ancient and modern, in one and the same work; his Iberian ancestors had combined the Gothic and Moorish styles in just this way.

1905. In his Pink Period Picasso's art has undergone a change; much of the bitterness has gone out of it. For a while he has discarded his humanitarian ideology, and the emotive, emaciated figures of his earlier phase give place to fuller, plastically molded forms. Harsh contour-lines disappear, volumes are stressed and color plays a part in building form. In his *Two Female Nudes* we find certain constructive elements that will be further developed in *Les Demoiselles d'Avignon.*

1907. A memorable year, since to it belongs the famous picture named above, which gives the first clear intimations of the full-fledged cubist aesthetic. It stood for nothing short of a revolution in the art of painting and a new vision of reality, in which the concept of atmosphere is replaced by that of space. Much has been written on the origins of the new art-form sponsored by *Les Demoiselles d'Avignon.* As regards the drawing, some have traced it to the influence of archaic arts, from those of the Greeks, Egyptians, Iberians up to Negro art. Indeed it was natural enough that, in seeking to discover for the art of painting (as scientists periodically do for science) a new point of departure, and in view of the fact that painting seemed to have marked time so to speak for several centuries, Picasso should look back to the Primitives for a lead. Here the discoveries of Cézanne and Seurat, the great precursors, stood him in good stead, since it was now a matter of taking greater liberties with nature and making it clear that between the work of art directly inspired by visual experience and that built up by the creative mind there was a difference in kind, not merely in degree.

Such were the circumstances under which cubist aesthetic took form. I well remember those gatherings in Picasso's studio, at which he sketched out to us its basic principles and his general plan of campaign, but I must admit that at the time we had some difficulty in grasping exactly what he was driving at. The period of logical exegesis came much later. What made things harder for us was that his ideas were the fruit of a lively poetic imagination, not of reasoning; as indeed was to be expected of a highly original creative genius.

1908. A general description of Cubism has been given in an earlier part of this book. Picasso's version of it reflected, as was natural, his own turn of mind, the idiosyncrasies of his inventive genius. Whereas Braque, as we shall see, relied heavily on Cézanne and his program of reducing nature to geometric forms, what Picasso appreciated most in Cézanne was his ambition not merely to reconstruct on canvas his initial sensory response but to convert it into something different. In any case it was not Cézanne the great pictorial architect alone who lay behind Picasso's Cubism. It might be said with equal plausibility that Picasso's transformation of the classical way of seeing the world owed as much to Piero della Francesca, to Poussin and to Corot as to the Master of Aix. The truth, however, is that there were fundamental differences between Picasso and all his predecessors; he had in a quite literal sense his own ideas and, bearing this in mind, we may find it easier to understand the many metamorphoses of his art in the course of his career.

Given the almost superhuman tasks he has set himself and the kink in his nature that has doomed him to an endless quest of ever new visions and interpretations of reality, it is not surprising if occasionally he betrays a certain unsureness, even indecision. For he is never

In pursuance of the comparative method of presenting the various art movements here adopted, we reproduce Picasso's Harlequin and his Family *for comparison with the two pictures named* L'Estaque *by Braque and Dufy respectively (see pages 104-105). The compositional arrangement of these two pictures is similar, can be found in many classical works, and was often followed by Cézanne. Briefly, it consists in flanking a landscape with trees placed well in front and right and left, which, acting like the pillars on either side of the proscenium of a theater, suggest spatial recession and lead the spectator's gaze into the heart of the picture. The Cubists, on the other hand, aimed at bringing the subject forward towards the spectator, and to implement this effect a new kind of frame was devised, convex instead of concave (i.e. recessive) as in the past.*

Braque and Dufy kept to Cézanne's procedures; their geometric forms existed only as aspects of, and derivative from, the subject represented, whereas Picasso's were pure plastic rhythms. The crooked arm on the right and the Harlequin's face on the left are mere, casual allusions to reality. Also the two first-named artists still shared Cézanne's respect for nature; whereas Picasso reduced nature to plastic signs, a procedure which was to become characteristic of "orthodox" Cubism. We may note, in fact, that the two canvases by Braque and Dufy are not yet dominated by the notion of re-creation in the mind that was basic to Cubism, and that, with them, a concept of pure space has not yet ousted that of an impressionist "atmospheric" ambiance.

PABLO PICASSO (1881). HARLEQUIN AND HIS FAMILY, 1908. (39¼ × 31¾")
E. VON DER HEYDT COLLECTION, ASCONA (SWITZERLAND).

satisfied with the provisional truths he lights on, nor does he regard art as a restful, unexacting mistress—as do some of his colleagues who have no qualms about turning out the same picture all their lives and accuse Picasso of never knowing his own mind. In fact nothing could be more human and less "diabolical" than this haunting sense of doubt and dissatisfaction which he sometimes accepts resignedly but which oftener, short-tempered as he is, throws him into fits of rage. In fact a spirit of revolt pervades all his activities: revolt against a social order whose form displeases him, revolt against the way in which so many of the human race behave, revolt against the imprecisions of the retinal image and the impossibility of attaining an Absolute—his lifelong obsession—beyond the reach of men.

1919-1924. In the course of his researches, during that is to say his experimental phase between 1919 and 1924, Picasso came to feel the time had come to call a temporary halt, to take breath as it were in the calmer atmosphere of classical art (which he has always deeply revered). And here he glimpsed new possibilities, in accordance with the Spanish tradition of combining different styles. It was child's play for him to learn the secrets of the great art of the past; that marvelous drawing which lies at the core of his achievement, and indeed means everything to him, came to his aid and he now produced works that, as has been justly said, "excelled Ingres and equaled Raphael." Starting out from reminiscences of Greece, Crete, Etruria, Pompeii and the Renaissance, he succeeded, amazingly, in fusing the impersonality of Classicism with that emotive expression of the self which is never absent from his work. In his painting, sculpture and engraving alike, Picasso always takes as his point of departure a clean-cut idea, though oftener than not it turns into "something quite different," as he tells us, in the process of working it out. None is more surprised than he when this happens, though actually it is natural enough, considering his temperament, the quickness of his responses to the promptings of an intuition that seems never to take into account what any other artist, even he himself, has done before.

1925. It was round about this date that, giving free rein at last to his poetic impulses, Picasso conceived the idea of conjuring up the elements of an imaginary world, the stuff that dreams are made of; as a result he was accused by an uncomprehending public of an obsession with the diabolic, with the ugly and grotesque, or at best of a childish wish to mystify. Some have gone so far as to describe this phase of his artistic evolution as "the period of monsters," having in mind no doubt the so-called *estilo monstruoso* of Spanish art to which reference has already been made. It would have been more accurate to describe this, using the term invented by Apollinaire, as Picasso's Surrealist Period, though actually the material he worked on stemmed not from the Unconscious but from instinct and intuition; and in particular from a strong feeling for those prototypal myths which have haunted the mind of man since the dawn of human life. In the art of Picasso we find a constant urge to build up a new world (has he not invented a new anatomy?) in which the microcosm and macrocosm of the ancient metaphysicians intermingle in a proliferation of strange, hugely swelling forms, incredible distortions, plastic inventions that fascinate or horrify, as the case may be.

1937. In this year Picasso's vast, underlying compassion for human suffering found a new form of expression inspired by the horrors of the Spanish Civil War, whose tragedy he commemorated in that great dedicated mural *Guernica*. Once again he recast his technique, and this time in terms of his vision of a world of pain and cruelty, sensuality and death; a world that he interpreted under a curious guise as half machine and half alive, and one whose workings could not better have been revealed by the most ruthless vivisection. The mood that inspired his *Guernica* has never left him, though he still is constantly directing his art towards new goals. Whether his theme is a sleeping figure, a tearful face, a dying man, a bird perched on a branch, a savage bull, or young people playing on a beach, always he abstracts from the complex of forms generated by these visual experiences such elemental signs as mouths, teeth, eyes or limbs which he treats as specific referents. In these works Picasso, so to speak, disincarnates the object; his art is as it were the equivalent of a cry, which can signify an emotion and, though a mere fleeting sound, achieve a poignant lyricism more evocative than any spoken or written words.

Georges Braque

★

A N EXPLANATION of the hesitations shown by Braque in subscribing to the program of the early stage of the cubist movement may be found in the difference between his artistic background and Picasso's. Picasso was born at Malaga; his family moved to La Coruña when he was ten, and soon after to Barcelona, where he lived for the next fifteen years. All three towns are seaports. Braque's family came to Le Havre when he was eight and he lived there until his twentieth year. Picasso never showed the least interest in the sea or in the colorful activity of the seaports where he spent his young days. Some forty years later, observing a young artist gazing intently at the blue expanse of the Mediterranean preparatory to depicting it on his canvas, Picasso asked him: "What are you trying to see? Is there anything out there?" Braque was very different; he loved the Channel, and memories of the sea haunted him even in his cubist period; nor are they absent in his later and most recent works. I remember one day watching Picasso in his studio drawing a Harlequin with his usual flawless accuracy. A couple of days later I met Braque at Honfleur; he was out on the beach, painting the sea. The limpid, ever-changing light, the skies and seas of Normandy fascinated him no less than they had fascinated the Impressionists. Whereas one always felt that Picasso's art training had been on classical lines, Georges Braque made no secret of his fervent interest in problems of atmosphere, light and color. Thus it may seem surprising that the two young artists should have one day joined forces and applied themselves to the same problem. Nevertheless, when we recall Braque's lifelong cult of order and clarity and his famous remark, "I like the rule that corrects emotion," this abrupt decision to work together seems natural enough. For Braque has always regarded nature as a repertory of forms strewn around in picturesque confusion, on which it is his function as an artist to impose order. Indeed his organizational sense and aversion for any "untidiness" are among the qualities to which he owes his unique place in modern art.

We have already mentioned that Picasso's father was a drawing-master; Braque's was a house-painter and decorator who did landscape painting in his leisure hours and even had some of his work accepted for the *Salon des Artistes Français*. As a boy Georges was often to be seen in his father's workshop where he was initiated into the mysteries of mixing that curious, glutinous paint which, applied by a skillful hand on walls, doors or dados, gives an eye-perfect illusion of wood or marble. Almost unconsciously he seems to have perceived poetic possibilities in these seemingly so banal commercial techniques and he developed a boyish ambition to promote them to the level of a fine art. As already mentioned, the glamour of Impressionism, from whose thrall he had some trouble in escaping, led him temporarily up blind alleys, and though he had a clear enough conception of his ultimate goal, it cost him a struggle to resist the lures of the impressionist way of seeing. He went about this prudently, methodically, and for a time joined forces with the Fauves, whose disciplinary measures marked a transition stage between Impressionism and Cubism. In this phase his emancipation was made easier by the fact that, great as was his love for nature, he clearly saw that impressionist methods could but lead him towards a vision of reality under its most fleeting, evanescent aspects and a manner of art that was far from satisfying his desire for solid pictorial construction and the expression of permanent values.

He soon perceived how well Cézanne's theories tallied with his personal conceptions and what, no doubt, made it all the simpler for him to see the merits of a geometric organization of the picture was that he had so often watched his father's skilled employees at their work, ruler in hand or merely resting the tip of a little finger on the surface to be painted so as to steady the movements of the brush, and, by the application of certain elementary rules of geometry, producing decorations which, though narrow in their range, were admirable of their kind. The cubist ventures of his next phase tended to stimulate his wholly objective devotion to the quest, to his mind paramount, of style at its purest, and to the creation of a personal language. Necessarily in this endeavor the natural appearances of objects had to go by the board, but that could not be helped; it was the first essential step towards a new vision, peculiar to himself. As we have seen, there was a basic incompatibility between the temperament of Braque and that of Picasso. While Picasso's art overwhelms the beholder, one might almost say "gets him on the raw," Braque's is persuasive and weaves a spell that is often irresistible. Not that it resorts to any questionable or insidious artifices; on the contrary, Braque's handling of the brush is forthright, unequivocal. He has no use for the short-cuts in which so many other Cubists indulged and which, as he realized, would militate against his constant concern for measuring, calculating, reckoning up—in other words for organizing the picture. His aim is of a special order; he has always sought to employ the personal language he has carefully planned out for "making a picture," and "the picture" is something he ranks above the expression of sensations and emotions. As already mentioned, he "likes the rule that corrects emotion," and he has always refused to expose his soul-searchings on canvas. Nor is there any trace in his work of Picasso's objective expressionism; the emotion of which he speaks concerns his sensibility as a colorist, and this he keeps within due limits by assigning to color a specifically constructive role. Thus Braque, in setting out to "make a picture" at this period, conceived it strictly in terms of the means of cubist technique, many of whose rules were of his own invention, and he had also to conceive it in its entirety since the aforesaid rules could be applied to good effect only in compositions whose general structure was concordant with their spirit. In any case his highly individual poetic vision prevented him from attaching overmuch importance to the notion of the subject. In taking (like most of the Cubists) quite commonplace objects, always the same ones, as his models, his reason was that he regarded these as type-forms or rather molds—somewhat like the forms of poetry and music, sonnets and fugues—which enabled him to create plastic arrangements governed by the idea expressed in his remark, "I think in forms and colors." He carried his indifference to the subject to the point of creating near-abstractions in the so-called Hermetic Period of Cubism and, in fact, non-figurative artists of today claim him as one of their precursors.

Nevertheless he was alive to the risks he was running in those labyrinthine adventures, often perilously novel and impossible to check up by any known standards, into which the promptings of his imagination led him. A remark he made at this time is significant: "Limitation of the artist's means creates style, gives rise to new forms and stimulates creation." This spirit of deliberate renunciation makes itself felt notably in the works he produced during the three phases of Cubism: Analytical, Hermetic and Synthetic. During the analytical phase he disintegrated forms more and more; indeed it was due to the lengths to which he carried this ruthlessly analytic process that Cubism entered on its next, hermetic phase, in which objects are so to speak volatilized and tend to lose almost all their individual traits. Perhaps in so doing he was guarding himself against a latent inclination to revert to impressionist procedures. But, thanks to his unfailing devotion to "the rule," he soon was led to reconstituting synthetically what he had dissected at the prompting of his coloristic imagination and reverted to that almost scientifically balanced composition which he had temporarily lost sight of. So exceptional is Braque's technique that it may be said to defy all attempts to pigeonhole it, the reason being that though the intellectual concepts behind it, the elements of conscious planning, may be ascertained and described, that strange, incommensurable thing, genius, has woven itself into their very texture. It is generally recognized that as a colorist, he is the equal of the greatest masters in that field. And in tackling the arduous problem of dissociating color from form so as to treat it as an independent element capable of creating with its own resources that new space he has in mind, Braque has succeeded in producing a color orchestration in which the tones, while exquisitely subtle, produce none the less an impression of entire solidity. Indeed Braque's colors take effect on the beholder's sensibility with a rare immediacy, inducing in him that mysterious thrill of satisfaction, that sense of perfect *rightness* and reposefulness, which Matisse had in mind when he said he wished his painting to act as a "cerebral sedative."

GEORGES BRAQUE (1882). LANDSCAPE, 1908. (31¾ × 25½")
KUNSTMUSEUM, BASEL.

In the Analytic Period of Cubism to which this work belongs there is greater similarity between the procedures of Braque and Picasso. Allusions to reality are to all intents and purposes ruled out, except for some details inserted in the picture to serve as "pointers." There are traces of stylization and also of chiaroscuro, this latter being used for emphasizing volumes —which, as Léger remarked, was encroaching on the field of sculpture. Also, the superposition of planes and the presentation of objects under their various aspects and in different colors show a similar tendency. Picasso and Braque have not yet carried abstraction to the point it reached in the Hermetic Period.

PABLO PICASSO (1881). SEATED WOMAN, 1909. (38⅞ × 31⅞") ROLAND PENROSE COLLECTION, LONDON.

For some aestheticians art is a game, and if classical perspective is but one of its rules, the Cubists replaced it with another. Picasso posited an entirely new conception of space in which the objects painted lie all on the same plane and, instead of receding into the canvas towards a vanishing point, exist solely on the picture-surface. Unlike classical perspective, which leads the eye into the picture through the "window" of the frame, by means of such familiar devices as *trompe-l'œil*, chiaroscuro and foreshortening, cubist perspective leads outwards from the picture-surface towards the spectator. Carrying this principle to an extreme, the Cubists enclosed their canvases not in the traditional frames which curve inwards, but in frames curving away from the picture.

PABLO PICASSO (1881). GIRL WITH A MANDOLIN, 1910. (39¼ × 29″)
ROLAND PENROSE COLLECTION, LONDON.

GEORGES BRAQUE (1882). STILL LIFE WITH VIOLIN AND PITCHER, 1909-1910. (45⅝ × 28⅝″)
LA ROCHE COLLECTION, KUNSTMUSEUM, BASEL.

GEORGES BRAQUE (1882). THE PORTUGUESE, 1911. ($45\frac{5}{8} \times 31\frac{3}{4}''$)
LA ROCHE COLLECTION, KUNSTMUSEUM, BASEL.

PABLO PICASSO (1881). THE CLARINET-PLAYER, 1911-1912. (41⅝ × 26¼″) DOUGLAS COOPER COLLECTION, LONDON.

ROBERT DELAUNAY (1885-1941). THE EIFFEL TOWER, 1910. (77 × 50¾″) KUNSTMUSEUM, BASEL.

WASSILY KANDINSKY (1866-1944). ABSTRACT COMPOSITION (WATERCOLOR), 1910. (19⅝ × 25½")
MRS NINA KANDINSKY COLLECTION, PARIS.

Reactions from Cubism

Towards Movement and Color

ALL THE PAINTERS with whose work we now shall deal are more or less affiliated to the Impressionists, and the impressionist conception of "atmosphere" is still more or less apparent in their procedures. For them Cubism had been merely a call to order, which they declined to obey. Thus they restored to color the prerogatives the Fauves had given it and the Cubists had repudiated, anyhow to begin with. Though no stress is laid on form and outline, the flimsiness of impressionist art is now replaced by the classical conceptions of ordered composition, planes and well-knit pictorial construction. Under the cross-fire of rays of light the outlines of objects either break up or melt away. None the less the light that falls on objects on the one hand and, on the other, the light that they reflect binds them together and thus new forms emerge from the intersections of these luminous planes. The intensity of this fusion depends on the greater or lesser refractive quality of the object, which thus contributes to the building-up of these new immaterial forms expressed by color. Indeed the material structure of the object sometimes disappears altogether in a haze of broken lights or color patches which set up movement paths in the canvas, and the new color orchestration of these painters is more of a musical and lyrical than of a plastic order.

ROBERT DELAUNAY (1885-1941). SIMULTANEOUS WINDOWS, 1911. (18 × 15¾")
JEAN CASSOU COLLECTION, PARIS.

Delaunay dedicated this work to Jean Cassou and on the back of the canvas is written in the artist's own hand : "This document had to be returned to a poet." In no other work did the artist's lyrical gift reach such a degree of luminous intensity. And we can see why Apollinaire was inspired by this painting to write one of his most beautiful poems, *Les Fenêtres*. It was he, too, who baptized as "Orphism, the New Dynamic Poetry" the type of art, musical in conception, in which Delaunay was developing a new form of color orchestration still impressionist in spirit.

Delaunay and Orphism

"Dislocation" of Cubism and Color Orchestration

THE NAME of Orphism was given by Guillaume Apollinaire to a movement launched by Robert Delaunay in 1912, which had among its adherents the Czech painter Kupka, the Americans Bruce, Morgan Russell and Macdonald Wright, and Sonia Terk, an artist whose brilliant conceptions greatly influenced the decoration and women's fashions of the day, and who became Delaunay's wife.

A great admirer of the Primitives, Delaunay had a particular affection for the Douanier Rousseau. He kept to the bright palette of the Impressionists and his best works are canvases conceived on an heroic scale, characterized by their poetic flights of fancy and a sensual delight in color for its own sake. If he submitted for a while to the influence of Cézanne, this was no more than a period of self-imposed discipline, an effort to control the drive of inner forces that often threatened to undo him, though he took care never to betray this. Cubism for him was never more than a potential source of instruction and its graphic lyricism had no appeal for him. He had an instinct for a very different kind of lyricism, exuberant and wholly personal, to which he has given brilliant expression in works of dazzling color. Indeed a passionate, almost physical love of color possessed him, though, to begin with, fearing "to make an exhibition of himself," he tried to repress it. It was not until his so-called Orphic Period that he indulged this passion to the full and broke with all traditional modes of representing the real world. In short Robert was literally obsessed with color. I can remember his holding forth to me on the subject one day with quite amazing eloquence, using exactly the terms a young lover might use to describe his first *grande passion*. One had the impression that certain colors, especially when intensified by the play of light, acted on him like an intoxicant and color was a kind of fifth element outside which he could not breathe.

Then, in 1911, almost as a symbolical gesture, Delaunay suddenly threw open his *Windows* to a fully integrated vision of his world of color. At one swoop he abolished any suggestion whatever of real objects, of depth or perspective, and this dramatic move was certainly impulsive, not in the least thought-out. None the less his conception of abstract art is the most intelligible and intelligent of all. Through these open *Windows* he lets in a cataract of lustrous colors, transformed by his imagination and his skillful brush into a glittering maze of broken lights. He sees light overflowing all the boundaries of space, conjuring up a wonderful diversity of rhythms governed by the laws of color contrasts (those famous "simultaneous contrasts"), to which the picture owes its throbbing vitality. They are, a grammarian might say, the syntax of the picture, that on which its meaning hinges. From his early enthusiasm for the dynamic possibilities of sporting events, the Eiffel Tower and even cathedrals, Delaunay moved on to colorful syntheses of movement, and thence to the most passionate effusions that pure color has ever achieved. Nothing could be farther from the truth than Boccioni's claim that Orphism was "only Futurism in other clothes." The two conceptions were utterly different. Delaunay's Orphism was the product of a physical rather than a purely artistic urge, and this was not the case with Futurism, not even with Boccioni. The futurist taking-off point was always the subject, whereas with Delaunay, as he has himself made clear, "color is both form and subject." Orphism and Futurism are diametrically opposed.

Writers on abstract art have usually and rightly considered Delaunay to be one of its purest exponents. Some abstract painters have tried to escape from the traditional art of nature-imitation by replacing it with evocative, realistically rendered geometric forms. Not so Delaunay; without stretching the point, we may perhaps say that his way of painting was like that philological process which, after abstracting the specific quality of an object, proceeds to a generalization and gives it a distinctive name. Thus Delaunay created pure objects endowed with particular qualities, and these objects owed their existence to that physical passion for color which was the unique source of his inspiration.

Futurism

Dynamic versus Static Painting

THIS NEW, startling movement was launched by the poet Marinetti who published the Futurist Literary Manifesto at Paris in *Le Figaro* on February 22, 1909. The gist of the Manifesto (to which the painters subsequently subscribed) was a declaration of war against traditionalism in art ("*passatismo*," as Marinetti called it) and an impassioned glorification of the future. Hence the origin of the name Futurism.

The first "Manifesto of Futurist Painters" was declaimed at the Teatro Chiarella in Turin on March 3, 1910, before an audience of three thousand people. It was signed by Umberto Boccioni, Carlo D. Carrà, Luigi Russolo, Giacomo Balla and Gino Severini. Futurism was not an impulsive, unpremeditated movement like Cubism, which even owed its name to a casual jest. Futurism was a concerted manifestation whose title and program had been deliberately chosen by its promoters.

The general intentions underlying the futurist movement are clearly expressed in a sentence of the Manifesto. "The gesture we seek to represent on canvas will no longer be an arrested moment within the universal dynamism; it will be the dynamic sensation itself." The idea was original and involved the presentation of a new vision of the universe. But—and this is one of the great differences between Futurism and Cubism—Futurism aimed at a realism entirely conditioned by retinal sensations, and at discovering the exact nature of appearances. For the Futurists "everything moves, all is in a state of flux, of headlong change. Given the persistence of the image on the retina, objects in movement multiply themselves endlessly and become distorted as they overflow each other like vibrations launched into space and weaving through it. Thus a trotting horse has not four legs but twenty and their movements are triangular . . ."

Obviously these highly ingenious notions called for a total revision of our whole attitude towards the work of art. The spectator, instead of being placed in front of the picture in the traditional way, now found himself posted at the very heart of the canvas. In fact it was rather like what happens in a theater. "A man in pain has exactly the same interest for us as the pain of an electric light bulb suffering from spasmodic interruptions . . . The expression in a work of art of simultaneous states of mind—that's what we aim at with all the fervor that is in us." And the Manifesto closed with an exhortation to "scorn all forms of imitation." Once we start to examine futurist works, it becomes apparent that the Manifesto did less than justice to them. The Futurists in short were worth more than Futurism. Moreover, praiseworthy as was their avowed aim of avoiding all forms of imitation, they were the first to forget about it. Nothing shows this more clearly than the case of the horse with twenty legs quoted in the Manifesto. Indeed it was only as a result of imitation pushed to its extreme limit that the Futurists were led to represent the full complexity of objects in motion by accumulating visual sensations and integrating them into a single plastic unit. True, the Futurists introduced a certain number of pictorial elements which they "inferred" among those which they "saw," and, also, stylized movements by means of force-lines intended to synthesize their dynamism. But this simply made imitation the more complete. Here, in fact, was the fatal flaw in a movement which, insofar as it contributed to a timely revolution in art, was altogether praiseworthy. Nevertheless the plastic aspect of the futurist compositions, their unmistakably dynamic brio, proved to be a mine of discovery for Dadaists, Surrealists and even for certain Cubists.

Born at Reggio in Calabria in 1882, Umberto Boccioni met his death in the First World War. Temperamentally daring and independent, he left his parents at an early age when they tried to prevent his taking up painting as a career. He went to Rome and studied with Giacomo Balla, who also joined the Futurists later. Boccioni's departure from his family circle left its mark on his personality, and departure runs like a leitmotiv through his short life.

UMBERTO BOCCIONI (1882-1916). STATES OF MIND I : THE FAREWELLS, 1911. (27¼ × 27¾")
NELSON A. ROCKEFELLER COLLECTION, NEW YORK.

Even in his series of vibrant compositions, *States of Mind,* and in their sub-titles *The Farewells, Those who stay, Those who leave,* we seem to sense a prescience of his early death. In 1914 he was imprisoned with Marinetti and Russolo for manifesting in favor of Italy's entering the war on the side of the Allies. These facts in themselves are indications of Boccioni's forceful temperament. It showed itself further in his fondness for taking human bodies and objects to pieces as though they were bits of machinery. He had the traditional Italian feeling for perfect technique, his style is always warmly human and even in his most romantic fantasies, though indulging in eye-bewildering contrasts, he never loses sight of the need for an over-all structural order.

Luigi Russolo, a musician as well as a painter, wrote the "Futurist Manifesto on the Art of Noises," and his painting tended towards the expression of an abstract dynamism which has certain affinities with music. In fact one of his best pictures was called *Music.* In such pictures as *Dynamic Volumes, Lines of Force of a Thunderbolt,* he was less concerned with realistic subject-matter than with the interpenetration of planes and a development of plastic masses in space somewhat analogous to the development of music in time. But he also painted such orthodox futurist works as *The Revolt* of 1911. He also designed sets and costumes for plays, in which he showed bold originality and a very real feeling for the grandiose.

Carlo D. Carrà studied at the Brera Academy and received a training on classical lines. His contribution to Futurism was classical in spirit. His drawing was synthetic, his execution pure and often severe. He was also a good writer and critic, and was largely responsible for the "Manifesto of Futurist Painters." But Carrà's means were never limited by the

139

UMBERTO BOCCIONI (1882-1916). THE FORCES OF A STREET, 1911. (39¼ × 21¾")
MRS NELL URECH-WALDEN COLLECTION, SCHINZNACH (SWITZERLAND).

Unlike the Cubists, the Futurists made reality their point of departure. Here Boccioni, in order to depict the dynamism of a street, has tried to make a synthesis of all its movements. Forms react upon each other in a welter of collisions; circular elements intensify, speed up the movement; sudden highlights multiply and heighten the tension between lines of force whose intersections create an effect of tumultuous depth.

discipline which had been instilled into him at the Academy. Carrà has an energetic, progressive temperament and his political ideas are vigorously displayed in his painting *The Funeral of the Anarchist Galli*. Carrà shows the same reformative instincts in his pictorial experiments and in his absolute rejection of all pretty, eye-flattering elements. Even in those compositions which are most full of movement—for example *The Jolts of a Cab* and *What the Streetcar told me*—the plastic elements are not artificially dislocated so as to simplify the task of picturing movement. They are rhythmically integrated. Carrà never loses sight of the idea of the picture he wants to make. Furthermore he has a remarkable feeling for the emotive and dynamic value of juxtaposed geometric elements. Indeed the most original quality in Carrà's work is the fact that he makes geometry live. His success in this respect

CARLO CARRÀ (1881).
THE MILAN GALLERIA, 1912. (35¼ × 23½ ″)
GIANNI MATTIOLI COLLECTION, MILAN.

is due to a mathematical sensibility which is thoroughly in the Italian tradition, and we should take his declaration that he "paints as a drunkard sings" with a grain of salt.

Born at Cortona in 1883, Gino Severini is essentially a consummate technician and a poet. He is highly cultured and well versed in the art of the past. In true Italian style, he has written about his own artistic aims and outlook in a series of admirable books. It was perhaps his knowledge and culture which saved him from the excesses of Futurism and from yielding too completely to the doctrinaire dynamism of the movement. Severini regarded the idea-sensation as something controlled both by retinal sensations and intellectual elements. Thus his art was based on a synthesis of both. He tried to combine the static qualities of Cubism with the mobile force of Futurism. He originally subscribed fully to the futurist

CARLO CARRÀ (1881). SIMULTANEITY : WOMAN AND BALCONY, 1912. (57¾ × 52¼″)
PRIVATE COLLECTION, MILAN.

GINO SEVERINI (1883). DANCER AT THE BAL TABARIN, 1912. (24 × 18″)
PRIVATE COLLECTION, MILAN.

conception in a work entitled *Dynamic Hieroglyph of the Bal Tabarin* (1912). But finding it insufficient, he sought inspiration in classicism, and was thus enabled to reintroduce into his work the notion of an object. But the originality of his futurist works is best revealed in his symphonies of multicolored tonalities.

Modern Painting in the United States

The Armory Show

THIS epoch-making International Exhibition of Modern Art took place in New York in February 1913, at the Armory of the 67th Regiment; hence the name under which it has become world-famous. The organizers were a group of American artists, notably Walt Kuhn and Walter Pach, who persuaded the painter Arthur B. Davies to take charge of it. 1100 works were shown and this was the first time that the American public was confronted by modern art on such a scale. There were angry protests; the artists were accused of being degenerate or, on the kindest view, lunatics, Marcel Duchamp's *Nude descending a Staircase* being a favorite target for the fury and derision of visitors to the exhibition. The organizers of the show had been careful in their choice of works, and with the object of bringing out the links that existed between modern art and that of earlier periods a few works by Ingres and Delacroix had been included. For the rest, Cézanne and Van Gogh, so far more or less unknown in America, were hung beside the Fauves and Cubists, and works by Kandinsky, Lehmbruck and Brancusi. France, Italy, Germany, England, Spain, Russia and Switzerland were all represented. Many great American artists figured in the exhibition—Whistler, Ryder and Twachtman amongst them—as well as other outstanding painters known to be admirers of modern European art—for example, Hopper, Robinson and Marin.

Despite the violent hostility of the press, the exhibition had considerable success. Public opinion was greatly shaken and the Art Institute of Chicago took over the exhibition to show it in that city. There the scandal was no less and Sheldon Cheney reports that some students even burnt effigies of the artists and organizers. When the exhibition moved on to Boston its reception was similar, except that on this occasion hostility was manifested by a stony silence. But the consequences of this famous exhibition as regards the evolution of modern art in America were far-reaching; indeed America's participation in the making of 20th-century art may be said to date from the Armory Show.

Vanguard Art in Russia

Larionov and Rayonnism

GENERALLY speaking, the artists who took the lead in shaping the course of modern painting belonged to the same generation; many indeed were born within a few months of each other. This is one reason why there have been many disputes about the exact dates of origin of the various movements. The variety of abstract art known as "Rayonnism," created by Michael Larionov, began, he tells us, with a painting he made in 1909.

Larionov, who was born at Tiraspol in 1881, was promoter of the artist groups quaintly named "The Donkey's Tail," and "The Jack of Diamonds." But his Rayonnist manifesto was not written till 1912 (published in 1913). Among the announcements it contained was the following: "Here begins a painting which can succeed only by following the laws of color and of its transposition on to canvas. Here begins the creation of new forms whose force and meaning depend solely on tonal strength and each tone's position in relation to others." Every form and every art style of the past was condemned out of hand. Here there are obvious links with Futurism, but Rayonnism claims to have been the first movement to sponsor such ideas. In 1910 Marinetti had had triumphal receptions at Moscow and St. Petersburg; four years later Larionov saw to it that he was greeted with rotten eggs! In 1914 the preface for the catalogue of a Rayonnist Exhibition organized in Paris for Larionov and Natalie Gontcharova was contributed by Guillaume Apollinaire.

JACQUES VILLON (1875). SOLDIERS MARCHING, 1913. (25½ × 36⅛″) LOUIS CARRÉ COLLECTION, PARIS.

The "Section d'Or"

★

IN 1912, the "Section d'Or" Exhibition took place in the Galerie La Boétie, Paris, the following artists being represented: Fernand Léger, Marcel Duchamp, Duchamp-Villon, Juan Gris, Agero, Picabia, Delaunay, Valensi, Lhote, Herbin, Metzinger, Marie Laurencin, Marcoussis, Gleizes, La Fresnaye, Segonzac, Moreau, Marchand, Dumont and Jacques Villon, promoter and principal organizer of the exhibition. This was the first time that the works of all these artists had been seen together, and the occasion was a memorable one. None the less the Section d'Or exhibition provoked the usual hostile criticism in the press.

The importance of this exhibition was due to the galaxy of artists figuring in it and to the fact that it was a sort of homage to Cézanne. Many of those exhibiting had already begun in their own way to try to follow the principles of Cézanne, and likewise the arrival of Cubism on the scene naturally tended to be reflected in their work. This exhibition, then, was a mixture of works by artists who later developed into thoroughgoing Cubists, and others who in the course of time became violent adversaries of the new movement. Since this group called itself "La Section d'Or" (The Golden Section), we may pause for a moment at this point to examine the part played by geometry in the evolution of Cubism.

The true character of that movement, even at this late date, is apt to be misinterpreted by art critics. In the first place, the artists associated with Cubism simply turned to geometry for guidance in the planning of their compositions. They used geometrical principles as a

MARCEL DUCHAMP (1887). NUDE DESCENDING A STAIRCASE, 1912. (58¼ × 35⅜″)
WALTER ARENSBERG COLLECTION, HOLLYWOOD.

*As we are unable to photograph the original of this important picture, we have had recourse to the color reproduction
contained in the famous "suit-case" of Marcel Duchamp's works, published in 1941.*

check and never as a source of inspiration. Certain so-called Cubists, of course, carried away by the excitement of the moment and the novelty of this unaccustomed way of seeing the world, talked of non-Euclidean geometry and the fourth dimension. But geometry was never an end in itself, not even with Purism or Neo-Plasticism. The "golden section" is an ideal proportion defined by mathematicians as being the relationship between the diagonal and the side of the square. It is a proportion that has always been employed, for seemingly it corresponds to some deep-seated human instinct. Thus we find it in the humblest peasant objects, in things made by men who were completely ignorant of geometry and mathematics: in tables, chests, cupboards, in the dimensions given sheets of paper, and even in those of painters' canvases. This proportion is utilized by painters quite instinctively and can be found, for example, in Seurat's *La Parade*. Any uprush of plastic lyricism requires to be kept in check by some overriding rule such as is provided by rhythm in verse, and painters have generally realized this. But the "golden section" was not the only geometrical proportion resorted to by the Cubists. Actually they made much more frequent use of the formal patterns André Lhote has called the "constants."

In 1912 the title "Section d'Or" was adopted as a sort of compromise. For the works on view in the Galerie La Boétie were very different from one another, and as time went on the divergencies of the artists responsible for them became ever more apparent. Gris, for example, tended towards an architectural lyricism; Delaunay, Léger and Villon appeared to be under the spell of colored forms; Lhote on the other hand turned his back on color so as not to be "distracted" from his experiments with forms; Segonzac objected to the "intellectualism" of Cubism and contented himself with bringing out qualities of texture; Herbin concentrated on discovering that repertory of pure signs which was later to be given a new significance by the abstract artists; Marcel Duchamp and Picabia, whose inspiration was more dynamic, anticipated the outbreak of Dada with their lively interest in the plastic aspects of bodies and objects in movement; Gleizes envisaged the possibilities of using Cubism in large-scale mural painting. Thus 1912 was a memorable year, since the Section d'Or Exhibition was destined to prove the starting point whence stemmed many of the art trends which achieved their flowering during the next twenty years.

It is interesting to note that the Section d'Or Exhibition scored a success unprecedented in the annals of avant-garde art. It was taken to Rouen, and in the course of the next few years was revived several times in Paris. Abroad, too, it attracted considerable notice. The times, in fact, had changed and "modernism" was no longer frowned on by the art-loving public, however heartily the old guard of academic-minded critics damned it.

It would seem that Jacques Villon's aim was in his manner to fulfill Cézanne's ambition of making Impressionism something solid and abiding like the art of the Old Masters. Obviously this was no easy task and many long years were to pass before the artist lit on a solution. The problem was to organize and give duration and durability to those fugitive effects which had meant all to the Impressionists. Villon was as much obsessed with color as Léger and Delaunay were, and at the same time no less concerned with problems of plastic form than Juan Gris. With Villon these two preoccupations were more instinctive than due to any process of reasoning. In fact he needed to have recourse to a poet's intuition if he was to fuse these two tendencies into a coherent whole. He began by never using anything but pure colors, the colors of the prism, and this simplification of his means involved him in the use of solids, the forms of which he borrowed from geometry. Madame de Staël's famous observation, "Architecture is frozen music" might suitably be applied to Villon's art. Any object the artist deals with—a face, a body, a river or a landscape—is adjusted to the disciplines of what we might call a geometry of the visual responses. Villon's great achievement is to fit colored, intensely luminous forms into the crystalline pyramidal structures he almost always uses as his framework. Thus he conjures up a private world, the creation of a poet's dream; and as in a block of crystal, faceted with prisms, so in Villon's universe light is trapped and made to do a work of analysis and measurement, to reveal its latent beauties and those "faults," as a geologist would call them, which singularly add to its appeal.

ALBERT GLEIZES (1881-1953).
LANDSCAPE WITH A WINDMILL, 1913. (22⅜ × 15⅜″)
JACQUES VILLON COLLECTION, PUTEAUX (SEINE).

Unlike orthodox Cubists, Gleizes counts on nature for his inspiration and would rather "analyze" a landscape than a guitar. This type of Cubism, common to Gleizes, Lhote and La Fresnaye, came to be known as "French Cubism."

Chronologically speaking, Metzinger is the third Cubist after Picasso and Braque. His early interest in Neo-Impressionism was the fruit of a scientific education; next, he was drawn to the geometrical problems arising from the pictorial architecture of Picasso and Braque. His habit of mathematical accuracy served him well in his evaluation of certain cubist theories, notably the incidence of depth on vertically laid out planes and the structure of the "new space" created by the Cubists; his approach to these problems showed no little originality. Indeed Metzinger's book *Du Cubisme*, written in collaboration with Gleizes and published in 1912, was the first of its kind, and is by way of being a classic on the subject.

Gleizes wrote several books expounding his theories of art; his breadth of view may best be conveyed by a quotation from one of them. "In the field of the fine arts Cubism has sponsored the most disinterested and authoritative attempt to refashion the moral and psychological outlook of our generation, by disintellectualizing the technique of painting and promoting human values." In his art Gleizes is always faithful to the high standards of purity and sincerity he advocates. The liberties Gleizes took more and more with objective reality and in his handling of forms led him to contemplate a twentieth-century renaissance of mural painting in terms of cubist aesthetic.

Lhote's admiration for classical art has led him to a use of boldly geometrized forms which, however, do not strictly conform to cubist theory. Starting out with studies after nature, he selects from these what he regards as the essential forms. In his quest of technical perfection, he seeks to reconcile a rather arid precision with a will to spontaneity. As a rule, the disciplined organization we feel behind his work is tempered by a plastic sensibility that gives it an agreeably poetic charm. Along with Delaunay, Gleizes, Villon and La Fresnaye, whose tendencies he enthusiastically championed, André Lhote was one of the most active promoters of Cubism's return to color. Marcoussis' personal contribution to Cubism (round about 1911) was the liberation of color from the restriction that had been imposed on it by Picasso, Braque and Juan Gris. Notably in his *fixés sur verre* he gave rein to his Slav imagination, without, however, breaking with that architectonic composition whose validity he had accepted once for all. His devotion to effects of light led to compositions of a delicate lyricism that enabled him discreetly to mitigate the rigors of Analytic Cubism.

Brother of Jacques Villon, of the sculptor Duchamp-Villon and of the painter Suzanne Duchamp, Marcel Duchamp is a brilliant talker who loves to make play with the deep emotions he discreetly hides under a veneer of smiling skepticism. Yet Duchamp can never quite conceal the smoldering unrest within him. He seems to take a special pleasure in divesting himself, so to speak, of his own personality. Thus, when he feels he is on the brink of self-betrayal, he usually turns the subject with a witty remark, or immerses himself in chess—

a game of which he is a past master. Knowing all too much about the follies and vagaries of the human mind, he toys with them, uses them as the material for brilliant paradoxes that convey home truths whose cynicism sometimes startles but never offends, so wittily and charmingly are they expressed. Given the man he is, one can understand that in his painting Duchamp seeks to achieve those certitudes which his innate skepticism denies him; for him painting is a means of striking a balance between conflicting aspirations, which, however, he does not make as plain as we might wish, perhaps owing to the difficulty of finding a new vocabulary capable of expressing them. Nevertheless his influence has been considerable and he ranks among the pathfinders of modern art.

Like his brother, Marcel Duchamp has a forceful temperament and this led him to look with favor on the first futurist venture, though it conflicted with his early tendencies towards Cubism. But he disapproved of the futurist method of picturing movement in terms of frankly realistic subjects. Duchamp loved movement in the same way as Delaunay loved color—absolutely; thus he did away with its purely representational aspects, and in handling a dynamic subject abstracted from it a symbol of movement in its purest state. It was this tendency to strip down the subject to essentials that led him to patronize the Dada movement and we shall hear of him again in that eventful year when simultaneous Dada exhibitions took place in Zurich and New York.

At the Section d'Or exhibition Picabia exhibited *Procession in Seville*. His alert mind was quick to respond to every stimulus however slight, whether it disconcerted, horrified or delighted him. Equally, he welcomed any symptom of an impending upheaval of an order of things that, anarchist that he was, he heartily detested. Living as he had to, in a world which, as he saw it, needs remaking through and through, he scrutinized everything and everybody with a critical eye. He refused to inhibit his freedom with established rules, and believed in going to extremes. When he brought any of his ventures to its logical conclusion he was frankly irritated and began all over again, trying to carry it a stage further in the hope of making a technical discovery which might come nearer to some vague, unformulated ideal. So it is not surprising if he destroyed many of his pictures. Yet, even if Picabia did not always find the solutions he counted on, he had at least the satisfaction of the born fighter—that feeling of battling one's way through a hostile world.

As early as 1909 in a watercolor named *Rubber*, Picabia too had tried his hand at the non-objective picture. The title *Procession in Seville*, inscribed by the painter on the canvas itself, is not meant to be descriptive; it is at once an element of the picture and a reminder that the subjection of reality, that is to say the retinal image, to the artist's creative mind is an aim of abstract art.

FRANCIS PICABIA (1878-1953). PROCESSION IN SEVILLE, 1912. (47 ¼ × 47 ¼″) PRIVATE COLLECTION, PARIS.

Roger de La Fresnaye

★

AMONGST the many 20th-century artists who died young was Roger de La Fresnaye, who was born at Le Mans in 1885 and died in 1925 as the result of an illness contracted in the trenches during the First World War.

La Fresnaye studied first at the Ecole des Beaux-Arts in Paris, but chiefly at the Académie Ranson. Later he was to say: "Everyone is shaped by the past. If one follows in the footsteps of others one is obviously an imitator, but even if one strikes out for oneself one is still an imitator since we can but modify what has gone before." This attitude, however, did not prevent his giving a new direction to the cubist movement.

La Fresnaye came of an aristocratic French family that traced its origins back to the 15th century. One might be tempted to describe him as congenitally averse from revolution in all its forms, but that would be doing him less than justice; he was one of those who, like Keyserling, believe that "revolutions are made in order to safeguard tradition." For him Cubism represented above all a stockpile of new elements which he could draw on as a means to revivifying classical tradition. From the start his love of nature in all her aspects made itself felt, and it dominated his art to the very end. Indeed to La Fresnaye's thinking, painting had no *raison d'être* apart from nature. In much of his work he keeps to typically classical composition; sometimes he is obviously influenced by such masters as El Greco and Poussin. Naturally enough, the structural disciplines of Cézanne and Gauguin, which had become law at the Académie Ranson, prevailed in his early works of 1910-1911, such pictures, for example, as *Eve* and the series of nudes in landscapes: sturdy, simply conceived works, typically French in their balanced restraint, their elegance and refinement.

It was never his purpose to body forth a purely personal vision of the world. His one concern was to present the data of our everyday visual experience in an harmonious, structurally satisfying form. This was the spirit in which he yielded to the influence of Cubism, which he personally regarded as something of a passing fashion; not so much a form of visual poetry as a promising repertory of structural elements. With disconcerting frankness he once said: "Painting in our time is incapable of vying with the work of the great masters and that is why our artists have to resort to tricks to justify themselves." He never shared the qualms felt by Picasso, Braque, Gris and Léger as regards natural appearances; though from 1912 on he took to depicting objects broken down into their component parts on cubist lines, he indulged in modeling and chiaroscuro as well as in flat planes of color. For as it so happened, La Fresnaye had a great liking for curves, circumferences and spheres, a taste he shared with Delaunay and Léger. But whereas with the latter the forms these represented were almost abstract entities, La Fresnaye's forms are wholly natural, like clouds or smoke. He always had much respect for geometrical organization. In his elegant still lifes he arranged familiar objects in such a way that their plastic elements formed a subtle counterpoint of forms bathed in a discreetly subdued, delicately artificial light. Indeed he created a special atmosphere around them, and the word atmosphere obviously, and quite rightly, suggests that La Fresnaye remained faithful to what had been the basis of impressionist art. He never endorsed the concept of absolute Space which the Cubists were in course of substituting for the effects of atmosphere and aerial perspective of the Impressionists.

Near the end of his life La Fresnaye deliberately abandoned the cubist dissociation of planes and reverted to a more realistic form of art. Though in this period he obviously drew inspiration from El Greco, he was far from indulging in the heaven-scaling fantasies of the great baroque master; he tended, rather, towards a slightly mannered, but wholly charming elegance. The realistic trend of the art of his last years did not involve a total break with Neo-Cubism; it was, rather, a new note La Fresnaye added to the neo-cubist concept, a note of melancholy suggested perhaps by the artist's presentiment of an early death.

ROGER DE LA FRESNAYE (1885-1925). SKETCH FOR "THE CONQUEST OF THE AIR," 1913. (37 × 28¼")
A.L. COLLECTION, PARIS.

FERNAND LÉGER (1881-1955). CONTRASTS OF FORMS, 1913. (21⅝ × 18″)
HERMANN RUPF COLLECTION, BERN.

Here Léger indulged in a "study" in the musical sense of *étude*. His immense technical skill was directed towards themes and variations of forms in which contrasts of curves, of angles and rectangles of various sizes combine in decorative, abstract patterns pointing the way to the superb murals he was subsequently to make. It is usual to group together under the common denomination of "Contrasts of Forms" all the works produced by Léger during this period of his career, when the whole trend of his art was frankly opposed to the procedures of all the cubist artists without exception.

Fernand Léger

★

LÉGER hailed from Normandy, as did Dufy, Friesz, Jacques Villon and Marcel Duchamp. And, like them, Léger began by yielding to the spell of impressionist light and the lures of color. Nevertheless, as early as 1905 he painted a *Corsican Village* that prefigured the new aesthetic which was to characterize the vanguard painting of the first half of the 20th century. His taste for architecture in the literal sense (he had studied architecture for two years at Caen) led him to take a special interest in Cézanne. Léger always felt a shrewd mistrust of all that goes by the name of tradition, meaning a set of procedures and rules-of-thumb that it is enough to apply correctly. Thus he set about transforming Cézanne's methods along personal, wholly original lines which, if following in a general way the cubist technique, owed nothing whatever to Picasso, Braque or Juan Gris. So striking was the originality of his conceptions that his influence soon made itself felt not only in France but also in Germany, where in 1913 he exhibited at the Der Sturm Gallery in Berlin, and in the United States, where in the same year works of his figured in the big Armory Show in New York. Great colorist though he was, Léger did not love color for its own sake. He saw in it a means of defining the forms he sought to integrate into a new kind of space, and he mistrusted all theorizings about color. In his last phase he stepped up local tones to an intensity and vividness far beyond their merely sensuous referents, and took to a form of composition in which forms are painted flat and defined by lines drawn in a single stroke—without recourse to such devices as breaks or syncopations of the drawing: calm yet forceful lines, inspired solely by the imagination, governed by its own mysterious laws.

Léger's new conception of space was inspired by that innate feeling for the monumental and architectural which characterizes all his work and is apparent in the *Nudes in the Forest* and *Contrasts of Forms* here reproduced.

In the first-named painting he interpreted the methods of Cézanne in the spirit of his own mechanistic conceptions. Cézanne had spoken of cylinders, cones and spheres. And Léger had noticed in the *Boy in a Red Waistcoat* (page 52) how the right arm of the model is a cylinder inserted into a triple concentric form where the top of the sleeve meets the armhole of the waistcoat, thereby creating a plastic combination whose effect is felt throughout that superb composition. He adopted here the same procedure, but simplified its elements and contented himself with bringing out their geometric values without letting them interlock as in Cézanne's work. To use his own term, he "disjointed" them, so as not to run the risk of emphasizing aspects of the subject that were merely accidental, and also so as to avoid a form of perspective which might lead him to mask the flat surface of the canvas and to indulge in quasi-sculptural effects, in the manner of Braque and Picasso. The fact is that his insistence on lines of force ruled out any interpenetration of volumes, for this, as he clearly saw, would tend to weaken the dynamism basic to his aesthetic. *Nudes in the Forest* (1910) is one of those works in which Léger's special handling of forms can be seen to best advantage. Between 1906 and 1908 he made a number of sketches which were included in his *Contrasts of Forms*. Always we feel that he is aiming at a synthetic rendering of forms in terms of the dynamism that meant so much to him; indeed he carried the simplification of objects to the point of creating almost wholly abstract geometric patterns.

The truth is that Léger never made nature his starting-off point or, rather, he assigned it a new role. For him (as for the scientist) the object is a complex of living molecules animating space and he treats this as functional to the picture-surface, conditioning its dynamism in terms of the play of light upon the object. Another habit of his is to combine, almost arbitrarily it would seem, quite heterogeneous motifs—a flower, a key, a human body, a tree, and so forth—and thus to conjure up scenes which could not possibly find expression in any language other than that of painting.

Juan Gris

★

THERE is no question that Juan Gris ranks beside Picasso and Fernand Léger as one of the most original of the group of artists who sponsored the development of Cubism. We should not overstress the Spanish element in his art. Gris was born in Madrid, but the only specific influence of Madrilenian tradition on his painting is to be found in the austerity and the rare distinction of his palette—which has led some to see affinities between his art and that of Zurbaran. This innate tendency towards self-discipline is apparent not only in his choice of colors but also in his compositional schemes and even in his sometimes startling innovations. He has occasionally been treated as a theory-monger, a mathematical-minded artist who showed much skill in finding solutions for problems set by others; the truth is, rather, that he invented his own theorems and undertook their demonstration on lines that were his alone. This is perhaps what Picasso meant when, talking of Gris, he once said to me, "He was the ablest of us all in that line." But before discussing what "that line" was, we may begin by pointing out that the problems whose elements Gris posited in his art were suggested to him by a strongly lyrical, creative imagination that gave expression in a very human way to the harrowing unrest, the dramatic tensions his temperament inflicted on him. And an early death was the penalty he paid for thus living, intellectually speaking, always at high pressure.

Juan Gris had an almost fanatical thirst for knowledge of all kinds, and this led him minutely to explore even the smallest problems that came his way. Paradoxically enough, his art, though seemingly so "scientific," was the fruit of a prodigiously fertile pictorial imagination. None of the promptings of his many-sided sensibility was checked or inhibited. True, he loved nature, but he did not see her "through his temperament" (according to the realist formula); rather he saw her in the mirror of his temperament. Nevertheless his imagination was severely controlled by a special, very personal logic, as daring as it was unerring, and always consistent with his desire for truth. A remark he made when about twenty-five: "I don't

JUAN GRIS (1887-1927). BANJO AND GLASSES, 1912. (11¾ × 22¾")
GALERIE LOUISE LEIRIS, PARIS.

yet know what I must do, but I have found out what I must *not* do," reveals his practice of testing, experimentally, all the possibilities of painting. This attitude led to a friendly dispute with Braque—on almost existentialist lines. Braque had written: "Nails are not made from nails but from iron," and to this Gris retorted: "I believe just the opposite. Nails are made from nails, for if the idea of the possibility of a nail did not previously exist in the maker's mind, there would be a serious risk of his making a hammer or a curling-tongs instead." This emphasis on the "idea" as the creative factor is characteristic.

He started out from certain artistic conventions which he deeply respected, whether they stemmed from Cézanne, Seurat or from older masters whom he revered; but he treated them as no more than hypotheses whose converse might equally well serve his turn. With Gris it was never the subject that took command. To his thinking, the subject would automatically grow out of the object he was creating, that is to say the picture. Thus inverting Cézanne's procedure, he said: "Out of a cylinder I make a bottle." And he explained himself still more explicitly when he added: "Cézanne goes towards architecture, I set out from it." When Gris constructed a picture, the basic elements he employed did not really acquire a meaning until their positions had been determined by the perfectly balanced organization of the picture space he had in mind. If he needed a circle and a patch of white at a certain spot, it was not until this white circle had been fitted into place that it became a recognizable object, a plate, the top of a glass or perhaps a halo. For Gris, as he himself said, the only possible technique was that of "a sort of flat, colored architecture."

After 1918 Juan Gris (who had only nine more years to live) began to build up his work methodically, without any sudden changes of direction, and to consolidate both his theories and his technique. Above all he sought to make of Cubism an aesthetic in its own right and not just a compendium of means intended to safeguard the classical sense of order. Despite the lyricism which gives his work its singular charm, he was always aiming at an architecturally ordered composition. In other words Gris' plastic poetry was always governed by the rules of a carefully thought-out prosody. Thus in his style we find a certain degree of preciosity. Yet though Gris appears a "difficult" painter, because his style is so subtle and refined, and because he was so relentless in his pursuit of perfection and the absolute, we can also see that he never lost himself in the wilderness of abstraction and never deliberately sought to be obscure. Gris agreed with that phrase of Voltaire: "How many people resort to abstraction in order to appear profound!" Gris was convinced that every picture needed to have points of contact with objective reality. The subtlety of Gris' painting is a natural consequence of his predilection for what Vauvenargues called "using terms which leave much to the imagination." This throws light on his insistence on an element of surprise as a necessary ingredient of the picture. However, since he was both a proselyte and a born dialectician, Gris' poetry often takes the form of a sort of ardently persuasive rhetoric. It was Gris who achieved a codification of cubist technique, and in fact he has been called the most cubist of all the Cubists.

The absolute impersonality of his aesthetic (behind which lurks a profoundly human, though involuntary sense of the tragic side of life) stands in sharp contrast to the so-called expressionism of Picasso. Lipchitz, an authentic visionary, said to Gris one day: "You're following up your mistake magnificently." As a result of his refusal to let any sentimental or emotive elements make their presence felt in his work, Gris surrounded it with an aura of secrecy which often seems difficult to penetrate. He went on enriching his original conceptions till the day of his death. Attempts have been made to present Gris as a mere theory-monger. Those who do so, however, ignore the moving, lyrical quality and the sublimity of his achievement, theories notwithstanding. For Gris' work is a monument of clarity, eloquence and distinction. And Diaghilev made no mistake when he commissioned him to design the sets for *La Fête Merveilleuse*, a ballet to be performed in the Hall of Mirrors at Versailles. For the disciplined splendor of Gris' art fitted in perfectly with that of the Grand Siècle.

Juan Gris will go down to art history as the Master who carried cubist aesthetic to the farthest limit of its potentialities.

Chagall and "La Ruche"

★

ROUND about 1900 there existed in the Vaugirard district of Paris (at the far end of the city from Montmartre) a sort of replica of the "Bateau Lavoir." Founded by the sculptor Boucher and intended to serve as a home for more or less indigent artists, this building, situated in the Rue de Dantzig—it still exists—was a nest of rather sordid studios. It owed its name "La Ruche" (the beehive) to its bizarre shape. Not only artists lived there; there were also workmen and nihilist refugees, one of these being Trotsky, whom Lenin sometimes came to visit. Amongst its artist population were young men soon to be famous: Léger, Soutine, Lipchitz, Archipenko, Kremegne, Laurens and, last but not least, Marc Chagall. We all—writers, artists, poets—used to forgather in a small nearby bar which was also patronized by slaughtermen from the Vaugirard abattoir just across the way.

Every painter who makes a truly personal contribution to living art has something in him of the Primitive, anyhow as regards those aspects of his work which show the most originality. And one of Chagall's claims to greatness lies in the fact that he has expressed, superbly, his poetic vision of a world bathed in the magic light of fairyland, a world that is not so much fantastic or even fanciful as whimsical, since always its inspiration stems from quite human realities. He is not concerned with "a universe supplementary to ours" as Alfred Jarry conceived it, but with the normal relations between quite ordinary objects viewed in a special way and from a curiously vitalistic, almost a religious angle. Thus there are obvious affinities between his most characteristic works and those of the 13th- and 14th-century European Primitives and illuminators. Chagall, too, has made illuminations—not mere illustrations—for esoteric texts whose inner meaning he has divined under the guidance of an imagination as versatile as it is prolific.

He has a preference for subjects whose elements he can shuffle up at will and re-arrange, not in the modern manner for purely painterly, compositional ends, but like the Primitives, with an eye to presenting them in terms of the emotional import he assigns to each, and of a poetic vision evoking that bygone age of myth and folklore when animals spoke and sometimes masqueraded as human beings. Thus he gives a woman a fowl's head, makes a street-lamp perambulate, shows a cow playing the violin, a poet with his head upside down, a winged he-goat proffering flowers. A favorite procedure of Chagall's—if the word procedure be not too prosaic to apply to the creations of a poet born—is to represent animals, objects and people floating in the sky. Indeed Chagall spurns the earth; his art can spread its wings, move freely, only in the pure, clear air of the stratosphere. The familiar objects peopling his dreamland—not so much a super-real as a supraterrestrial dreamland—straddle each other, scatter like startled birds, and re-arrange themselves in wholly unrealistic patterns like those of children's pictures. Only in the placing of his brilliant colors do we find a studied lay-out; for the rest, he distributes as the fancy takes him, in a space of his own invention, the fabulous denizens of his private wonderland, much as early painters peopled their skies with winged cherubs' heads, angels, banners, phylacteries, celestial palaces.

But however much he loves to soar on wings of the imagination, Chagall has always shown a vast compassion for suffering humanity, and this sedater side of his art touches us profoundly. When he is illustrating the Old Testament, painting Crucifixions or those admirable portraits of Rabbis in which the rules of classical order are observed to such effect, his work has a grave dignity, combined with warmly human feeling, expressed in color-schemes that border on austerity.

In short Chagall's art is in a class apart; born of the dreams and nostalgic yearnings of the Slav soul, the world he conjures up is a maze of iridescent color and subtle nuances that he handles with consummate mastery and bathes in an appropriate light, whether that of familiar skies or the visionary light of his far dreaming.

MARC CHAGALL (1887). SELF-PORTRAIT WITH SEVEN FINGERS, 1912-1913. (74 × 49½ ")
REGNAULT COLLECTION, MUNICIPAL MUSEUM, AMSTERDAM.

Chagall uses a geometric lay-out not to simplify but, on the contrary, to give more forceful expression to his images. A harmony is established between the structure of the face—square cheek and long elliptical eye—and the color nuances of the insets. The evocations of his native village and Paris, dispersed through the picture, correspond to the colors laid out on his palette. Already in this picture we find those blendings of colors of which he was subsequently to make great use : blues or greens melting into greys, yellows and pinks. Three large compositions by Chagall, of which this is one, figured in the Dutch "Independents" Exhibition (1914) and were bought by a connoisseur.

161

his Romantic Period that Kandinsky produced his most emotive, least premeditated works; works which grip the beholder without giving him time to think, draw him irresistibly into a swirling dance of color and leave him, when he turns away, a little dazed—the after-effect of great emotional music, too. In fact Kandinsky's art, like much modern music, generates a sheerly sensual pleasure stepped up to its highest pitch, whose precise causes cannot be determined or explained.

Marc's temperament was very different from Kandinsky's. Before deciding for art he had thought of taking up theology or philology as his life's work and it was only after meeting Kandinsky and (during a visit to Paris) Delaunay that he saw that painting would enable him to express the poignant but always well-controlled emotions which certain aspects of reality inspired in him. His first teacher, an animal-painter, imparted to him his love for animals. These in fact became his favorite subjects, just as the articles of daily use in their studios had been for the Cubists. He studied Fauve art, then Cubism, then Kandinsky's abstract art, and in his glowing, luminous pictures we have a sort of synthesis of the three aesthetics. There are traces of indecision in his work, as if he were not yet sure that he had found his appointed path, and since he died at the early age of thirty-six (in 1916 in the fighting at Verdun) we can only guess at what this might have been. Distinctive of his art is his use of translucent, poetically emotive colors organized in a well-planned yet flexible architectonic framework. Its undertone of melancholy reflects that profound dissatisfaction with the world which is so clearly expressed in his writings; an early, discreet intimation of that spirit of revolt which was soon to assert itself so fiercely at Zurich, then at Berlin, in the Dada movement.

In 1912 Klee had taken part in the Blue Rider Exhibition at Munich. Then in his thirties, he had been painting since 1898, under the joint influences of Van Gogh and Ensor. In 1903 he did some etchings in the so-called "grotesque style." He was still unsure of his path and developed a brief enthusiasm for the work of Von Marées, which he saw in that artist's exhibition at Munich in 1909. However his meetings with Kandinsky and Franz Marc, whose personalities much impressed him, helped to dispel this somewhat misplaced admiration, and he describes in his Diary the strong emotions his new friends' work aroused in him. But he did not subscribe at once to their revolutionary theories; at a Blue Rider exhibition he showed watercolors, pen and wash drawings remarkable for their delicate, limpid, luminous effects, their poetic undertones and characteristic indications of a desire to break with the data of reality and its shackles on the freely ranging imagination. It is clear, however, that besides seeking to create a new, fanciful kind of beauty he was also trying his utmost to develop a personal style, and to this end he made innumerable sketches and studies in which we see the beginnings of that highly original technique which is distinctive of all Klee's mature work. As early as his Blue Rider period he was testing out curious effects of light and translucent tones: experiments which, however, he was careful not to press too far and which indeed reveal a certain cautiousness, not to say timidity, in his progress towards those unique achievements of his later period.

It was during a stay at Kairwan that he truly found himself and extricated himself from the mesh of conflicting influences which had hitherto impeded the flowering of his true personality, that of a born poet and color magician. Now he wrote in his Diary: "Color is my mistress. I no longer need to run after her. She has claimed me for her own, for ever."

It was, however, not until about 1925, the year of the first Surrealist Exhibition in Paris (in which he figured), that Klee gave definitive form to his aesthetic; we shall examine the work of his maturity later in this volume.

Abstract Art

★

I T IS an interesting point that very few French artists figure among the pioneers of purely abstract art. True, in Léger's *Contrasts of Forms* there is a special kind of abstraction, marked by Léger's distinctive touch, and the same may be said of Delaunay. But characteristic of all that is most personal in the work of these two great artists is its solid basis in reality. Léger used abstraction merely as a *means* of constructing form, while Delaunay seems to have owed his leanings towards abstraction to his wife Sonia, who was Russian. For the great pioneers of abstract art were almost all Russian born: Larionov, Kandinsky, Malevitch, Gabo, Pevsner, Tatlin, Lissitzsky, Rodchenko. Next we have the Czech Kupka; the Dutch artists Mondrian, Van Doesburg, Vantongerloo; an Italian, Magnelli; a German, Freundlich; a Hungarian, Moholy-Nagy. French art employs abstraction only to a limited extent and cautiously; it may simplify, eliminate, elide but never wholly loses touch with reality. In short the French artist regards pure abstraction as a mirage, and refuses to be allured by it. Abstract art in its early phase seems to have been the expression of a special state of mind, a vague poetic yearning to escape from the thrall of stern reality, and as such it never found much favor with the French or, we may even say, the Latin temperament. None the less, as we shall see, this conception of an "abstract" art—to use the rather unsatisfactory epithet with which it has been saddled—came ultimately to appear legitimate and logical enough even in the eyes of those who at first were prejudiced against it owing to the over-categorical nature of the aforesaid epithet. In its early phase, anyhow, it could not be regarded as mere gratuitous invention, creation *ex nihilo*, or an effect of, so to speak, spontaneous generation, since even in the case of its most uncompromising exponents it usually owed its origin to an emotion stemming from reality, an emotion which then was stepped up to its most intense expression, by reason of the artist's craving for an absolute or as Malevitch called it "supreme" perfection, its ultimate refinement.

There were, however, some who made complete abstraction their taking-off point, a procedure difficult to justify unless they hoped to bring off the *tour de force* achieved by Juan Gris and, instead of starting out from reality and proceeding thence to the construction of the picture, to begin with an abstraction and then to re-create reality in its guise.

The forms taken by the aesthetic whose various manifestations are generally known as abstract art may be divided into two categories: relative abstraction and absolute abstraction. The former draws inspiration from some given aspect of reality, the latter is an entirely mental creation, a complex of plastic relations of a purely imagined order.

Most abstract painters have practiced both manners of expression. But, though Mondrian has assured us of the contrary, they did not all of them begin as Cubists. None the less they took over the basic principles of Cubism, principles which indeed have influenced not only abstract art but all the outstanding and typically modern forms of present-day art. One of these is the idea, basic to contemporary aesthetic, of creating a world conceived purely in terms of art. Another is a mistrust of retinal impressions as being not only of a too exclusively physical nature but often inadequate or inaccurate. And, as corollaries, the primacy of the mind over the senses, and of the intellect over intuition; also a clean-cut distinction drawn between nature and art, a tendency to reject all accidental qualities in favor of essentials: in other words, a desire for simplification, elimination of all that is superfluous, a sort of asceticism in which the artist's subjective responses are replaced by strict objectivity. Thus, ceasing to be the "whimperer" Matisse once ridiculed, the modern abstract painter plays the part of an architect or constructor (hence "Constructivism").

It is a moot point where and when abstract art made its first appearance. Picabia dated his *Rubber*, a work that seems wholly abstract in conception, to 1909. In a watercolor of 1910 Kandinsky painted a dynamic medley of color patches having no representational

WASSILY KANDINSKY (1866-1944). COMPOSITION, 1914. (39 ¼ × 30 ⅝ ")
MUSEUM OF NON-OBJECTIVE PAINTING, NEW YORK.

The romantic profusion of colors in this picture reminds us of a remark made by Renoir when showing one of his most
colorful wild-flower pieces to a friend: "Isn't it just as beautiful as a battlepiece by Delacroix?"

significance and suggested to him, he said, by the multicolored spots on a woman's dress (in which case we here have "relative abstraction"). Picabia did not follow up the trend of his *Rubber*. Kandinsky, however, gave a scientific basis to his aesthetic; in his abstract compositions of this early period there were no subjects in the ordinary sense but color impressions arising from the sight of a given object. These looked rather like the ornamentation, deriving from geometry, used in architecture: the Greek key, bead-and-reel patterns and so forth. The names Kandinsky gave his pictures are revealing: *The Black Curve* (1912),

The use of circles is nothing new in art; we find it in the haloes of the Primitives and the lay-outs "in festoons" of many classical painters. Delaunay's handling of "circular rhythms" is dynamic more than decorative, as might be expected of an artist for whom "simultaneous disks" not only exalt color but signify the movement of the vital force. *Homage to Blériot* is, above all, a homage to the sky. The clouds (sources of light in his 1910 "Towers") have become symphonies of many-colored disks which, with their intersecting planes, set up massive rhythms, perfectly integrated, despite their violence, into the picture-surface.

ROBERT DELAUNAY (1885-1941). HOMAGE TO BLÉRIOT, 1914. (98¼ × 98¼") PRIVATE COLLECTION, PARIS.

Landscape with a Red Patch (1913). Some years later the names became more abstract: *Diagonal Line, Two Reds, Polychrome Circle* and the like. Kandinsky believed the artist would benefit by scrutinizing the craters on the moon, flower petals, cigarette ash, in the same way as Leonardo contemplated clouds or Picasso misted shop-windows.

It was in the same spirit (this was before he gave the name Suprematism to his theory of art) that Casimir Malevitch (1878-1935) made his first ventures in abstract art, to which he came by way of Fauvism and Cubism. One of his compositions, *Woman with Water Pails* (1912), shows the influence of Léger, notably his *Nudes in the Forest* and *Contrasts of Forms*, and the pictures he showed at the Second Blue Rider Exhibition (1912) were in this vein. Even when he carried abstract art to its highest pitch, Malevitch usually started out from reality, particularly the geometric lay-out of fields as seen from the air. By gradual degrees he came not only to strip the object of its poetic overtones, but to express what he termed "the feeling of the *absence* of the object." At this stage he painted circles or black squares on plain white backgrounds and declared that a surface painted in this way is more "alive" than the representation of a face with two eyes and a smile stuck on it. However Malevitch subsequently seems to have abandoned this extremist position and in some of his works we find traces of subjectivism, since they evoke notions of sensations. Thus at the same time as he named one of his works *Suprematist Composition utilizing the Triangle*, he called others *Sensation of Flight* (outline of an airplane), *Sensation of Mystic Will* (a cross), *Sensation of Dispersal, Sensation of Attraction* and the like. Basic to Malevitch's theories is his desire to attain the "supreme aim" of art (Suprematism) by freeing painting and architecture "from all sociological or materialist associations."

PIET MONDRIAN (1872-1944). COMPOSITION NO. 14, 1914. ($36\frac{7}{8} \times 25\frac{1}{2}$ ")
SCHIJVENS VAN ASSENDELFT COLLECTION, ZEIST (HOLLAND).

In this endeavor Malevitch was, it seems, outdone by his compatriot Rodchenko, who launched at Moscow an "Anti-objectivist" movement and carried his exclusion of all artistic or emotive considerations to the point of using only a ruler and compasses for his compositions. When he exhibited a picture, *Black on Black*, a circle intersected by two ovals, Malevitch riposted with a *White Square on White*. Abstract art could go no further.

The Constructivists, as their name indicates, were in favor of construction, the antithesis of abstraction, and did not disdain to have recourse to the semblance (though only the semblance) of reality. True to their name again, they gave their forms the aspect of sculpture or, more precisely, of real objects located in space, and did not, like such abstract painters as Malevitch, Rodchenko and Mondrian, deliberately reject traditional methods but merely made a point of employing unusual materials, or materials hitherto unused in art. It is obvious that Tatlin, Gabo and Pevsner got their ideas from the cubist *papiers collés* and the sculptural inventions of Lipchitz, Laurens and Picasso. All sorts of materials were employed, vulcanite, wood, wire, glass, celluloid and various metals to which sometimes color was applied; the objects thus constructed had often an exciting quality due to an intriguing play of lines and the boldness of their planes, which their makers could handle with complete freedom since they did not relate to the appearance of any existing object.

The abstract compositions of Franz Kupka (1871), who was one of the true originators of abstract art, stem from other conceptions but they too always keep a foothold in reality. That there were certain preconceived ideas behind them is evident from their titles: *Warm Chromatics, Study for a Fugue, Fugue in Two Colors,* for example, which indicate that at this stage Kupka was inspired by music, and in fact he was the forbear of the so-called "musical painters" (e.g. Valensi, Blanc) who banded themselves together round about 1920 and who succeeded in being neither abstract nor figurative. One has the impression that Kupka himself aimed less at "abstracting" anything than at constructing color-forms in the spirit of Baudelaire's "correspondences."

"Color is both form and subject." This remark of Delaunay's may suggest why he showed so much interest in contemporary scientific researches into the nature of color. He was impressed by Chevreul's work on the subject and especially his "law of simultaneous contrasts," which enabled him to produce some really marvelous effects. One day I had a letter from him signed "Delaunay the Simultaneous!" He was particularly struck by the theory of the changes which come over colors that are placed side by side, when, as Chevreul pointed out, the alterations they undergo are due to the fact that the complementary of one color is added to the color of the other; also if two colors have not the same height of tone, the color which is dark will appear still darker and, for the same reason the other will seem brighter than it really is (assuming that this latter effect is not "killed" by the former). Thus Delaunay abandoned all idea of figural representation and constructed by color alone. The result was that he dispensed with subjects in the ordinary sense and his compositions were purely abstract color patterns. Unlike most abstract painters Delaunay did not build up an ideology around his methods, and his works differ from other productions of abstract art in not being dominated by some preconceived idea foreign to the art of painting.

On the other hand Mondrian (1872-1944), before the "De Stijl" period (1917), started out, despite the seeming rigorism of his formulas of abstract art, from the idea of representing some existing object, then little by little stripping it of its accidental features. He gave a demonstration of this method in four successive compositions, the first of which depicted a tree quite naturalistically, the next two progressively eliminated its distinctive aspects, and the last was a sort of working-drawing, containing only such plastic elements as furnished a vague reminiscence of the "first state" devoid of any anecdotal referents. This was, in effect, a process of progressive disincarnation, and the names he gave some of the works in which this operation had been carried to its highest pitch—*The Pier, The Ocean, New York City*— are merely reminiscences of the objects which originally inspired them. It was only in the "De Stijl" period that the titles of Mondrian's works became abstract and he took to naming most of his compositions simply "Painting."

Papiers Collés

★

THE INTRODUCTION of typographical characters into cubist pictures was perhaps suggested by the inscriptions and "legends" figuring in Old Master paintings and illuminated manuscripts. What is certain is that these old inscriptions had an informative purpose and, as often as not, a decorative one, since the ornamental properties of Gothic lettering, in particular, were skillfully exploited.

With the Cubists it was another matter, and at first the implications of this new procedure somewhat perturbed them. For while the trend of their aesthetic was towards annihilation of the "subject," the introduction of lettering seemed to bring them, indirectly, back to realism; it was almost like reinstating the object in the picture. Finally, however, letters came to be treated as purely plastic elements.

This idea was carried a stage further when the Cubists began to introduce into their pictures bits of imitation marbling and grained wood. One purpose of this was to defeat imitation and *trompe-l'œil* at their own game, and to imitate imitation in a witty manner. Also, by evoking natural appearances to enable their pictures to combine the poetic qualities of cubist art with the most prosaic aspects of reality. And Braque applied himself to discovering means of implementing this conception in an orderly, workmanlike manner. Thus for their painted imitations of grained wood the Cubists went so far as to procure the graining combs used by professional painter-decorators.

A synthesis of this phase of Cubism was most completely achieved by what are known as *papiers collés*. Such compositions were generally made on sheets of white drawing paper on to which were stuck pieces of newspaper, colored paper or wallpaper with decorative patterns. The strips of paper were cut into shapes appropriate to the composition and the artist integrated them into it by drawing over them in pencil or ink, sometimes too in gouache or watercolor. Appearances notwithstanding, the effects were not intended to be comic or even whimsical. On the contrary, the idea behind these *papiers collés* was always that of welding elements of reality into the picture, elements which by thus being brought face to face were made to yield a lyrical and plastic value. *Papiers collés* were above all regarded as an experimental test designed to confirm the poetic aspirations of these painters, aspirations as to whose validity they needed reassurance. In this sense *papiers collés* were experiments, but they were regarded above all as simple, practical illustrations of the way in which seemingly extraneous elements like paper might be integrated into pictorial architecture; ten years later the Surrealists were to create a new, highly poetic form of art, starting out from this procedure.

The next stage of this technique was the introduction into the picture of other elements of reality in the most literal sense: sand, textiles, glass, oilcloth and the like. These materials were of course used in the first instance for introducing novel color and textural effects. But the way they were used showed that the artists' intention was also of a lyrical order, that is to say they sought to transmute the significance of these material objects, just as poetry gives new overtones to commonplace words.

When the Dada group adopted this procedure, they used it for a different purpose. For Hans Arp, Marcel Duchamp, Man Ray, Schwitters and Max Ernst, *papiers collés* served more as destructive than as constructive elements; they were intended to "destroy" all the old traditions of painting which, to the Dadaists' thinking, must be rejected lock, stock and barrel, if a new, vital form of painting was to make good. (Unless, of course, the Dada movement was out for mere destruction, for its own sake.) With Surrealism this ambition was achieved; surrealist *collages* are not merely plastic elements, they also help to express—with a willful defiance of the technical conventions of the past—the new vision of a universe built with "the stuff that dreams are made of."

GEORGES BRAQUE (1882). THE FRUIT DISH, 1912. (24 ⅜ × 17 ⅝ ″) DOUGLAS COOPER COLLECTION, LONDON.

GEORGES BRAQUE (1882). WOMAN WITH GUITAR, 1913. (50 ⅜ × 28 ⅝″) PRIVATE COLLECTION, PARIS.

PABLO PICASSO (1881). VIOLIN, 1913. (25½ × 18″) HERMANN RUPF COLLECTION, BERN.

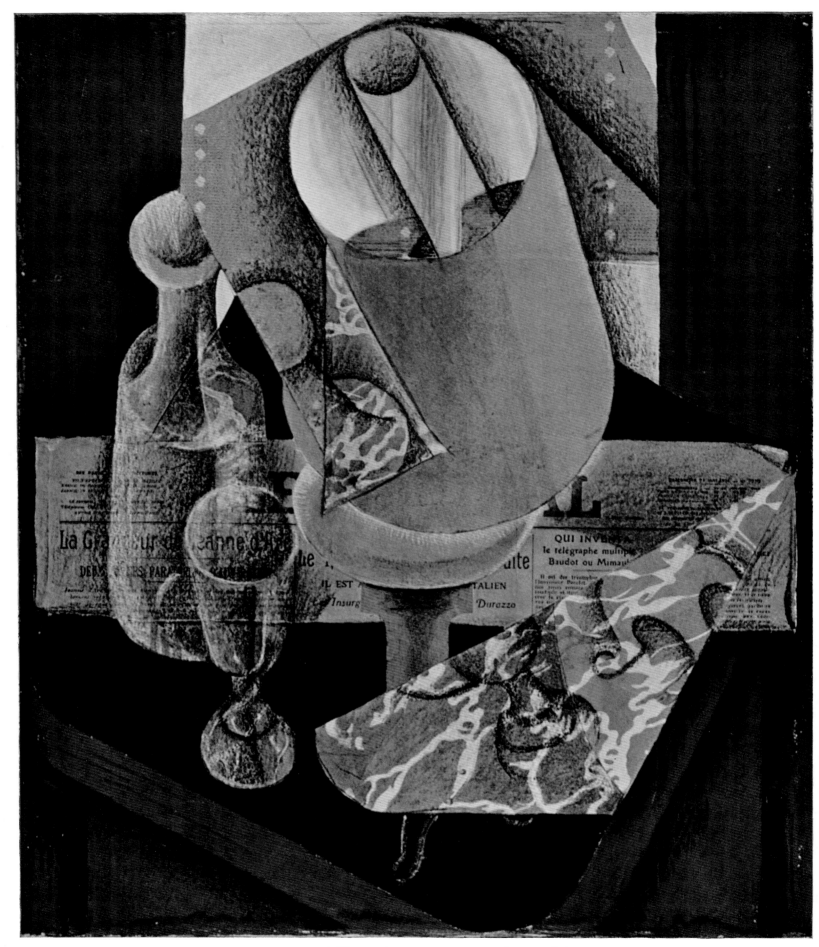

JUAN GRIS (1887-1927). THE LAMP, 1914. (21½ × 18″)
PRIVATE COLLECTION, PARIS.

The artist's highly original technique is seen to advantage in this work built up with what he called "abstractions,"
which, however, in the process of painting developed into objects. As usual Gris synthesizes the picture-surface by
integrating all the diverse elements into a well-knit composition strictly architectural in conception.

Wyndham Lewis and Vorticism

★

THE YEARS immediately preceding the First World War were a period of great promise in England both in literature and art, and in June 1914 there appeared the first number of the review *Blast*, whose editor was the painter Wyndham Lewis.

Wyndham Lewis, who was born in 1884, is also a distinguished writer; his novels *Tarr* and *The Apes of God*, like the apocalyptic fantasia of *The Childermas*, are works of high originality. The sub-title of *Blast* was "Review of the Great English Vortex," and from this the term "Vorticism" was derived. The poet Ezra Pound took a leading part in the movement and amongst those grouped round Lewis were the painters Edward Wadsworth, W.P. Roberts, Frederick Etchells and the sculptors Gaudier-Brzeska and Epstein. And in his Manifesto Lewis "blasted" his pet aversions, amongst them "the Britannic Aesthete (cream of the snobbish earth), Humor (quack English drug for stupidity and sleepiness), Sport (Humor's first cousin and accomplice)."

The program of the movement was to free English art from the morass of error in which it had been bogged for a century and more, and set up in its place a genuinely 20th-century art. The vortex being "the point of maximum energy," the aim of Vorticism was to bring all forms of art into line with machinery in an extremely direct way, but not "to sentimentalize machines, as did the Italians."

In fact one of the features of the first issue of *Blast* was its attack on Italian Futurism. "Automobilism (Marinettism) bores us. We don't want to go about making a hullabaloo about motor cars, any more than about knives and forks, elephants or gaspipes." None the less the young English artists' desire to build up the picture architectonically, on the lines suggested by Cézanne, led them naturally enough to turn to machinery in which the presence of "cylinders, cones and spheres" is far more clearly indicated than in the works of Nature. Naturally enough, but in the last analysis unjustifiably from the aesthetic point of view. For since the machine was in itself already an artifact, whatever inspiration the artist drew from it lacked one of the essentials of true creative art: originality.

It is interesting to note that in the second (1915) number of *Blast* Wyndham Lewis diverted his attacks from Futurism to Cubism and wrote: "The whole of the modern movement is under a cloud. That cloud is the exquisite and accomplished, but discouraged, sentimental and inactive personality of Picasso. We must disinculpate ourselves of Picasso at once."

The time was, in point of fact, propitious for the appearance of a new kind of art in England, where the public had its eyes opened to strange, new forms of beauty by the Russian Ballet; and it was largely thanks to its décors that British art, which, since the collapse of the aesthetic movement in the late 'nineties, had been in a backwater, began to move again. The movement headed by Wyndham Lewis was in a sense a reaction against the aestheticism of the Beardsley period still out of favor, not merely in Philistine but also in avant-garde circles, and in the shining smoothness of cylinders and crankshafts the artists discovered forms that would do away with the frills, furbelows and fussiness of the Victorian age.

It is interesting and significant, perhaps, that one of Wyndham Lewis' early and not least remarkable paintings, *Plan of Campaign*, built up of parallel lines and blocks of color (representing divisions of armies locked in combat) should have been exhibited in June 1914 —before anyone in England had the least idea that war was impending. In 1918, after two years' service with the heavy artillery in France, he returned to London, and one of the first pictures he painted after his return (for the Canadian War Memorial) was *The Gun Pit*, splendidly evocative of the majesty of big guns in action.

The historical significance of *Blast* is perhaps greater than its actual contribution to art; for, with it, almost for the first time, an art emerged in England that synchronized with similar art movements across the Channel.

1915-1923

1915   In Paris Ozenfant launches the magazine **L'Elan** • Among other portraits Picasso paints Vollard's • Back in Paris Gris does illustrations for Reverdy's **Poèmes en Prose** • Wounded at Carency, Braque undergoes a head operation, then is invalided out of the army • Utrillo called up, but rejected as physically unfit • Magnelli's first abstract paintings • Marcel Duchamp and Picabia arrive in New York • Demuth's first exhibition at the Daniel Gallery, Matisse exhibition at the Montross Gallery, New York • The Stieglitz group publishes the magazine **291** • Chirico's "Metaphysical Painting" in Italy **(Melancholy of Leaving, The Seer)** • Carrà moves away from Futurism and comes under Chirico's influence • Hans Arp exhibits abstract works at the Tanner Gallery, Zurich: **Papiers déchirés et collés** • Malevitch publishes **The Non-Objective World** at Moscow, in Russian • Franz Marc's **Feldskizzenbuch,** a notebook of abstract sketches, made at the front • Refugees in Amsterdam, Frits van den Berghe, Gustave de Smet and André de Ridder form the **Open Wegen** group and keep in touch not only with Le Fauconnier and the Dutch painters of the groups known as **Hollandsche Kunstenaarskring** and **Het Sienjaal** (Sluyters, Charley Toorop, Leo Gestel, Hildo Krop and others) but especially with the Belgian artists who have taken refuge in England: Permeke, Tytgat, Daeye, Van de Woestyne.

1916   Matisse paints **The Piano Lesson** and **Moroccans at Prayer** • Villon, Segonzac and many other painters serve at the front in camouflage units • Death of Odilon Redon in Paris, of Rijk Wouters in Amsterdam, of Boccioni in Italy • Franz Marc killed in action at Verdun • The Rumanian poet Tristan Tzara, the German writers Hugo Ball and Richard Hülsenbeck and the painter-sculptor Hans Arp found the **Cabaret Voltaire** in Zurich and launch the **Dada** movement (February 8) • Arp's "automatic" drawings and reliefs • Carrà's first metaphysical pictures at Ferrara • Tatlin's counter-reliefs in Moscow • At Oslo Gabo does "constructions" out of various materials • Villon Exhibition at Oslo.

1917   In Paris Pierre Reverdy founds the review **Nord Sud** in collaboration with Apollinaire, Aragon, Breton, Max Jacob, Philippe Soupault • Rouault begins his illustrations for **Les Réincarnations du Père Ubu** • Léger paints **The Card Party** • Death of Degas • Dufy is given a post at the Musée de la Guerre, Paris • Braque paints **Woman with a Mandolin** • In Rome Picasso does sets and costumes for Diaghilev's **Parade**, with libretto by Jean Cocteau, music by Erik Satie, choreography by Massine. This ballet opens at the Châtelet Theater, Paris, in May • Matisse paints **Interior with a Violin** at Nice and begins his series of **Dark Interiors** • Morandi's Metaphysical Period, at Bologna • "Radiantismo" Exhibition in Rome and translation of the **Rayonnist Manifesto** of Larionov and Gontcharova • Dada Gallery in Zurich shows works by Arp, Chirico, Max Ernst, Feininger, Kandinsky, Klee, Kokoschka, Marc, Modigliani, Picasso. Tristan Tzara publishes the review **Dada** • Marcel Duchamp launches the magazines **Wrong-Wrong** and **The Blind Man** in New York • Van Doesburg founds the review **De Stijl** at Leyden, with the painters Mondrian and Van der Leck, the sculptors Vantongerloo, Arp, Brancusi, the architects Oud, Rietveld, Van Eesteren, Wils, the poet Antony Kok and, among other foreign artists, Severini and El Lissitzky. **De Stijl** does not cease publication until 1932 • In Barcelona Picabia publishes the first number of the review **391** • First performance of Apollinaire's **Mamelles de Tirésias** in Paris, with sets by Serge Férat • Maurice Denis illustrates Alfred de Vigny's **Eloa** • Gabo and Pevsner in Moscow • Chagall elected Commissar of Fine Arts for the Vitebsk region.

1918   Publication in Paris of Apollinaire's **Calligrammes**; he dies on November 9 • Ozenfant and Jeanneret publish **Après le Cubisme**, the Purist Manifesto (November 10) • Léonce Rosenberg opens the Galerie de l'Effort Moderne, Paris • Modigliani Exhibition at the Berthe Weill Gallery closed down by the police • Léger paints **The Tug Boat**, which marks a return to the object, but situated in a mechanical civilization • Death of Duchamp-Villon on October 7 • Matisse meets Renoir at Cagnes • Miro's first one-man show in Barcelona • Tristan Tzara publishes the Dada Manifesto in Zurich, in **Dada 3** • Picabia arrives in Zurich • In Berlin Hülsenbeck founds the "Dada Club" and Hausmann the magazine **Der Dada**, whose three numbers contain contributions by Baader, Hausmann, Hülsenbeck, Tzara, Heartfield, Herzfelde, Mehring, Picabia • At Lausanne, the Pitoëffs produce **L'Histoire du Soldat**, libretto by C.F. Ramuz, music by Stravinsky, sets by Auberjonois • George Grosz joins the Berlin Dada group • First **"De Stijl" Manifesto** in the review of the same name (a rallying call to all who believe in the artistic and cultural revolution of our time, urging them to a common effort in its advancement), signed by Van Doesburg, Van't Hoff, Huszar, Mondrian, Kok, Wils, Vantongerloo • Apollinaire writes the preface for Derain's one-man show at Paul Guillaume's, Paris • Picabia illustrates his own **Poèmes et dessins de la fille née sans mère**, Matisse **Les jockeys camouflés** by Pierre Reverdy, and Dufy **Monsieur Croquant** by Remy de Gourmont.

1919   Braque Exhibition at the Galerie de l'Effort Moderne, Paris • Launching of the review **Littérature** • Death of Renoir at Cagnes, on the Riviera, at the age of 78 • Mondrian returns to Paris where he remains until 1939 • Miro meets Picasso • Picasso does sets for the Diaghilev ballet **Le Tricorne** (music by De Falla), and Derain for **La Boutique fantasque** • Matisse Exhibition at Bernheim-Jeune's • At the Concerts Delgrange, Paris, works by Georges Auric, Louis Durey, Arthur Honegger, Darius Milhaud, Francis Poulenc, Germaine Tailleferre • Soutine stays at Céret • In Rome Chirico, Carrà and Morandi contribute to the review **Valori Plastici** (1919-1922) • At Weimar the architect Walter Gropius founds the Bauhaus. Feininger one of the first teachers • In Zurich **Dada 4-5** (cover by Hans Arp) comes out as a **Dada Anthology**. Picabia and Tzara return to France. Dada group formed at Cologne by Baargeld (author of the pamphlet **The Ventilator**), Arp and Max Ernst, who begins his **Fatagaga** series of collages. Kurt Schwitters' **Merz** collages at Hanover • Suprematist-Non-Objectivist Exhibition in Moscow. Rodchenko shows his picture **Black on Black**, Malevitch his **White Square on a White Ground**. Chagall decorates the Jewish Theater, does sets and costumes. Kandinsky appointed Professor of Fine Arts at the University of Moscow. Carl Hofer takes a teaching post at the Berlin Academy • Suicide of the sculptor Lehmbruck • Illustrated books: René Dalize's **Ballade du pauvre macchabée mal enterré**, André Breton's **Mont de Piété**, Vlaminck's **A la santé du corps** (Derain); Cendrar's **La fin du monde** (Léger); **Six poèmes de Whitman** (Lurçat); Salmon's **Le Manuscrit trouvé dans un chapeau** (Picasso); Paul Dermée's **Beautés de 1918** and Reverdy's **La Guitare endormie** (Juan Gris).

1920   Modigliani dies in Paris at the age of 36 • Picasso paints "classical" subjects and draped bathers • Matisse works on his series of **Odalisques** • Ozenfant and Jeanneret found the review **L'Esprit Nouveau**, which continues publication until 1925 • Léonce Rosenberg publishes Mondrian's **Le Néo-Plasticisme** • Dada Festival at the Salle Gaveau, Paris. Marcel Duchamp exhibits a Monna Lisa with mustaches • First Paris exhibition of Max Ernst's **collages** • Lipchitz Exhibition at Rosenberg's • Matisse does sets and costumes for the Russian ballet **Le Chant du Rossignol** • Illustrated books: Mallarmé's **Les Madrigaux** (Dufy); Voltaire's **Candide** (Paul Klee); Cocteau's **Escales**, Eluard's **Les animaux et leurs hommes, les hommes et leurs animaux**, Coleridge's **Le dit de l'ancien marinier**, Thomson's **Corymbe de l'automne** (André Lhote); Tristan Tzara's **Cinéma, calendrier du cœur abstrait** (Hans Arp); Soupault's **La rose des vents** (Chagall); Gide's **Le Prométhée mal enchaîné** (Bonnard); Salmon's **Le Calumet** and Gabory's **La cassette de plomb** (Derain); Kipling's **Les plus beaux contes** (Van Dongen); Vanderpyl's **Voyages** (Vlaminck) • Dada Exhibitions in Berlin (174 works) and Cologne (the famous riot in the Winter Beerhouse) • Max Ernst and Hans Arp publish the review **Die Schammade** • Paul Klee and Schlemmer teaching at the Weimar Bauhaus • In Moscow Pevsner and Gabo bring out the Realist Manifesto, reviving the controversy over Tatlin's Constructivism • Publication at Brussels of the review **Sélection** and opening of a gallery of the same name, sponsoring Cubism in Belgium.

1921   In Paris Picasso paints two versions of **Three Musicians** and does sets for the Russian ballet **Cuadro Flamenco** • Severini publishes **Du Cubisme au Classicisme** • Meeting of Beaudin and Gris • Braque does woodcuts for Erik Satie's **Piège de Méduse** • In Barcelona Siqueiros publishes a Manifesto advocating "a revolutionary art, thoroughly Mexican" • Léger paints **Three Women** and does sets for the Swedish ballet **Skating Rink** • Illustrated books: Duhamel's **Trois journées de la tribu** (Vlaminck); Max Jacob's **Ne coupez pas, mademoiselle** (Juan Gris); Gide's **Paludes** (La Fresnaye); Radiguet's **Les Pélican** (Laurens); Malraux's **Lunes en papier** (Léger); **Communications**, written and illustrated by Vlaminck • In New York Duchamp paints **Why not sneeze?** and Man Ray invents **Rayographs** and goes on to explore other possibilities of photography, in a Dada and Surrealist vein • Van Doesburg founds a "De Stijl" group at Weimar in close collaboration with the Bauhaus • In Moscow Kandinsky founds the Academy of the Arts and Sciences of All the Russias • Archipenko in Berlin • Viking Eggeling bases a film on his **Diagonal Symphony** • In Paris Marinetti lectures on a new kind of art: Tactilism.

1922   In Paris Picasso paints **Frightened Women by the Sea** and does sets for Cocteau's **Antigone** at the Théâtre de l'Atelier • International Dada Exhibition at the Montaigne Gallery, Paris • Max Ernst arrives in Paris, illustrates Eluard's **Les Malheurs des Immortels** and paints **Au Rendez-vous des Amis**, containing portraits of Breton, Aragon, Eluard, Desnos, Crevel, Arp, Soupault • Léger does sets for the Swedish ballet **La Création du Monde**, music by Darius Milhaud • Braque shows at Salon d'Automne • Illustrated books: Benjamin Péret's **Le passage du Transatlantique** (Hans Arp); Gabory's **Le nez de Cléopâtre** (Derain); Claude Anet's **Notes sur l'amour** (Bonnard); Dermée's **Le volant d'artimon** (Marcoussis); Reverdy's **Cravates de chanvre** (Picasso) • Kandinsky and Moholy-Nagy begin teaching at the Bauhaus. The latter takes charge of publishing the "Bauhausbücher" • Ilya Ehrenburg and Lissitzky publish the constructivist review **Objekt** in Berlin • Dada campaign in Holland led by Schwitters and Van Doesburg, who publishes the review **Mecano** • "Manifesto of the Union of Worker-Artisans, Painters and Sculptors" signed in Mexico City by Siqueiros, Orozco and Rivera, who launch the review **El Machete** • Villon Exhibitions at the Société Anonyme, New York, and in Paris with Latapie • George Grosz breaks with the Dada group • The Swiss sculptor Giacometti works in Bourdelle's studio, Paris • Bianchini takes Dufy to the races to observe the dresses of the women, but Dufy has eyes only for the horses and paints many pictures on this theme.

1923   In Paris Picasso paints three versions of **Seated Harlequin** • Chagall returns to Paris. He has just written **My Life** and starts the illustrations of Gogol's **Dead Souls** for Vollard (96 engravings). The book did not appear until 1949 • Léonce Rosenberg organizes an exhibition of works by the "De Stijl" group at the Galerie de l'Effort Moderne, Paris • Max Jacob writes the preface for Beaudin's first exhibition at the Percier Gallery, Paris • Le Corbusier publishes **Vers une Architecture** • Braque does sets for the Diaghilev ballet **Les Fâcheux**, music by Poulenc • Juan Gris does sets for Diaghilev's ballet **La Fête merveilleuse**, performed in the Hall of Mirrors at Versailles, then for **La Colombe**, music by Gounod, and **L'Education manquée**, music by Chabrier, at Monte-Carlo • In New York Marcel Duchamp gives up painting, leaving unfinished his glass panel **The Bride stripped bare by her Bachelors even**, begun in 1915. He is elected president of the **Société Anonyme** • Rivera begins his decorations for the Ministry of National Education in Mexico • Archipenko goes to the United States • Illustrated books: Vollard's **Le Père Ubu à la guerre** (Jean Puy); Max Jacob's **La couronne de Vulcain** (Suzanne Roger); Tristan Tzara's **De nos oiseaux** (Hans Arp) • Mark Tobey teaches at the University of Washington, Seattle • Man Ray film: **Le Retour de la raison**.

1915 ★ 1918

New Trends and Movements Outside France

The year 1915 witnessed the rise of several movements and tendencies in countries that were spared the horrors of active warfare, and such was their variety and originality that they exercised considerable influence not only on the art of the day but also on post-war art.

In Holland Mondrian, who had now left Paris, made his first researches into the possibilities of abstractionism and reduced his compositions to carefully planned arrangements of vertical and horizontal lines.

As for the United States, Marcel Duchamp and Picabia from 1915 onward collaborated in the 291 review and prepared the ground for what was to be known as "Dadaism." In 1916 a club newly founded in Zurich, the "Cabaret Voltaire," launched, under the leadership of Hans Arp and Tristan Tzara, the Dada movement, which spread to Germany in the following year, being sponsored in Berlin by Richard Hülsenbeck, while Max Ernst acted as its propagandist in Cologne. It was also in 1917 that a Dada movement arose in Paris, where in the following year the magazine Littérature *made its appearance under the auspices of Aragon, Eluard, Breton, Soupault and (beginning with the second issue) Tristan Tzara.*

In Italy between 1915 and 1918 Chirico was entering on his Metaphysical Period and Carrà, whom he met at Ferrara, joined forces with him.

The year 1917 saw a general revival of artistic activities all over Europe, and a host of literary and artistic reviews lent their support to the new tendencies in art. At Barcelona Picabia, with Marie Laurencin, Arthur Cravan and Albert Gleizes, began to edit 391, a sequel to the New York 291 magazine; it ran for fifteen numbers published in various cities, Barcelona, New York, Zurich and Paris. Next came Sic (in Paris), edited by Pierre Albert Birot. Pierre Reverdy, too, in co-operation with Apollinaire, Aragon, Soupault and Max Jacob, was responsible for a new review, Nord Sud. Meanwhile at Zurich Tzara had founded the "Dada" magazine, while in New York, with the collaboration of Marius de Zayas, Walter Arensberg and Man Ray, Marcel Duchamp launched two new reviews, The Blind Man *and* Wrong-Wrong. *Finally, with Van Doesburg as editor,* De Stijl, *sponsoring Neo-Plasticism, made its appearance in Holland.*

From Mondrian to "De Stijl"

★

In NEO-PLASTICISM non-figurative art underwent a transformation that was in a sense a natural consequence of the co-existence, already mentioned, of two forms of abstract art, relative and absolute. Art movements have a way of pressing their theories to extremes and this extremism usually turns out to be the prelude to their dissolution. This was what happened with Neo-Plasticism, which in the end brought abstract art to an impasse. In fact, whenever we find attempts being made to regenerate Neo-Plasticism, they invariably come to nothing; the same procedures are repeated without any real advance.

Neo-Plasticism made its "official" appearance only in 1917, though as a matter of fact Theo van Doesburg, its promoter, had published in 1916 a book entitled *A New Movement in Painting*, which, while drawing inspiration simultaneously from the conflicting theories of Mondrian and Kandinsky, set forth clearly enough the essentials of Van Doesburg's new doctrine. He had difficulty in finding a title for this and his choice, "De Stijl," was hardly happy (nor, for that matter, was "Neo-Plasticism"). Such sobriquets as those of the Impressionists, Fauves and Cubists were apter. Mondrian, in his turn, published, with Léonce Rosenberg, in his magazine *L'Effort Moderne*, a French translation of *Die neue Gestaltung*, one of the Bauhaus publications, in which he put forward views opposed to Kandinsky's basically expressionist procedures. To this book was partly due the conflict which arose within the Bauhaus group between the advocates of "pure" pictorial architecture and those who preferred a less rigorously ordered form of painting.

Mondrian presented in a new light that doctrine of the primacy of the mind over retinal sensation which had prevailed in all vanguard art since Cubism. In speaking of an "equivalence" between nature and the mind, between the individual and the universal, and in

PIET MONDRIAN (1872-1944). COMPOSITION NO. 10, PLUS AND MINUS, 1915. (33⅜ × 42½")
RIJKSMUSEUM KRÖLLER-MÜLLER, OTTERLO.

contemplating a social order dispensing with the personality of the individual, he sponsored an ideology that proved a godsend for the Dada group and, later, for the Surrealists.

When Mondrian came to Paris he was determined to see his venture through to its logical conclusion. He did not gradually strip away non-essentials but made abstraction his starting-off point. Symbolically perhaps, he now discarded his long romantic beard—anyhow, since Impressionism beards were no longer worn in artistic circles—in favor of the American businessman's smoothshaven chin.

Mondrian had now withdrawn from the venture into which he had been led seemingly by Kandinsky, Marc and Klee. While wishing to abolish others' personalities, he was set (though perhaps as yet he was unaware of this) on safeguarding his own. His view of abstraction as a process of "abstracting" the essence of the object by progressive elimination, an illustration of which we have cited in the four "states" of his picture of a tree, was leading him towards a new art-form, Neo-Plasticism, which was abstract only in name. Absolute form, with all the schematic rigorism this implies, was now his aim. He went about this in various ways; for one thing he restricted himself to straight lines, since curves were too emotional; also he ruled out modulated or broken colors as being unclear and sentimental, and used only the primaries; finally, he gave the plane, to his mind the basic plastic element, the leading role. By a process of reasoning that was wholly logical, given his aim of substituting the universal—that which *is* and never changes—for the accidental, he was led to formulate a new conception of the balanced composition of the picture, which was that it should contain large non-colored or empty areas and relatively small colored or occupied spaces. And whereas paintings of the past expressed for the most part relations between objects of visual experience, Mondrian sought to exhibit such relations in and by themselves. The name he gave this new aesthetic was "Morphoplasticism."

There is no denying that Mondrian's views seem highly rigid, not to say pedantic, and some have seen in his work a mere parade of calculated virtuosity. Actually, however, Mondrian's attitude was that of a professional artist who takes his vocation with high seriousness—and, in the last analysis, has not every true artist always been inspired more by the beauty of lines and colors and the relations between them than by the concrete subject of the picture ? Mondrian was wholly in earnest in all he did and said. He sincerely felt he had a mission, and if his lucubrations strike us sometimes as tediously didactic, this was because he stood by his principles wherever they might lead. This desire to strip the object down to bare essentials, coming as it did after the relative freedom of his early work, and also a sort of religiosity in his approach to art, might suggest he was a victim of "repressions." That was not so; rather, he was a sage, a puritan, one might almost say a saint, but a saint who had never felt or feared temptation. And it is interesting to speculate what form Mondrian's art theories would have assumed under the brush of a repentant sinner.

Theo van Doesburg, who commenced as a poet, was the most active personality of the new movement. He brought tidings of it with his pen, his works and with the spoken word to many great European cities. He had studied all recent art movements enthusiastically but with a nice discernment, for he was an acute critic, before coming in contact with Mondrian whose aesthetic he hailed as a veritable revelation. He was convinced of the supremacy of the mind over the eye and it was in the light of this belief that he interpreted Mondrian's procedures. Also he gave a more precise meaning to that concept of "beauty" (too long regarded as a monopoly of academicism) by describing it as a symbolic expression of the Universal and the Divine. To his thinking aesthetic emotion derived from the presence of these two entities in a work of art. Still convinced that only verticals and horizontals should be used by the artist, he saw in them the "essential directions," since they alone could provide that hieratic, symbolical interpretation of the Universe which was "the very soul of form." He had a gift for clear thinking and equally lucid exposition which enabled him to clarify the aims of Neo-Plasticism, in the light of his definition of plastic art as "inorganic form stemming from a spontaneous impulse."

Vantongerloo was the mathematician of the group, and his form of abstraction derived from geometrical simplifications; in fact he harked back to Cézanne's formula of reducing all the forms of nature to cylinders, cones and spheres. He, too, employed analysis as a means of getting down to the basic structure of the object, through the exclusion of non-essentials. At first sight his work calls to mind the methods of Bracelli and Villard de Honnecourt; all the same, like Van der Leck and Van Doesburg, Vantongerloo did not keep to this rigorist program. Indeed he ended up by indulging in curves, modeling, color effects and a variety of tones, and it was Mondrian and Mondrian alone who kept to the ascetic discipline of absolute abstraction.

THEO VAN DOESBURG (1883-1931). COMPOSITION, 1915. (10⅛ × 4⅝″) PRIVATE COLLECTION, PARIS.

UMBERTO BOCCIONI (1882-1916). CHARGE OF LANCERS, 1915. TEMPERA AND COLLAGE ON CARDBOARD.
(13⅜ × 20″) PRIVATE COLLECTION, MILAN.

Evolution of Futurism

★

TRUE, one of the aims of the Futurists was, as Boccioni put it, "to synthesize what we remember and what we see." But they made no secret of another ambition, that of expressing the very essences of things seen. Obviously for achieving this it was necessary to fall back on those methods of simplification and elimination which had characterized early Cubism and been carried still further by Kandinsky, then by Mondrian. In fact the Futurists were haunted like so many artists of the day by the idea of a pictorial world that was neither an imitation nor an interpretation of the real world, but *signified* it. Also, as we have already seen, they aimed at representing objective reality under novel aspects (such as the development in space of bodies in motion), but aspects that were none the less realistic, and not in any sense transcending visual appearance, as it had been transcended in the art of the Cubists and abstract painters.

In Boccioni's case, however, we find that his art became less and less figurative, further and further removed from observational data. However, this did not involve the concept of a single plane like Mondrian's or combinations of abstract colors like Kandinsky's. The guiding idea behind Boccioni's *Charge of Lancers* is that of violent movement; in fact almost the only impression we get from this picture is the surging onrush of the lances from an empty space which, too, is "signified"—in this case by "collage" of a war news clipping. This is rather an evocation of the dynamism of specific objects than of dynamism in the abstract.

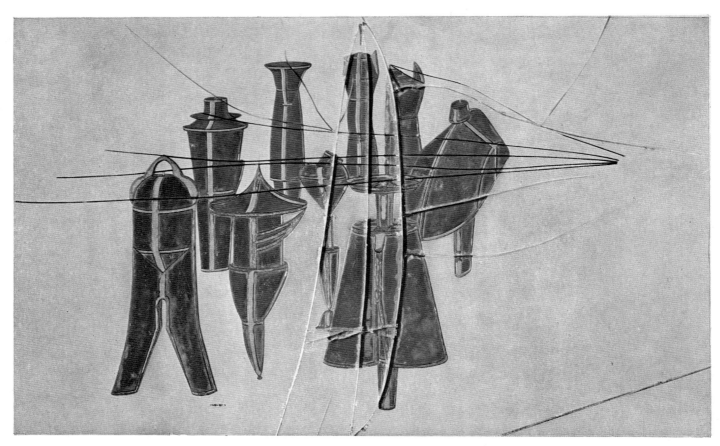

MARCEL DUCHAMP (1887). NINE MALIC MOLDS, 1914. (28¼ × 48¾")
ROCHÉ COLLECTION, PARIS.

Consisting of strips of copper between panes of glass that Duchamp cracked deliberately, this fragment of a picture
was incorporated later in the famous *Bride stripped bare by her Bachelors even*. The *Nine Malic Molds* represent the
bachelors : the gendarme, the cuirassier, the city policeman, the priest, the bell-hop, the delivery boy, the flunkey,
the undertaker's man, and the station-master.

The Dada Movement

★

UNQUESTIONABLY Marcel Duchamp should be regarded as the progenitor of the Dada
movement. However in his earliest works (for example in the portrait of his father
in the manner of Cézanne, made in 1910) and especially in the famous *Nude descending a
Staircase*, there were as yet no signs of the anti-artistic tendencies he was to carry to such
lengths when he embarked on what was nothing short of a calculated destruction of all
traditional art values. It was not until 1915 or thereabouts that he seriously contemplated
the possibility of making a clean sweep of all the conventions, practices and the very *raison
d'être* of painting since time immemorial. Obviously this meant discarding not only all
preconceived ideas and academic standards, but also even the technical aptitudes he had
acquired; also that the picture must be given a wholly new function, as to whose exact nature
he was not yet quite sure but which certainly was basic to the art of the future. One of the
various means of clearing the ground was, as he saw, to employ the language of the cari-
cature, and to produce witty, satirical or frankly brutal travesties of accepted art, with the
intent of making all painting seem ridiculous; or, alternatively, he might substitute for
the time-honored themes of painting (which he regarded as hopelessly out of date) new,
completely irrational subjects and give them titles even more preposterous.
Here again we have symptoms of that revolt against the dictates of the thinking mind and
common sense which, as we have seen, had already been making itself felt among the
younger painters and writers. But now a frontal attack was directed at the whole art of

painting, its technical means of expression included. As yet there was no question of any nihilist, anarchist or anti-moral campaign; that blessed word "Dada" had not yet been culled from the dictionary. Once again the matter at issue was essentially and exclusively of a technical order: a revision of the traditional motifs and means of painting. Looking at Marcel Duchamp's early efforts, we are reminded of that famous Hogarth engraving in which the artist secured a richly comic effect by deliberately indulging in all the "errors of perspective" he could think of; or of those amusing 16th-century paintings whose landscapes, when inspected from a certain angle, reveal caricatures of well-known personages; or again of those quaint anticipations of *papiers collés* in which advertisements, popular prints, calendar-pictures were drawn or painted with an illusionist realism as precise as it was pointless. Probably Duchamp, as we have already suggested, was *au fond* merely amusing himself; his sole aim was to parody and ridicule the efforts made by so many of his contemporaries to conjure up a new world of the imagination: efforts which to his mind were futile if the artist relied solely on the employment of the hitherto accepted means and methods. It was with this in mind that Duchamp arrived at the notion of "transposition" as the only logical basis for the creation of a world enabling him to transcend the familiar world of appearances. Thus the position taken up by Duchamp as regards the real world was inspired by the notion of a total inversion, a reshuffling of its contents, for this to his thinking was the only way of throwing new light on the ultimate relations between objects and the operations of the mind. It was a difficult task he set himself, and perhaps he was not wholly successful in it. But he took his stand, plausibly enough we must admit, on a theory which was in keeping with his personal philosophy; namely that if one knows what one is looking for—which is always a moot point—one never knows what one is going to find—that anyhow can be taken for granted.

There is no question that Marcel Duchamp's ideas had a considerable influence on art; the Surrealists, notably, were to regard him as one of their forerunners and masters.

Such were the conceptions behind the so-called "ready-mades" which Marcel Duchamp exhibited at New York. They were manufactured objects, articles in common use—one of them being a porcelain plumbing-fixture—signed by the artist and presented as authentic works of plastic art. It is obvious that this was both a challenge to and a rejection of all conventional ideas of rationality in art. The reaction of the New York public to Duchamp's productions can easily be imagined; the time was not yet ripe. Duchamp's exhibits were turned down by the jury of the New York Independents' exhibition and he welcomed this as a pretext for resigning from the Society.

With Duchamp were associated Picabia, de Zayas, Arensberg and Man Ray. Picabia, too, had gone to New York in 1915 and his contribution to the Dada movement was well calculated to rouse the indignation of the American public. It was not so much the traditions of academic art that he attacked as the prestige of the machine, and the habit of seeing in machinery one of the noblest works of man. Amongst several pictures in this vein Picabia painted one entitled *Parade amoureuse* (Amorous Display) featuring *inter alia* parts of a carburetor. It is amusing to find that Picabia's efforts in this direction have borne fruit; quite recently an American inventor, we are assured, has constructed an immensely complicated machine, whose distinctive feature is that it serves no purpose whatsoever.

Man Ray, on the other hand, found a field for his remarkable talents in experimental photography, and produced what he baptized, after his own name, *Rayographs*; in these, the medium being photography, the ideas behind Duchamp's "ready-mades" were given a new and striking application.

In the work of all these artists, Duchamp, Picabia and Man Ray, we find (pending the launching of the assault on social and moral values sponsored by the Dada groups in Zurich and Berlin) a witty, sometimes rather malicious challenge of the accepted notions of law and order, and a fondness for paradoxical situations—not unlike that uncommendable but wholly human instinct which rejoices in the sight of a policeman being laid out by burglars or a lion-tamer eaten by his lion.

HANS ARP (1887).
COLORED WOODEN
FORMS, 1917.
$(12\frac{1}{2} \times 8\frac{1}{4}'')$
OWNED BY THE ARTIST.

Influenced by the wood-engravings published by Kandinsky in his book *Klänge* (1913), Arp, in his compositions of superimposed, colored pieces of wood, invented, around 1917, a completely original style in which chance and conscious design co-operated. Associations welling up from his Subconscious suggested forms resembling those of nature. Their style gives the critic the option of assigning certain works by Arp to Surrealism or abstract art as he prefers.

With the foundation of the Cabaret Voltaire in Zurich during the First World War the revolt, heralded by Duchamp, against the dictates of the reasoning mind and all art standards of the past, was amplified, and literary men now took a hand in "the destruction of all recognized values" in ethics as well as art. This program reflected the bitterness and disillusionment of the younger generation, who resented the constant degradation of the freedom and dignity of the individual caused by the war, and made it the chief target of their invectives. Zurich was then the temporary home of many Russian refugees including Lenin; of pacifists who had fled from Germany; of anarchist-minded poets and painters such as Tristan Tzara, Hugo Ball, Richard Hülsenbeck and the Alsatian Hans Arp. It was in February 1916 that the Cabaret Voltaire was founded; it had an exhibition gallery, a stage and club premises. Lectures were given, poems and manifestos read to excited, often uproarious audiences. The word "Dada" (i.e. hobby-horse) was lit on by Tzara when leafing through a French dictionary looking for a name for the group, and he started a review bearing that name, which published not only articles and poems but reproductions of works by Picasso, Hans Arp and Modigliani. In the Cabaret Voltaire gallery works by Kandinsky, Paul Klee, Chirico, Modigliani, Prampolini, Van Rees and Max Ernst were exhibited and created much stir in avant-garde circles.

By way of anti-war propaganda, they had the ingenious idea of confusing issues by publishing false or tendentious news: of bogus assassinations, suicides, accidents, duels, kidnappings, thefts of state papers—not to mention exhibitions of ultra-modern pictures which might be regarded—anyhow by their enemy, the bourgeois—as "subversive."

Thus the Dada movement in Zurich took a very different form from that which it had had in New York. Later, in Berlin, it had yet another trend. In Zurich its chief concern was the manifestation of a fierce antipathy for the established order and all that seemed to shore it up: science, painting, poetry, philosophy and even music. Meanwhile the Zurich group, being in Switzerland, were not exposed to the dangers of war or the famine conditions then prevailing in Germany, or to the police action soon to be set on foot against the leaders of the movement in Berlin. Arp was the only representative of Dada painting in Zurich. While fully in sympathy with the aspirations of the group, as an artist he followed his own bent and his work had not the aggressive, caricatural quality we find in that of Duchamp and Picabia. In collaboration with Sophie Täuber, who became his wife, he made abstract *papiers collés*, then plastic colored objects that he called "upcrops of the cerebral heart": relief constructions in the surrealist vein, and also sculpture in the round—manifestations of that "concrete art" which, to quote Arp's own words, "wishes to transform the world."

After the works like *Procession in Seville* (see page 153) of his Dada period, Picabia reverted to the representation of objects—but of mechanical objects serving no purpose whatsoever. The colors are bright, the whole atmosphere is gay and lively, but we sense an implied criticism of the social order in this elaborate machine at once so carefully contrived and so supremely futile.

FRANCIS PICABIA (1878-1953). AMOROUS DISPLAY, 1917. (39 × 28¾") PRIVATE COLLECTION, PARIS.

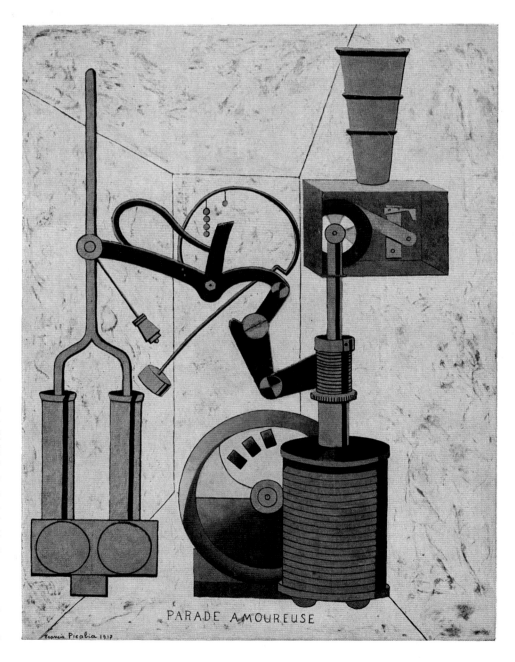

PARADE AMOUREUSE

GIORGIO DE CHIRICO (1888). THE SEER, 1915. (35¼×27½″) PRIVATE COLLECTION, NEW YORK.

Metaphysical Painting

★

IT WAS Chirico himself who by using the term *pittura metafisica* made a distinction between his work before the First World War and his later work. This epithet "metaphysical" not only seemed to match his grandiose ambitions, but suggested (in its root meaning) just what he was aiming at: to discover behind the enigmatic silence and aloofness of the natural world its latent meaning, intimations of the supernatural.

We must not forget that Chirico was born in Greece, a land of crystal-clear light that defines and shows up objects with an almost eerie precision and enables one to see so far beyond the range of ordinary vision that one almost fancies oneself gifted with a supernormal second sight. Something of this is reflected perhaps in Chirico's strange depictions of deserted streets, tall lugubrious factory chimneys, gloomy shadow-haunted arcades, vast empty squares peopled with mysterious antique statues that seem half alive, and illusory perspectives reaching out into infinity. His pictures give us a feeling that he is always trying indefatigably to discover the secret life behind the sights of everyday and to communicate it to the beholder. Chirico was obsessed with the idea of perfection, it was an almost physical craving with him; but this perfection had little to do with craftsmanship. It concerned, rather, the "something beyond everything" glimpsed by that great mystic Thomas Traherne; something that certainly exists though always it lies just out of reach of our perception, even of our imagination—that tantalizing Unknown dreamt of by the poet and the metaphysician. Chirico's world is haunted by the poet-painter's disquietude when confronted with the static, frozen impenetrability of enigmas he seeks in vain to fathom. The arcades of his palaces are so many hugely gaping eyes whose depths reveal nothing but a void impossible to plumb. He questions them with a sort of desperate persistence, as one repeats a word over and over again till it is drained of meaning, a mere sound signifying nothing. Nevertheless Chirico made one discovery, pregnant with consequences for modern art: that strange, unwonted conjunctions of inanimate objects evoke as it were a colloquy between them, a meaningful drama in progress behind their disquieting stillness. In fact Chirico created a poetry of the immobile which, under the most abstract aspects, conveys a feeling of agonized suspense, an expectation of some impending catastrophe of, presumably, a supernatural order. Unlike the Cubists and Abstractionists, he does not disintegrate the object but shows it in its natural state, but—and this is the factor of surprise—as it left its maker's hands and before being given the place for which it is intended and where we would expect to see it. Thus, in *The Seer*, a tailor's dummy in an incongruous setting, idly contemplating a blackboard covered with an architectural diagram, seems to take on an enigmatic life of its own and we almost sense a secret presence stirring behind the paneled flooring.

But the poetic effects obtained by Chirico from emotive anomalies of this order gave place to dynamic values when in 1915 his Metaphysical Period began. There had been a human element in his early work, strange as it was, and this he now eliminated. Solitude, nostalgia of the infinite, melancholy and incertitude, which had so far been his favorite themes and whose strange enchantments he had so poignantly conveyed, ceased to interest him. We may well believe that the static atmosphere to which his earlier works largely owed their haunting quality began to seem oppressive and now, perhaps under the influence of Futurism, he developed an interest in forms in movement, culminating round about 1925 in his pictures of galloping or rearing horses. Also he took to peopling his canvases with elements of a kind he had not hitherto employed, pseudo-human figures in the forms of mannequins or robot-like forms built up with geometrical instruments, set squares and so forth, and reminiscent of some of Bracelli's figures. There is no question that these uncanny effigies give the beholder a feeling of being plunged into a supernormal world; the only links with reality are in their titles: *The Seer, The Disquieting Muses, Hector and Andromache, The Troubadour.*

GIORGIO MORANDI (1890). METAPHYSICAL STILL LIFE, 1920. (26¾ × 24¼")
PRIVATE COLLECTION, MILAN.

The Dada approach to art was wholly anarchistic—all was to be destroyed and nothing put in its place; Chirico, on the other hand, seeks to build up a new world organized in terms of metaphysics. Yet, if he certainly has created some very remarkable works on these lines, they go little further than the dreamworlds that other artists have conjured up in the past with more or less success. He, too, had discovered a "new thrill," but soon realized that he had exhausted its possibilities, and struck out in a new direction. And that direction brought him back to a conventional realism, devoid of any poetic atmosphere, and to a new conception of art that led him to repudiate his past.

Giorgio Morandi has never joined forces with any art movement, never set forth in writing his views on art and never visited Paris. He has always lived a completely secluded life in his native town in Italy, Bologna. His art reflects his life; of neither has the even tenor been ruffled by any disturbing event or any interference from without. Characteristic of Morandi's art is its complete integrity, his devotion to the commonest objects of daily life which he exalts like his Latin forbears to the rank of household gods, his *Lares et Penates*, and in whose

cult he finds all the inspiration he desires. His color is subtle, light and delicate in tone without any touch of harshness; his composition solid, architectonic. Indeed the noble serenity and harmony of Morandi's art has almost a religious quality, something of the "peace that passes understanding," and it is this gift of investing quite ordinary things with the glamour of another world that affiliates his aesthetic to that of the *scuola metafisica*.

Unlike Chirico, Carrà came by way of Futurism to Metaphysical Art. Despite the fact that he was one of the original Futurists he did not share in Marinetti's disdain for what the Futurists called *passatismo*, and never lost faith in the aesthetic and traditions of the great Italian masters. True, he did not indulge in any slavish imitation of reality, but aimed, rather, at "realizing the image of form" and expressing "the very essence of existing things." This, to his mind, was the only way of achieving "true architectural austerity," of winning through to "a new reality" and metaphysical painting in its most authentic form. Thus Carrà never wholly rejected natural appearances, but included in his metaphysical compositions realistic elements which, when this seemed called for, he stylized and used only as more or less topical allusions. He was convinced that *"ordinary things* are the only real links we have between the essence of the world and ourselves," and that "they alone make manifest its secret splendors."

In his Metaphysical Period Carrà often resorted to elements charged with suggestive magic—but not always; for sometimes, too, he employed realistic motifs so as to keep contact with the objective world which had supplied the starting-off point of the picture. Here he goes even further and succeeds in re-creating reality by means of curious objects whose concatenations (with their shadows) on tilted planes are strangely disturbing. Yet, in keeping with the Italian tradition, the organization of the picture-surface is mathematically ordered, and indeed this very order heightens the effect of eeriness produced by the ensemble.

CARLO CARRÀ (1881). THE DRUNKEN GENTLEMAN, 1916. (23½ × 17½") PRIVATE COLLECTION, MILAN.

Expressionism

★

As already pointed out in connection with the work of Van Gogh and that of Munch, "Expressionism" is one of the very few names of art movements which were not either foisted on them (as was the case with Impressionism, Fauvism and Cubism) by hostile art critics, or invented by the artists themselves (Futurism, Dadaism, Surrealism). The particular "-ism" with which we are here concerned owed its name to some writer on art, very likely Herwarth Walden, who often used it to describe certain tendencies that were not impressionist, realistic or classicizing, but above all revolutionary. Moreover Expressionism has often been confused with Realism; indeed the name Expressionist is applied (as in fact Walden applied it) to such a diversity of artists that no sooner does one attempt to define it in terms of any preciseness than it becomes evident there are a host of exceptions that do not so much prove the rule as stultify it.

Around 1914 Expressionism (the term is used here in its widest connotation), after withstanding the attacks of "purer" forms of art—Cubism, Futurism, Abstractionism—, continued in the path marked out by Van Gogh and Munch. It soon transpired that this was not a movement in the ordinary sense, promoted that is to say by a group of artists sharing a community of views and ideals, but rather a tendency stemming directly from Romanticism. Its aim was (and is) to make painting as it were a *speculum hominis*, a mirror held up to the artist's Ego and a vehicle for the unfettered expression of his soul-searchings.

In this connection we must bear in mind that these artists were individual cases, using the word "case" almost in its medical sense; in fact many of the most typical and authentic Expressionists suffered from neuroses, more or less pronounced, and came under medical supervision at one time or another. Nothing is gained by burking the all too obvious fact that such men as Van Gogh, Munch, Kirchner, Pascin and Soutine were obsessed throughout their careers by morbid *idées fixes*; that four of them attempted to commit suicide and several succeeded in the attempt. Thus they cannot be judged by normal standards; their extreme egocentrism was, ultimately, pathological.

Another interesting and perhaps significant fact is that the most homogeneous manifestations of what we have described as the expressionist tendency have always been specifically Nordic; that the countries of origin of its most representative figures were Holland, Germany, Russia and Scandinavia. In the United States, too, it has found its most notable exponents and most fervent admirers amongst artists and connoisseurs of Nordic origin. On the other hand, Latin countries, France, Italy and Spain, have always tended to be allergic to the manifestations of Expressionism.

None of the Expressionists of the period with which we are now concerned, for example Kirchner, Soutine, Pascin and Kokoschka, showed much interest in the social or ethical problems which were being so eagerly debated by the intelligentsia of the day. Whereas the Dada movement stood for a revolt against a social order that was held to have been more or less responsible for the First World War and was therefore utterly pernicious, the Expressionists did not take sides; all that interested them was the utterance of things private and inward, personal problems. This had not been the case with Van Gogh, Gauguin and Munch, who took up a well-defined position as regards the world around them. The Expressionists did not overtly question the dictates of Reason; simply, they ignored them. Nor did they give much thought to their technical equipment; as long as they could express their inner anguish, little mattered the means employed. Matisse had them in mind when he made the ironic observation that the painter is frequently by way of being a "whimperer" *(pleurnichard)*, a man who may well be dogged, as he professes, by bad luck, but who is interested less in the hardships and injustice of the human situation in so far as these affect his fellow men, than in the inconveniences they may cause him personally.

In Kirchner we have an exponent of what has been called "psychological Expressionism." He studied the work of the Fauves, the Cubists and above all the early German Masters. His highly strung temperament led him to the use of strident color, but his favorite medium was the woodcut, whose technique he rejuvenated and which represents the most characteristic part of an œuvre pervaded through and through by a sense of feverish unrest. He suffered from a nervous complaint, attended by partial paralysis, and was classed as "physically and mentally unfit" for military service. In the post-war period he was greatly distressed by the turn of events in Germany, and, to make things worse, he now fell victim to an incurable intestinal disease. Finally, in despair, he took his own life.

Our purpose in giving reproductions of the two self-portraits of Kokoschka and Soutine is to remind our readers of the predilection shown by Expressionists in general for making psychologically searching studies of their own faces. True, almost every painter has at some time or other in his career felt moved to depict his face, whether from a psychological or a purely plastic viewpoint. But artists whose chief interest lies in painting for painting's sake have never been fond of using themselves as models. True, some painters who, by reason of the universality of their genius, are not to be ranked among the exponents of expressionist self-analysis, have occasionally studied their own faces, with a view to a specific interpretation of the human personality. Picasso and Rouault are cases in point. But though the latter has lent his features to several of the figures in his compositions, he obviously has never had any definite intention of producing likenesses of himself. As for Picasso, all his self-portraits date to his Blue, Pink and Negro Periods; he made none thereafter.

Expressionists, on the other hand, have never had any qualms about exteriorizing their personalities by way of introspective studies of their features and long self-scrutinies in a mirror—dialogues with their reflected selves. Time and again such thoroughgoing Expressionists as Soutine and Kokoschka psychoanalyzed themselves in this manner; and the same is true of Munch who, we have already remarked, made no less than a hundred self-portraits. However there is nothing morbid about Kokoschka, though like all Expressionists he often bodies forth emotions of a purely personal order, which in his case take the form of intensely emotive allegories or apotheoses. Thus the surging rhythms of *The Tempest* dramatically symbolize his passionate love for Alma Mahler, widow of the famous composer. In general, however, he conceals his feelings under a veil of discreet allusions couched in poetic forms. In fact his art may be said to lie midway between Expressionism and Realism in view of his ever-increasing interest in technique and the universal, objective quality he imparts to his conceptions. After the period of allegorical pictures, he developed a new method of rendering landscape, making (as he described them) "portraits" of scenes of nature. But the distinctive quality of his art is undoubtedly a tendency—though never pressed to its extreme limit—to give expression primarily to his ego, to things private and inward. This can be felt even in his searchingly analytic, passionately expressive interpretations of the psychology of his sitters. As already mentioned, Kokoschka, unlike most Expressionists, is much interested in technique and we can see that Van Gogh's particularly attracted him at one stage of his career. In its course he wandered far afield, on his way from Pöchlarn (in Austria) to London where he now lives. Amongst the countries where he has stayed for long or short periods are Germany, Switzerland, Tunisia, Italy, Turkey, Spain, Portugal and Holland.

Perhaps some explanation of the reasons why no picture by Rouault figures in this section of the present work seems called for. Between the years 1917 and 1927 he virtually gave up painting pictures and devoted himself to book illustration. Thus we shall deal again with Rouault's art as from the date when he reverted, definitively, to easel-painting.

In a general way it may be said that during this period the Expressionists showed no inclination to curb their passionate subjectivism. This is perhaps to be regretted when we consider what they might have done had they directed their vast creative energy towards some altruistic ideal. It is only at a somewhat later period, in the work of realists like Gromaire and Alix (e.g. *The Itinerant Workman* and *The Surrender*), that we begin to find traces of human fellow-feeling, generous indignation and a sense of social responsibility.

OSKAR KOKOSCHKA (1886). SELF-PORTRAIT, 1917. (30 × 24½″) VON DER HEYDT COLLECTION, WUPPERTAL.

Here the vacillating, undecided posture suggests the artist's state of mind in 1917, when he was about to move on from his "psychological" manner to a more "cosmic" outlook.

CHAÏM SOUTINE (1894-1943). SELF-PORTRAIT, 1918. (21½ × 18″)
HENRY PEARLMAN COLLECTION, NEW YORK.

Poignant as is the anguish written on his face, Soutine was not aiming primarily at a psychological evocation of it ; the portrait issued as naturally from his brush as the sound of his voice from his lips. Usually the Expressionists did not trouble overmuch about technique ; Soutine, however, if quite instinctively, probed persistently into his medium, so as to wrest from it the secrets of its being, like an anatomist exploring the secret places of a body. Here, in any case, the artist did not set out to make a likeness of himself ; this is less a portrait than a "head."

After the First World War

★

In the following pages we describe the events and tendencies that shaped the course of painting subsequently to 1918. We shall examine the post-war trends of Cubism, the "return to the object," reminiscences of Old Master art and classical design, Expressionism, the swerve back to realism, the advance of popular art and that of abstractionism, and the activities of the Bauhaus guild of artists and artisans.

The year 1918—year of the Armistice and also of Apollinaire's death—saw artistic activity, hitherto confined to Montmartre and Montparnasse, spread over the whole of Paris. A taste for painting suddenly became generalized; new galleries opened and exhibitions multiplied. Visitors to the Salon d'Automne, the Indépendants and the art dealers' shops now were better equipped to appreciate modernistic art. The Russian and Swedish Ballets, with their sets and costumes designed by the leading painters of the day, played a part in fostering the new spirit. Although in 1917 that witty Picasso-Satie ballet *Parade* had come in for general abuse, Diaghilev's new ballets were unqualified successes: *Tricorne* (Picasso 1919), *La Boutique Fantasque* (Derain 1919), *Le Chant du Rossignol* (Matisse 1920), *Les Fâcheux* (Braque 1923), *L'Education Manquée* (Juan Gris 1924). For its part, Rolf de Maré's Swedish Ballet Company performed *Skating Rink* and *La Création du Monde*, both with sets by Léger, *Relâche* by Picabia and *La Jarre* by Chirico (1925), while E. de Beaumont's *Les Soirées de Paris* presented *Salade* by Braque (1924) and Picasso's *Mercure* (1924). Famous producers of the Russian theater also sought the collaboration of modern painters and the names of Gordon Craig, Stanislavsky, Tairoff, Meyerhold and Granowsky became widely known and respected. The cinema too was a tempting field for artists. Léger executed revolving scenery for Lherbier's *L'Inhumaine* (1925) and composed his film *Le Ballet Mécanique*, while Picabia collaborated with René Clair on *Entr'acte*. In the motion picture, then passing through an exciting, experimental phase, painters found new, dynamic possibilities.

Modern painting also brought about a revolution in the art of poster design. Taking their lead from Léger's pure, flat colors, such excellent artists as Colin, Cassandre and Carlu selected plastic elements that symbolized the subject of the poster and presented them in striking shapes and colors that caught and held the eye.

A new generation of poets appeared—Aragon, Eluard, Breton, Tzara, Soupault and Desnos —and their works were illustrated by painters. There were frequent gatherings of poets, musicians and painters, not to mention the entertainments sponsored by *Littérature*, *L'Effort Moderne*, Germaine Bongard, and the first, boisterous Dada demonstrations.

New literary and art reviews filled the gap left by *Les Soirées de Paris*, *L'Elan*, *Sic* and *Nord Sud*, which had ceased publication. Art galleries—*L'Effort Moderne*, the Galerie Berthe Weill, the Galerie Bernheim—began to issue their own bulletins. And finally, from 1920 on, the magazine *L'Esprit Nouveau*, edited by Ozenfant and Jeanneret (Le Corbusier), became a rallying point for five years of avant-garde literary and artistic activity.

Montparnasse now replaced Montmartre as the center of Paris art life, and its cafés were frequented by an increasingly cosmopolitan clientele; the "Dome," the "Rotonde," the "Jockey" and, at Saint-Germain-des-Prés, the "Flore," the "Brasserie Lipp," and the "Deux-Magots" were among the most famous haunts. Picturesque balls were organized by artists at the Académie Scandinave, the Gymnase Huyghens and Bullier's, and Paul Poiret gave sumptuous receptions—one of them on a house-boat on the Seine. Even the fashion world was affected by contemporary painting. Sonia Delaunay designed dresses and fabrics with "orphic-simultaneous" color-schemes, Dufy painted textiles for Bianchini, and Germaine Bongard and Gabrielle Chanel relied heavily on the co-operation of modern painters, while one of the big Parisian stores successfully launched a dress material named "Picassine." The number of collectors increased, dealers prospered, and sometimes even the artists themselves reaped benefit. Their names became known the world over; painting, in short, was fashionable.

One of the theatrical events of the time calls for special mention. At Lausanne in 1918 the recently formed Pitoëff company, which was soon to achieve such fame in Paris, produced *L'Histoire du Soldat*, a poetic drama by C. F. Ramuz with music by Stravinsky (conducted by Ernest Ansermet), and costumes and sets by René Auberjonois. (After Picasso's famous sets for *Parade*, it was the second time a great painter was called on to make the decors for a ballet.) This was a memorable occasion in view of the eminence of the collaborators and the excellence of the production. Auberjonois commemorated it with a picture, his moving *Homage to Ludmilla Pitoëff*, and Ramuz wrote about it in his book on Auberjonois. "1918. This was the year in which we worked together on *L'Histoire du Soldat*; you painted the sets and designed the costumes, while Stravinsky composed the music and I was responsible for the words. How well I remember those strenuous months when we pooled our efforts in the service of a shared ideal; it was a case of 'team-work' in the very best sense of that rather over-worked modern term." The persons figuring in this composition, from left to right, are: Georges Pitoëff, Ludmilla Pitoëff, Ernest Ansermet, Stravinsky, Ramuz, Auberjonois.

RENÉ AUBERJONOIS (1872). STUDY FOR "HOMAGE TO LUDMILLA PITOËFF," 1920. (22½ × 19½")
KUNSTMUSEUM, BASEL.

GEORGES BRAQUE (1882). THE CAFÉ-BAR, 1919. (62⅛ × 31½ ″) LA ROCHE COLLECTION,
KUNSTMUSEUM, BASEL.

GEORGES BRAQUE (1882). THE SUGAR BOWL, 1920. (12 1/4 × 21 3/4 ")
PRIVATE COLLECTION, SWITZERLAND.

Evolution of Cubism

★

IN 1918 Ozenfant and Jeanneret published a book entitled *Après le Cubisme* in which the two artists set out to prove that Cubism had reached its peak and was indeed already on the downgrade. They put the Cubists on their guard against a trend towards decorative stylization, and even professed to discover traces of Impressionism in their recent work. As a corrective, Ozenfant and Jeanneret expounded a new aesthetic—Purism—whose purpose was to restore the discipline and austerity of the movement at its inception and, stemming the rising tide of Dadaist irrationalism, to defend the claims of reason and orderly procedure now imperiled by the licence given to the senses. Soon their ideas had rallied considerable support, and the result, as we shall see in the following chapter, was a frank return to the subject and by the same token a swerve away from the somewhat baroque turn Cubism had recently been taking.

For the time being, however, a superb series of canvases illustrated a phase during which Picasso, Braque and Gris made a point of incorporating in their compositions fragments of actual visual experience exactly as they saw them—a procedure that obviously ran counter to that supremacy of the mind which was basic to the cubist creed. Indeed it almost seemed as if the retinal image was by way of superseding the imagination.

True, seemingly Picasso continued to abide by cubist composition. In actual fact, however, he had by-passed the static principles of Cubism and he now distributed his geometrized forms dynamically, with arabesques and spirals, of a new, disconcerting fancifulness, flickering across the picture-surface. The pure and vivid colors of this phase suggest influences of the Russian Ballet. In the manner of the Romanesque decorators, he surrounds the central motif with a sort of ornamental frame and abandons the austere linework with which hitherto he had been reducing objects to their bare essentials. Instead, he indulges in a wealth of

PABLO PICASSO (1881). THE SCHOOL-GIRL, 1919. (36½ × 29½ ″) DOUGLAS COOPER COLLECTION, LONDON.

Reverting about 1917 to a more colorful form of Cubism, Picasso did not flinch at using harsh, flat tones reminiscent here of a shuffled deck of gaudy playing cards. All forms are reduced to a complex system of geometric planes, whose clashing colors set up a dancing movement on the picture-surface, much like the colorful patterns of the Russian Ballet.

leafage, flowers, fans, birds and beasts, hardly distorting them at all, and the effect is one of an almost bewildering richness and intricacy. It must have been clear to Picasso that he had reached a limit and must now strike out in a new direction.

For his part, Braque had almost forgotten the "rule that corrects emotion" and gave untrammelled expression to his feelings under forms as varied as they were delightful, which, far from running riot, fell into place with an order and discipline of their own.

Juan Gris was conscious of having failed so far to achieve the synthesis towards which he had nevertheless been steadily progressing. Meanwhile his palette, hitherto restrained by an extreme circumspection, began to include a richer scale of colors. Though only a few years before he had made it clear that there was no place in his art for the things of the senses, he now felt that the time had come to modify this self-denying ordinance and pay court to color, whose glamour he had formerly mistrusted.

Art movements are apt to be short-lived. And though perhaps by now Cubism had nothing really new to offer, the literal demonstration of its theories having reached a conclusion, the spirit of the movement remained none the less a living force in the modern art-world, and it is plain to see that cubist inspiration, under various forms, has had a stimulating effect on the painting of our time.

JUAN GRIS (1887-1927). STILL LIFE WITH FRUIT DISH, 1918. (25½ × 21¼")
HERMANN RUPF COLLECTION, BERN.

JACQUES VILLON (1875). THE GAME, 1919. (36¾ × 28¼″)
GALERIE LOUIS CARRÉ, PARIS.

We have selected this work of Villon's because it is so good an illustration of the structural methods counseled by Leonardo: the use of "guide lines" and a carefully organized ground-plan. Noteworthy, too, is the pyramidal lay-out, favored by so many of the great masters of the past, which here, combined with flat-patterning, gives an effect of thickness ; also the way in which the artist achieves space-creating depth by the use of staggered planes of color. This is a robust, virile work and the staidness of Villon's color-scheme is a somewhat new departure.

214

Return to the Object and the Subject

★

THE YEAR 1918 witnessed the revival of a tendency which was to be of capital importance in the art of the near future. It took the form of a return, discreet to begin with, towards the object and the subject. We feel that painters now are seeking to escape the consequences of the extreme insistence on purely aesthetic values which had led them to a point that had come to seem uncommonly like a dead-end. Needless to say there was no question of absolutely breaking with the cubist theory of the primacy of painterly considerations in the making of the picture, nor of returning to the mere expression of emotions. But a need was felt to enlarge the field of inspiration; to consider the claims of landscape and the human body and the possibilities they offered for a more dynamic conception of the subject, as against the static impassivity of the still life. There was, in fact, a feeling that a new epoch was impending in which the painter would give more thought to ordinary human sentiments. Despite a belief, common especially among the more simple-minded, that the ending of the war would usher in a sort of millennium, our artists could not forget so easily the tragic years they had been living through and the havoc these had wrought on their sensibility. True, *Guernica* was still far off, but the time was near when the human figure was to reappear either under the enigmatic, but living aspects Gris and Léger were to give it, or under a more expressive form in Picasso's work.

Round about 1918 Léger, who had served at the Front during the war, began to give his work a more human atmosphere. The period of Mechanical Forms was followed by one of Animated Landscapes. Figures, trees and animals were introduced in an evocative manner under simple, stylized aspects; as wholly plastic elements yet unmistakably endowed with life. In short, Léger now treated the object not only as functional to the architecture of the picture but as a living form. In the return to nature implied by the use of plants and animals in his compositions, he did not bend nature to this service but, rather, served her in so far as she provided the "dictionary" of which Delacroix had spoken.

As regards Picasso, much has been written about the reasons behind his so-called return to classicism. As a matter of fact all his life long Picasso has kept in touch with natural appearances, and his handling of line has always been in the classical tradition. The work he did during this period for Diaghilev's Russian Ballet and the many sketches this necessitated lay outside the main stream of his activities, and did not deflect him from his study of the problems of Cubism. He now made portraits, illustrated Ovid's *Metamorphoses*, and there has been talk about his "Pompeian Period," his "Ingres Period" and so forth. But more perhaps than any other artist Picasso loves nature, loyally and sincerely. He never proposed, like Juan Gris, to make of Cubism an exclusive, self-sufficient aesthetic and an end in itself; the expression of his responses to life has always been his paramount concern.

Moreover his desire to be true to life, in other words to make his picture *live*, has prevented him from ever losing touch with classical form. The classical conception of the necessity of striking a perfect balance between the content of the picture and its over-all structure is to his mind the most salutary of traditional disciplines. Thus whether he permits himself the most startling, poetically imaginative liberties or applies himself to expressing quite literally his love of life, he makes a point of integrating these two tendencies, that is to say of effecting a total fusion between form and subject. Neo-classical procedures furnish him with a sort of prosaic schema which he can elevate to purest poetry thanks to the rare combination of technical virtuosity and high imagination that is peculiarly his.

As for Juan Gris, to all appearances he kept to his method of starting off from an arrangement of colors and thence proceeding to a subject. None the less we seem to glimpse as it were a subconscious urge behind these purely coloristic elements that leads them to assume human forms suggested by realistic touches: the figural motifs he had abandoned in early youth.

FERNAND LÉGER (1881-1955). ANIMATED LANDSCAPE: A MAN AND A DOG, 1921. (25 ½ × 36″)
DOUGLAS COOPER COLLECTION, LONDON.

FERNAND LÉGER (1881-1955). TWO WOMEN WITH FLOWERS, 1922. (28 ¾ × 45 ⅝″)
GALERIE LOUIS CARRÉ, PARIS.

PABLO PICASSO (1881). TWO FEMALE NUDES, 1920. DOUGLAS COOPER COLLECTION, LONDON.

Amedeo Modigliani

★

WHEREAS Picasso (who visited Italy at the time when the Russian Ballet was in Rome) now took to making works inspired by Antiquity and the Renaissance, Modigliani, whose feeling for the great Italian tradition was innate, gave rein to the emotionalism characteristic of his race.

When in 1906, a newcomer from his "cara Italia," he boldly embarked on his Parisian venture, Modigliani quite rightly guessed that he would find amongst us the stimulus needed to free him from the shackles of the academicism then prevailing in his country. And he promptly sought out and frequented the most "advanced" circles in Paris. Our first impression of this young man of twenty, all high-spirited ambition, was a shade discouraging; he struck us as being rather stand-offish and over ready to take offense. It was only by degrees we realized that he was fundamentally warm-hearted and shyly hid an almost boyish sentimentality under his air of gruffness. Following the wise advice of Brancusi the sculptor, he began by imposing on his sensibility the discipline of the new technical procedures. Then contact with Pre-Hellenic statuary, Negro art and Brancusi's bold simplifications led him to create works of sculpture hieratic in aspect but vibrant with inner life. As early as 1908, reverting to painting, he produced some large canvases which belong to the intermediate phase of his art, between the realism of his Italian beginnings and the constructive discipline he imposed more and more on his sensual exuberance. For acquaintance with Cézanne and contacts with the Cubists deflected him towards an architectural style of composition in which his early practice of sculpture doubtless played a part. But though fully alive to the excellence of this aesthetic, he realized that its rigors could but inhibit the expression of his emotions; thus his Cézannesque-Cubist phase was relatively short-lived.

Towards 1914 he became intimate with an English poetess, Beatrice Hastings, who had, it seems, a good deal of influence on his development. Her temperament was much like his own and, in sympathy with it, he began to exteriorize his very personal and sensitive reactions to the human face and body—a procedure that he was to follow throughout his career, always adding new refinements. Thus in his art we observe that curious blend of idealism and realism which, in many ways, is typically English. Beatrice Hastings, in fact, encouraged him to "find himself," and the moods of depression and exhaustion accompanying this struggle to discovery led him to the heavy drinking and drug-taking which hastened his untimely end. Some have seen Florentine or Umbrian influences in his painting, and no doubt he appreciated Botticelli and Mantegna and other less plastic than intellectual Italian masters. Indisputably present in his art are traces of the Pre-Raphaelite manner of painting, which Beatrice greatly admired. In his portraits of women, with their elongated faces, their long, swan-like necks, their dreamy faraway gaze, the slightly morbid, languorous grace of their beautifully posed bodies, there is not a little of that voluptuous realism combined with almost mystical idealism which distinguishes the work of the Pre-Raphaelite Brotherhood. True, he does not try to point a moral, as they were prone to do; but, like them, he imparts a characteristic suavity both to the expressions of faces and the attitudes of bodies. On the other hand, he disciplined his tendencies to emotionalism by the use of strictly classical composition. But it was the spiritualization of the human body that was at once the chief concern and the solace of this man of many contradictions—at once so kind-hearted and so truculent, always prompt to quarrel with and to contradict his friends, yet genuinely fond of them—whose erratic life hovered constantly between comedy and tragedy, intermittent phases of buoyant rapture and acute nervous depression.

As a friend, we found him "difficult," his irascibility and reluctance to meet others half way did not make for easy intercourse; but, now that we see him in time's mellowing perspective, we can only do homage to the purity of his inspiration, his singleness of heart.

AMEDEO MODIGLIANI (1884-1920). SEATED WOMAN. PRIVATE COLLECTION, PARIS.

CHAÏM SOUTINE (1894-1943). CHILD WITH A TOY, 1919. (32 ¼ × 26″)
OWNED BY MR CHARLES IM OBERSTEG, GENEVA.

Chaïm Soutine

Passionate Expression of an Unquiet Soul

Escaping from the dreary surroundings of the Smilovitchi ghetto in Lithuania, Soutine made his way, perhaps on foot, to Paris as to a promised land where, he fondly hoped, the artist's wildest dreams came true. He was speedily disillusioned. No sooner had he arrived than he found himself in that Parisian "ghetto," *La Ruche*, whose denizens were compatriots, political refugees, many of whom lived in terror of their lives. So depressing was the atmosphere and so hopeless seemed his plight that Soutine tried to hang himself and was only saved *in extremis* by his compatriot Kremegne.

He never managed to get used to life in Paris, in fact he felt as much "lost" there as he had felt in his humble native village, where he was the tenth child in a family of eleven children and was always being pestered, unsuccessfully, by his father to learn his trade, that of a tailor. For a while he continued to live in that nest of dingy studios, the *Ruche* or "Beehive," next door to the Vaugirard municipal slaughterhouse. In a nearby bar he hobnobbed with the butchers and slaughtermen who frequented it, clad in blood-stained overalls and with long, murderous-looking knives stuck in their belts. Though probably he shared his compatriot Chagall's fondness for vivid, high-pitched colors, he rarely indulged in them, and whereas the latter lavished brilliant greens, blues, yellows on his canvases, Soutine when he used these colors kept them relatively low in tone. Nevertheless by some alchemy that was his secret they acquired the rageful, flaring intensity we associate with his art. Owing no doubt to his daily contacts with the Vaugirard slaughtermen he was drawn to painting carcasses of animals and pieces of tainted meat stained with the hues of decomposition. And, by a curious transference he carried over those livid, gruesome colors even into his figure pieces and landscapes. We are reminded of the ghastly 15th- and 16th-century statues of skeletons to which some shreds of flesh still cling, crawling with worms; or, again, of those horrifying, greenish bishops slumped in their coffins in the "Triumph of Death" at the Pisan Campo Santo.

Soutine had something of the quality of a Primitive out of tune with the modern world, trying in vain to find his path and at the mercy of his moods. He did his best to "improve his mind," read all sorts of books indiscriminately, ranging from the Bible to popular novels, not to mention poetry and philosophical treatises; likewise he spared no pains in seeking to discover the secrets of the Masters of the past, from Rembrandt to Cézanne (he once owned to never having looked at Van Gogh "seriously"). Yet never did he succeed in finding in the manifestations of the great thinkers and artists to whom he turned for guidance anything that threw light on his personal problems, or on the meaning of a world which he accepted as inevitable but in which he always felt himself a stranger, ill at ease. One might almost say he suffered from an unreciprocated love of life. Though for a while he had a boundless devotion for Rembrandt, he never enjoyed that feeling of complete satisfaction which his friend Chagall experienced when, after passionately studying the work of the old Dutch master, he exclaimed triumphantly: "Rembrandt loves me!"

The very special conditions under which Soutine's art came to its flowering indicate how difficult it is to regard Expressionism as other than a complex of individual tendencies in which the achievement of each great artist stands alone. Obviously Soutine is a case in point. He does not fit into any known category and his most distinctive trait is that obsession with death and destruction which leads him to distort, even to mutilate all the subjects he touches with a bitter, almost sadistic joy. His technique, in fact, is wholly governed by impulse, and the one principle he resolutely keeps to is that of saying what he has to say, no matter by what means. Thus he always sacrifices the plastic qualities of his art to the emotion of the moment. That underlying melancholy and tragic sense of life which he so poignantly expresses give Soutine's pictures the curious appeal of an old Negro Spiritual magnificently rendered by a Negro with a husky voice.

Persistence of Classical Landscape

★

T HOUGH we can see in retrospect that the course of art through the ages is an evolutionary process, and change is a condition of survival, we also find that in every age there have been excellent artists who not merely withstood that process but swam against the stream. Cubism, abstract art, the Dada movement and their striking achievements had made their mark on early 20th-century painting, but there was in France a group of artists, and very fine ones, whose love and respect for nature prevented them from yielding to such influences and falling in line with the trends of the age.

Despite the far-reaching changes that the art of landscape painting has undergone from the days of the Primitives to the coming of Impressionism, the artists I have in mind approach it, rather, in the spirit of the great tradition which runs from Fouquet to Corot; that is to say they aim at rendering landscape in their pictures as they *feel* it, after seeking out in Nature her significant, emotive values or, if needs be, adding these by dextrous, highly personal touches. These were what Bonnard had in mind when he said, "Many little lies go to make a great truth," and added by way of justification that "unqualified sincerity may make the picture look ridiculous and even indefensible." For the rest, our landscape painters cultivated the utmost humility as regards nature, and showed as a rule the greatest patience in waiting for an emotion that would surely come in its good time. Their attitude was one of fervent contemplation, objective not subjective, for unlike the Expressionists they had no wish to parade their own personalities. By the same token, they mistrusted that romantic interpretation of nature which uses her as a sort of pleasure-ground, a source of sentimental thrills. The only emotion transmitted by the picture was functional to the initial "shock" the artist underwent when he happened on a certain scene, and this he interpreted under an ideal form, using of course all the resources of his technique but being careful to ensure an over-all unity that concealed the scaffolding of the picture and the rather self-conscious calligraphy sometimes visible in works of the masters of the past.

All the artists we have in mind—Derain, Ceria, Asselin, Vergé-Sarrat, Dufresne, Segonzac, Luc-Albert Moreau, Lotiron, Coubine, Gernez, Savin, Waroquier and others—were frankly hostile to all cut-and-dried theories and systems, but even more to any revolutionary adventures. And as already mentioned, they were equally against incursions of the romantic "ego." To their thinking the impressionist revolution had been, to say the least of it, misguided. For Impressionism had not shown due respect for Nature and Nature was, in their eyes, sacrosanct. The Impressionists had made Nature the subject of an experiment, which far from being an attempt to unveil her beauties and to extol her, analyzed her for purely scientific ends; it was like a cold-blooded surgical operation performed solely for the purpose of forcing her to disclose some vital secret. True, the idea of evoking the natural scene under its ever-changing aspects hour by hour (on the strength of the ancient dicta that "everything is in a state of flux" and "you can never cross the same river twice") was certainly original and had much to commend it. None the less this attitude was too objective. And unless one pressed it, as Monet for example pressed it, to the point of inspired abstractions, it led to a certain artificiality, to a mere set of formulas the use of which was justifiable only if (as in the case of Cézanne or Degas, Manet or Renoir) it was frankly recognized as such, and employed solely for building up a "solid and abiding art" like that which Cézanne advocated and practiced.

For great as was their devotion to nature, and mindful as they were to safeguard the spontaneity of their compositions, the landscape painters of this period were devotees of a sort of classicism and the expression of their responses was conditioned by this. They were all too ready to follow the counsels of Manet and Renoir, enjoining the painter to study the great masters in the museums. True, they gave more thought to rhythmic arrangement than to schematic lay-out. Occasionally—we find this in Dufresne, Segonzac, Moreau— they even borrowed some of the structural formulas of Cubism, though they were quick to repudiate these *instanter*. But they subjected themselves to certain disciplines as regards color, line and form; they simplified, synthesized, pruned away irrelevancies. Thus the freshness and liveliness of the sketch are often absent from their landscapes. Even the color has a reticence that contributes to the solidity of the composition. Violent colors are ruled out, and the use of subdued, neutral tones and earthy hues is carried to such a pitch that some of their pictures look like monochromes. Moreover, these landscape painters, once they have settled on their palette, keep persistently to the same range of colors, with the result that some have been accused of painting the same picture over and over again all their lives. Yet such men as Ceria, Lotiron and Vergé-Sarrat show a fine feeling for atmosphere and for light as well, and though they deliberately rule out dramatic effects, their landscapes have a subtly emotive quality and sometimes reveal a passionate response to natural beauty that they have vainly tried to discipline.

By and large, however, such art seems strangely out of keeping with the spirit of our time. Nevertheless it has been suggested that it may have a return to favor in the second half of the present century. For this to happen a change of climate would be needed, the coming of a more peaceful era, of which at present there are, unhappily, few indications. In any case it is probably out of the question to put the clock back and to nullify the effects of the revolution that has taken place in painting during the last fifty years, paralleled only by that of the Italian Renaissance.

ANDRÉ DERAIN (1880-1954). LANDSCAPE WITH OLIVE-TREES, 1919. PRIVATE COLLECTION, PARIS.

CONSTANT PERMEKE
(1886-1952).
TWO SAILOR BROTHERS,
CA. 1923. (11 × 20″)
KUNSTMUSEUM, BASEL.

At first sight an unbridgable gulf seems to separate this stark almost forbidding work, quite devoid of any anecdotal or emotive appeal, from that imaginative opulence which is basic to traditional Flemish art; Permeke, we feel, is a far cry from Rubens and Brueghel. Yet, on a closer scrutiny, we are able to discern profound affinities between the Old Flemish Masters and the modern Flemish expressionist school, of which Permeke is certainly the major representative. In the works of the former, once they are stripped of all contemporary referents, we find the same vigorous treatment of volumes, the same aggressively emphatic renderings of faces and bodies.

the second group were Constant Permeke, Gustave de Smet and Frits van den Berghe; they adhered more closely than the first to the old Flemish tradition sponsored by Hieronymus Bosch, Brueghel, Rubens and Jordaens.

The First World War scattered the Laethem group; Permeke, who had been wounded in the siege of Antwerp, fled to England, as did Tytgat, Daeye and Van de Woestyne. De Smet and Van den Berghe went with Le Fauconnier to Amsterdam. Floris Jespers stayed at Antwerp, Brusselmans in Brussels. Each went on working independently; when at last they met again they found to their surprise that all had been progressing on the same lines: towards a starkly virile style, depictions of lush fields, massive buildings, broad-shouldered peasants with huge hands. Their art celebrated the daily round of Flemish life: tending the cattle, meals in dark, low rooms, cheerless Sunday walks, kermesses, love-making in the countryside, placid deathbeds—all in fact that Van Gogh at the time when he lived under the selfsame skies had been trying to express.

After the war the Flemish artists' headquarters was the "Selection" Gallery in Brussels, whose slogan was "National Expressionism." The term "Expressionism" hardly fitted, since the art now taking form in the Belgian group had none of the transcendental or tragic implications of the work of such men as Munch, Nolde, Kirchner or Kokoschka. Essentially an art of fine craftsmanship, Flemish painting never seeks to convey ideas but simply to depict the daily life of a small, hard-working race and the simple grandeur of those humble folk whom Michelet had once half pityingly, half scornfully, described as little better than animals. Permeke, De Smet and (to a lesser extent) Van den Berghe were unaffected by that cult of the machine from which Léger and Delaunay, poets (e.g. Cendrars) and some musicians, Honegger for example, were drawing inspiration. The people they depict do not belong to any period; they typify the peasantry of time immemorial, and it was this eternal quality in the life of the tiller of the soil that the Flemish painters emphasized.

Constant Permeke, however, did not keep to this rather narrow range of subjects; there is nothing anecdotal in his art and his forms have a rugged power. He does not seek to charm us with his colors and the lugubrious, almost monochrome color-scheme of *The Two Sailor Brothers* here reproduced is typical, with its earthy browns upon a faintly glimmering ground. Another characteristic work by Permeke is one he has ironically named, in Flemish, *Den Welgezingen*, the Blissful Man, showing a man lying on the ground, curled up like an animal, sleeping off his drink, or his fatigue.

The Popular Tradition

★

DESPITE the fact that the Douanier Rousseau has figured in the Louvre since 1946, many visitors still contemplate his work with an affectionate but slightly condescending smile. For them, he remains "the nice old fellow" Apollinaire called him, an endearing representative of unsophisticated, ingenuous folk art at its purest, whom romantic-minded writers have invested with a legendary glamour.

Art historians have never quite agreed as to how to classify that picturesque company of artists who have entered into art history under the aegis of the Douanier. Should we call them modern primitives, folk painters, naïve artists or more familiarly, just Sunday Painters? They have been discussed in numerous monographs and articles in France and abroad; by Uhde, Gautier, Jakowski and, in the United States, by Sidney Janis. Group exhibitions of their most representative works have taken place; in Paris, at the Galerie Simon in 1921, at the Galerie Royale in 1937, at the Kunsthaus in Zurich and the Museum of Modern Art, New York, in 1938 and again in New York in 1939 (Exhibition of Contemporary Unknown American Painters). In the catalogues we find the names of many French artists: Rousseau, Vivin, Bombois, Boyer, Bauchant, Peyronnet, Séraphine Louis, Dietrich, Jean Eve, Rimbert, Lefranc, Dechelette, Narcisse Belle, Trouillard; of an Englishman Scottie Wilson; of an Italian Metelli; of the Americans Hirshfield, Sullivan, Kane, Pickett, Grandma Moses and Horace Pippin. Owing to the fact that the art of folk painters does not change as rapidly as that of professionally accredited artists, they stand for something relatively permanent, that basic human stuff of art from which a completely fresh start can be made when one is called for and with which professional artists too often have lost touch. In the last analysis, there is no fundamental difference between the work of a mediaeval rustic artisan and a landscape by Metelli, Vivin or Pickett. In all we find, persisting through the centuries, the same approach to nature and the same viewpoint; whereas professional landscape painters modify their way of seeing from generation to generation.

The naïve artist is in his fashion a chronicler of his age; for he does not confine himself to painting his own (usually humble) surroundings, but often depicts political and social events that have fired his imagination. Thus while Hirshfield paints the "pin-ups" of his dreams and Bombois circus scenes, Dechelette boldly tackles such "big" subjects as the United Nations conference in Paris; Sullivan, the marriage of the Duke of Windsor and Mrs Simpson; Bauchant, episodes from Roman history and Holy Writ.

Still the chief interest of their painting does not lie in its documentary value, as a visual chronicle of past or current events, however piquantly these are presented. As a matter of fact, the position of these naïve painters has a certain ambiguity. Formerly the art historian totally ignored them, whereas today they are given, as of right, a place in every general survey of contemporary art. One reason for their prestige is that they have revealed, or at least suggested to many modern artists, the possibility of a quite new kind of painting. Thus when the Cubists sought to blaze new trails, the only guides they found were African, Oceanian and Mexican sculptors and, amongst the Europeans, "primitive" artists who had retained that freshness of approach which enabled them boldly to express themselves through signs and in a language of their own invention.

Thus these unschooled artists have taken their place in contemporary art history as more than charming "innocents." We have come to discern how much there is in common between Paul Klee and Louis Vivin, Hirshfield and the Surrealists; between Séraphine Louis and the non-figurative school. In short these once rejected painters have come into their own. One of them, the greatest, is in the Louvre. What of the others? we may wonder. Will the future confirm the prestige they now enjoy, or is this but a passing fashion? In any case there now is talk of giving African art a place in the Louvre.

Non-figurative Art after 1918

★

THE NAME of "abstract art" was appropriate enough when the method employed by its practitioners was a "taking away" *(abstrahere)*, that is to say a removal stage by stage of the superficial aspects of an object, with a view to disclosing its basic plastic elements. It was thus that Mondrian (as we have seen) produced an abstract picture of a tree and one of the façade of a cathedral; Huszar, of the head of a young girl; and Van der Leck *Men riding Donkeys*—to name but a few outstanding examples of this procedure.

Actually, however, "non-figurative" would seem to be a more suitable epithet than "abstract." The latter term was suitable enough when the painter's method was one of elimination as described above. But from now on he makes the abstract his point of departure; he ceases trying to extract from an object its basic elements and takes to building up architecturally ordered compositions by means of plastic signs, creations of his mind alone. It is rather like what happened with Cubism in its hermetic and *papiers collés* periods. There is now no question of interpreting the thing seen under any form whatsoever; the painter visualizes formal arrangements of line or color in his mind—without reference to the outside world. Thus "non-figurative" (or non-representational) is a suitable description of a type of art which, from the period we are now considering, has persisted and developed up to the present day. As things stood in 1918, the non-figurative movement seemed to have succeeded in formulating to some extent its means, as illustrated in Mondrian's Neo-Plasticism and Kandinsky's abstract Expressionism respectively. And there was now a tendency to give these two forms of non-figurative art a new direction in which both participated.

Mondrian, who had confined himself hitherto to almost purely linear composition, no longer ruled out color. But, as might be expected, color was not given by him the dominant, constructive role assigned to it by Kandinsky and Delaunay. None the less when Mondrian introduced any new element into his work this was never gratuitous or unpremeditated. And when he took to using color, he refused to allow it to interfere with his conceptions of an Absolute unconnected with appearance. For Mondrian there is no question of constructing with color; nor does he now revert to the neutral, if richly modulated tones of the time when he employed the cubist palette. He does not yet ask of color its specific dynamism, its illusionist effects, the magical play of color patches and smooth, sweeping brushstrokes. Nothing of the kind. The streak of puritanism in his nature leads him to treat color as a strictly scientific phenomenon due to the absorption of light by surfaces. The function he assigns it is to fill spaces mapped out geometrically—usually squares, though occasionally rectangles. As regards his choice of colors, he limits himself to complementaries, put on quite flat without any visible traces of the brush within compartments mapped out by ruled black lines of considerable thickness. Mondrian's theory is that color should lie smoothly and evenly on the picture-surface, and must not be weakened by any modulations due to form; on the contrary, it must be set off by areas of non-color, that is to say of white, black or grey. It would seem that Mondrian's asceticism now can go no farther. For if he had carried this cult of absolute "purity" to its logical conclusion, nothing would have been left but to reduce his compositions to a few cut squares of, for example, white paper, and to dispense with brushes, pigment, pencils, even canvases.

Nevertheless, we feel that he still had a secret, unavowed hankering after the world of visual experience, and presently he modified his geometric rigorism and even, as in earlier days,

PIET MONDRIAN. PAINTING NO. I. ⟶

In this picture Mondrian has banished all forms—diagonals or curves—suggesting any natural structure, nor has he allowed the slightest freedom to his brush. The surface is divided into strictly rectangular areas. As with his later work, it is only in his choice of colors that traces of organic life can still be felt. Here the relatively delicate modulations from color to color have, perhaps, a faint suggestion of "atmospheric" painting, or, anyhow, of the cubist use of monochrome.

PIET MONDRIAN (1872-1944). PAINTING NO. 1, 1921. (38 × 24")
MÜLLER-WIDMANN COLLECTION, BASEL.

drew inspiration from scenes of real life. Indeed he went so far as to give one of his most famous compositions the name of a Negro dance, *Boogie-Woogie*. Though, as might be expected, this color mosaic gives no idea of the choreographic frenzies the name suggests and any "human" element is entirely lacking, it proves that towards the close of his life his self-imposed asceticism was beginning to pall.

That the period we are now concerned with witnessed the climax of pure abstractionism is evidenced by the turn taken by Kandinsky's art. Between 1910 and 1914 he had obviously been enthralled by the wonderful possibilities of the effects of light and color suggested by his vision of the world, and produced some compositions of a sensuous loveliness by means of combinations of patches of color—indeed he stressed the "patchwork" nature of these works in their titles, *Picture with Three Patches*, *The Black Patch* and so forth. Actually in several of these compositions there are traces of figurative art that take us by surprise coming as they do in the midst of a frenzied riot of dabs of color, wholly chaotic and brilliantly, violently stimulating. But by dint of this very disorderliness, almost one might say meaninglessness, Kandinsky links up with the most absolute abstraction as manifested, though in a diametrically opposed manner, in the carefully planned constructions of such geometric-minded abstractionists as Mondrian.

None the less, round about 1920 there comes an almost startling change in Kandinsky's art, and one that brings him in line with Mondrian. He now seems, strangely enough, to submit himself to frankly architectural disciplines, and takes to adapting his forms to those of geometry. He goes about this by degrees. Instead of a disordered mingling of tints and forms, outpourings of the untrammelled sensuality we spoke of above, he now employs a sort of color calligraphy, much more discreet in nature, in which the color patch is replaced by line. And this line is controlled by a geometric lay-out, seemingly quite incompatible with Kandinsky's spontaneous temperament. There is no longer any question of more or less fantastic arabesques and he now uses quite regular curves played off against straight lines. Both are located in a space of a special kind, conceived in terms of Kandinsky's new pictorial architecture, while an over-all balance is created by arrangements of squares, triangles and rectangles as precisely drawn as in Mondrian's "diagrams."

The change is noteworthy. Whereas Kandinsky's early "splotchings" were wildly dynamic, uncontrolled by the mind, his art now is static, almost rigorously ordered. The only exception to this radical abstractionism is in the names he gives his pictures, names which show that he still bears in mind the impressions giving rise to them: *Floating Lightness*, *Quiet Thrill*, *Serenity*. Kandinsky seems to have entered on this calmer phase, perhaps simply because he needed a rest, but perhaps because he also felt the time had come to revise his earlier manner. In any case he now lightens the texture of his pictures, stressing their completely abstract qualities. So much so that in some of them, he (like Mondrian) denies himself even the luxury of occasional curves; as in the simple grouping of squares and rectangles which he names *Thirteen Right Angles* (actually there are forty!).

Artists of all periods have tended to be refractory to discipline and Kandinsky was no exception. He soon reverted to freer, more emotive forms of expression, and himself baptized this as his Romantic Period. Nevertheless he kept in mind the valuable lessons of his geometric phase and the necessity of making the picture a well-knit ordered structure; moreover, in the abstract works of his best disciples we can see that they profited by this salutary example. Under the influence of this strict but humanized discipline Kandinsky's art developed a restrained power that had been lacking in his earlier, impressionistic compositions.

Much the same thing happened with Delaunay and Magnelli, to cite two typical cases. The abstractness of Delaunay's *Circular Forms* was tempered with more human qualities in his sequence of *Runners*. As for Magnelli, who in 1915 was producing abstract, exclusively geometric works whose only possible name was the one he gave them, *Paintings*, his later compositions, while still more abstract, were not devoid of expressionist, even metaphysical tendencies, as suggested by the meaningful titles he bestowed on two of them, *Composed Reflection* and, notably, *Fabulous Calm*.

The Bauhaus Painters

★

AMONGST the ideas that have always appealed to vanguard artists is that of pooling their means and joining forces in a common cause; unhappily it usually turns out that such groups break up under the influence of internal dissensions, however sincere the enthusiasm of their individual members. It was such an ideal that led to the foundation of the Staatliches Bauhaus at Weimar in 1919, when a number of artists got together and drew up a working program in which their aims were set forth with both poetic fervor and precision. It was the architect Walter Gropius who took the lead in the new venture. The concluding phrase of the Manifesto ran as follows: "Let us then create a new guild of craftsmen free from that class-dividing arrogance which sets up an impassable barrier between the artist and the artisan. Let us all join in planning, seeking to bring into being, shoulder to shoulder, that new structure of the future in which architecture, sculpture and painting are harmoniously reunited. Millions of workers will help us to build up this glorious edifice in the skies of the future—a crystalline image of their faith in a new age."

The idea was obviously one of creating a sort of phalanstery *à la Fourier*, reviving the system of the mediaeval guilds. But the Bauhaus group had no intention of harking back to the past and to academic German art; they stood for the most modern art developments and were prepared to respect the independent efforts of individual artists, provided these fell in line with that united effort which was the keynote of the program drawn up by Gropius, the eminent founder of this "Advanced School of Creative Art," as he described it.

When we remember that amongst the teachers at the Bauhaus were not only Gropius but also Paul Klee, Oskar Schlemmer, Moholy-Nagy, Feininger and Kandinsky, the high importance of the venture becomes manifest. But the very fact that artists with such strong and inevitably conflicting personalities were on the teaching staff, was bound to undermine the cohesion of the group and thus to lessen its chances of survival. This was, in fact, the reason why symptoms of disruption soon appeared. There was a latent incompatibility between the architectural conceptions, the notions of measure and order, basic to the original program of the group, and the romantic, highly personal aspirations of men like Klee and Kandinsky. But worse was yet to come. From 1925 on, when the Bauhaus moved to Dessau, there was a slowing down of its activities due to the hostility of the National Socialists to all they stigmatized as "degenerate art." Finally, in May 1933, it had to be closed down.

Though the personalities of Klee and Kandinsky seemed hardly in keeping with the ideology of the Bauhaus, those of some other members of the teaching staff were more in line with it. Moholy-Nagy (1895-1946), whose aesthetic was affiliated to Russian Constructivism, was in charge of the metal workshop at the Bauhaus. His abstract compositions on plates of aluminum or polished steel were remarkable for their unusual light effects, the sudden gleams he conjured up on the surface of the metal. From 1925 to 1930 he supervised the editing of the famous series of Bauhaus books. In the thirties he migrated to Chicago, where in 1937 he founded a New Bauhaus on the lines of the old.

The art of Oskar Schlemmer (1888-1943) was in keeping with the conceptions of the founders of the Bauhaus; he was in fact a German Purist, aiming at purely plastic harmonies and avoiding all accidental or incidental forms.

Lyonel Feininger, too, remained faithful to the Bauhaus tradition throughout his long career, and his art is a sort of epitome of the group's aesthetic. Executed in a cubist technique devoid of any dryness, his compositions are thoroughly architectural in conception, and his geometrically ordered patterns, with their sumptuous color orchestration, imaginative yet well-controlled, have a fine emotive quality. After returning to the United States for good in 1936, Feininger, up to his death at the age of eighty-four on January 13, 1956, kept to his strikingly original mode of expression imbued with conviction and sincerity.

LYONEL FEININGER (1871-1956). GATEWAY AND TOWER I, 1924-1926. (24 ½ × 18 ½″)
DOETSCH-BENZIGER COLLECTION, BASEL.

The aim of the Bauhaus was to create an association of architects, sculptors and painters enabling them to pool their ideas, experiment with new techniques and in collaboration to produce work on thoroughly modern lines. Faithful to this program, Feininger made a point of introducing architectural concepts into his painting, without however abandoning the expression of his poetic vision of the world. Though in a general way he drew inspiration from the procedures invented by the Cubists round about 1908, he did not like them confine himself to a restricted range of colors. When an artist seeks to body forth his dreams, he usually does so at the expense of the formal structure of the picture. Feininger is an exception. All he jettisons is the factor of thickness ; surfaces of objects become transparent but their forms are geometrically precise ; everywhere there is an harmonious give-and-take between the architectural concept and the dream.

Paul Klee

A New World of Poetic Imagery

NOTHING, perhaps, is more characteristic of the artists of the first half of the present century than the tendency of each to build up his private world—and none of these private worlds is more remarkable than Paul Klee's. For it is above all a wonderland, as unreal as that of the fairy tale, in which anything may happen, a pumpkin be metamorphosed in the twinkling of an eye into a coach for Cinderella, a beanstalk scale the skies. Much as a Roman poet once said that everything he wrote became a line of poetry and Braque assures us that he "thinks in forms," so Klee thinks in terms of magic transformations. Some have laid stress on his "general culture" (a vague term at best and of doubtful relevance as regards an artist), his interest in literature, poetry and, above all, music, and no doubt these contributed to the flowering of his peculiar genius. But more to the point is the singular keenness of his visual perceptions, a sort of second sight; his ability, like those who as we say can read between the lines, of "reading between" the things he sees. In this sense only we may speak of culture with reference to Klee. He never indulged in—never wished to indulge in—scientific research in the strict sense of the term. Nor can we say that he was directly influenced by such early forms of art (however much he relished them) as Chinese, Indian, Egyptian, Pre-Columbian or Persian painting. No doubt he was keenly sensitive to the exotic charm of the East, to the works of the great oriental poets and story-tellers, in particular Firdousi and Hafiz, and to the glamour of the Arabian Nights. But the only use Klee made of the East, for his explorations of the realm of myth and buoyant fantasy that was his happy hunting-ground, was to borrow a Flying Carpet that transported him out of Space and Time into a world of fabulous encounters, incredible coincidences. These he depicts less as an artist than as a modern Prospero, less favored than Ariel's master, since, because he knew too much, some malefic fairy queen has prisoned him in the husk of an earthbound painter limited to the seven colors of the prism for the imaging of his escapades into the preposterous.

Basic to the essential magic of Klee's art is a curious alchemy by grace of which he transmutes unconsidered trifles that have caught his eye into objects of a totally different nature, and in this he differs from so many of his contemporaries who, it often seems, merely rearrange elements of visual experience in new patterns and modify them relatively little. For everything Klee sets eyes on conjures up automatically before him, through a nexus of "associations" irrational but systematic, images that have nothing at all to do with the retinal image, and these he promptly interprets in a language unlike any other pictorial language and stamped with the imprint of his unique, intriguing genius. Often indeed, without the need of any external stimulus, he finds himself composing little poems in paint that seem to have welled up, fully integrated, from that marvelous imagination of his, an imagination constantly replenished from those mysterious sources whence rise the metaphors of poets, the melodies of great composers—and also those disconcertingly apt remarks which children so often make. Perhaps it is not surprising that many have seen in Klee's art an adult equivalent of the art of children. But the analogy must not be pressed too far; a child's imagination is uncontrolled—in the sense that it allows free play to the vagaries of chance and is at the mercy of the moment. Thus even the best children's pictures are rarely more than lucky flukes, or one might say "arrested falls," since they are not so much trying to conjure up a new world in their imagination as to extricate themselves from their own world, a world by which they still are baffled. Klee, on the other hand, had no difficulty in breaking loose from a material environment which he studied for its own sake only at the very outset of his career as an artist; and he soon discovered his vocation: that of initiating us into that peculiar world of his whose wonders and delights unfurled themselves unceasingly upon the screen of his vivid imagination. He has described the evolution of his art as follows:

PAUL KLEE (1879-1940). VILLA R, 1919. (10⅛ × 8¾") KUNSTMUSEUM, BASEL.

"We used to represent things visible on earth, things we enjoyed seeing. Now we reveal the underlying reality of visible things and thus express our belief that visible reality is merely an isolated phenomenon, outnumbered by other, unseen realities. Thus things take on a vaster, more varied significance, often seemingly in contradiction with rational experience. Hence a tendency to stress the element of the essential in the random." He never troubled to review his technical means, and left to his inspiration the task of making its own rules. He always starts off without any fixed intention, from something he has chanced to see, then improvises on this theme with careless rapture, hardly knowing whither it will lead him or where he had better call a halt. Though one of the most striking things about his pictures is the rhythmic orchestration pervading them through and through, this rhythm has emerged quite naturally, not as the result of conscious planning. And the same holds good for his plastic organization; his mastery of form, line and color is innate, almost one might say automatic. Thus, when he talks of himself he never parades his ego, nor does he indulge in exhibitionism like so many of the Expressionists.

Moreover, in discussing art he is careful not to commit himself too precisely and keeps to generalities. "Color and I are one," he once remarked—and let it go at that. In his work we find the same discretion; it is always elegantly balanced and he never allows emotion to run wild. The furthest Klee goes, in fact, in the way of self-expression is in his use of allegories or parables suggesting his responses to the manifestations of life and nature. Thus he compares the creative process to the growth of a tree. "Within the artist a rich sap rises from the earth, permeating him and his visions, and he plays the part of the tree-trunk." It is interesting to note that when he describes the functioning of his inspiration, he frequently employs metaphors of an oriental tinge. As regards technique, he adapts it to the mood of the moment. Thus of the numerical proportions governing the interrelation of the picture's elements, he says: "These figures may seem cold and dead, but it is not so. They are full of the breath of life."

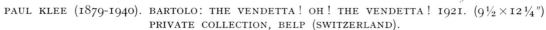

Paul Klee's world remains a very human one, to which he rarely omits to add a touch of whimsy, as in this *Vendetta*. Klee knows the "tears of things" but smiles through them. His sense of humor never leads him into mere facetiousness; it echoes the "laughter in heaven" of the Immortals. Wayward as it may seem, his calligraphy is always purposeful and to the point. For this great artist never allows his fancy to override his keen intelligence.

PAUL KLEE (1879-1940). BARTOLO: THE VENDETTA! OH! THE VENDETTA! 1921. (9½ × 12¼")
PRIVATE COLLECTION, BELP (SWITZERLAND).

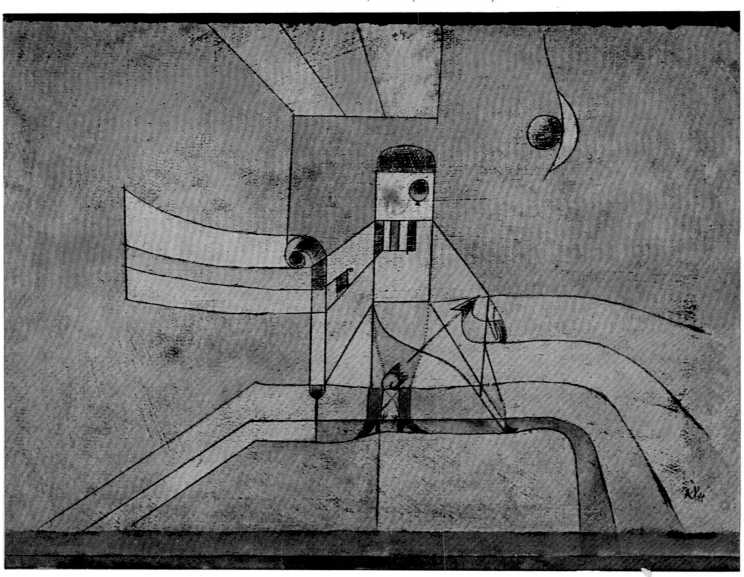

PAUL KLEE (1879-1940). THE ORDER OF THE HIGH C, 1921. (12½ × 8¾")
ROLAND PENROSE COLLECTION, LONDON.

PAUL KLEE (1879-1940). SENECIO, 1922. (16 × 15″) KUNSTMUSEUM, BASEL.

Klee's great devotion to the Douanier Rousseau is comprehensible. His method, in a word, is to have no method. If he played fast and loose with almost all the traditional rules of painting, this is because his sensibility alone guided his brush—which, unlike Goya's, knew better than he what he must do. In this connection, the affinities between Klee's art and popular painting, songs and music, are evident. He himself was a fine musician and a great admirer of Bach, but perhaps his spontaneous art, so full of brilliant improvisations, has more of the qualities peculiar to "hot" jazz. In it, too, we find a lively inventiveness, a wealth of colorful surprises, a direct poetic appeal and, with these, a mysterious power which grips us so effectively that we never pause to speculate what its subconscious origins may be.

This representation of an imaginary personage, whom the artist has baptized, for reasons unknown and perhaps not to be known, with the name of a Pacific island, sponsors his idea of organized escape from everybody and everything. The absence of any realistic referent heightens, in his opinion, the value of each element, and the conjunction of these elements generates an "extra" figure—a projection of the Subconscious—as compelling as any real figure. Thus Max Ernst conjures up sequences of irrational, hallucinating images, hinting of secrets behind the vagaries of chance. This work is obviously the outcome of some intense obsession and a stimulus which, though it may have consisted, originally, of some actual visual experience, has in the picture been given a totally different form. The spontaneity of this method (so characteristic of Max Ernst's art) and its poetic implications justify us in regarding the artist as the pioneer of surrealist painting; moreover, of all the group none has kept so persistently to the original program of the movement.

MAX ERNST (1891). CELEBES, 1921. (50 × 43 ¼") ROLAND PENROSE COLLECTION, LONDON.

Towards Surrealism

The Rise of Dada in France and Germany

NO SOONER was the war over than the Swiss Dada group, with some unadventurous exceptions, made a general move from Zurich to Paris. Immediately on their arrival Aragon, Tristan Tzara, Max Ernst, Soupault, Breton, Eluard, Man Ray, Ribemont-Dessaignes and Arthur Cravan organized a series of provocative demonstrations at the Palais des Fêtes and in the Berlioz and Gaveau concert-halls. The Dadaists believed in shock tactics, these gatherings were invariably uproarious and, as often as not, ended in free fights which only ceased when the police arrested the belligerents or cleared the hall. Several Dada reviews made their appearance: *Le Bulletin Dada, Dadaphone, Cannibale* and—much the most successful—*Littérature*. At the Au Sans Pareil Gallery Max Ernst, Picabia, Man Ray and Chirico exhibited *collages*, compositions deliberately anti-artistic in conception, whose novelty aroused much interest, if little real admiration.

As in New York and Zurich the Paris Dada movement was almost wholly indifferent to art *qua* art; it was essentially an intellectual revolt against the social order. In its program (anyhow in its definitive form, when the group had more or less agreed upon their aims) we find a satirical intent and a revolutionary desire to make a clean sweep of the past. Thoroughly disgusted with the follies and ugliness of the world around them, these excited young men denounced with equal fervor and contempt all its institutions and activities: war, the judiciary, the Church and State. But it is common knowledge that such outbursts of indignation, frequent in the course of history, have rarely done much, if anything, to remedy the order, or disorder, of the world at large.

The Dada movement died a natural death when its members realized that, in condemning the intelligence itself and placing the imbecile on an equal footing with the man of brains, they, too, were using their intelligence and in the last analysis employing exactly the same logical methods as those they anathematized. Having destroyed everything, the only course left to the conscientious Dadaist was to destroy himself. Thus Arthur Cravan gave a symbolic demonstration of the logical conclusion of the Dada adventure when, going on to the platform to give a lecture on "Suicide," he announced that he would begin by killing himself, produced a revolver and fired several shots. Anyhow in 1922 the Dada group broke up as uproariously as it had begun, with an exchange of insults and reciprocal accusations of "deviationism."

A Dada movement was launched in Germany in 1917 by Richard Hülsenbeck; its first demonstration was staged in Berlin in 1918, several painters, writers and sculptors, amongst them Raoul Hausmann and George Grosz, taking part in it. Hausmann exhibited *photomontages* and sculpture in the Marcel Duchamp manner. Grosz made his name with savage caricatures of German militarism and the middle class.

The Berlin Dada group had a strongly political bias, the chief targets for attack being the decadent imperialism responsible for a disastrous war and all the human suffering it had entailed. Hausmann founded a review *Der Dada* and amongst its contributors were Tzara, Grosz, Baader, Hülsenbeck, Mehring and Picabia. It featured *collages, photomontages* and faked photographs in which a "dream reality" was evoked by absurd ensembles of objects. In Cologne Dada was sponsored by Max Ernst and Baargeld. The latter founded a Dada newspaper *Der Ventilator* which was suppressed by the British Army of Occupation. Ernst produced a series of *collages* entitled *Fatagaga*, while Arp collaborated on a review *Die Schammade*. Meetings were held at the Winter Beerhouse—until the police intervened. The promoter of the movement at Hanover was Kurt Schwitters, who published a series of *collages* titled *Merz*. After taking refuge in England he made so-called "Merz constructions" which, however, were not conceived in the purely destructive spirit of Picabia's and Marcel Duchamp's productions, but revealed certain positive tendencies that were subsequently exploited by Surrealism.

1924-1938

1924 André Breton publishes the **Surrealist Manifesto** in Paris. Launching of the review **La Révolution Surréaliste** • Picasso paints the curtain for the ballet **Le Train Bleu** and designs sets and costumes for **Mercure** • Juan Gris lectures at the Sorbonne on "The Possibilities of Painting" • Braque does sets for **Salade** • Film: Léger's **Le Ballet Mécanique** • First Klee Exhibition in New York at the Société Anonyme.

1925 First Group Exhibition of the Surrealists at the Galerie Pierre, Paris, with Arp, Chirico, Max Ernst, Klee, Man Ray, Masson, Miro, Picasso, Pierre Roy • At the International Exhibition of Decorative Arts Dufy exhibits dress material printed in mordant colors in Poiret's house-boat on the Seine • Death of La Fresnaye at Grasse • Mondrian's book **Die Neue Gestaltung** (New Representation) published in the Bauhaus series.

1926 Max Ernst publishes **Histoire naturelle**, rubbings, and holds an exhibition in Paris • Klee and Chagall have their first one-man shows in Paris and New York respectively • Opening in Paris of the Galerie Surréaliste (March 26), which does not close until 1929 • Calder comes to Paris • Van Doesburg publishes the **Manifesto of Elementarism** (**De Stijl**, no. 75-76) • Christian Zervos launches the **Cahiers d'Art** in Paris • Duchamp produces **Anemic Film**.

1927 Matisse wins the Carnegie Prize • Death of Juan Gris and Sérusier • Gabo and Pevsner do strange geometric scenery for Diaghilev's ballet **La Chatte** • Tanguy, Arp, Max Ernst exhibitions in Paris.

1928 Derain wins the Carnegie Prize • Miro paints his **Dutch Interiors** • André Breton publishes **Le Surréalisme et la peinture** • Picasso at Dinard: series of **Women bathing**.

1929 Opening of the Museum of Modern Art, New York • Breton publishes the **Second Surrealist Manifesto** • Chirico does sets for **Bal**, Ballets Russes de Monte-Carlo • Sets by Rouault for Diaghilev's ballet **Le fils prodigue** • Max Ernst publishes his collage-novel **La femme 100 têtes** • Death of Diaghilev at Venice • International Exhibition of Abstract Art in Zurich • Dali and Luis Bunuel produce the film **Un chien andalou**.

1930 Chirico does sets for **The Life of Orestes** at the Krolloper, Berlin, and illustrates Apollinaire's **Calligrammes** • Dali publishes **La femme visible** • Van Doesburg launches the review **Art Concret** • First number of magazine **Le Surréalisme au service de la révolution** • Picasso wins Carnegie Prize • Pascin commits suicide.

1931 Dakar-Djibouti ethnographical mission, led by Marcel Griaule • **L'âge d'or**, second film by Dali and Bunuel, is shown at Studio 28, Paris • Chagall illustrates the Bible, Braque the **Theogony** of Hesiod, Segonzac Virgil's **Georgics** and Picasso the **Metamorphoses** of Ovid • Death of Van Doesburg • Matisse travels to Tahiti • Sculpture-objects by Giacometti • Miro does sets for the ballet **Jeux d'enfants** at Monte-Carlo.

1932 **Abstraction-Creation** group founded in Paris, with Mondrian, Gabo, Pevsner, Vantongerloo, Gorin, Hélion, Herbin, Domela, Del Marle, Vordemberge-Gildewart and others • Skira publishes Mallarmé's **Poésies** with etchings by Matisse • Expelled from Dessau the Bauhaus moves to Berlin • First Calder Exhibition (mobiles) in Paris • Picasso Retrospective at Georges Petit Gallery, Paris.

1933 Following Hitler's seizure of power, Schmidt-Rottluff is expelled from the Berlin Academy of Fine Arts and Schlemmer forced to quit his teaching post. Schwitters goes into exile, settling near Oslo, while Klee returns to Switzerland. Kandinsky leaves Germany, settles at Neuilly, near Paris. The Berlin Bauhaus is closed down • Last numbers of **Le Surréalisme au service de la révolution**. First number of the review **Minotaure**, launched by Skira • Matisse completes the mural decorations commissioned by Dr Barnes for his museum at Merion, Pa.

1934 Dali illustrates **Les Chants de Maldoror** for Skira • Marcel Duchamp publishes **La Boîte**, containing reproductions of his works • Max Ernst publishes his collage-novel **Une semaine de bonté** • Breton publishes **Qu'est-ce que le Surréalisme?** illustrated by Magritte.

1935 Death of Signac and Malevitch • Dali publishes **La Conquête de l'Irrationnel.**

1936 International Surrealist Exhibition in London • Outbreak of the Spanish Civil War: Picasso named Director of the Prado • Marin Retrospective at the Museum of Modern Art, New York • Sophie Täuber-Arp launches the review **Plastique** at Meudon, near Paris.

1937 Paris World's Fair: decorations by Delaunay, Dufy, Gromaire, Bonnard, Léger, Lhote, Munch, Bissière, Chastel, Coutaud, Gischia, Pignon, Lapicque, Manessier and others • Léger does sets and costumes for Lifar's ballet **David triomphant** at the Paris Opera • Exhibition in Paris of "Maîtres de l'art indépendant," including Rouault, Braque, Matisse • Feininger returns to New York, Beckmann takes refuge in Amsterdam. In Germany the National Socialist government ruthlessly confiscates thousands of works by the best modern artists • Moholy-Nagy founds the **New Bauhaus** in Chicago • Picasso paints **Guernica**, engraves **Songes et mensonges de Franco**.

1938 International Surrealist Exhibition at the Galerie des Beaux-Arts, Paris • Second Salon d'Art Mural in Paris: Matisse, Picasso, Léger, Delaunay, Gleizes, Villon, Lurçat, Derain • Carl Hofer wins the Carnegie Prize.

Surrealism

★

THE FORM of sensibility which Surrealism illustrates is not without precedents in the history of art. The element of novelty is that the Surrealists have sought to give it precision, a well-defined aesthetic, and thus to body forth a wholly new conception of the relations between Man and the world that he regards as "real," a world that to the Surrealists' thinking it is possible and indeed obligatory to transcend.

We have seen how in the course of its development Modern Painting has oscillated between two tendencies, sometimes divergent and sometimes interacting. These attitudes were determined by the answer given the question: Is painting intended to give pleasure or to serve as an indispensable mode of knowledge of the outside world? In Surrealism we seem to have a movement inspired by that spirit of scientific research to which reference has already been made and which invites painting to contribute to a deeper understanding of life and our reactions to it; an understanding which cannot be arrived at by contemplation of the phenomenal world.

For the Surrealist, visual experience is something to be transcended. The inadequacy of the retinal image had, as we have seen, been recognized by Cubism, which sought to represent that which was perceived by the mind's eye and shaped by conscious thought. Primitives of all periods followed the same methods in their depictions of fabulous events, in their evocations of the magical and esoteric, and thus had contributed to the exploration of the secret places of the mind of Man. But the Surrealists went much further in this direction and in fact maintained that there was a total cleavage between objective reality and the stuff of human consciousness. There was no longer any question of depicting a selected subject and the artist sought, rather, to express a reality existing wholly in his consciousness.

Thus surrealist art was not intended to be a source of pleasure or even of visual thrills. It involved an introspective study of the Self and its object was to get down to life's ultimate significance and to discover an inner world replacing the objective world the eye perceives. In short Surrealism set up to be a branch of science as well as an art form, and when a Surrealist speaks of "poetry" with reference to his work, he is far from having in mind the lyricism we associate with certain manifestations of traditional art. This indeed, like other traditional forms of expression, was excluded from the surrealist program, and the poetic quality envisaged by the Surrealists was more of the nature of the scientific imagination which gives birth to new inventions.

It was from the Subconscious alone that Surrealism drew its inspiration and one of its aims was to unify and reconcile the promptings of the Subconscious. This unity was envisaged in terms of a rigorously methodical system combining in an organic whole such logically contradictory entities as "life and death, the past and the future, the real and the imaginary," to quote from the list drawn up by André Breton, who in 1924 published the famous Surrealist Manifesto. The artist was called on to create a poetic unity between the perceptions of waking consciousness and representations of dream states that had hitherto been ignored. "I believe," wrote Breton, "that in the future the two apparently contradictory states—the dream and reality—will merge into a reality-absolute, a surreality."

Obviously, so far as painting was concerned, this entailed the rejection of all time-honored art procedures and the creation of wholly new ones, since the surrealist painter's concern was to give objective expression under deliberately anti-conventional forms to subjective images no less unorthodox. The task he thus assigned himself was evidently difficult to perform, but the way was made easier when in their campaign against the rational the Surrealists had recourse to material supplied by dreams, nightmares, hallucinations, delirium and even by insanity which, agreeing with Eluard, they regarded as a manifestation of the "pure reason" in its freest, most authentic form.

JOAN MIRO (1893). MATERNITY, 1924. (36 × 28¾″)
ROLAND PENROSE COLLECTION, LONDON.

Miro seizes on the most significant details of his subject and isolates them so as to give them greater emphasis. Here these are the mother's breast and the child, which figure in opposite corners of the picture, seen full face and in profile. Fine-spun, delicate lines ensure the continuity between the various elements, and assign each its place in space.

JOAN MIRO (1893). HARLEQUIN CARNIVAL, 1924-1925. (26 × 36½")
ALBRIGHT ART GALLERY, BUFFALO, N. Y.

IN HIS early compositions such as *The Farm*, when he was still under the influence of his formative years in Catalonia, Miro employed the imaginary space we have spoken of in connection with the Cubists and which is one of the distinctive, and not least attractive, features of all Primitive art. Even at this early stage he treated objects as independent entities, little worlds apart, which move and have their being without reference to the spatial relations which in the "real" world would determine their positions on the picture-surface and vis-à-vis each other. Like the Primitives Miro located objects in a space created solely in his imagination and according to the relative importance he assigned them, their hierarchy so to speak, and invested each with a specific magical or ritual aura. When he joined forces with the Surrealists and the concept of poetic transmutation released him from any obligation as regards the object, Miro continued to represent a world existing only in the imagination and peopled it with all the forms suggested to him by his prolific fancy, and also with splashes of vivid color that now were freed from any obsession with local tones. Henceforth he devoted himself to the depiction of a universe entirely composed of hieroglyphic signs, a new vocabulary of his own, which were to be interpreted, like the Egyptian hieroglyphs, not singly but in terms of their combinations and of the special meanings he ascribed to them. Thus in Miro's later art hieroglyphic signs have taken the place of the objects he depicted in his Catalan period. But all these galaxies of tiny suns and moons, of "Women-Birds-and-Stars," are intended to produce the "shock" of which Matisse had spoken on the beholder. They remind us of the symbols and allegories dear to oriental art, and their effect is heightened by Miro's use of pure, brilliant colors and his dextrous handling of tones. Devoid as they are of any realistic connotation, Miro's compositions suggest above all a *will to metamorphosis*,

247

the result of that myth-making propensity which characterizes the romantic mind. It was Géricault who said, "I set out to make a picture of a woman and it ends up as a lion," and, similarly, the fauns and centaurs of mythology started off with human forms before being metamorphosed into hybrid, half-animal beings.

One has the impression that the elements of Miro's pictures, his hieroglyphic signs, are strewn upon the canvas without any apparent connecting links (the truncated phrases of some modern poems produce much the same effect). In fact one has the impression of a sort of celestial globe on which the constellations are arrayed in glittering immobility. But that immobility is deceptive; these signs are caught up in a rotary movement and actuated by a centrifugal force that, without dispersing them, holds them on their orbits, like tiny stars which might fancy themselves freely moving but are subjected to the tug of gravitation and the initial impulse conditioning their courses. And this initial impulse, the ordered rhythm of their gyration, has been imparted to them by their creator, the artist.

Miro is one of the few surrealist painters who have shown an active interest in the technical problems of art, and he has made contributions of his own in various fields. He has much of the spirit of the craftsman and this has led him to try his hand at such various modes of artistic expression as engraving, sculpture and ceramics. To all these ventures he has brought the almost juvenile enthusiasm and gay temerity that are characteristic of his art. Thus he has paid little heed to the "psychic automatism" preconized in the Surrealist Manifesto, nor has he been satisfied with the over-simplified, not to say academic, means which other Surrealists found sufficient for their purpose—that is to say, the interpretation in a clear, forthright style of ideas which are often far from forthright. Miro's approach to art has always been of an essentially painterly order; potent as is his imagination, he has subordinated its demands to the expression of his marvelous feeling for color, and indeed he ranks beside Matisse, Léger and Klee as one of the greatest colorists of modern times.

ANDRÉ MASSON (1896). CHILDREN EATING A FISH, 1928. (6½ × 9½")
HERMANN RUPF COLLECTION, BERN.

YVES TANGUY (1900-1955). FOUR O'CLOCK IN SUMMER: HOPE, 1929. (51¼ × 38″)
PRIVATE COLLECTION, PARIS.

In the art of Tanguy we see the furthest point reached in the exploration of the unknown. For he no longer needs, like Chirico, to have recourse to elements of reality diverted from their natural contexts or, like Ernst, to make use of unusual substances. He builds up a world antecedent to the world of sight, and bathed in a crystalline air peopled with strange, inchoate forms. This is no coldly abstract creation, but as it were a preview of another reality, yet to be.

SALVADOR DALI (1904). A GIRAFFE AFLAME, 1935. (13¾ × 10¾″)
KUNSTMUSEUM, BASEL.

One of the reasons why the Surrealists denounce so vigorously everyone who does not share their views is the disgust inspired in them by the (to their mind) scandalous indifference of most painters to social conditions and contemporary politics. For they believe that the world is heading for disaster and that the artist, as a good citizen, should do his best to remedy this state of affairs. Hence their scorn for the "bureaucratic practitioners" of the still life of three apples on a plate, nude women on sofas, and smiling landscapes—tedious stereotyped subjects that have nothing in common with their aspirations for a new and better world.

By 1925 André Masson had been completely won over to this view. His art is rageful, dramatic, charged with dark forebodings. One feels that his mind is constantly haunted by presentiments of evil, of massacres, worldwide havoc. He is, in fact, the most highly strung of all the modern romantic revolutionaries. His work is steeped in an atmosphere of eroticism and cruelty; he conjures up scenes of carnage, crime and creatures preying on each other, and if a collective title for his pictures were needed, that of the famous book by Maurice Barrès, *Du sang, de la volupté et de la mort*, would be perfectly appropriate. Nothing could be further from Masson's purpose than to depict actual events or episodes of history and like all Surrealists he mistrusts "artistic" themes. He relies solely on the alchemy of his imagination, which automatically transmutes all the subjects visualized by it. In any case Masson does not regard the outside world as an object but as a subject of which he himself forms part, that is to say he feels himself not an onlooker but inside it, and implicit in his art is a sort of pantheism that lies at the source of his wholly logical and integral "automatism."

But Masson's mistrust of art has not prevented him from giving free rein to his personal abilities as an artist and these are of a very high order. In his work line and color are governed by the rhythms of an elemental dynamism, that of the world into which he has integrated his personality. A world of sudden, violent death, always at the mercy of unpredictable upheavals akin to those periodic cataclysms which take place in the bowels of the earth and to which are due so many chance "meetings" (like those which fascinated Lautréamont), for example the presence of fauna of the Ice Age alongside tropical vegetation. And from these strange encounters, from the clash of opposing fields of force, arise those tensions and bursts of livid light which give Masson's art its compelling power.

Though in basing their art on the prompting of the subliminal self and a cult of the irrational the Surrealists were led to ban the processes of logic, their revolt against the thinking mind was not, like that of the Dadaists, merely iconoclastic and satirical in intent. One of the major figures of Surrealism, Tanguy had no sympathy with the anarchism of Dada, but aimed at using the irrational for constructive ends. Though he lived much in Paris, Tanguy came of Breton stock and the glamour of the ancient land of Brittany, its folktales and superstitions, was ever present in his mind. In the "Brief Dictionary of Surrealism" play is made with his name, which to a French hearer suggests the two words *temps* (time) and *gui* (mistletoe), and he is entitled "Guide to the age of the Druid adepts of the Mistletoe." In the unfathomed depths of skies and seas Tanguy sought to discover the secrets of a hidden life beyond the ken of science and the scope of normal vision. For only to the artist is it given to perceive the eerie presences that fill the upper air, or the sunken cathedrals, celebrated in music by Debussy, and the queer, amorphous creatures, like figments of a mad poet's dream, that haunt the sea-depths. It was not until he was twenty-two that Tanguy took to painting, after the sight of a picture by Chirico had given him a sudden revelation of the mysterious significances latent beneath the surface of everyday reality. Such is the amazing intensity of Tanguy's imagery and its imaginative richness that we can only glimpse its meanings; yet he convinces us that this strange world of glimmering forms and embryonic entities really exists, though in order to perceive it we might need a Wellsian transfer into the Fourth Dimension.

Even in his teens, as an art student at the School of Fine Arts, Barcelona, Salvador Dali was regarded as a subversive element; indeed, his teacher and fellow students were thoroughly scandalized by his enthusiastic championship of Chirico's Metaphysical Art and its challenge to traditional realism. Nevertheless he spared no pains in learning the secrets of academic technique and he showed a quite remarkable aptitude for reproducing the illusionist effects obtained by such painters as Cotan and Zurbaran in their still lifes. He has deliberately cultivated this gift for intensely naturalistic representation and complete verisimilitude, throughout his career.

The impression produced by most of Dali's pictures is less one of spontaneous inspiration than of methods well thought-out and systematized. Indeed Dali himself makes no secret of this, for he has expounded his theory of art, with its premises and corollaries, in detail and with logical precision. From what he writes we gather that he is hostile to several Dadaist and Surrealist conceptions, in particular the notion that the artist should avoid any sort of submission to the dictates of the reasoning mind.

Then, again, whereas the Surrealists make a point of rejecting lock, stock and barrel all the means of traditional art, Dali has always been quite ready to employ them and indeed shown much interest in those painters of the past who, though interpreting familiar subjects with considerable freedom and creating rhythmic orchestrations of their own, remained faithful after their fashion to the data furnished by the retinal image and to the patterns into which these naturally fall. Dali was particularly attracted by the Romanesque Catalan painters and their weird, symbolical interpretations of themes culled from the New Testament, especially the Book of Revelations; also by their allegorical imagings of strange animals. Indeed whatever may be the association of ideas behind his *Giraffe Aflame*, this picture has quite obvious affinities with those Catalan frescos in which we see the wings of angels or the haunches of St Luke's ox starred with gaping human eyes. But it is above all to the color-schemes and to the patina of ancient canvases that he has recourse in order to intensify the more bizarre aspects of that illusionist realism of which he is a past master.

The careful planning basic to his technique is paralleled by his personal aesthetic. Herein he differs from such artists as Miro, Masson and Tanguy who have always aimed at exteriorizing deeply felt emotions under forms spontaneously suggested by the promptings of their Subconscious and uncontrolled by any set plan. Dali, on the other hand, has built up his "metaphysical" universe bit by bit and systematically, using as his material not only dreams but hallucinations and more or less deliberately provoked states of delirium. To this end he has studied text-books of psycho-pathology and come to the conclusion that all great artists suffer from that form of mental disease known as paranoia. This may be defined as the gradual development, usually under the impact of external stimuli, of a permanent state of delirium which dominates the mind, conations and activities of the paranoiac, though he may not suffer from any organic complaint. This pathological condition, which gives rise to various phobias and mental aberrations, is one which, to Dali's thinking, can be organized and directed towards artistic creativity. He describes the paranoiac-critical activity as "a spontaneous method of irrational apprehension based on a critical-interpretational association of the phenomena of delirium." As Breton has rightly pointed out the use of this would-be scientific jargon itself springs from what a psychiatrist might call a "benign" form of paranoia, that is to say one which involves no permanent derangement and manifests itself sporadically. It would seem that, with all his earnestness, Dali has a sense of humor that enables him to exploit to whimsical effect the "errors of logic" which he preaches and practices. In so doing he often shows more sleight of mind than truly poetic emotion, notably when he invests objects carefully selected for this purpose with a symbolism deriving ostensibly from "paranoiac delusions." "Bear well in mind," he has said, "that those limp watches of which there has been so much talk are nothing else than paranoiac-critical camembert cheeses—soft, fantastic, existing in Time and Space."

Successful as are some of Dali's compositions, it must be admitted that the general effect of his work was to lead Surrealism to that dead-end which so many art movements come up against when, in default of any authentically pregnant inspiration, an artist falls back on systems and artificial stimuli. Dali's mistake was to replace the untrammelled spontaneity called for by Surrealist art by somewhat labored fantasies, rationalized irrationalities.

SURREALISM AROUND THE WORLD. REPRODUCED FROM "MINOTAURE," NO. 10, 1937.

The fact that Max Ernst never went through any art school and that the subject he studied at the University of Bonn (from 1909 to 1914) was philosophy may throw light on his highly original approach to art. None was better qualified than he to appraise what lay behind the conflict between the logic of the reasoning mind and Dada's deliberate unreason when, after serving and being wounded in the First World War, he too decided that there was something rotten in the state of Europe and that the disastrous years he had lived through proved the stupidity, indeed malevolence, of the powers-that-be in every European country. Before coming to Paris to join forces with his French colleagues in their campaign against the old order, Ernst had launched a Dada movement in Cologne. Hitherto his only incursion into the world of art had been an exhibition of his paintings at the First Autumn Salon, sponsored by Der Sturm in 1913 at Berlin, and these pictures showed abilities nothing short of startling in a self-taught artist. The part he played, however, in the German Dada movement was primarily of a political order, an expression of his disgust with the aftermath of defeat, the ignominious collapse of German imperialism and the moral and physical degradation he saw prevailing on all sides.

It was not until 1919 that he resorted to the medium of art to give expression to these feelings, and on the methodical lines to which his training in philosophy had schooled him he set to ridiculing traditional aesthetic by "collages" in which fragments of photographs or engravings were arranged in irrational, anecdotic combinations, in terms of "the exploitation of the chance meetings of two incongruous realities on a plane of unsuitability." This was, in fact, a typical surrealist procedure, and it constituted the first step towards the discovery of "a universe supplementary to ours," not merely plausible but veridical. Ernst relied on the vagaries of chance as a means to the discovery of psychically disturbing associations of elements not normally seen together, the classical example of which was Lautréamont's "chance meeting of a sewing-machine and an umbrella on a dissecting table." However in 1925 Max Ernst decided to try his hand at a new technique involving the use, conventional though this might be, of brush and pencil. It turned out that he was an accomplished draftsman, gifted with all the traditional excellences in that field: boldness and sureness of line, disciplined concision and expressive power. It was in the course of these experiments that he invented a new technique which he named *frottage* (rubbing). This consisted in rubbing paper with charcoal or a graphite pencil over a more or less uneven surface, such as a gnarled floorboard, a thickly veined leaf, a strip of sacking or a rough wall, and the effect was like that of "brass-rubbing." In the patterns thus produced he saw images of a weirdly obsessive order like those which Leonardo and Botticelli had discerned on irregularly mottled surfaces, for example a wall against which a sponge soaked with various paints had been thrown. Children, invalids and day-dreamers, also, have this knack of discovering "hidden" images of figures or objects on curtains, woodwork and the like.

We must add that Max Ernst soon advanced beyond this rather elementary procedure and that he has succeeded, by methods nearer to the normal, in creating hallucinating visions in which fragments of visual experience are arranged in combinations of an unusual, disturbing kind, sometimes monumental in conception and always powerfully emotive. And the choice and arrangement of these pictorial elements in his work are always marked by a refreshing spontaneity, a far-ranging imagination and the visionary fervor of an authentically poetic temperament.

As we have seen, Surrealism introduced all sorts of new practices in painting, drawing and sculpture, the novelties ranging from *frottages* to the making of objects with substances that no sculptor had ever dreamt of employing hitherto.

Man Ray decided to make photography his starting-off point, but to add something of his own to the purely mechanical operation of the camera. It is well known that a skillful photographer can produce synthetic, character-revealing portraits of his sitters, especially if the latter co-operate with him intelligently, and some of the portraits made by Man Ray on these lines have become justly famous. Another kind of photograph Man Ray brought to perfection was the quite realistic representation of carefully arranged objects whose very

MAX ERNST (1891). THE CITY, 1936. (23½ × 31½″) PRIVATE COLLECTION, ZURICH.

immobility produced on the beholder the same disturbing sensations as the intense stillness of the objects in Chirico's pictures of his pre-metaphysical period. But these almost entirely mechanical procedures gave little or no scope for the expression of the artist's personal emotion, and now Man Ray devised the technique of what was called the "rayograph." In his "rayograms" he associated with his models objects or fragments of objects calculated to create that atmosphere of "chance encounters," a dislocation of everyday reality, which is basic to surrealist art and to which it largely owes its weirdly hallucinating effects.

The form of automatic painting which Dominguez called "decalcomania" is somewhat in the same spirit. Dominguez' method was to smear a flat surface with paints of various colors put on haphazard, then to apply to it a sheet of white paper, and by pressing this down or moving it back and forth, to secure a transfer (hence the name *décalcomanie*, meaning "transfer"); the result of the process being a picture charged with mysterious messages emanating presumably from the Subconscious. Paalen invented a similar process that he named smoke-pictures *(fumages)*. His method was to drop blobs of ink of various colors on a sheet of paper and then spin it in the open air or blow on it so that the colors fanned out in all directions, the result being a picture as "automatic" as anyone could wish for.

Meanwhile, under the general description of "objects with symbolic functions" the Surrealists constructed all sorts of queer objects of no practical utility whatever but answering to purely poetic requirements. Their object was to draw attention to those strangely suggestive coincidences and resemblances which stimulate the mysterious workings of the subconscious and give us glimpses of a world beyond our ken. At the 1938 International Surrealist Exhibition in Paris many such curious artefacts were shown and their effect was certainly startling and, as all who visited it will agree, unforgettable.

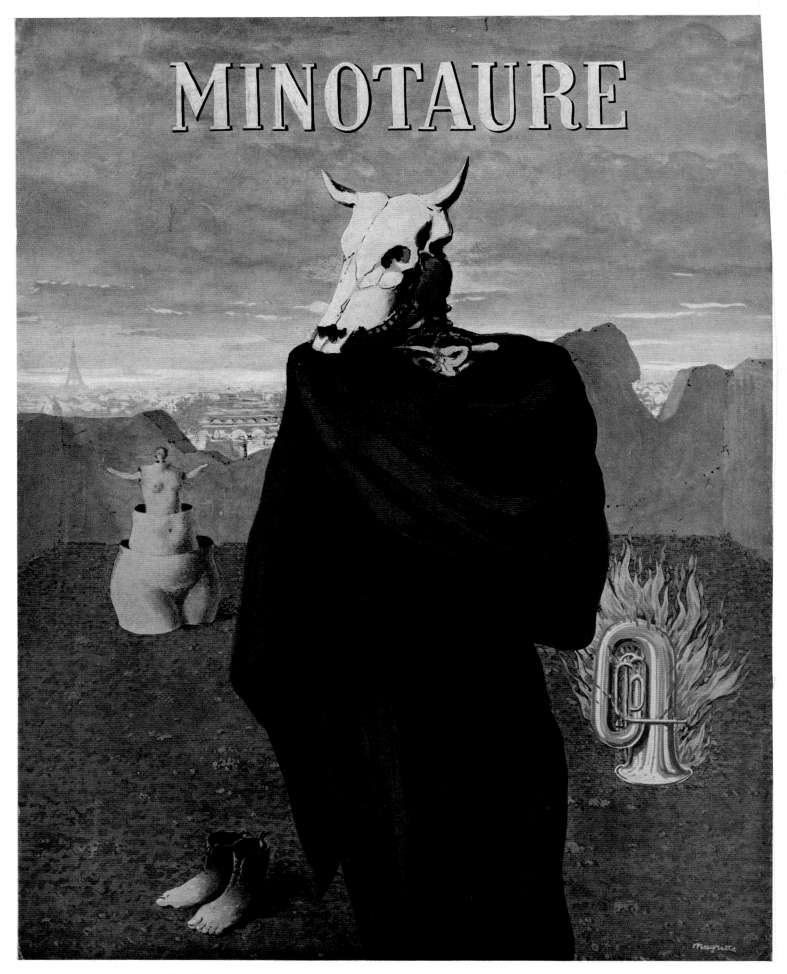

RENÉ MAGRITTE (1898). COVER OF "MINOTAURE," NO. 10, 1937. REPRODUCED FROM THE ORIGINAL GOUACHE.

Several surrealist artists seem to have had almost uncanny premonitions of future events. This weird form, a bull's skeleton draped in a black toga and standing erect upon the shattered fortifications of the City of Paris, might well be a grim prophetic symbol of the catastrophe which was soon to overwhelm France.

Despite the fact that Surrealism was international in scope and dealt in universal values, several surrealist artists were obviously influenced by their racial background and the traditions of their native lands.

Thus, for example, the Belgian Surrealists René Magritte, Paul Delvaux and Mambour seem never to have felt any wish to discard the realistic tendencies congenital to Flemish art. And though the directive ideas behind their compositions are certainly the same as those of such artists as Max Ernst, Masson, Arp, Tanguy and Miro, there is a marked difference in their handling of the content of the picture.

René Magritte never disintegrates the object. Associations of ideas may suggest to him the bringing together of incongruous elements in the characteristic surrealist manner, but he does not have recourse to far-fetched technical procedures or startling distortions of reality; he depicts these objects under frankly realistic aspects which in themselves suffice to create a poetic atmosphere tinged with magic. Magritte in fact has that instinctive, wholly human craving for the Marvelous, for revelations of what lies behind the veil, which is common to so many artists, not Surrealists alone. He himself has declared that the physical reality of the object whose secret significance the artist wishes to elicit must be regarded as initial to the creative act, and on no account whatever must he lose sight of it.

Delvaux, too, has no truck with automatism, paranoiac visions, or chance meetings of unlikely objects. On the face of it his imagery is frankly naturalistic, but he charges it with disturbing intimations, a sense of the mysterious secrets latent in the commonplace. His compositions are peopled with plump nude women, whose faces are exactly, almost obsessively alike, but whose wide-open eyes suggest a curious expectancy, as if they were waiting for a summons from some messenger of the Beyond.

Generally speaking, Surrealists outside France seem to have concerned themselves less with creating a new world, than with eliciting the vital secrets of the world we know. In the throes of their crusading fervor, the orthodox Surrealists—and the Dadaists before them—had never paused to consider the sad but certain truth that human nature changes but little with the ages, despite the laudable attempts so often made to better it. Or perhaps the provocative, rather querulous tone of their early pronouncements was due to the fact that they guessed as much, and hated to admit it. Nevertheless there is no doubt that Surrealism acted as a healthy stimulus and fanned to a flame the unrest that had been smoldering in the minds of artists; an unrest whose reasons they had hitherto ignored but which, they now perceived, was due both to the inadequacy of traditional conceptions of the human situation and to the cramping effect of academic form. And by directing their attention to a vast domain of the human mind that had been neglected hitherto, Surrealism did art a real service.

It was partly with this in mind, but also because they refused to endorse the view that the intellect was to be regarded as wholly nugatory, that the non-French Surrealists indulged so often in procedures that were primarily descriptive and devoid of any specifically creative purpose. Far from disdaining reality, they drew from it motifs deriving quite as much from scenes of the world around them as from psychological adventures, those "headlong dives into our inmost selves" advocated by André Breton.

In short, they reverted to the poetic methods employed by Chirico in his researches prior to his Metaphysical Period. The Chilean artist Matta Echaurren was far from repudiating traditional techniques and displayed an amazing gift for color. "The wonderful will flash forth," he said, "like the fluorescence of a ruby bathed in ultra-violet light," and he gave free rein to his poetic imaginings in fantastic journeys into astral worlds. The Austrian Paalen explored the magical possibilities of totemism, while the Rumanian artist Brauner found in monsters and their curious ambivalence intimations of a universe of signs and wonders. Many other artists interpret reality in terms of magic: amongst them, the British painters Leonora Carrington, W. S. Hayter and John Tunnard; the Americans Sullivan, Peter Blume, Howard, Ferren; the Italians Donati and Guglielmi. Son of a Cuban mother and a Chinese father, Wilfredo Lam has conjured up tragic evocations of strange imaginary scenes in a world of atavistic folklore, and devised for their expression a startling, highly original technique.

MAX BECKMANN (1884-1950). CENTER PANEL OF THE TRIPTYCH "DEPARTURE," 1932-1935.
(84¾ × 45⅜"). MUSEUM OF MODERN ART, NEW YORK.

PABLO PICASSO (1881). THE MUSE, 1935. (51¼×63¾″) MUSÉE D'ART MODERNE, PARIS.

PREMONITIONS OF CATASTROPHE

IN THE COURSE of its successive phases, Picasso's art had assumed many forms and his imagination had led him to indulge in a vast, almost bewildering diversity of manners of expression. But soon the humanly emotive side of his artistic personality—which for so many years he had masked with a show of smiling or superb indifference—was to come dramatically to the fore. It is clear that he had a presentiment of the Spanish Civil War whose tragedy and horrors were soon to wring his heart. And now his exasperation with the world at large and his innate truculence led him to apply himself to tearing to pieces systematically whatever he laid hands on, though not without an eye to reconstruction with the shattered fragments. With a sort of savage glee he now dissects his model, disembodies, disintegrates it; then forces it into conformity with the laws of a predetermined architectural concept. Notable in his compositions is the frequency of acute angles and such few curves as he employs are serrated with jagged notches. Colors seem to be governed by the drive of some inexorable obsession and in this phase Picasso displays a violence unprecedented in his art—perhaps in the whole world's art.

Beckmann, too, had forebodings of the disasters that were to befall his country and the world. *Departure* was painted between 1932 and 1935. In 1937 he fled Nazi Germany and made his home in Amsterdam. In 1947 he went to America; he taught for two years in St. Louis and more briefly in Brooklyn, where he died in 1950. Beckmann was one of the outstanding figures of a period which reckoned not a few authentic visionaries amongst its artists.

1939-1955

1939 First exhibition of "Réalités Nouvelles" at the Galerie Charpentier, Paris • In England, Stanley Spencer, Henry Moore, John Piper, Paul Nash and Graham Sutherland are appointed official war artists.

1940 With the fall of France artists are scattered, museums closed, works of art evacuated.

1941 Exhibition of "Jeunes peintres de tradition française" at the Galerie Braun, Paris: Pignon, Beaudin, Coutaud, Gischia, Marchand, Suzanne Roger, Borès, Bertholle, Lapicque, Le Moal, Estève, Singier, Manessier, Desnoyer • New painting in Brussels: "Apport 41" Exhibition (Bertrand, Van Lint, Camus), held again each year until 1945 • Marcel Duchamp publishes **La Boîte en valise,** the famous "suitcase" of reproductions of his works.

1942 Matisse illustrates the **Florilège des Amours de Ronsard** for Skira • In New York Breton, David Hare, Max Ernst and Duchamp launch the review **VVV.**

1943 Braque Retrospective at the Salon d'Automne, Paris • Picasso produces his **Shepherd Holding a Lamb.**

1944 Picasso Retrospective at the Salon d'Automne • Death of Kandinsky • Lipchitz decorates the façade of the Brazilian Ministry of Education, Rio de Janeiro • First Motherwell, Pollock, Baziotes exhibitions at Peggy Guggenheim's gallery, New York (Art of this Century) • Skira publishes **Labyrinthe.**

1945 Opening of the first Salon de Mai, Paris, organized by the younger painters who have recently come to the fore • Matisse Retrospective at the Salon d'Automne • Laurens illustrates **Les Idylles** of Theocritus • Derain illustrates Rabelais' **Pantagruel** for Skira • Second exhibition of "Réalités Nouvelles," Paris • The Picasso-Matisse Exhibition at the Victoria and Albert Museum, London, gives rise to violent controversy • Stemming from the "Apport" group of the war years, the "Jeune Peinture Belge" group is founded at Brussels.

1946 Matisse illustrates **Les lettres portugaises** • Uproar over the Dubuffet Exhibition at the Galerie Drouin, Paris • Magnelli Exhibition and large scale Kandinsky Retrospective, Paris • Picasso does ceramics at Vallauris (French Riviera) • Church of Assy (Haute-Savoie): sculpture by Braque and Lipchitz, a mosaic by Léger, altarpiece painted by Matisse, tapestry for the apse by Lurçat, stained-glass windows by Rouault, Bazaine, Berçot, Brianchon • The "Fronte Nuovo delle Arti" founded at Venice by the young painters Birolli, Cassinari, Corpora, Guttuso, Leonardi, Morlotti, Pizzinato, Santomaso, Turcato, Vedova, Viani • Younger English painters coming to the fore: Adler, Colquhoun, MacBryde, Vaughan, Trevelyan, Bacon.

1947 International Surrealist Exhibition, Galerie Maeght, Paris • Francis Gruber wins the "Prix National," Paris • Braque publishes his **Cahiers,** and Matisse, **Jazz** • Hans Richter's **Dreams that Money can buy** wins a prize at the Venice Film Festival • Bernard Buffet's first one-man show • Death of Bonnard.

1948 Founding in Paris of the "Cobra" experimental group: Appel, Constant, Corneille, Doucet, among others • Venice Biennale, 14 nations represented: first Picasso Exhibition in Italy; exhibition of the Peggy Guggenheim Collection; Braque and Morandi win prizes for painting, Chagall for engraving, Henry Moore for sculpture.

1949 Masson illustrates Malraux's **Les Conquérants** for Skira • Matisse begins decorations for the Dominican Chapel, at Vence and exhibits at Lucerne • Young American painters: The Intrasubjectives, Baziotes, de Kooning, Gorky, Gottlieb, Graves, Hofmann, Motherwell, Pollock, Reinhardt, Rothko, Tobey, Tomlin.

1950 Socialist realism: Fougeron in Paris **(The Land of Mines),** Guttoso in Italy • Léger does sets and costumes for Darius Milhaud's **Bolivar** at the Paris Opera • Venice Biennale: Matisse, Severini, Carrà win prizes for painting, Zadkine, Mascherini, Minguzzi for sculpture, Masereel for engraving; Blue Rider Retrospective; Mexican Pavilion with Rivera, Siqueiros, Orozco, Tamayo • In Boston Dufy does sets for Anouilh's **Ring around the Moon.**

1951 Laurens and Villon Exhibitions at the Musée d'Art Moderne, Paris • Decoration of a church at Audincourt: stained-glass windows by Léger, mosaics by Bazaine • First Biennale at Sao Paolo: Max Bill wins first prize for sculpture • Traveling exhibition in the United States of "Advancing French Art," with Schneider, Soulages, Hans Hartung, Estève and others.

1952 Uproar at the Salon d'Automne in the room devoted to Socialist Realism; the police remove the pictures • Gromaire, Nicholson, Bazaine, Ubac win Carnegie Prizes • Bissière wins the "Prix National" • Venice Biennale: Dufy and Casorati win prizes for painting, Nolde for engraving, Calder for sculpture; Die Brücke Retrospective • Rouault Retrospectives at Amsterdam, Brussels, Paris • Dufy Retrospectives at Geneva, Copenhagen.

1953 Opening of a surrealist gallery in Paris, "L'Etoile Scellée"; among the exhibitors are Toyen and Simon Hantaï • Braque decorates the ceiling of the Salle Henri II in the Louvre • Picasso paints **War** and **Peace** • Chagall Exhibition at Turin • Large-scale Picasso Exhibitions in Rome, Milan and Lyons • Reopening of the Bauhaus, at Munich, with Max Bill as director • Léger decorates the general assembly hall of the United Nations, New York • Death of Raoul Dufy, John Marin and Francis Picabia.

1954 27th Venice Biennale: Max Ernst wins first prize for painting, Arp for sculpture, Miro for engraving. Death of Derain and Matisse.

1955 Manessier, Tamayo and Birolli awarded Carnegie Prizes. Death of Tanguy, Léger and Utrillo.

Dramatic Painting

★

THE CATASTROPHES that have befallen the Western world since the outbreak of the Spanish Civil War have had an unmistakable effect on the trend of modern painting. Though, as we have seen, some artists still devote themselves to the realization of their dreams of beauty in a spirit of serene indifference to all but the claims of art, many have been profoundly affected by the course of world affairs during the last twenty years.

Nevertheless this tragic sense of life is nothing new in art. There have always been artists whose highly strung temperaments and romantic aspirations—combined with that feeling of horror and dismay described by Pascal, when our eyes are opened to "the nothingness of our earthbound condition"—have led them to stress the darker aspects of the world around them. When Delacroix painted *The Massacre of Chios* or made sketches of flayed tigers, and when Picasso painted *Guernica* and the *Bull's Skull*, both alike were interpreting an obsession with death that derived quite as much from their personal temperaments as from events taking place in the outside world. And the case of Delacroix serves to remind us that this haunting sense of life as basically tragic has manifested itself throughout the course of painting; from the Italian, German, Spanish and French Primitives to El Greco and Caravaggio, and thence to Picasso in our time. Thus the presence of this feeling in so much modern art need not be attributed to influences of Dada and Surrealism.

If in this connection we have chosen illustrations from the works of artists of different nationalities, it is not only to show that this poignantly dramatic form of expression is worldwide today, but also to demonstrate the identity of its sources of inspiration and the means employed by those who practice it. There is no question that the ruthlessness of the age we are living in could hardly fail to give rise to evocations of scenes that are harrowing, horrifying or even frankly sadistic as the case may be; but it is significant that our artists imbue these scenes with a sort of mournful resignation, and in fact seem less concerned with voicing a message than with their primary function as artists: that of expressing form.

Thus the dramatically emotive art of today is conditioned by technical means of a quite special nature; for example, the range of colors employed has much to tell us. It will be noticed in the pictures we reproduce that bright tones are almost wholly lacking. Even when the color orchestration calls for a certain intensity of hue, colors are muted by an atmospheric ambiance charged with baleful intimations. The means employed for giving emotive intensity to the picture—and this is characteristic—are dramatic distortions of line and form. Masses are bound with heavily stressed contour-lines that intensify their impact on the eye and harsh contrasts emphasize the tragic aspects of the theme. The drawing, too, is of a special order, severely disciplined. As we have pointed out with reference to Picasso (and the same holds good for Rouault, Tamayo and Beckmann), curves are almost wholly excluded from the composition; the few that subsist are constricted to such a point that at first sight they look more like angles. Vertical lines are slashed across with horizontals, while angles intersect, splinter upon each other. In short the over-all effect is one of violent contrasts—and contrasts have always been the most favored means of expressing dramatic emotion.

Indeed, after studying these various technical procedures we almost feel that a list might be compiled of the rules of dramatic expression in art. But there would, admittedly, be exceptions to these rules of which Delacroix, who said: "There are no parallel lines, and straight lines are monsters," would certainly not have approved. For the artists with whom we are now concerned, far from fearing this "monstrous" quality of the straight line, had recourse to it deliberately, to stress the tragic sense of life behind their art.

All the elements of Picasso's *Bull's Skull* and *Cat and Bird* contribute to this effect of cruelty and horror; behind both pictures is that obsession with death of which we have already spoken, combined with suggestions of ravenous hunger and murderous violence, death's

PABLO PICASSO (1881). THE BULL'S SKULL, 1942. (51 × 38″) PRIVATE COLLECTION, PARIS.

minions. The color-scheme of *Cat and Bird*, with its various shades of brown picked out with streaks of livid white on a glaucous monochrome ground, admirably befits the uncompromising savagery of the theme.

The dominant hue of the *Bull's Skull* is violet, a color which the Old Masters, with the exception of Zurbaran, usually excluded from their palettes. Nevertheless in Christian color symbolism violet is the martyr's color, and it is peculiarly fitted for creating a tragic atmosphere. Here Picasso combines it with somber greens and blues, and that grey to which so many Spanish masters were addicted, especially El Greco. Areas of black and gleams of dazzling white intensify the over-all dramatic impact, attenuated only by some skillfully located bands of ochre.

In the case of George Grosz (who had left Germany and come to the United States) the "depression" was hardly needed to give his art its bitingly satiric turn; in his depictions of individuals there were many reminiscences—a legacy of his Dadaist days—of the horrors of the First World War. Alton Pickens, too, in his scenes of family life, often strikes a somewhat tragic note. Nor had Thomas Benton forgotten the war. Ben Shahn painted his unforgettable portraits of Sacco and Vanzetti, while Lawrence stressed in his work the plight of the colored man in a "white" civilization. Philip Evergood, Hyman Bloom, Walter Quirt and Abraham Rattner evoked more or less tragic scenes in the guise of allegories, with an emphasis on their human content.

PABLO PICASSO (1881). CAT AND BIRD, 1939. (31¾ × 39¼")
PRIVATE COLLECTION, PARIS.

RUFINO TAMAYO (1899). ANIMALS, 1941. (30⅛ × 40ʺ)
MUSEUM OF MODERN ART, NEW YORK.

But by and large it is in Mexican painting that we find the bitterest, most vital expressions of the artists' disgust with the political conditions of the day. The social upheavals that took place in the early years of this century and notably the aftermath of the 1910 Revolution inspired Mexican artists to what was little short of a modern renaissance. Moreover their contacts with the ancient autochthonous art of the country led the best Mexican painters to repudiate the traditions of the San Carlos School of Fine Arts and to re-create a specifically Mexican art by harking back to pre-Columbian art or "folk" traditions.

Several Mexican artists had studied in Europe and shown a keen interest in the achievements of the Paris group. One of these was Diego Rivera; his approach to art is essentially painterly and his work has not the violent emotionalism of Siqueiros, Tamayo and Orozco.

Siqueiros has expressed with dramatic intensity of feeling the horrors of the Mexican civil wars, and his work has something of the willful savagery of pre-Columbian art. Technically his art has the full-blooded power of Aztec and Maya works. Influences of popular Mexican art can be seen in the vibrant, strongly contrasted colors implementing the disciplined power of his composition.

Orozco's frescos, too, contain reminiscences of the civil wars and there is an unqualified truculence in his compositions, traversed by movement lines of an extraordinary dynamism. In Rufino Tamayo's work, with its recalls of pre-Columbian art, we seem to have the most authentic expression of the Mexican art heritage. True, he had begun by studying at San Carlos, but he made long stays in Paris and the poetic aura of Western art was to him a revelation; for he realized that here at last was something that answered to his aspirations. Late cubist art suggested to him ways of linking up, beyond academicism, with the lyrical fervor and elemental grandeur of archaic Mexican art. His painting is nourished by that somber fatalism and deep religious instinct which is inherent in the Mexican mentality and gave rise to images of cruel deities greedy for human sacrifices. Such themes are basic to Tamayo's art, but he transposes them on to the plane of everyday life, and his pictures have such innocuous titles as *Sleeping Musicians, Lovers gazing at the Moon, The Melon Eater*.

Tamayo's method of combining tragedy with grim humor is quite in the Mexican tradition. Mexican painting owes the prominence it now is justly given to the fact that, while retaining to the full its autochthonous characteristics, it has contributed in no small measure to the revival of the poetic emotion that animates so much present-day Western art.

Lonely Eminence of Rouault

★

W<small>E HAVE</small> already drawn attention to the fact that round about 1917, after a phase characterized by many pictures on social and religious themes, there was a lull in Rouault's activities as a painter and he devoted himself chiefly to book illustration. During the next ten years he made illustrations (commissioned by Vollard) for a number of books and, save for occasional canvases, only resumed painting in 1927. Thus it seemed desirable to postpone appraisal of his art until this point in our History of Modern Painting; that is to say the period when what we describe as "dramatic painting" was in the ascendant. For his work is of this nature and can best be studied in this context.

"I've been crazy over painting since the cradle!" When Georges Rouault said this he was not exaggerating. He is not the son of a Breton for nothing, with all the bull-dog tenacity of the Breton breed, and throughout his long life he has shown in his impassioned art a continuity, a fixity of purpose rare in the world of painters. A propos of his birth, we may mention that it was greeted, like that of princes, with salvoes of artillery. It took place, probably at night, in a cellar in the Belleville district of Paris during the Commune, when the city was being bombarded from Versailles. Rouault was a very delicate child—none could have guessed that he was destined to outlive the age of eighty—and never joined in his schoolfellows' boisterous games. In fact even as a boy he seems to have lived in a world of his own, and his favorite recreation, we are told, was making drawings in chalk on the red-tiled kitchen floor.

The atmosphere of his youth certainly favored this early interest in art. His aunts, who were devoted to him, painted charming fans that figured in the windows of Duvelleroy's shop in the Boulevard des Italiens. His father was an expert French-polisher, employed by the famous House of Pleyel for polishing their magnificent pianos. His grandfather, who rejoiced in the delightfully rustic name of Champdavoine (i.e. oatfield), was a great picture-lover, told the boy stories of Courbet, Daumier and Manet and showed him reproductions of their works. And, lastly, when he was fifteen his father apprenticed him to a stained-glass worker. Thus circumstances conspired to foster the youngster's natural penchant towards art, but beyond and above all this he had from his earliest days an idiosyncrasy that was to persist throughout his career: his deep religious fervor.

His father, a pious man, had a simple, unquestioning faith that he transmitted to his son. He developed much enthusiasm for the teachings of Lamennais and was so indignant when he learned that this writer's works had been condemned by the Catholic authorities that he sent his son to a Protestant school. But Georges did not stay there long; as the result of a punishment unjustly inflicted by a master, his father promptly withdrew him from the school. The boy's religious faith was unimpaired by these experiences. It was, and has remained, the mainspring of Rouault's genius. Always he has felt a boundless love for his fellow men, embracing all alike, even the outcasts of the social order; the Christian charity which is so often preached, so seldom practiced. And behind it is the *fervor* of which we have already spoken. There is something of the enthusiasm of the evangelist in his desire to promulgate the "good word" of his militant art, and his tone, we must admit, is sometimes slightly sermonizing. Indeed in conversation with Rouault one often has the feeling he is preaching rather than talking; not so much addressing his companion of the moment as the world at large.

That fervor—the word recurs inevitably when one speaks of Rouault—makes itself felt also in his passionate cult of craftsmanship and technique.

He was employed for some time by a restorer of stained-glass windows, who also made some new ones for the Church of Saint-Severin, and in these young Rouault collaborated. His instinctive fidelity to nature made itself felt in this work and attracted the attention

GEORGES ROUAULT (1871). JOAN OF ARC. (18⅞ × 26¼″) PRIVATE COLLECTION, PARIS.

GEORGES ROUAULT (1871). FAMILY OF CLOWNS, CA. 1940. (79 × 45″) PRIVATE COLLECTION, PARIS.

of the painter Albert Besnard (whom Degas mockingly described as "a fireman who had caught fire"). But when Besnard invited him to work on the stained-glass windows he had been commissioned to make for the Paris School of Pharmacy, Rouault declined, not wishing to "let down" his employer. This very special branch of craftsmanship much appealed to him and throughout his career he has been haunted by the translucencies of colors framed in dark lead strips as we see them in the great French cathedrals.

We may wonder why in his early works he kept so rigorously to dark tones, the "dull, reddish opacities" spoken of by Gustave Geffroy. Perhaps it was that Rouault, nothing if not conscientious in his methods, even at his most venturesome, thought it wisest to proceed from the known to the unknown, that is to say to begin with drawing before confronting the perilous enchantments of color. He had in fact that saving cautiousness of many great painters which preserves them from errors due to over-confidence. But before long he perceived the part, no small one, that color was to play in his art. The procedure Rouault now adopted, and with characteristic singleness of purpose he has kept to throughout his career, consisted of using strongly accented streaks of color, brief and vivid as lightning flashes, which at first gave the impression that his technique might be assimilated to that of the Fauves. Actually, however, his aim was not to construct with color, but to emphasize and boldly to define the purport of each color-note in a chromatic orchestration.

As a young man, he conscientiously applied himself to getting the most he could out of the uninspiring curriculum of the Ecole des Beaux-Arts. But he did not let this silence the inner voice of his genius, though as yet he hardly understood its promptings and must often have been rather alarmed by the sudden uncontrollable impulses that surged up within him, impulses that ran wholly counter to the conventions which his teachers inculcated. Fortunately he there met Gustave Moreau, his only master, and Moreau, who was quick to see the gifts of his pupil, did not try to curb them but, though personally he was out of sympathy with them, was generous enough to encourage his young pupil and to help him in every possible way. And Rouault has never made a secret of his almost fanatical devotion to Gustave Moreau.

From the start his attitude to painting was of a religious, almost abstract order; he regarded it as a vehicle for expressing his beliefs, opinions and predilections, always in the light of his Christian faith. He indulged in indefatigable researches, made innumerable sketches, studies, projects for pictures; his compositions were full of startling accents, vivid strokes and counterstrokes, patches of color sometimes of an almost savage violence, which none the less he kept under control, organized and integrated into an organic unity, even when seeking to express the psychological make-up of an individual with total objectivity. This it is that differentiates him from the Expressionists. He never tries to construct a private, egocentric world, to lay bare his personality and exhibit it in an emotive light. Moved by his fervent love for all mankind, he directs his compassion towards suffering humanity and if he is apt to linger on the seamy side of life, it is not to reproach men with their vices, since his Christian charity leads him to believe that very likely, in the last analysis, they are not wholly responsible for their failings. Thus when he depicts judges, prostitutes and pimps (in point of fact such subjects do not bulk large in his work), he does not "flay" his victims, as has been said, or "immolate them at the feet of a barbarian Christ." All his effigies of Christ reflect the vast pity that is his. True, he may go to extreme lengths in distorting forms and features, stress tones and underline contrasts, but this is more for stylistic ends than with any psychological intent.

Some have thought to detect a sadistic vein in Rouault's art and in his highly personal interpretations of the phenomena of life. But though the sheer force of his inspiration and his ebullient technique lead him, it sometimes seems, to overload his line and give it an aggressive virulence, this is not due to any wanton impulse. No doubt he has a keen eye for the evils of the social order, but always he envisages the possibility of a redemption; and it is this attitude, that of a fundamentally good-hearted castigator, which we sense both in Rouault's painting and in his company.

The Joy of Painting

★

IN USING this title we have in mind not only those dwellers in ivory towers who, blissfully remote from the social and political upheavals of the age, asked nothing more of their art than the joy of depicting the forms and colors of the world. For it cannot be denied that the artists whose work reflects what we have named "the tragic sense of life" experienced a pleasure of sorts—if only a morose delectation—in putting on to canvas their personal reactions to the contemporary scene, its perils and perplexities.

All the same there is a basic difference between these two conceptions of art and of the artist's function. Briefly, the point at issue between them is this: Should painting be regarded as a means of enlarging our experience of life, or simply as a source of pleasure?

Most artists who aim at bodying forth their personal views on the human predicament tend to scrutinize the objective world attentively with a view to using the discoveries thus made for building up what seems to them a new and better world. Obviously such an attitude implies a somewhat pessimistic view of man's estate and a desire to remedy it. And what these artists ask of painting is that it should collaborate, so to speak, with them and help to widen their understanding of life and the possibilities of amending it.

According to the other school of thought the artist's task is to record in his picture the pleasurable emotions aroused in him by contemplation of the natural world. Those who hold this view are apt to use expressions which mean nothing to the advocates of "intellectual" painting. Thus they talk of the beauty of a volume, a form, a color, and we find Matisse speaking of "lovely blues, lovely reds and those physical properties of the pigment which stir our senses so delightfully." All that is beautiful, in fact, is necessarily pleasure-giving and the painter's proper study. These are the optimists; there is so much beauty to be found in life that they can accept its flaws with an indulgent smile. Nor, to their mind, are the ways of men so ugly or futile as the philosophers of gloom would have us think; while, as for scenes of nature, these are sources of delight which the artist can exploit without any mental reservation. His task is solely to discover the best means of expressing all the beauties of the world around him: the gem-like brilliance of colors at their most exquisite, form at its most perfect, the magical play of surface effect, the flowing grace of arabesques. To this end he may indulge in the boldest flights of fancy as regards the composition and take the utmost liberties with a view to decorative effect.

Obviously there is no question in such art of using painting as a means to discovery or an enlargement of our apprehension of the world. When Matisse spoke of art as a "cerebral sedative" and compared it to "a comfortable armchair" in which one can relax after the day's work, he meant that the painter's function was to express sensory responses of an agreeable order, all the more reposeful since they require no intellectual effort. The quest of "knowledge" on the other hand, the desire to penetrate beneath the surface of appearances, involved the artist in all sorts of perplexities and soul-searchings and was, to his thinking, a disheartening venture since the field of such research was infinite and the artist ran the risk of getting nowhere. Nothing could be more different from the joy he had in mind, a joy without the faintest tang of bitterness, whose aftertaste lingered agreeably on memory's palate when the initial thrill produced by one's first sight of the picture had passed away. The joy of painting is the outcome of a sort of *grande passion*, and love, as we know, is apt to sublimate its object; to read into it more than the factual truth. Thus the painter who cultivates this joy does not weary himself seeking to detect in Nature beauties which quite often she does not possess; like the lover, he endows her with them. And by these gifts he associates her with his joy, which comes to him serenely, without the least effort, as it came to that single-hearted lover of Nature, Corot, who said: "It doesn't do to search; one has but to wait and watch..."

GEORGES BRAQUE (1882). PATIENCE, 1942. (57¼ × 44½″)
PRIVATE COLLECTION, U.S.A.

PIERRE BONNARD (1867-1947). FRUIT, 1946. (22 ¼ × 13 ¾ ") GALERIE MAEGHT, PARIS.

WITH Bonnard, who always declared that he was purely and simply an Impressionist, and with Braque the Cubist and Matisse the Fauve, we enter on the last section of this volume, which ends with what we have described as "optimistic painting." True, we include in this category artists whose aims and conceptions of the architectonics of picture-making have little or nothing in common, except the fact that none of them indulges in soul-searchings of a religious or metaphysical order, in brooding self-pity or in the expression of social preoccupations. For in the very heyday of the Fauves, Cubists, Futurists, Neo-Classicists and Surrealists, there were other painters—men of high ability and no less "modern" in the best sense of the word than the leaders of the new schools—whose work is all serenity; a great family of artists among whose many forbears were Chardin and Corot, and more particularly the Impressionists, cheerfullest of whom was obviously Renoir. Speaking of Bonnard, Francis Jourdain remarks on "the unfailing good humor, so welcome and so rare, that we sense in his painting" and adds that "Bonnard has no quarrel with the scheme of things and takes an optimistic view of life." As for Braque, Jean Paulhan shrewdly observes that "each of his pictures gives an impression at once of gay expectancy and plenary achievement." And did not Matisse entitle one of his most famous pictures *Le Bonheur de vivre*? It is above all by his orchestration of colored forms that Matisse so skillfully suggests a peace of mind unruffled by any intellectual consideration. Thus he does not want us, in the first instance, to try to puzzle out exactly what the picture *means*. "The work of art," he said, "has its own absolute significance implicit within itself and should convey this directly to the beholder before he stops to wonder what the picture represents." Here we have an obvious allusion to that "initial shock" on which Matisse always laid so much stress, a concept linking up his work with the amazing color abstractions of Monet's final phase. Color in fact is Matisse's natural element, in the world of color his art attains its plenitude; it arouses in him vague, pleasurable emotions like those we get from the rustling of leaves in a summer breeze, a waft of perfume, or a last sudden gleam of light on a bird's wing when night is falling.

HENRI MATISSE (1869-1954). STILL LIFE WITH OYSTERS, 1940. (25½ × 32″) KUNSTMUSEUM, BASEL.

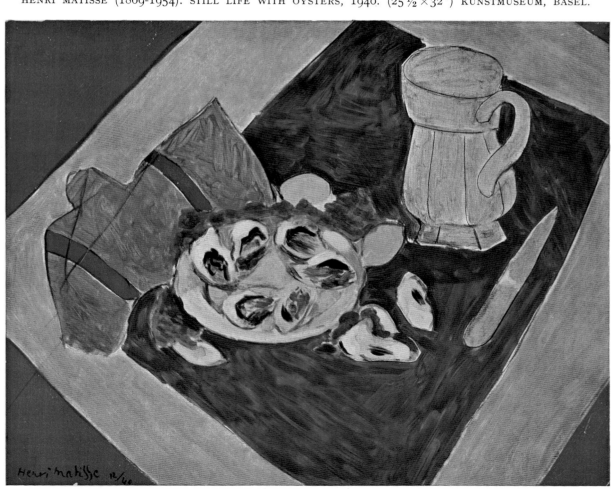

HENRI MATISSE (1869-1954). INTERIOR, 1947. (21 ½ × 18″) PRIVATE COLLECTION, PARIS.

Matisse once declared that he never concerned himself with the psychological values of a face; and this is clearly proved by the canvas reproduced here. In Matisse's interiors light is rendered by the same methods as those he used in outdoor scenes; color is employed not to illuminate, in the usually accepted sense of the word, but to heighten tones, though its absence does not necessarily imply the presence of a shadow.

ALTHOUGH in Braque's *Patience* there are reminiscences of Cubism, it also goes to prove that Impressionism continued to exert an influence which made its latent presence felt even in the work of artists who sought to break away from it. In this masterly canvas we see Braque's peculiar excellencies at their splendid best: emotion, serene mastery and perfectly balanced composition.

The new concept of space implicit in Braque's form of Cubism involves concessions to the impressionist notion of atmosphere. Indeed a swing-back of opinion in favor of the great 19th-century movement has made itself felt among not a few of the leading representatives of abstract art. Thus André Lhote, reversing Cézanne's famous dictum, has boldly declared that the modern artist's duty is "to make of the art of the Old Masters something solid and abiding like Impressionism."

★

THIS *Still Life with Fruit* (page 273), Bonnard's last work, has many affinities with Monet's *Waterlilies*. Its atmosphere is saturated with color, and in it forms and outlines seem to dissolve into a soft, translucent, circumambient mist. Bonnard has come to treat color as a sort of abstraction, wholly conditioned by basic relations of light and shade, in which the actual hues are little more than conventional allusions. In Bonnard's still life it is plain to see how the color elements interpenetrate and blend, each borrowing from each its neighbor's hues. By these means the artist achieves extraordinary light effects, which are far more in the nature of spontaneous effusions, stemming from the Subconscious, than due to any predetermined plan or technical device. These effects are implemented by the priority given invariably by Bonnard to complementaries as against primary colors; following Verlaine's advice he "prefers nuances to simple colors."

★

BLACK is a color and may even be a cheerful color, so Matisse once said with reference to this *Interior*, with its symphony of blue and its window giving on a sunlit view of Vence. In the *Still Life with Oysters* reminiscences of the artist's Fauve period emerge: thick contour-lines, broad planes of flat color. The color, too, is once again intense, aggressive, and as in the past pure tones of the utmost brilliancy are juxtaposed without any intervening passages of neutral hues. Also we find recalls of his geometric period (1913-1918) in the architecturally ordered structure, here allied with the exuberance of Fauvism.

Likewise in *Still Life with Oysters* we find the flat tones and graphic methods of *Le Bonheur de vivre* (1905), combined with the geometric patterning of the 1908 *Desserte*. Though the composition is based on a strictly rectangular lay-out (the "Golden Section"), whose regularity is emphasized by the use of the three primaries, the dish of oysters itself, between the green serviette and the mauve jug, embodies a complementary, in quite the classical spirit. This still life is an excellent example of that "pure painting" or "painting for its own sake" with which Maurice Denis once reproached Matisse. Nevertheless this was one of the great artist's most significant, worthwhile and personal contributions to the advancement of modern art.

★

FOR a relatively short time, following Matisse's lead, Marquet did homage to the vehemence of Fauvism; no doubt his natural loyalty to a friend for whom he had so much affection prevented him from acting otherwise. But at the back of his mind were memories not only of the rebellious young man he had been at the Ecole des Beaux-Arts, but also of the art student who at the Louvre (almost on the sly) copied Chardin, Claude Lorrain and Poussin, or, rather, interpreted them in his own manner. Thus his definitely classical temperament led him to break, almost effortlessly, with the conceptions of the Fauves.

ALBERT MARQUET (1875-1947). THE EASEL, ALGIERS, 1942. (10¼ × 8¼″) PRIVATE COLLECTION, PARIS.

Though he had long since given up the dazzling palette of his "Fauve" phase, Marquet abandoned for the nonce the
tranquil color orchestration of his river scenes and landscapes and indulged once again in bright, gay colors.

RAOUL DUFY (1877-1953). HOMAGE TO MOZART. (35 × 45⅝")
DIANE ESMOND COLLECTION, NEW YORK.

In the result Marquet took to using a sober, highly refined palette enabling him to give a very personal atmosphere to his landscapes, without any of the dazzling color effects he indulged in during the golden age of Cubism. Yet in the last years of his life it would seem that he once again succumbed to the spell of color. And in *The Easel* he has returned, if not to the stridencies of Fauvism, to the use of decidedly brighter colors.

★

DESPITE similarities there is a basic difference between Matisse and Dufy; the former seeks to move us, the latter solely to give pleasure. The picture reproduced here might be described as a graceful tribute to music, to the condition of which, Walter Pater has told us, "all art constantly aspires." This was the third "Homage to Mozart" that Dufy painted; he dedicated other works to Bach and Chopin. He found in music a frequent source of inspiration; the subjects of many of his paintings, etchings and drawings are concerts, orchestras and above all soloists. Dufy's aim was less, perhaps, to embellish facts of visual experience than to toy with them as the fancy took him. When a friend once accused him of playing fast and loose with nature, he replied: "But nature, my dear sir, is only an hypothesis." An hypothesis against which he sets up another, no less problematic in its way, that of a charmingly artificial world of the imagination in which boldly syncopated arabesques weave through a sky all in transparent nuances, and take part in a sort of ballet accompanied by an invisible orchestra that sets its light, fantastic rhythms. The very special luminosity he imparted to his seascapes by means of a few, discreetly muted colors and his simply, delicately poignant color harmonies have here given place to a sonorous color orchestration.

Towards the close of his career Dufy embarked on an experiment as novel as it was audacious. Could it be that he, erstwhile champion of a rich diversity of colors, recalled how once the Fauves had questioned the efficacy of color pure and simple? In any case he now took to using what he called "tonal color," and aimed at creating harmonies in a single color, based on variations of tone set off by passages of white.

This must not be confused with monochrome painting (in which the suggestion of depth is a *sine qua non*), nor with *grisaille* compositions in which light-and-shade plays a leading part. It was above all with the object of conjuring up a new world of purest fantasy that Dufy applied himself to devising a new syntax, a vocabulary, indeed an alphabet, peculiar to himself. The artifice with which he clothes his emotion might seem merely capricious and arbitrary, were it not for the genuinely human feeling infusing it, even in its extravagances and its most wayward flights of fancy.

In *The Red Violin* Dufy seems to be toying with a discipline somewhat like that of plainsong, but there is something in his touch that palliates its rigor, much as the charm of a singer's voice will sometimes temper the severity of the Gregorian mode.

One has a feeling that Dufy, reacting from the rich color orchestration of the Fauves, is here indulging in a sort of melodious recitative which, while freely flowing, is elegantly ordered. He was over seventy when he painted this picture, and old age has its consolations. In *The Red Violin* he has transformed the superficial, transient pleasure he once got from toying with forms and colors, into something deeper, a more solid and lasting joy. Music and musical instruments had always had a strong appeal for him and several times before this he had painted violins; but never before with such simplicity, such a fine feeling for abstraction and with that unequivocal precision and clarity which Braque was aiming at in his phase of *papiers collés*.

RAOUL DUFY (1877-1953). THE RED VIOLIN, 1948. (15 × 21″)
MUSÉE D'ART ET D'HISTOIRE, GENEVA.

Experimental Color

★

As we have seen, Bonnard, Matisse, Marquet, Braque and Dufy assign to color the function of expressing sensation—the same sensation as that which had meant so much to the Impressionists. For the five artists named above the subject of the picture matters little; often quite commonplace, it serves chiefly as a pretext for an arrangement of colors and colored forms. True, they keep in mind the formal, architectonic structure of the picture; but the ideas behind this architectural concept are rarely of an abstract nature and as a rule derive from facts of visual experience of an agreeable order bearing out their hedonistic view of life. Indeed it may be said that they have little concern for purely speculative considerations of a technical order and the problems these entail; nor do they aim at a pictorial lyricism wider in scope than that which came to its flowering in Impressionism. Their handling of color falls in line with the impressionist ideal of "painting as a bird sings." Thus in the art of these masters of color the joy of painting is happily untouched by any tragic sense of life; their chief concern is to give expression in the most effective manner to their sensory responses and to their delight in all the manifold beauty of the world. In short their conception of color is by and large in harmony with the intentions of the leading painters of the close of the 19th century.

This cult of color (for it is nothing short of that) is shared by the painters to whom we now shall turn, but they give it a different and in a sense more ambitious directive. In the art of Marin, Mondrian, Kandinsky, Léger, Miro, Chagall, Villon and Beaudin color is not merely a source of pleasure; it sets the artist problems and is treated experimentally. Though these painters, too, investigated nature and discovered some of nature's secrets, they used their discoveries for loftier ends and indeed assigned to painting functions of an order hitherto undreamt-of. Their approach was twofold, intellectual and spontaneous (that is to say in accordance with the free expression of instinct), but in both cases based on deductions from the premises of Impressionism, Fauvism and Cubism. Mondrian, for example, made no secret of his admiration for Matisse, Picasso and Léger, thus indicating that though he rejected the influence of "reality," he was quite prepared to accept that of works of art which to his mind gave a more authentic vision of nature. (Kandinsky had the same experience when confronted by the color patches on a woman's dress.) Thus color was handled by these painters as a substance capable of giving poetic expression to certain data of the thinking mind. It was the same desire to escape from the tyranny of the purely sensual that led Léger to build up an aesthetic based on machinery. We might almost say that painting, carrying its autonomy a stage further, now had recourse to "second states" of nature; in other words that art was no longer called on directly to interpret reality, but was treated as a language made for the expression of specific emotions stemming not (as in the past) from contacts with the real world but from operations of the mind.

In the work of these artists color is in fact no longer charged with associations deriving from the scenes of nature (as in the work of the five French exponents of "the joy of painting" mentioned above); abstract in the sense that it has no objective referent, it is not a means to celebration of seen beauty but an instrument of exploration and discovery.

Largely as a result of the new direction given art, there was an extension of the painter's activities; no longer confining himself to easel painting, he branched out into fields usually regarded as extraneous to art proper: posters, shop-window displays, dress materials and wall decoration. Mondrian rightly said that every true artist is far more moved by the beauty of lines and colors and their relations between themselves than by what they represent. The public of today has been won over to this view; in the modern world color enjoys a prestige it never knew before. And if the ascendancy of color in the public taste is so well assured today, this is an outcome of the researches and discoveries of our 20th-century painters.

JOHN MARIN (1870-1953). TUNK MOUNTAINS, AUTUMN, MAINE, 1945. (25×30″)
PHILLIPS COLLECTION, WASHINGTON.

WE BEGIN this, the final section of the present volume, with a late work by John Marin; its intense vitality is nothing short of amazing when we remember that this great artist was seventy-five years old when he painted it. Born in 1870 at Rutherford, New Jersey, he was trained as an architect, but at the age of twenty-nine he enrolled in the Pennsylvania Academy of the Fine Arts and decided to devote himself to painting. When he was thirty-five he went to Paris where he lived for some five years (excluding a stay in America in 1909-1910), and came under the influence of Whistler and Méryon. He was in his fortieth year when (in 1909) he gave his first exhibition at the Stieglitz Gallery. Though the watercolors he then exhibited were remarkable for their easy, fluent execution, they had not yet acquired that truly Whitmanesque forcefulness which we find in his later evocations of New York City, of mountains and the sea. Yet no sooner was he back in the United States than he discovered what was henceforth to be his ruling theme: the City, with its great buildings soaring skywards, its mighty bridges, the busy traffic and the lights of its streets —in short, the trepidant rhythms of New York during an active period of its growth. And in these scenes he has admirably symbolized the dynamism of the modern world.

Here Marin's starting-off point was the reduction of the subject to basic signs, mere allusions to its content. Moreover, with his bold color patches he achieves an effect of almost overwhelming power without recourse to the primaries, usually employed for such effects.

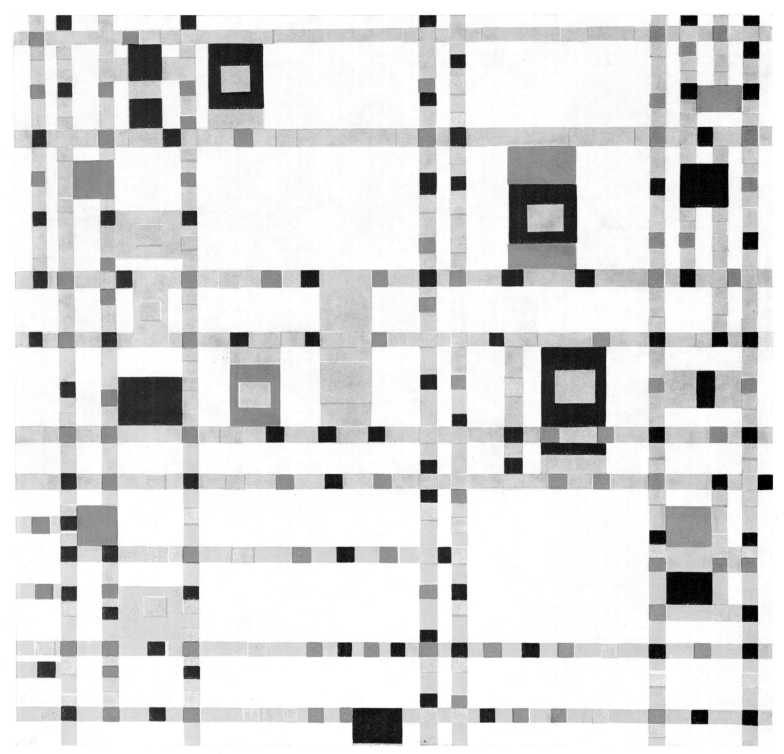

PIET MONDRIAN (1872-1944). BROADWAY BOOGIE-WOOGIE, 1942-1943. (50 × 50")
MUSEUM OF MODERN ART, NEW YORK.

THIS GAY, brilliantly colorful composition comes as something of a surprise when we
remember Mondrian's austere handling of line and color in his earlier work. In 1940
he had migrated to New York, and it would seem that there, at long last, he fell under the
spell of color; or was it the dynamic tempo of American life that made the staticism of his
earlier art seem overdone? It is perhaps revealing that now, in his sixties, this inveterate
bachelor suddenly decided to learn to dance, bought a gramophone, and took to frequenting
the Harlem dance-halls. It was from watching the perforated music-rolls of a barrel-organ
that he got the idea of this singular composition. Though all his last canvases were inspired
by the erratic rhythms of Boogie-Woogie (after which he named them), his lifelong feeling
for absolute precision kept him to the use of rigidly straight lines marking off rectangular
compartments. One feels that his "discovery" of color came too late, for when he died he
was only just beginning to explore its possibilities.

From that moment early in his career when his eyes were opened to its delights, Léger never wavered in his allegiance to color, and in fact devoted himself to extending its field of action to the utmost. For, as he saw it, color is by far the most effective means of imparting new and vital significances to the visible world. In that often-quoted remark, "I think in forms and colors," Braque made it understood that he drew a distinction between them in his mind; in other words that under certain circumstances he could conceive of form without color and vice versa. Léger, on the other hand, thinks in color ("color" not "colors," be it noted) in a quite literal sense. With most modern artists the procedure of constructing with color alone is the outcome of a thought-out plan, an intellectual operation. It is not so with Léger; when we say he thinks in color, it is not any intellectual process we have in mind; the truth is rather that he becomes aware of objects through their color as a blind man through his sense of touch. In fact we have here a physical peculiarity which conditions his way of thinking and painting as well as his way of seeing. Another of Léger's characteristics is his organizational sense and his feeling for carefully balanced composition; thus he was always mindful to equate his colors to an abstract architectural concept. Moreover he did not treat color on expressionist lines, as a means of exteriorizing emotion, nor as a source of sensory responses that can be put to the service of some purely plastic conception. He treated it, rather, as an autonomous entity, providing all the materials needed for the build-up of the picture. In brief, it might be said that color alone supplies the bricks and mortar of Léger's pictorial architecture.

FERNAND LÉGER (1881-1955). PLANT IN FRONT OF TREETRUNKS, 1952. (21 ¼ × 25 ⅛″) GALERIE LOUIS CARRÉ, PARIS.

PAUL KLEE (1879-1940). THE HARBOR, 1938. (26½ × 64⅞″) KUNSTMUSEUM, BASEL.

DURING his early period Klee applied himself to mastering the technique of drawing, and showed little or no interest in color. This may explain why, as we have already mentioned, he once declared that for him color was a mistress who came to him of her own sweet will without his needing to go in quest of her. Hence, too, perhaps, the delightful surprises of his palette, a range of colors in whose choice technical considerations play no part and which owes all to the creative imagination.

Thus in Klee's art color never has the constructive role assigned it by so many modern painters nor is it ever used to specify "locality." It is not subjected to any traditional disciplines or treated *à la Corot*, as merely a "charming, ever-welcome visitor." Klee feels that color can be trusted to take charge of everything in the picture and gaily lets it run.

One might almost say that the autonomy of color championed by the moderns finds its happiest expression in Klee's art. All the more so because in his case it is not conditioned by any system, private aesthetic philosophy or social preoccupation. By the same token, Klee seems to give no thought to the accepted rules as to the disposition of the picture-surface; he treats Space not as a means to the organization of the picture, but as a natural datum conditioning the life of all around him and his own world in particular.

KANDINSKY has another view of the function of color. In the course of his career his feeling about it underwent a drastic change. To begin with, as we have seen, color in his case implemented an abstract, purely physical and sensual response to variations of intensity in its scale and compass, on essentially musical lines. In short, he made the most of the affective qualities of the medium, and organized these in terms of a very free and flexible conception of the exigencies of form. But, after his first abstract period, he developed a less materialistic, more elevated conception of it. He now subjected it to geometric disciplines, adjusting it to architecturally ordered forms—a surprising volte-face when we remember the unbridled freedom of his colors in the previous phase. The reason was that Kandinsky now assigned a new function to color; instead of using it for the sake of its purely *physical* effects on the senses, he now gave it a *psychical* referent and a spiritual purport.

The methods of Kandinsky and those of Mondrian were followed up by a number of artists, amongst them Schneider, Hartung, Deyrolles, Vasarely, Duthoo, Dewasne, Domela; a Swiss artist Max Bill; the Americans Morris, Glarner, Wolf, Shaw, Xceron and Hilla Rebay —all of whom rank among the leading exponents of abstract art.

WASSILY KANDINSKY (1866-1944). LIGHT CONSTRUCTION, 1940. (28¼ × 16¼″)
HERMANN RUPF COLLECTION, BERN.

USUALLY in Chagall's pictures we find the color-scheme follows the classical system of being restricted to one or two dominants and their derivatives. But he steps up these colors to their maximum intensity and organizes the pictorial architecture accordingly, often accentuating graphic arabesques so as to increase the structural solidity of the color pattern. In any case Chagall's color effects, for all their seeming exuberance, are always subordinated to his flawless drawing. In his *Red Sun* Chagall uses the three primaries, which, however, he modulates with grey in the manner of the great colorists of the past. But, brilliant as are his colors Chagall never employs them purely for their own sake. There is nothing abstract about his art and in its poetic imagery we always find an emphasis on the human content. Each of his pictures represents an instant of his life, the after-image of a dream or perhaps some fairytale he has told himself. And amidst the joyous profusion of his colors, their rainbow tints and eye-filling richness of surface, we trace, if we scan them closely, nuances like wistful smiles and the dark cast of pity for human sorrow.

★

COLOR serves Miro as a material for the magic garments of the personages and objects of his private wonderland, garments enabling them to look their best in the scenes he conjures up: of cabalistic incantations, fairy weddings, military pageants, sacrificial rites and so forth. In his art there is no question of arranging masses or colored planes with an eye to plastic symmetry. His colors are just picturesque items: flowers, stars, gems, flames, pretty girls, or what you will; sometimes even preposterous mustaches. But all these forms are meta-morphosed, broken down into their constituent parts, which the beholder has to re-assemble like the pieces of a puzzle, as best he can. Sometimes these elusive fragments remind us of the tiny, queerly shaped fish that flicker to and fro in the spectral, falsifying light of an aquarium.

Miro, indeed, often gives the impression of a mischievous demiurge amusing himself with the world he has created by changing the colors originally given to objects, or by removing the distinctive aspects of one and grafting them upon another; thus reducing to a fascinating chaos the cosmos he has made and altering the significances he assigned to creatures and things, perhaps in all seriousness, when he called them into being.

JOAN MIRO (1893). PAINTING ON CANVAS, 1953. (76¾ × 148⅝″) GALERIE MAEGHT, PARIS.

MARC CHAGALL (1887). THE RED SUN, 1949. (55 × 38½″) OWNED BY THE ARTIST.

JACQUES VILLON (1875). FARM-YARD WITH PIGEON-HOUSE, 1953. (23½ × 31¾″)
GALERIE LOUIS CARRÉ, PARIS.

WHEN this work by Villon is compared with those reproduced on pages 145 and 214, we see that the artist has modified his palette in the direction of an emphasis on brilliant color that comes as something of a surprise, especially when we remember how drawing had always played the leading part in his compositions.

During the early phase of Cubism Villon was one of the first to try to reconcile form and color. Though his rich palette glowed with all the hues of the rainbow, he discreetly toned them down; perhaps, not without reason, he felt that he was trying out a new mode of art whose legitimacy might be questioned by the more orthodox Cubists. Meanwhile, without letting himself become involved in problems of pure plasticity, still less in those of expressing solely personal sensations, he applied himself to "revealing the inmost soul of things," by simplifying and synthesizing on the lines preconized by the Cubists.

But in so doing he was careful always "to keep his feet in contact with the earth," as he put it, that is to say, to call on Nature to supply the driving force of his creative impulse. "We must elicit from the countless possibilities of a landscape, a still life or a figure what seems to us to correspond to it most perfectly—no easy task." This is where he joined issue with the Cubists, and he reproached certain artists for not making Nature their starting-off point but by-passing her so to speak. He accused these artists of "falling back on an art that had been brought to maturity, worked out and indeed sucked dry by others," and "of parading on their canvases the emotions they derive from it, emotions that are second hand at best —pale reflections of other men's emotions."

Since 1940 or thereabouts Villon has stepped up the intensity of his colors to a remarkable degree, and in his recent compositions he employs pure colors, chiefly the primaries.

THE ARTISTS of the generation following that of the Fauves and Cubists kept to one of the main directives of the latter movement and sought to represent the world, not under its trivial, fleeting or "picturesque" aspects, but as an organic whole—as in fact it truly is. Nevertheless, their approach was not wholly objective, that of detached observers of the phenomenal world; in their conception of the artist's field of activity they included operations of the thinking mind and sought to co-ordinate the universe with Man.

This was the program of a group of artists who set out to reconcile two conceptions of their predecessors and adapt the purely materialistic handling of color practiced by the Fauves to the lyrical vision and architectural disciplines of the Cubists. Obviously this involved eclecticism which—after the way of eclecticisms—ran the risk of impairing the characteristic virtues of both its antecedents. Perhaps, however, in this case it was chiefly a matter of technique and the basic concept remained the same: that of starting out rather from suggestions coming from outside than from promptings of the inner consciousness. Also, the artist was invited to identify himself with Nature in her creative functions rather than to confine himself to analyzing objects under their invariable aspects.

André Beaudin may be regarded as the figurehead of the group who, by and large, followed these directives, though to each is due the credit of an original, personal contribution to this new development. Other outstanding figures are Borès, Pignon, Manessier, Bazaine, Le Moal, Gischia, Singier, Tal Coat, Roux, Lapicque, Suzanne Roger, Kermadec, Estève and Ghika. To begin with, following the lead of Matisse, Beaudin planned his composition in flowing arabesques playing across the picture-surface; soon, however, it seemed to him that they lacked weight and substance when compared with cubist realizations, and especially those of Juan Gris. In Beaudin's art, as in his temperament, we can detect two separate trends, now reconciled, now conflicting. Thus his natural impetuosity often comes up against his no less innate sense of the necessity of order, and his dynamic outbursts are confined by firm design that limits their expansion without, however, diminishing their gusto.

In short the artists named above, whose tendencies derive in general from those of Matisse and Picasso, played much the same part, after Fauvism and Cubism, as the Nabis and Divisionists had done after Impressionism.

ANDRÉ BEAUDIN (1895). THE MEETING, 1952. (15 × 18″) PRIVATELY OWNED, BELFORT.

Conclusion

★

A S REGARDS the great painters whose art has been discussed in the foregoing pages we were able to follow their careers from earliest youth up to their death, or a ripe old age—for not a few of them are, happily, still with us. But at this point we are confronted by a new generation and younger men whose genius or talent is still in active process of formation, and regarding whose place in the history of art it is hardly possible as yet to form an estimate.

At the close of the first half of the present century such was the diversity of tendencies that Picasso was led to say, "There are no longer any schools, there are only individual painters." One has in fact the impression that at this stage of its long progress art is marking time; painters today are taking stock of the vast heritage bequeathed them by their illustrious elders before striking out in new directions. Meanwhile, however, we may subdivide the most modern tendencies into three main categories.

First, we have what now is called figurative art. Uninfluenced both by the conceptual objectivity of Cubism and by the asceticism of abstract art, many painters still keep to the traditional method of painting "from nature"; that is to say, directly recording aspects of reality supplied by visual experience. The artist takes as his model an object he has before his eyes, not an imagined entity, and he often shows a preference for the human figure, which Derain once described as the "supreme test in art." Moreover the figurative artist aims at expressing the feelings inspired in him by man not as an isolated unit but as member of a community and sharing in its responsibilities.

Next we have abstract art; it has already made amazing headway in recent times and is steadily gaining ground. The movement towards giving form and color complete autonomy vis-à-vis the subject, which began in the 19th century, has done much to promote the theory of the non-objectivists: that the expression of form without any objective referent can give rise to emotions of a specific, self-sufficient order.

Finally there are some artists who seek to reconcile these two tendencies, figurative and abstract, by interpreting the underlying rhythms that permeate reality. Thus they have recourse to the world of things, but only with a view to eliciting "correspondences," interrelations that the ordinary beholder fails to perceive and which give intimations of the inmost life of the phenomenal world. Thus reality is presented not under its traditional aspects but under the form of equivalences expressed solely by signs.

It would be rash to try to predict what new developments the future has in store. This much however, may be affirmed: that there are many highly gifted living artists whose work is rich in promise. Some of them believe that the discoveries of the last fifty years have not yet been exploited to the full and can be carried several stages further. Obviously we might reply that, none the less, they gave rise in their day to many masterpieces, and it is for the younger generation to make good their claim. Let us hope they will succeed and sponsor revolutions in painting no less dramatic than those achieved by their forerunners. It must, however, be admitted that in the work of the younger men there are as yet no signs that point to any radical changes in the near future, so closely are contemporary tendencies bound up with the discoveries of the recent past. But, as ever, art is in the process of becoming and it may well be that men of genius will emerge "out of the blue"—and yet again transform the whole course of art.

BIOGRAPHICAL
AND BIBLIOGRAPHICAL NOTICES

SELECTED BIBLIOGRAPHY

GENERAL INDEX

LIST OF COLORPLATES

Biographical and Bibliographical Notices

★

ARP, HANS (1887)

1887 Born at Strasbourg, Alsace, September 16. Attended Strasbourg School of Arts and Crafts.

1904- First visit to Paris. First contacts with modern painting.

1905 At the Weimar Academy under Professor Ludwig von Hoffmann (1905-1907).

1907 Settled at Weggis, Switzerland. Met painters W. Gimmi, W. Helbig, O. Lüthi, D. Rossiné, with whom he was soon to found Der Moderne Bund.

1911 Exhibited at first exhibition of Der Moderne Bund at Lucerne. Visited Kandinsky at Munich in whose work he found confirmation of the lines on which he himself was working. Kandinsky asked him to collaborate on the book Der Blaue Reiter (The Blue Rider).

1914 In Paris. Met Max Jacob, Modigliani and Cravan at Marie Vassiliev's canteen in the Avenue du Maine. Introduced by Max Jacob to Picasso.
Met Apollinaire with Delaunay.

1916- With Ball, Tzara and Hülsenbeck founded the Dada

1919 movement in Zurich. Worked on the publications Cabaret Voltaire, Dada, 391, Der Zeltweg. Illustrated 25 Poèmes by Tzara, Phantastische Gebete by Hülsenbeck, etc., with wood engravings of new and strange beauty. 1917: woodcuts and wood reliefs.

1919- At Cologne. Collaborated with Baargeld and Max Ernst

1920 on the dadaist publication Die Schammade. Series of Fatagaga pictures with Max Ernst (Fabrication de tableaux garantis gazométriques). Short stay in Berlin. Met El Lissitzky and Kurt Schwitters.

1921- With Breton, Max Ernst and Tzara took part in first

1922 dadaist demonstration in the Tyrol. Collaborated on publication: Dada au Grand Air (Dada in the Open). Married Sophie Täuber.

1923 In Hanover. Collaborated with Kurt Schwitters and helped to edit review Merz. Set of lithographs entitled 7 Arpaden published by Merz.

1925 Settles in Paris. Active collaboration with the Surrealists. Exhibited at first general surrealist exhibition at the Galerie Pierre.

1926- Reconstructed the restaurant L'Aubette at Strasbourg

1928 together with Sophie Täuber and Van Doesburg.

1930-1932 Torn-paper period. Sculpture in the round.

1940 After fall of France, fled with Sophie Täuber to Grasse. In autumn 1942 took refuge in Switzerland.

1943 January 13: Sophie Täuber killed accidentally at Höngg near Zurich.

1948 Wittenborn, New York, published Arp's On My Way (poems and essays 1912-1947). First important monograph on Arp.

1950 Traveled to United States. Commissioned by Harvard University to construct a large mural relief.

1954 First prize for sculpture at the Venice Biennale.

(Information supplied by the artist.)

BIBLIOGRAPHY

Arp, "On My Way, poetry and essays 1912...1947" (Documents of Modern Art, 6), New York 1948. With contributions by R. Motherwell, C. Giedion-Welcker, G. Buffet-Picabia. Bibliography by B. Karpel.

A. Breton, Le Surréalisme et la peinture, Paris 1928. — G. Bazin, in L'Amour de l'Art, with biographical and bibliographical notes, Paris 1934. — D. Gascoyne, A Short Survey of Surrealism, London 1935. — A.H. Barr, Cubism and Abstract Art, Museum of Modern Art, New York 1936. — Id., Fantastic Art, Dada, Surrealism, Museum of Modern Art, New York 1936. — J. Brzekowski, Lodz 1936. — J. Levy, Surrealism, New York 1936. — Dictionnaire abrégé du surréalisme, Paris 1938. — A. Breton, Anthologie de l'humour noir, Paris 1940. — M. Seuphor, L'art abstrait, ses origines, ses premiers maîtres, Paris 1949. — G. Buffet-Picabia, Paris 1953.

AUBERJONOIS, RENÉ (1872)

1872 Born August 18 near Lausanne of a Swiss father and a French mother. Receives a classical schooling in Switzerland and Germany, and then devotes himself entirely to painting.

1898 Follows courses at an art school in Kensington, London.

1901 Enrolls at the Ecole des Beaux-Arts, Paris, then works in the private studio of Luc-Olivier Merson, where he gets into his stride and evolves a style of his own. Living uninterruptedly in Paris for the next thirteen years, he witnesses the triumph of Cézanne and the revolutionary innovations of Cubism. This is the crucial period in his development as an artist. Beginning of his lifelong friendship with C.F. Ramuz.

1914 Leaving Paris upon the outbreak of war, he returns to Switzerland. Lives now at Lausanne, though making almost yearly trips to Paris, Rome, and the Valais.

1917 Does sets and costumes for Ramuz' L'Histoire du Soldat, music by Stravinsky.

1927 Paints a large mural decoration for a pavilion at the Lausanne Fair. Little notice is taken of this until the Auberjonois Retrospective Exhibition at Geneva in 1946, when critics acclaim it as a masterpiece of improvisation.

1943 At Lausanne Ramuz publishes a book on Auberjonois, the testament of their friendship.

1948 Retrospective Exhibition at the Venice Biennale (some 30 paintings ranging from 1906 to 1947).

BIBLIOGRAPHY

Hans Graber, Basel 1925. — Paul Budry, Lausanne 1923. — C.A. Cingria, Formes et Couleurs No. 4, 1942. — C.F. Ramuz, Lausanne 1943.

BEAUDIN, ANDRÉ (1895)

1895 Born February 3 at Mennecy (Seine-et-Oise). Art studies at the Ecole des Arts Décoratifs, Paris. Called up for military service in 1915.

1921 The turning-point in his career as an artist: after making a trip to Italy, he strikes up lasting friendships with André Masson and, above all, with Juan Gris, whose influence on him is to be decisive.

1923 First exhibition of his work at the Percier Gallery, Paris, preface by Max Jacob. His painting of this period is eminently sober, almost grey. Only much later are his eyes opened to color. Begins to do sculptures.

1932 First one-man show in London. Now in full possession of his means, he strives for an ever greater simplification.

1936 Etchings for Virgil's Bucolics, published by Skira. Period of large dancing nudes. From 1937 on paints bulls' heads and horses.

1945 Illustrations for Paul Eluard's Doubles d'ombre.

1946 Illustrates Georges Hugnet's Oiseaux, ne copiez personne. Paints many portraits.

1949 First exhibition in New York, preface by Paul Eluard. Landscapes: the Seine quays.

1950 Illustrates André Frénaud's Les Paysans.

1952 Illustrates Francis Ponge's L'Araignée.

1953 Retrospective Exhibition of Beaudin's paintings, sculptures and book illustrations at the Kunsthalle, Bern (preface by D.H. Kahnweiler).

BIBLIOGRAPHY

Maurice Raynal, Anthologie de la peinture en France de 1906 à nos jours, Paris 1927. — E. Tériade, in Cahiers d'Art, Paris 1928. — Herbert Read, Art Now, New York 1933. — Jacques Baron, in Minotaure, Paris 1935. — Maurice Raynal, in Arts et Métiers graphiques, Paris 1937. — Léon Gischia and Nicole Védrès, La Sculpture en France depuis Rodin, Paris 1945. — Anthologie du livre illustré par les peintres et graveurs de l'Ecole de Paris, Geneva 1946. — Peintres du XXᵉ siècle, Geneva 1947.

BECKMANN, MAX (1884-1950)

1884   Born February 12 in Leipzig, son of a miller from Helmstädt (near Braunschweig). Begins painting at the age of 13.

1900   Enters the Weimar Academy of Fine Arts where he studies under Frithjof Smith, a Norwegian painter. Early enthusiasm for the painting of Hans von Marées.

1903   Makes a trip to Paris, visiting the Louvre and the Exhibition of French Primitives.

1904   Spends six months in Florence.

1905   In Berlin. Influenced by Cézanne and the German Impressionists.

1906   Wins the "Florenz Preis" at Weimar and begins to make a name for himself. Exhibits with the Secession; gets married.

1908   Influenced by El Greco.

1909   Publishes a set of lithographs on the story of Orpheus and Eurydice.

1910-   Named a member of the Secession committee, but hands
1911   in his resignation after a year, preferring to work and exhibit wholly on his own. Does lithographs on biblical themes.

1914-   Serves with a German hospital unit on the French and
1918   Belgian fronts.

1918   Falls ill, but works hard at drawing and etching during his convalescence. His style undergoes a change, and his paintings are the anguished expression of a world in upheaval.

1921-   Writes four plays which have never been performed.
1922   An easing of the tension; reverts to quieter, more peaceful themes, painting landscapes and portraits. But the political and social unrest in Germany again has its effect on his painting, and his style grows somber and stark.

1925   Appointed professor of painting at the Frankfort School of Fine Arts. Second marriage, this time with the daughter of the painter von Kaulbach.

1929-   Wins the second Carnegie Prize (1929). Now spends
1932   several months each year in Paris, exhibiting at the Galerie de la Renaissance (1931) and at the Galerie Bing (1932). Retrospective exhibition, Kunsthalle, Basel (1930). Forced out of Frankfort by the Nazis, goes to Berlin. Begins a triptych: *Departure* (1932-1935).

1934   Begins doing sculpture.

1937   Goes into exile, settling in Amsterdam, where he remains until 1947.

1939   First Prize at the Golden Gate International Exhibition, San Francisco.

1943   Illustrates *The Book of Revelation* and does a set of drawings inspired by Goethe's *Faust*.

1947   Goes to the United States. Lives in St. Louis and directs a practical studio class in painting at Washington University. Illustrates Milton's *Paradise Lost*.

1950   Dies December 27 in Brooklyn. His last work is a triptych: *The Argonauts*. In his Diary for December 24 he wrote: "I am very tired. Final touches on *The Argonauts* this morning." And on December 26: "It is snowing; worked all day on the 'head' " (a detail of the triptych). At midnight he announced to his wife: "Yes, it's done now. There's not a single brushstroke left to add. At last it's finished."

BIBLIOGRAPHY

Kaiser, Berlin 1913. — Hartlaub, Paris 1930. — Neumann, Munich 1931. — W. Schöne, Berlin 1947. — J.T. Soby, *Contemporary Painters*, New York 1948. — Harold Clurman, New York 1948. — Reifenberg and Hausenstein, Munich 1949. — See also the catalogues of Beckmann's exhibition at the Buchholz Gallery, New York, and the catalogue (with biography and bibliography) of the City Art Museum, St. Louis (1948).

BOCCIONI, UMBERTO (1882-1916)

1882   Born at Reggio, Calabria, Italy, October 19.

1898-   In Rome, 1901: Met Gino Severini. At Giacomo Balla's
1902   studio where he encountered Impressionism and Neo-Impressionism.

1902-   In Paris. Influenced by the Neo-Impressionists. Traveled
1904   to St. Petersburg.

1909   Met Marinetti. February 20: Publication of first *Futurist Manifesto* by *Le Figaro*, Paris. Tried to apply theories of Futurism to painting.

1910   February 11: *Manifesto of the Futurist Painters* published by Boccioni, Carrà, Russolo, Balla, Severini.

1911   December: Traveled to Paris where introduced by Severini to Picasso, Braque, Dufy and others.

1912   February 5-24: First Futurist Exhibition at Bernheim-Jeune Gallery, Paris. April 11: Published *Technical Manifesto of Futurist Sculpture*.

1913   June 20 to end July: Exhibition of Futurist Sculpture at Galerie La Boétie, Paris.

1914   September: First manifestations by leaders of Futurism in favor of Italian intervention in the war on the side of the Allies.

1915   Italy at war. Boccioni volunteered for army.

1916   August 16: Fell from his horse while riding near Verona. August 17: Death of Boccioni.

BIBLIOGRAPHY

G. Coquiot, *Cubistes, futuristes, passéistes*, Paris 1914. — R. Longhi, *Scultura futurista: B.*, in *La Voce*, Florence 1914. — A. de Witt, in *Dedalo*, 1914. — C. Carrà, Milan, 1916. — H. Walden, *Einblick in Kunst*, Berlin 1917. — F.T. Marinetti, 1924. — *L'Amour de l'Art*, Paris 1934. Bio-bibliographical notes. — A.H. Barr, *Cubism and Abstract Art*, New York 1936. — F. Pastonchi, in *Cahiers d'Art*, Paris 1950. — J.T. Soby and A.H. Barr, *Twentieth-Century Italian Art*, New York 1950.

BONNARD, PIERRE (1867-1947)

1867   Born October 13 at Fontenay-aux-Roses near Paris. His father, head of an office in the War Ministry, hailed from the Dauphiné province; his mother, Elise Mertzdorff, was an Alsatian.

1877-   Had a classical education, at which he did well, at the
1885   Vannes Lycée and Louis-le-Grand.

1885-1888   Under pressure from his father, studies law.

1888   Ecole des Beaux-Arts, Paris.

1889   A decisive year. Gauguin's art, on view at the Volpini exhibition, is a revelation. A group is formed: the "Nabis." Bonnard makes a poster, *France-Champagne*, preceding Lautrec's posters (1891), which he sells for a hundred francs. Gives up his law studies; decides to be a painter.

1890   Military service ar Bourgoin. *The Review* (Private Collection, Switzerland). His sister Andrée marries his friend Claude Terrasse, the composer. Shares a studio, 28, rue Pigalle, Montmartre, with Vuillard, Maurice Denis and Lugné-Poe.

1891   Exhibits 9 pictures at Salon des Indépendants, which are praised by Gustave Geffroy, the critic. The Natanson brothers launch *La Revue Blanche*, in which he at once collaborates. The Nabis have their first exhibition in Le Barc de Boutteville's Gallery.

1892   Again exhibits in Salon des Indépendants (March-April) and at Le Barc de Boutteville's (November). Small stylized black and grey panels, much admired by Roger Marx and Albert Aurier.

1893   Has a studio 63, rue de Douai. Color lithographs for *La Revue Blanche* and *L'Escarmouche*. Lugné-Poe founds the Théâtre de l'Œuvre; Bonnard helps with the sets and costumes. Meets Vollard.

1895   Vollard publishes *Quelques aspects de la Vie de Paris*, with 12 lithographs by Bonnard. Tiffany exhibits at the Salon a set of stained-glass windows, one of which, *Maternity*, is from a design by Bonnard. Bonnard sometimes accompanies Lautrec in his nocturnal jaunts in Montmartre.

1896   Bonnard's first one-man show, in Durand-Ruel's gallery, is discussed at length by G. Geffroy and T. Natanson. Collaborates with Terrasse at the *Théâtre des Pantins*.

1898   Bonnard illustrates *Marie*, a novel by Peter Nansen; his first illustrated book. In the spring begins the illustration of Verlaine's *Parallèlement*, commissioned by Vollard; the sketches are intermingled with the printed matter, giving the first indication of a form the modern illustrated book was often to take.

1899   Large-scale group exhibition at Durand-Ruel's as a "homage" to Odilon Redon. Bonnard enters into contact with Bernheim-Jeune Gallery.

1901   Exhibits a large triptych at Salon des Indépendants.

1902   Vollard publishes *Daphnis et Chloé* with Bonnard's illustrations.

1903   Exhibits at the first Salon d'Automne. *Bourgeois Afternoon.*

1904 Illustrates Jules Renard's *Histoires Naturelles*. One-man show at Bernheim's: intimate scenes, women dressing.

1905 Two pictures at Salon des Indépendants, five at Salon d'Automne.

1907-1910 Travels in Belgium, Holland, England, Italy, Spain, Tunisia.

1912 Buys a small house at Vernonnet near Vernon: *Ma Roulotte*. From now on till 1938 he divides his time between the Seine Valley and the South (Grasse, St. Tropez, Le Cannet). Declines Legion of Honor decoration. Has studio in Paris, 22, rue Tourlaque. His palette has grown brighter, as a result of the Provençal atmosphere. Large decorative panels.

1913 Travels in Holland and, with Vuillard, in England.

1914-1918 Lives at St. Germain-en-Laye.

1918 Spends the summer at Uriage. Has a studio in Paris, 56, rue Molitor.

1920 Thirty drawings for André Gide's *Prométhée mal enchaîné*.

1923 Death of Claude Terrasse.

1925 Buys a small house at Le Cannet, near Cannes. Watercolors. His Paris residence: 48, Boulevard des Batignolles.

1926 Visits the United States.

1930-1932 Arcachon. Winters at Le Cannet.

1932- Spends summers at Deauville and Trouville.

1938 Seascapes.

1940 Deaths of Madame Bonnard and Vuillard. Bonnard retires permanently to Le Cannet (a brief stay in Paris, in 1945). His lyrical emotion rises to a last, vivid intensity. His final achievement is a decorative work: *Saint François de Sales Visiting the Sick*, an altar picture for the church at Assy, Haute-Savoie.

1944 Publishes *Correspondance*.

1947 Dies, January 23, at Le Cannet.

BIBLIOGRAPHY

Correspondance, Paris 1944. — Interviews and observations collected in *L'Art et l'Affiche*, 1898. — *Verve*, August 1947. — *Arts de France*, 1947.

T. Natanson, *Revue Blanche*, 1896. — L. Cousturier, *L'Art décoratif*, 1912. — F. Fosca, Paris 1919. — G. Coquiot, Paris 1922. — L. Werth, Paris 1923. — C. Roger-Marx, 1924 and 1931. — C. Terrasse, Paris 1927 (with catalogue of graphic work by J. Floury). — A. Fontainas, Paris 1928. — G. Besson, Paris 1934. — J. de Laprade, Paris 1944. — A. Lhote, Paris 1944. — T. Natanson, Gischia, L. Werth, G. Diehl, Paris 1945. — P. Courthion, Lausanne 1945. — J. Leymarie, *L'Amour de l'Art*, Paris 1946. — F. Jourdain, Geneva 1946. — G. Besson, *Arts de France*, 1946. — G. Jedlicka, Zurich 1947. — J. Beer, Paris 1947. — J. Rewald, New York 1948.

Special numbers of *Le Point*, 1943. — *Formes et Couleurs*, 1944. — *Verve*, 1947.

BRAQUE, GEORGES (1882)

1882 Born at Argenteuil-sur-Seine, near Paris, May 13. His father owned a decorator's business and was a "Sunday painter" of some talent.

1890 His family moved to Le Havre.

1893 At school. Attended evening classes at local Art School.

1899 Apprenticed to his father.

1900 Settled in Paris, in Montmartre.

1902-1904 Two months at the Ecole des Beaux-Arts (under Bonnat), then at the Académie Humbert. 1904: Spent the summer in Normandy, near Honfleur. Moved into his first studio.

1906 Exhibited six canvases at Salon des Indépendants. Summer at Antwerp with Othon Friesz. Autumn at L'Estaque. Fauve influence.

1907 Exhibited with other Fauves at the Indépendants; sold all his canvases. Summer at La Ciotat, autumn at L'Estaque. Met Kahnweiler, who signed a contract for all his work, and Picasso.

1908 Spring and summer at L'Estaque. Marked influence of Cézanne. Submitted seven canvases to the Salon d'Automne, but the jury having refused five, he withdrew all seven and showed them with others at Kahnweiler's. In *Gil Blas* of November 14, 1908, Vauxcelles accused Braque of reducing everything to "little cubes."

1909 Exhibited at the Indépendants. Vauxcelles refers to "jumbles of cubes" (*Gil Blas*, 25th May). Derogatory in origin, the word "cubism" becomes current.

1910 Analytical Cubism. Began using oval canvases.

1911 First canvases incorporating letters of the alphabet. *The Portuguese*. Summer at Céret with Picasso.

1912 Synthetic Cubism. Summer at Sorgues with Picasso. First *papiers collés*; introduced sand and imitation grained wood into his canvases.

1914-1916 At the front where he distinguished himself by his courage. Two citations. Wounded in 1915. Underwent head operation.

1917 Summer at Sorgues. Painted in large tracts of flat color.

1919 Large exhibition at Galerie Léonce Rosenberg.

1922 Neo-classical period. Exhibits at the Salon d'Automne.

1923 Sets for *Les Fâcheux*, Diaghilev's ballet.

1924 Sets for *La Salade*, Soirées de Paris ballet, and for *Zéphyr et Flore*, Russian ballet. Settled at 6, rue du Douanier, in a house constructed by himself and Auguste Perret.

1927 Introduced bright colors into his work.

1929 Frequent stays at Varengeville. Landscapes.

1930 Gets farther away from the outward appearance of things, then reverts to a closer approximation of the real world.

1931-1932 Tapestry-cartoons for Madame Cuttoli. Fishing-boats and cliffs. At this time, his canvases are covered with a very thin coat of paint and frequently engraved with drawings in the neo-classical style. Illustrates Hesiod's *Theogony*.

1939 Sculptures in limestone. Horses' heads, plaster fishes cast in bronze or lead. Plaster reliefs, sometimes colored.

1940 Fled to the Pyrenees to escape German invasion. Came back to Paris in the autumn. Introduced naturalistic elements into his painting (household objects).

1943 General exhibition at Salon d'Automne (26 paintings, 9 sculptures).

1945 Awarded Legion of Honor decoration.

1946 Exhibition in Tate Gallery, London, with Rouault. Paints *Billiards* (in several versions). Beginning of series of lithographs *Helios*.

1947 Completed *Cahier de Georges Braque* (aphorisms and lithographs).

1948 Awarded the First Prize for Painting at the 24th Biennale, Venice.

1953 Large-scale decoration for the Room II ceiling, at the Louvre. Exhibition in Bern and Zurich (Switzerland).

BIBLIOGRAPHY

G. Apollinaire (Preface to the catalogue of B.'s exhibition at the Galerie Kahnweiler), Paris 1908. — Id., *Les Peintres cubistes*, Paris 1913. — *Soirées de Paris*, special number for G.B., Paris 1914. — G. Coquiot, *Cubistes, futuristes, passéistes*, Paris 1914. — M. Raynal, Rome 1924. — C. Zervos, *Cahiers d'Art*, No. 1/2, Paris 1932. — G. Isarlow, *Orbes*, No. 3, Paris 1932. — *Cahiers d'Art*, No. 1/2, Paris 1933. Published for B.'s exhibition at the Kunstmuseum, Basel. With contributions by Apollinaire, Bissière, Breton, Cassou, Cendrars, Einstein, Lhote, Salmon, Soffici, Zervos, etc. — C. Einstein, Paris 1934. — A.H. Barr, *Cubism and Abstract Art*, Museum of Modern Art, New York 1936. — S. Fumet, New York 1945. — F. Ponge, Geneva 1946. — P. Eluard, *Voir*, Geneva 1948. — J. Grenier, Paris 1948. Published in English: London 1948. — H.R. Hope, Museum of Modern Art, New York 1949. With bibliography.

CARRÀ, CARLO (1881)

1881 Born at Quargnento, Italy, February 11. Left school at age of twelve to earn living as decorator. At same time worked at School of Decorative Arts, Brera.

1900 First visit to Paris. Decorated pavilions at World's Fair. Summer in London.

1909 Met Marinetti and Boccioni.

1910 Signed *Manifesto of Futurist Painters*.

1911 Second visit to Paris. Met Apollinaire, Modigliani, Picasso. Influenced by Cubism.

1912-1913 Exhibited at Futurist Exhibitions in Paris, London, Berlin, etc. Friendship with the architect Sant'Elia. Collaborated in review *Lacerba*. Brief contacts with Diaghilev and Stravinsky.

1915 Moved away from Futurism. Military service at Ferrara where he met Chirico.

1916 First metaphysical paintings under Chirico's influence. *The Drunken Gentleman*.

1917 Four important metaphysical works: *Solitude; Mother and Son; The Metaphysical Muse; The Enchanted Room*.

1919 Joined "Valori Plastici" group. Wrote for review *Valori Plastici* and became art critic of the newspaper *Popolo d'Italia*. Published: *Pittura metafisica*.

1925 Exhibited at Third Biennale, Rome.

1932 Traveled to Munich, Prague and Dresden.

1937 Visited Algiers, Malta, Palermo.

1950 Exhibition at the Biennale, Venice.

BIBLIOGRAPHY

G. Raimondi, Bologna 1918. — G. de Chirico, *Pittura metafisica di C.C.*, *Il convegno*, Milan, August 1920. — A. Soffici (*Arte Moderna italiana* 11), Milan 1928. — P.M. Bardi, Milan 1930. — R. Longhi (*Arte Moderna italiana* 11), Milan 1937. With bibliography. — G. Raimondi (*Arte Moderna italiana* 38), Milan 1942. With bibliography. — C. Carrà, *La mia vita*, Milan 1943. — G. Pacchioni, Milan 1945. With extensive documentation.

CÉZANNE, PAUL (1839-1906)

1839 Born at Aix-en-Provence, 23, rue de l'Opéra, Jan. 19. The family hailed from a village named Cézanne (Cesena) on the Italian side of Mont Genèvre, but was of French stock. His father Louis-Auguste Cézanne, a hat-maker, married in 1844 one of his work-girls, Honorine Aubert, by whom he had already had two children, Paul and Marie (born on July 4, 1841) who was always tenderly devoted to her brother.

1844 Attended dame-school in the rue des Epinaux, until 1849.

1847 His father took over the Banque Barges then in liquidation and launched it as a new concern, the Banque Cézanne et Cabassol. Located at 24, rue des Cordeliers, then 14, rue Boulegon, at Aix.

1849 Day-boarder at the Ecole St. Joseph.

1852 Boarder at the Collège Bourbon (now Lycée Mignet) until 1856; day-boy from 1856 to 1858. Thorough classical education, backed by religious teaching. Amongst his schoolfriends were Baptistin Baille and notably Emile Zola with whom he remained very intimate until their quarrel in 1886.

1856 Works under Gibert at the Aix School of Drawing. Second prize in 1858. Also studies music; much enthusiasm for Wagner.

1859 Takes degree in Letters (classified "moderately good"). Begins the correspondence with Zola who is now at the Lycée Louis-le-Grand, Paris. His wish is to go to Paris to study painting, but his father insists on his entering the Law School at Aix. This year, Cézanne *père*, whose bank is prospering, buys a country house near Aix, "Le Jas de Bouffan," where young Cézanne spends the summer and installs a studio.

1860 He tries to persuade his father to let him devote himself to painting, and his mother and sister Marie back him up in this. Besides Zola and Baille, with whom he subsequently loses touch, his friends at this time are a sculptor Philippe Solari (his faithful friend until his death, who did his bust in 1904), Numa Coste who was to become a journalist, Emperaire a painter, and Valabrègue an art-critic. Is now influenced by Loubon and the paintings in the Caravaggio manner in the Aix Museum.

1861 April. His father yields at last and goes with him to Paris. He lodges rue des Feuillantines, attends the Suisse Academy, where he meets Guillaumin and Pissarro, the latter of whom greatly influences him. Visits the Louvre and Salon. In September, after a setback at the Ecole des Beaux-Arts, has a fit of homesickness, goes back to Aix and takes a post in his father's bank, though he still attends drawing classes in the evening. He now does murals at Le Jas de Bouffan: *The Four Seasons* (Musée du Petit-Palais, Paris), *Interior* (Museum of Modern Art, Moscow), inspired by illustrations in a fashion paper.

1862 Nov.-1864, July. Second stay in Paris. Works at the Suisse Academy; becomes very friendly with Pissarro, Guillaumin, Oller, Guillemet, Bazille, Monet, Sisley, Renoir. With Zola visits the 1863 Salon des Refusés. He still admires above all Delacroix and Courbet. Embarks on a series of intensely romantic works, executed in dark, dramatic, "lurid" (as he calls them) tones, a manner which is to persist until 1872.

1864 Again loses heart and returns to Aix. From 1864 to 1870 shares his time between Paris and Aix. The pictures he sends in to the Salon are invariably rejected.

1865-
1867 Introduced to Manet who admires his Still Lifes. Does portraits of *Valabrègue*, *Emperaire* and of *The Artist's Father Reading L'Evénement*, the newspaper which published Zola's first articles on Manet.

1867-
1869 Long stays in the South. When at Paris constantly moving; rue de Chevreuse, rue de Vaugirard, rue Notre-Dame-des-Champs. Baroque compositions with erotic tendencies: *The Rape*, *The Orgy* (Coll. Lecomte, Paris), *The Temptation of St Anthony*.

1870 During the war lies low at L'Estaque, near Marseilles, where he lives with Hortense Fiquet, a young model he met in Paris.

1871 After the Commune returns to Paris and lives in the same house as Solari, 5, rue de Chevreuse.

1872 Birth of his son Paul (Jan. 4). Now living in the rue de Jussieu; in the spring goes to Saint-Ouen-l'Aumône; then visits Pissarro at Pontoise.

1873 Settles down at Auvers-sur-Oise, near Dr Gachet. Paints *The Hanged Man's House* (Louvre) and several landscapes showing Pissarro's influence. Meets Père Tanguy.

1874 Takes part in the First Impressionist Exhibition, thanks to Pissarro's good offices, and despite the opposition of the other exhibitors. His canvases, *Landscape at Auvers*, *The Hanged Man's House*, and *A Modern Olympia* were those most derided by the public. A short stay at Aix.

1875 Now living at 120, rue de Vaugirard; later, Quai d'Anjou. Meets Chocquet.

1876 Spends summer at L'Estaque. Refuses to join in the Second Impressionist Exhibition.

1877 Works at Pontoise, Auvers. Shows 17 canvases at Third Impressionist Exhibition (still lifes and landscapes), but the public is still hostile.

1878 Retires to L'Estaque; spends some months with his mother, now seriously ill. Trouble with his father about his way of living. Zola aids him financially. Cuts loose from Impressionism.

1879 Again rejected at the Salon, despite Guillemet's intervention. From May 1879 to February 1880 spends a quiet year with his family at Melun, often visiting Zola at Médan.

1880 Living at 32, Rue de l'Ouest, Paris, from Feb. 1880 to May 1881. Makes Huysmans' acquaintance. Spends summer with Zola at Médan.

1881 With Pissarro at Pontoise, May to Oct. Short stay at Aix in November.

1882 Renoir visits him at L'Estaque. Accepted at the Salon as "Guillemet's pupil." In Paris February to September. Settles at Le Jas de Bouffan, Aix.

1883 Works in neighborhood of Aix and at L'Estaque. Then roams Provence with Monticelli. In Dec. visited by Renoir and Monet.

1884 A mysterious love-affair which ends unhappily. June and July stays with Renoir at La Roche-Guyon. Returns in August to the South, where he stays until 1888. Works chiefly at Gardanne, a small town perched on a hilltop near Aix. The "classical" element in his style is growing more and more pronounced.

1886 Marries Hortense Fiquet (April); breaks with Zola, who in his novel *L'Œuvre* modeled one of the characters, an unsuccessful painter, on Cézanne. On Oct. 23 his father dies, leaving him comfortably well off.

1887 Exhibits with the "Les Vingt" at Brussels.

1888 Stays in Paris. Country rambles in the Ile-de-France.

1889 Entertains Renoir at Le Jas de Bouffan. Exhibits at the "Décennale" (World's Fair) thanks to Chocquet's insistence.

1891 A pleasure trip to Switzerland and in the Jura region. First attack of diabetes.

1892 Stays at Fontainebleau. To this extremely fertile phase of his career belong the 5 versions of *The Card-Players*, the series of *Baigneuses*, and that of the *Montagne Sainte-Victoire*.

1894 Spends autumn at Giverny in the home of Monet, who introduces him to Rodin, Clemenceau, Gustave Geffroy.

1895 First exhibition at Ambroise Vollard's. His work is cold-shouldered by the public, but thought much of by artists and some connoisseurs. *Portraits of Gustave Geffroy* and *The Boy in a Red Waistcoat*.

1896 In Paris January to June. At Aix June to September. During this period he takes a cure at Vichy and makes a short stay at Talloires beside the Lake of Annecy.

1896 Makes the acquaintance of the young poet Joachim Gasquet who becomes his warm admirer.

1897- Often works at Montbriant in the estate of his brother-
1898 in-law, Conil. Here he paints some fine views of the Valley of the Arc overhung by Montagne Sainte-Victoire; he also paints at Le Tholonet in a room fitted out as a studio at the *Château-Noir*. He also rents a *cabanon* (shanty) at the Bibemus quarry, above the Aix barrage. Oct. 15 his mother dies. Visits Paris.

1899 Sells Le Jas de Bouffan and settles in a small flat at 24, Rue Boulegon at Aix, with a devoted housekeeper, Mme Brémond. Exhibits three canvases at the Indé-pendants.

1900 Figures at the Centennial Exhibition; his fame is steadily increasing, abroad as well as in France. The Berlin Nationalgalerie purchases one of his pictures. Maurice Denis paints his *Hommage à Cézanne* (Musée d'Art Moderne, Paris), showing Bonnard, Denis, Redon, Roussel, Sérusier and Vuillard grouped round the Aix Master.

1901 Exhibits at *La Libre Esthétique*, Brussels, and at the Indépendants. Buys some land on the Les Lauves road north of Aix and has a studio built on it.

1902 The death of Zola, Sept. 29, despite their rupture, is a great blow to him. Mirbeau tries to secure his nomina-tion to the *Légion d'Honneur*, but fails.

1904 Stays some weeks at Paris and Fontainebleau. An entire room at the Salon d'Automne devoted to his work. This is his year of triumph. Young admirers come to Aix to pay their respects; provincials such as Léo Larguier, Joachim Gasquet, Charles Camoin, and Parisians, Edmond Jaloux, Roussel, Maurice Denis, Emile Bernard.

1905 He exhibits again at the Salon d'Automne and the Indépendants. Finishes the *Grandes Baigneuses* on which he had worked seven years.

1906 On Oct. 15., caught in a rainstorm while painting in the open his *Cabanon de Jourdan*, he collapsed on the road-side. A passing laundry cart picked him up, and he was taken home. He died on Oct. 22.

BIBLIOGRAPHY

Correspondence, compiled and edited by J. Rewald, Paris 1937; London 1941.
L. Venturi, *Cézanne, son art, son œuvre*, Paris 1936, 2 vols. Indispensable, 1634 items (805 paintings), 1619 illustrations. Preceded by an excellent critical study. Exhaustive biblio-graphy (561 items). (New and enlarged edition in preparation.)
A. Vollard, Paris 1914. — J. Gasquet, Paris 1921. — E. Bernard, Paris 1921. — G. Rivière, Paris 1923. — L. Larguier, *Le Dimanche avec Paul Cézanne*, Paris 1925. — E. Jaloux, *Souvenirs*, in *L'Amour de l'Art*, 1920. — C. Camoin and M. Laforgue, *Souvenirs*, in *L'Amour de l'Art*, 1921.
J. Meier-Graefe, Munich 1910. — J. Rivière, Paris 1910. — E. Faure, Paris 1910. — G. Severini, *L'Esprit Nouveau*, Nov.-Dec. 1921. — J. Meier-Graefe, Munich 1922. — T. Klingsor, Paris 1923. — A. Salmon, Paris 1923. — R. Fry, New York-London 1927. — E. d'Ors, Paris 1930. — G. Mack, London 1935; French edition 1938. — M. Raynal, Paris 1936. — J. Rewald, *Cézanne et Zola*, Paris 1936. — R. Huyghe, Paris 1936. — F. Novotny, Vienna 1938. — A.C. Barnes and V. de Mazia, New York 1939. — G. Jedlicka, Zurich 1939. — J. Rewald, Paris 1939. — L. Venturi, *Watercolors*, London 1943. — R.M. Rilke, *Lettres sur Cézanne*, Paris 1944. — E.A. Jewell, New York 1944. — P.M. Auzas, Paris 1945. — E. Loran, Los Angeles 1946. — B. Dorival, Paris 1948. — A. Lothe, Lau-sanne 1949. — M. Raynal, Geneva 1954.
Special numbers of *L'Amour de l'Art*, 1920 and 1936. — *La Renaissance*, 1936. — *L'Art Sacré*, 1936.

CHAGALL, Marc (1887)

1887 Born at Vitebsk, Russia, July 7. His father worked in a fish shop. A local academic painter, Tene, gave him his first lessons.

1907 Painted first important pictures. *Death*.

1908 Goes to St Petersburg, where he studies at the Imperial School of Fine Arts.

1910 A St Petersburg patron offered to send him to Paris or Rome in lieu of payment for seven pictures. Chagall chose Paris and settled at *La Ruche* near the Vaugirard slaughterhouse.
Friendship with poet Blaise Cendrars, Canudo, publisher of the review *Montjoie*, the painters La Fresnaye, Delaunay, Modigliani and poets Max Jacob and André Salmon.

1914 Introduced by Apollinaire to Walden, who organized his first one-man show at Berlin in the offices of the review *Der Sturm*. Chagall sent 200 canvases, which were still in Germany at outbreak of war. Visited his exhibition at Berlin en route for Vitebsk to marry his fiancée. Decla-ration of War.

1915 Married Bella. Called up; placed on reserve list.

1917 The Revolution. Elected Commissar of Fine Arts for the Government of Vitebsk. Founded a school.

1919- Granowsky, director of the Jewish theater at Moscow,
1922 commissioned mural paintings for the foyer. At work in the theater, and on his autobiography.
Left Russia. Went to Berlin where the publisher Cassirer brought out first series of engravings (illustrations for *Mein Leben*).

1922- Returned to Paris during winter. Cendrars brings Vol-
1923 lard to his studio.

1923 Vollard commissioned illustrations for Gogol's *Dead Souls* (96 engravings). Chagall worked on them till 1927; published only in 1949.

1924 First retrospective exhibition at Galerie Barbazange-Hodebert, Paris.

1926 First one-man show in New York.

1927-1930 Illustrations for La Fontaine's *Fables* (100 plates).

1931 Traveled to Near East to collect local color for illustra-trations of the Bible commissioned by Vollard. The work was unfinished at Vollard's death.
His autobiography, *Ma Vie* (My Life), is published in Paris.

1933 Retrospective exhibition at the Basel Museum.

1935 Traveled to Poland.

1936- Deeply stirred by the signs of war and the Jewish perse-
1939 cutions. Painted dramatic works, notably crucifixions. Carnegie Prize.

1941 Invited to the United States by Museum of Modern Art. Arrived there 23rd June. Lived quietly in the country. Mexico. Sets and costumes for *Aleco* (Tchaikowsky).

1944 Bella died. Work interrupted for a long time.

1945 Started work again with decors and costumes for *The Fire Bird* (ballet, music by Stravinsky).

1946 Retrospective exhibition at Museum of Modern Art, New York, then at Chicago Art Institute.

1947 Returned to Paris. Retrospective exhibition, taken later to Amsterdam and London.

1948 Awarded International Prize for Engraving at 24th Biennale, Venice. Worked at Orgeval near Paris.

1949 Settled in Vence (South of France) where he discovered the art of pottery.
Two large mural paintings for the Watergate Theatre, London.

1951 Retrospective exhibition in Zurich and Bern. Trip to Israel.

1952 Exhibition at Nice. Musée des Ponchettes.

1953 Retrospective exhibition in Turin.
(Information supplied by the artist's daughter.)

BIBLIOGRAPHY

A. Efross and I. Tugendhold, Potsdam 1921. — T. Däubler, Rome 1922. — K. With *(Junge Kunst. 35)*, Leipzig 1923. — *Sturm-Bilderbuch*, I, Berlin 1923; 2nd ed. With a poem by Blaise Cendrars. — B. Aronson, Berlin 1924. — E. Szittya, *Malerschicksale*, Hamburg 1925. — M. Raynal, *Anthologie de la peinture en France de 1906 à nos jours*, Paris 1927. — W. George, Paris 1928. With bibliography. — P. Fierens, Paris 1929. — *Sélection*, 6, Antwerp 1929, With bibliography and contributions by Chagall, W. George, J. Maritain, M. Raynal, A. Vollard. — R. Schwob, Paris 1931. — H. Miller, Berkeley 1944. — G. Schmidt, *Labyrinthe* No. 3, Geneva 1944. — L. Venturi, New York 1945. With bibliography. — Id., *Painting and Painters, from Giotto to C.*, New York 1945. — J. J. Sweeney, New York 1946. With important bibliography by H. B. Muller. — P. Eluard, *Voir*, Geneva 1948. — R. Maritain, Geneva 1949. — C. Estienne, Paris 1951. — U. Apollonio, Venice, 1951.

CHIRICO, Giorgio de (1888)

1888 Born at Volo, Greece, July 10, of Italian parents. Two years at the Fine Arts Academy, Athens.

1905 Copied the old masters in museums of Milan and Flo-rence: Uccello, Piero della Francesca, Botticelli, etc. Studied under Hackl at Munich Academy (1909-1910?). Decisive influence of Nietzsche and Wagner, Böcklin and Klinger.

1910 Metaphysical paintings of towns.

1911- Settled in Paris. Met Picasso. Apollinaire, Max Jacob,
1915 Paul Guillaume. 1914: First paintings with busts and geometric elements. 1915: Returned to Italy. Military service at Ferrara where he met Carlo Carrà who in 1916 did his first metaphysical paintings under Chirico's influence.

1919 Joins "Valori Plastici" group.

1924 Returned to Paris. Collaborated with Breton and Surrealists.

1925 Exhibited at first general Surrealist exhibition at Galerie Pierre, Paris.

1926 Decors for *Death of Niobe* by Alberto Savinio at Teatro Odescalchi, Rome.

1929 Published *Hebdomeros*, a dream novel. Decors for *The Ball* (Ballets Russes de Monte-Carlo).

1930 Decors for *The Life of Orestes*, opera by Krenek, at the Kroll-Oper, Berlin.

1933 Frescos at the Palazzo della Triennale, Milan. After this Chirico returned to academicism and repudiated his earlier work.

BIBLIOGRAPHY

Dodici opere di G. de Ch., Rome 1919; with contributions by A. Soffici, Apollinaire, Vauxcelles, Raynal, R. Marx, Carrà, Estienne. — R. Vitrac, Paris 1927. — J. Cocteau, Paris 1928. — W. George, with some writings by the artist, Paris 1928. — B. Ternovetz, Milan 1928. — *Sélection*, No. 8; issue devoted to G. de Ch., Antwerp 1929. With contributions by Bardi, Courthion, poems by Ch. — J. T. Soby, New York 1941. —R. Carrieri, Milan 1942. — A. Pica, *12 opere di G. de Ch.*, Milan 1944. — Lo Duca (Arte Moderna italiana. 10), Milan 1936. New edition 1945. With bibliography. — J. Faldi, Venice 1949. With bibliography.

DALI, SALVADOR (1904)

1904 Born at Figueras, near Barcelona, May 11.

1921- Wild career at School of Fine Arts, Madrid.

1924 Influenced by Chirico and Carrà's "metaphysical" style.

1925- Exhibited canvases in contradictory styles, but always
1927 very minutely painted, at Madrid and Barcelona.

1928 In Paris. Met Picasso and the surrealist painters and writers.

1929 First Paris Exhibition at Galerie Goemans.

1930 Published *La Femme Visible*, in which he outlined his theories.

1931 Collaborated with Bunuel on film *L'Age d'Or*.

1931- Interpretations of the William Tell legend and of
1934 Millet's *Angelus*.

1934 Illustrated *Les Chants de Maldoror* by Lautréamont (Skira). First journey to United States.

1937 Traveled in Italy. New appreciation of Raphael and the Baroque.

1940 Settled in California.

1941 Retrospective exhibition at Museum of Modern Art, New York.

1942- Published his autobiography: *The Secret Life of Salvador*
1944 *Dali*. Portraits of notable personalities.

1950 Started work on large panel representing the Virgin pregnant.
Pays the Pope a visit in Vatican City.

1953 In Barcelona, organizes a festival.

BIBLIOGRAPHY

R. Crevel, Paris 1931. — J. Lacan, *De la psychose paranoïaque dans ses rapports avec la personnalité*, Paris 1932. — D. Gascoyne, *A Short Survey of Surrealism*, London 1935. — R. Huyghe, *Histoire de l'art contemporain*, Paris 1935. With documentation by G. Bazin. — A. H. Barr, *Fantastic Art, Dada and Surrealism*, New York 1936. — J. Levy, *Surrealism*, New York 1936. — M. Block, *Current Biography*, 1940. With bibliography. — A. Breton, *Le surréalisme et la peinture*, New York 1945. — J. T. Soby, Museum of Modern Art, New York 1946. With important bibliography by B. Karpel. — P. Eluard, *Voir*, Geneva 1948.

DELAUNAY, ROBERT (1885-1941)

1885 Born in Paris, April 12.

1902- Apprenticed to Ronsin, a stage designer in Belleville.

1904 Painted in Brittany during his holidays. Influenced by the Pont-Aven school.

1905 Devoted himself entirely to painting. Influenced by the Neo-Impressionists. Friendly with Metzinger who was working along the same lines.

1907 One of the first admirers of Henri Rousseau, he introduced the Douanier to his mother who described her travels in India and inspired the famous painting *La Charmeuse de serpents* which she commissioned.

1908 Still lifes with blues and greens predominating. These colors later re-appeared in his cubist paintings. Developed an enthusiasm for Egyptian and Chaldean art in the Louvre. Painted *Paysages au Parc de Saint-Cloud* influenced by Cézanne.

1909 Began *The Tower of Notre-Dame* and the series called *Saint-Séverin* and *Cities*.

1910 Painted his first *Eiffel Tower*, a dynamic work full of light. Married Sonia Terk.

1911 The German painter Elisabeth Epstein—friend of Kandinsky, Jawlensky and their circle—visited Paris. She pointed out Delaunay's work in the famous Room 41 at the Indépendants to Kandinsky who was then working with Marc on the organization of the Exhibition of the Editorial Staff of the Blue Rider. At Kandinsky's invitation Delaunay sent 3 pictures. Became friendly with Apollinaire, Le Fauconnier and Gleizes.

1912 Exhibited at the 2nd Blue Rider show. Macke, Marc and Klee met Delaunay in Paris and were greatly influenced by his work. Klee translated his article *Sur la lumière* and published it in the review "Der Sturm," No. 144/145, January 1913. Painted: *The City of Paris* and *Windows* (Orphic period).

1913 Traveled to Berlin with Apollinaire for his exhibition at the "Der Sturm" Gallery. Apollinaire's lecture on modern art. Through Apollinaire Delaunay met Blaise Cendrars. Frequented Chagall, Archipenko and the Americans Bruce and Frost. Exhibited *L'Equipe du Cardiff* at the Indépendants. Traveled to Berlin where he exhibited at the first German Autumn Salon at the "Sturm Gallery."

1914 Painted *Homage to Blériot*. Traveled to Spain (Fuenterrabia) where he was caught by the war.

1915- Settled in Madrid. Painted *Nude reading* and *The Gitano*.

1917 Spent the summer in Lisbon. In the spring of 1917 in touch with Diaghilev's Russian Ballet.
Meets Stravinsky, Diego Rivera and others.

1918 Scenery for *Cleopatra*, Diaghilev ballet, with costumes by Sonia Delaunay. Painted Massine's and Stravinsky's portraits.

1921 Returned to Paris. The Dadaists and future Surrealists met in his home at Neuilly.

1922 Large retrospective exhibition at Galerie Paul Guillaume. Painted portraits of Soupault, Breton, Aragon, Tzara, Claire and Ivan Goll.

1924 Paris landscapes with the *Eiffel Tower* from the Louvre. Series of *Runners*.

1925 Mural paintings *City of Paris* for the "Palace of the French Embassy" at the International Exhibition of the Decorative Arts, Paris.

1930 Painted: *Play of Multicolored Disks* or *The Joy of Living*. Started working on plaster reliefs. Series of *Rhythms* and *Rhythms without End*.

1937 Large decorations in the "Palace of the Railway" and the "Palace of the Air" at the Paris exhibition.

1938 Decorated the Sculpture Room at the Salon des Tuileries with Gleizes, Villon, Lhote and Sonia Delaunay. Met Kandinsky with whom he had corresponded.

1939 Launched the first exhibition of *Réalités Nouvelles* (Galerie Charpentier, Paris).

1940 After the German invasion took refuge in Auvergne. Winter 1940/41 at Mougins.

1941 Died at Montpellier, October 25.
(Information supplied by Mrs Sonia Delaunay.)

BIBLIOGRAPHY

E. von Busse, *Die Kompositionsmittel bei R. D.*, Der Blaue Reiter, Munich 1912. — U. Boccioni, *Simultanéité futuriste*, Der Sturm Nos. 190/191, Berlin 1913. — P. Bommerstein, *Die Überwindung der Perspektive und R. D.*, Der Sturm No. 149, Berlin 1913. — G. Apollinaire, *Notes, Il y a*, Paris 1925. — H. Arp and El Lissitzky, *Die Kunstismen*, Zurich 1925. — B. Cendrars, *Profond aujourd'hui*, Paris 1926. — G. Bazin, *L'Orphisme, L'Amour de l'Art*, Paris 1933. With bio-bibliographical notes. — A. H. Barr, *Cubism and Abstract Art*, New York 1936. — C. Giedion-Welcker, *Werk* No. 8, Winterthur 1946. — J. Cassou, Preface to the catalogue of the R. D. Exhibition, Galerie L. Carré, Paris 1946. — R. S. Davis, *Institute acquires Cubist Masterpiece, Bulletin of the Minneapolis Institute of Arts,*

Minneapolis, October 4, 1947. — H. Arp, *Onze peintres vus par Arp*, Zurich 1949. — M. Seuphor, *L'art abstrait, ses origines, ses premiers maîtres*, Paris 1949. — F. Gilles de la Tourette, Paris 1950. — A. Gleizes, unpublished.

DENIS, MAURICE (1870-1943)

1870 Born at Grandville, Nov. 25. His father was an employee on the Ouest railway, his mother Hortense Adde, a milliner. Taken when three months old to St-Germain-en-Laye, where he lived for the rest of his life. A brilliant pupil first at the Pension Villon, then at the Lycée Condorcet. Taught drawing by a Brazilian artist, Balla.

1888 Académie Julian. Converted to the Pont-Aven theories of aesthetics by Sérusier.

1890 Exhibits a pastel, *The Choir-boy*, at the Salon; publishes an article on art in *Art et Critique*.

1891 Joins in the Nabi exhibition at Le Barc de Bouteville's Gallery. Nicknamed "the Nabi of beautiful icons."

1893 Helps in designing sets and costumes for Lugné-Poe's *Théâtre de l'Œuvre*. Makes illustrations for *Le Voyage d'Urien* by Gide.

1895 First journey to Italy; he now reverts to the classical, humanist art-tradition. Visits Tuscany and Umbria.

1897 Second journey to Italy; André Gide takes him to Rome.

1903 Goes with Sérusier to the Beuron Monastery. Vollard publishes his 216 woodcuts illustrating *L'Imitation de Jésus-Christ*.

1905 Travels in Spain with Mithouard (Avila).

1906 Pilgrimage, with Roussel and Emile Bernard, to Aix, to pay respects to Cézanne. He has already painted his *Hommage à Cézanne* (1900, Musée d'Art Moderne, Paris).

1908 Teaches, with Sérusier, at the Académie Ranson.

1907- Stays in Italy which speed up his tendencies towards
1908 Neo-Classicism. He now travels widely; to Moscow (1909), Dominica (1913), Switzerland (1914), Siena (1921), Algeria and Tunisia (1921), the United States and Canada (1927), Rome (1928), and in 1924 goes on pilgrimage to the Holy Land, to Greece and Italy.

1911 Illustration for *Sagesse* by Verlaine (Vollard).

1919 With Desvallières founds the Studios of Sacred Art for the revival of religious painting. His work alternates between intimist easel-pictures and big decorative works, religious and other: the Chapelle Sainte Croix at Le Vésinet (1899), Théâtre des Champs-Elysées (1912), cupola of the Petit-Palais (1924-25), the Saint Louis Church at Vincennes (1927), the Lycée Claude Bernard (1938), the League of Nations building, Geneva (1939).

1943 Dies in a motor-car accident, Nov. 3.

BIBLIOGRAPHY

An able writer and critic, Maurice Denis published a number of books and articles which attracted much attention: articles in *Art et Critique*, 1890. — *L'Occident*, 1907 and 1908. — *Théories*, Paris 1913. — *Nouvelles Théories*, Paris 1921. — *Charmes et Leçons de l'Italie*, Paris 1913. — *Histoire de l'Art Religieux*, Paris 1939. — *Sérusier, Sa Vie, Son Œuvre*, Paris 1942.

G. Geffroy, *La Vie Artistique*, 1891. — P. Jamot, *Gazette des Beaux-Arts*, 1911. — P. Alfassa, *Mercure de France*, 1912. — J. L. Vaudoyer, *Art et Décoration*, 1913. — L. Cousturier, *Art décoratif*, 1913. — M. Lafargue, *L'Amour de l'Art*, 1924. — F. Fosca, Paris 1924. — M. Brillant, Paris 1929. — *L'Art sacré*, Special number, Dec. 1937. — S. Barazetti, Paris 1945. — P. Jamot, Paris 1946.

DERAIN, ANDRÉ (1880-1954)

1880 Born June 10 at Chatou, where his father kept a pastry-shop. Wished to see his son an engineer and had him study for the Ecole Polytechnique. But as early as 15 Derain was already painting.

1898- Attends the Académie Carrière where he meets Matisse.
1899 Makes friends with Vlaminck, also living at Chatou.

1900 As he is copying Ghirlandaio's *Bearing of the Cross* at the Louvre, the attendants take exception to his interpretation and turn him out.

1901- At the Van Gogh Exhibition, he introduces Vlaminck
1902 to Matisse. At Chatou, he and Vlaminck work in the same studio. They do landscapes at Saint-Germain-en-Laye, Carrière-Saint-Denis, Le Pecq. First illustrated book: *D'un Lit dans l'Autre*, a novel by Vlaminck.

1904 Studies at Académie Julian.

1905 Military service; afterwards he joins Matisse in the South of France. In 1905 all the pictures in his studio are bought up by Vollard. Matisse visits Derain and Vlaminck at Chatou and advises them to exhibit at Salon des Indépendants.
Shows some landscapes at Salon d'Automne with Matisse, Rouault, Vlaminck, Manguin.
Exhibits at Berthe Weill's.

1907 Makes a contract with the Kahnweiler Gallery. Concurrently with a study of wood-engraving, he tries his hand at sculpture.
Works towards simplified form; studies volumes.
Stays at Martigues where he comes to grips with the problem of composition.

1908 Does ceramics, fired by Metthey, and paints *Les Baigneuses*; strong influence of Cézanne and of Cubism. Abandons pure color and breaks with Fauvism.

1909 Stays at Montreuil-sur-Mer. Does woodcuts for Apollinaire's *L'Enchanteur pourrissant*: one of the best 20th-century illustrated books.

1910 Stays at Cagnes. Paints *Le Pont de Cagnes*, typical of his lifelong interest in building the picture architecturally. Autumn: first trip to Spain where he meets Picasso (Cadaqués). Paints his first still lifes.

1912 Beginning of his Gothic period. Leanings towards stylization. Paints landscapes in the Lot Department. Returns to Paris in the winter. Figure studies.

1914 Portraits of Paul Poiret. Paints one of his masterpieces: *Saturday* (Museum of Modern Art, Moscow), as well as *The Two Sisters*, *The Chevalier X...* and *The Drinker*. Paints *The Last Supper*, which marks the end of Cubist influence in his work.

1914- Called up during the war, he makes masks from shell-
1918 cases. First one-man show at Paul Guillaume's (1916).

1919 Does sets for the Russian Ballet, *La Boutique Fantasque*.

1920- Rambles throughout the South of France. Landscapes

1930 at Bandol, Sanary, Cahors. Trip to Italy in 1921.

1924 Paints *Arlequin et Pierrot* and *La Table de Cuisine*.

1928 Carnegie Prize awarded him for *La Chasse* (Pittsburgh Museum).

1931 Large exhibition at Paul Guillaume's.

1935 Makes his home at Chambourcy (Seine-et-Oise).

1945 Portraits, sanguines. Illustrates Rabelais' *Pantagruel* (color woodcuts).
Does stage-sets in London.

1954 July 20: Knocked down by a motor-car.
September 8: Dies in a private hospital at Garches, near Paris.

BIBLIOGRAPHY

A. Basler, Ed. Crès, Paris. — Album of the *Chroniques du Jour* No. 3. — *Albums d'Art Druet* No. 31, Paris. — Daniel Henry, Leipzig 1920. — Elie Faure, Paris 1923. — Carlo Carrà, Rome 1924. — A. Salomon, *Chroniques du Jour*, Paris 1929. — *Pour ou contre Derain*, in the *Chroniques du Jour*, No. 8, 1931. — J. Leymarie, Geneva 1948.

DUCHAMP, MARCEL (1887)

1887 Born at Blainville near Rouen, July 28. Brother of the sculptor Raymond Duchamp-Villon and the painters Jacques Villon and Suzanne Duchamp. Went to school in Rouen. Started painting at the Académie Julian, Paris.

1910 First painting: *Portrait of Father* (influenced by Cézanne).

1911 Joined the Section d'Or. Painted the first sketches for *Nude descending a Staircase* and *The Coffee Grinder*.

1912 Painted *The King and Queen traversed by Quick Nudes*, *The Virgin*, *The Bride*, *The Virgin becomes a married Woman* and *Nude descending a Staircase*. This last picture was exhibited at the Section d'Or in October and in the following year at the Armory Show, New York.

1914- First "ready-mades" described as "scandalous." In
1915 1914 he signed a lithograph by an unknown painter and gave it the title of *Pharmacie*. He made several "ready-mades" from everyday objects (bottle-holders, snow-shovels, etc.), and gave them fantastic titles.
June: first voyage to the United States where he became the central figure of the Stieglitz group, which created an "anti-painting" and "anti-art" movement similar to the Dada movement in Zurich. *The Bride Stripped bare by her Bachelors, even*, on which he worked from 1915 to 1923. André Breton sees them like this: *The Bride* (hanged woman), *Nine Malic Molds*, *Shears*, *Water Mill*, *Scissors*, *The Sieve*, *The Chocolate Grinder*, *The Area of the Splatter*, *Eye Witnesses*, *The Bride's Dress*. The

"suitcase" with 93 pictures in facsimile which Duchamp made in 1934 throws some light on the making of these compositions.

1916 Foundation member of the Society of Independent Artists in New York.

1917 Editor of reviews *The Blind Man* and *Wrong-Wrong*.

1918 Mural painting *Tu m'*.

1920 Made an abstract film with strange optical effects using circles and spirals. *Jeux de mots*: "Rose Sélavy et moi nous estimons les ecchymoses des Esquimaux aux mots exquis," published in 1922 in *Littérature* No. 5 and in 1939 by G.L.M. in Paris. He used the pseudonym Rose Sélavy ("Arroser c'est la vie") to sign several less interesting works. With Katherine Dreier founded the Société Anonyme for the promotion of modern art in the United States.

1923 Left *The Bride Stripped bare by her Bachelors, even*, unfinished and devoted himself entirely to chess and experiments in mechanics and optics.

1926 *Anemic Film* (Circles and Spirals) in collaboration with Man Ray and Marc Allégret. Wrote a book on Chess. Organized a large exhibition of modern art in New York at the Société Anonyme and prepared the catalogue.

1934 Published the "Suitcase" containing the 93 studies which served for *La Mariée mise à nu*.
Rotoreliefs and *Cœurs Volants*.

1941 Published a "Suitcase" containing small reproductions of his principal works. With Breton organized a surrealist exhibition in New York. Edited the magazine *VVV* with Breton and Max Ernst in New York (1942-1944). The collection of the Société Anonyme was presented to Yale University: Duchamp and Katherine Dreier remaining its trustees.

1947 At the International Surrealist Exhibition in Paris, the "Rain Room" and the "Labyrinth" were constructed by Duchamp, who also created the famous object on the catalogue (a woman's breast in plastic).

1950 Most of Duchamp's works are in American collections (like Katherine Dreier's and L. and W. Arensberg's). Lives and works in New York.
(Information supplied by the artist and by Mrs Katherine S. Dreier.)

BIBLIOGRAPHY

A. Gleizes and J. Metzinger, *Du Cubisme*, Paris 1912. — G. Apollinaire, *Les peintres cubistes*, Paris 1913. — A. J. Eddy, *Cubists and Post-Impressionism*, Chicago 1919. — K. Dreier, *Western Art and the New Era*, New York 1923. — A. Breton, *Les pas perdus*, Paris 1924. Important article on D. — D. Gascoyne, *A Short Survey of Surrealism*, London 1935. — A. H. Barr, *Cubism and Abstract Art*, New York 1936. — Id., *Fantastic Art, Dada, Surrealism*, New York 1936. — G. Buffet-Picabia, *Cœurs volants, Cahiers d'Art*, Nos. 1/2, Paris 1936. — P. Guggenheim, *Art of this Century*, New York 1942. — K. Dreier and M. Echaurren, *D's Glass, an Analytical Reflection*, New York 1944. — S. Janis, *Abstract and Surrealist Art in America*, New York 1944. — A. Breton, *Phare de la mariée*, in: *Le Surréalisme et la Peinture*, New York 1945. — G. H. Hamilton, *Yale Associates Bulletin*, No. 2, 1945. — *View*, series V, No. 1, New York 1945. Number devoted to M.D. With contributions by Breton, Buffet-Picabia, Calas, Desnos, Janis, Kiesler, Soby, etc. — J. J. Sweeney, *Eleven Europeans in America, Bulletin of the Museum of Modern Art*, No. 4/5, New York 1946. — K. Kuh, Catalogue of the Exhibition at Art Institute of Chicago, *20th Century Art from the... Arensberg Collection*, Chicago 1949.

DUFY, RAOUL (1877-1953)

1877 Born June 3 at Le Havre. Has eight brothers and sisters.

1891 The family has a hard time making ends meet and, at 14, Dufy has to take a clerk's job in a coffee importing firm.

1895 First drawing lessons at Ecole des Beaux-Arts, Le Havre, under Professor Lhullier, former pupil of Cabanel and admirer of Ingres. Dufy and Friesz (also from Le Havre) paint together.

1899 On military service.

1900 Comes to Paris on a grant of 100 francs a month allotted him by the Le Havre Municipality. Enrolls in Bonnat's class, Ecole des Beaux-Arts.
His *Fin de Journée au Havre* exhibited at Salon des Artistes Français.
At the Louvre, he feels "crushed" by the masterpieces.

Henceforward he avoids the museums and spends his time in front of Durand-Ruel's windows where the Impressionists are shown. At Vollard's he sees pictures by Cézanne.

1901 The Van Gogh Exhibition at Bernheim's makes a lasting impression on him.

1903 Exhibits at Salon des Indépendants.

1905 At Salon d'Automne, Matisse's *Luxe, Calme et Volupté* opens his eyes to a new world.

1906 First exhibition at Berthe Weill's and at Salon d'Automne.

1907 Abandons pure color. Getting his bearings, Dufy moves in the direction already indicated by Cézanne and applies himself to the problems of colors investigated by Matisse and Picasso. His palette changes; in the period 1907-1911 his pictures show a great severity of style. Interest in architectural construction. Their bright, gay colors gone, his pictures no longer sell.

1908 He and Braque work together at L'Estaque.

1909 Visits Munich, accompanied by Friesz.
Paints his first boating scenes on the Marne.

1911 Friendship with the poets Fernand Fleuret, Vincent Muselli, Roger Allard, Guillaume Apollinaire. Does woodcuts for the latter's *Le Bestiaire*.
From this work and his friendship with the fashion-designer, Paul Poiret, he conceives the idea of doing woodcuts for printing on textiles. Poiret is won over and advances him 2500 francs to set up a small plant, boulevard de Clichy. Installs a steam boiler for 350 francs; hires a chemist at 500 francs a month, and one other employee (formerly a waiter at the Hotel Ritz), whom he instructs in handling the vaporizer. Dufy made the designs, engraved the plates, decided on the coloring; with the resultant fabrics Poiret made up dresses which were an immediate success.
Impressed by the venture, the big Bianchini firm takes Dufy on its staff.

1917 Makes illustrations for Allard's *Elégies martiales*.

1918 Illustrations for *M. Croquant*, by Remy de Gourmont.

1920 Illustrations for Gourmont's *Pensées inédites*.
Stays at Vence, where he paints a great many landscapes. Does ceramics in collaboration with the Catalan potter, Artigas.

1921 Does tapestries in mordant colors (artistic application of a mechanical process).

1922 Trip to Sicily, where the small Sicilian carts and wagons, so gaily splashed with color, enchant and stimulate his painter's eye.

1923 Makes illustrations for *Friperies*, by Fernand Fleuret.

1923-1925 Bianchini advises him to go to the horse-races, so as to observe the dresses of the women; but Dufy has eyes only for the horses. His racing pictures date from this time. Tired of the work at Bianchini's, Dufy gives up his copyright in exchange for cancellation of his contract.

1925 Makes illustrations for *La Terre frottée d'ail* by Coquiot. Travels to Morocco with Poiret, where he does a series of paintings.

1926 Exhibition at the Bernheim Gallery.
Makes illustrations for Apollinaire's *Le Poète assassiné*. Paints a triptych representing the road from Vallauris to Antibes.
Sets for the ballet *Palm Beach*.

1927 Series of watercolors of Nice.

1928 Paints for the most part in the Bois de Boulogne (Paris).

1929 Deauville.

1930 Illustrations for *La Belle enfant ou l'amour à quarante ans*, by Montfort.

1932 Does pottery with Artigas.
Designs a drawing-room suite for the great Beauvais tapestry factory.

1936 Illustrates *Mon Docteur Le Vin* for the Parisian wine-merchant, Nicolas.

1937 Works on large-scale decorations for the Palais de l'Electricité (World's Fair Exhibition) and for the Palais de Chaillot.

1940 Illustrations for *Aphorismes et Variétés* by Brillat-Savarin.

1940 Dufy moves to Perpignan.
Executes large-scale decorations for the entrance-hall of the monkey-house at the Jardin des Plantes, Paris. The work comprises two large panels.

1942 Makes a copy of Renoir's *Moulin de la Galette*.

1944 Scenery for Salacrou's *Les Fiancés du Havre*.
Dufy has come to the conclusion that "color is not painting." In contrast with Matisse, who has never wearied of chromatism, Dufy confines himself to what he calls "tonal painting," i.e. reducing the number of colors to a minimum. Thus he has painted pictures in a single tone, as for example *The Red Violin*, in which, apart from the white, red is the sole color employed.
Dufy also painted a *Dark Seascape*. This picture calls to mind a remark once dropped by Matisse, to the effect that, with black, a painter can convey all colors.

1950 Goes to Boston for treatment of his polyarthritis. Sets for *Ring around the Moon (L'Invitation au château)* by Jean Anouilh.

1951 Return to France.

1952 Lives at Forcalquier. First Prize at the Biennale, Venice. Retrospective Exhibition in Geneva.

1953 Retrospective exhibition in Museum of Modern Art, Paris. Exhibition at the Ny Carlsberg Glyptotek, Copenhagen. Died, March 23, at Forcalquier.

BIBLIOGRAPHY

Sélection, Antwerp 1928. — C. Zervos, *Cahiers d'Art*, Paris 1928. — M. Berr de Turique, Paris 1930. — F. Fleuret, Paris 1931. — René-Jean, Paris 1931. — C. Roger-Marx, in R. Huyghe's *Histoire de l'art contemporain*, Paris 1935. — R. Escholier, *La Peinture française au XXᵉ siècle*, Paris 1937. — J. Cassou, *Trésors de la Peinture Française*, Geneva 1946. — P. Camo, Lausanne 1947. — B. Dorival, *Etapes de la Peinture Française Contemporaine*, Paris 1948. — J. Cocteau, Paris 1948. — M. Gauthier, Paris 1949. — C. Roger-Marx, Paris 1950. — P. Courthion, Geneva 1951. — G. Besson, Paris 1953. — A. Werner, New York 1953. — J. Lassaigne, Geneva 1954.

ENSOR, James (1860-1949)

1860 Born April 13 at Ostend of an English father and Flemish mother. The family runs a small business, selling "Souvenirs of Ostend." The shop is filled with *bric-à-brac*—jewelcases made of sea-shells, Japanese and Chinese vases, tiny ships fitted inside bottles—that stir the boy's imagination.
First drawing lessons from a little known Ostend artist named Van Cuick.

1877 Attends the Académie des Beaux-Arts, Brussels, until 1879.

1879 Returns to Ostend (44, rue Longue, then 27, rue de Flandre), where he makes his home for the rest of his life. His first sketches show the influence of Van Gogh.

1880 His personal style asserts itself.

1881 Joins the art society *La Chrysalide*.

1882 Joins the *Essor* group.

1883 A section of the *Essor*, including Ensor, breaks away and forms the group known as the *XX* (17 painters and 3 sculptors).

1884 First exhibition of the *XX* at Brussels; the group puts on a number of exhibitions in the years to come, in which many foreign artists take part.

1886 First etchings.

1888 Paints his famous *Entrance of Christ into Brussels*.

1891 *Libre Esthétique* group.

1899 The magazine *La Plume* puts out a special issue on Ensor, with contributions by Camille Lemonnier, Edmond Picard, Emile Verhaeren, Maurice Maeterlinck. Retrospective Exhibition at the Palais des Beaux-Arts, Brussels.

1900 "Discovers" Negro art at the Palais de Tervueren.

1930 A Baronetcy is conferred on Ensor by King Albert I. Ensor Exhibition in Paris (Galerie des Beaux-Arts). To get his *Entrance of Christ* (now in the Casino of Ostend) into the gallery, a balcony has to be dismantled.

1949 Rumors of Ensor's death had gone round and obituary notices were frequent. Actually he died on November 19, in his 90th year.

BIBLIOGRAPHY

E. Demolder, Brussels 1892 and Paris 1899. — V. Pica, Bergamo 1902. — E. Verhaeren, Brussels 1908. — H. von Garvens-Garvensburg, Hanover 1913. — P. Colin, Postdam 1921. — G. Le Roy, Brussels and Paris 1922. — F. Cuypers, Paris 1925. — P. Desmeth, Brussels 1926. — A. Dörner, H. von Garvens-Garvensburg and P. Fränger, Hanover 1927. — P. Fierens, Paris 1929. — A. de Ridder, Paris 1930. — P. Colin, Leipzig 1931. — J. Teugels, Ostend 1931. — L. Schwob, Brussels 1936. — P. Desmeth, Brussels and Paris, new edition 1937.

— L. van Puyvelde, in *Gazette des Beaux-Arts*, Paris 1939. — J. Muls, Brussels 1942. — P. Fierens, Paris 1943. — Id., Paris and Brussels 1944. — F. Cuypers, Bruges 1946. — F. Fels, Geneva 1947.

ERNST, Max (1891)

1891 Born at Brühl near Cologne, April 2.

1898- At school, then studied philosophy at Bonn University.
1914 No art school training.

1913 Exhibited at the first German Autumn Salon, Berlin. First visit to Paris.

1914 Met Arp at the *Werkbund* exhibition, Cologne. Went through the war in the Artillery.

1919 With Baargeld and Arp brought Dada to Cologne. With Arp executed *Fatagaga* series of *collages (Fabrication de tableaux garantis gazométriques)*. Published *Bulletin D.*, and with Baargeld *Fiat Modes* (8 lithographs).

1920 With Baargeld published *Die Schammade*. Dada Exhibition at the Winter Beer-Cellar closed by the police. First exhibition of *collages* at Paris (Galerie "Au Sans Pareil").

1921 In summer: first Dada demonstration in the Tyrol with Arp, Eluard, Tzara and others.

1922 Went to Paris. Illustrated *Répétitions* and *Les Malheurs des Immortels* by Eluard. Contributed to *Littérature*. First experiments in automatic writing with Breton, Crevel, Desnos, Eluard, Péret, Picabia.

1924 Active participation in the Surrealist movement.

1925 First rubbings. Exhibited at the first Surrealist Exhibition at the Galerie Pierre. With Miro, did decors for *Romeo and Juliet* (Russian Ballet).

1926 *Histoire naturelle*, published by Jeanne Bucher.

1929 Collage-Novel, *La Femme 100 Têtes*.

1934 *Une Semaine de Bonté* published by Jeanne Bucher. Fresco for the *Mascotte-Bar*, Zurich.

1937- Decors for *Ubu Enchaîné* by Alfred Jarry at the Théâtre
1940 des Champs-Elysées. Sculptures and fresco for his own house at Saint-Martin-d'Ardèche.
Interned in French concentration camps.

1941 14th July arrived in the United States.

1942 Special number of the magazine *View* devoted to Max Ernst. With Duchamp and Breton edited the review *VVV*, at New York.

1945 Worked on Hans Richter's film: *The Dreams that money can buy*.

1947 Illustrations for *A l'intérieur de la vue* by Eluard.

1949 Returned to Paris.

1950 Exhibition at Galerie Drouin, Paris.

1954 First prize for painting at the Venice Biennale.

BIBLIOGRAPHY

Œuvres de 1919-1936, in *Cahiers d'Art*, Paris 1937. Contributions by Arp, Breton, et al. — *View*, New York, April 1942. Special Max Ernst number, including catalogue of the M.E. exhibition, Valentin Gallery, New York. — *Beyond Painting*, Wittenborn, New York 1948. Contributions by Arp, A. Breton, Eluard, Ernst, Tzara. Extensive bibliography by B. Karpel. — *At Eye Level, Paramyths*, Beverly Hills 1949. Catalogue of exhibition at the Copley Gallery, Beverly Hills. Contributions by Bousquet, Breton, Ernst, Eluard, Péret and others.

FEININGER, Lyonel (1871-1956)

1871 Born in New York, July 17.

1880 Studied the violin with his father. Gave concerts at the age of 12.

1887 Visited Germany to study music. Arrived at Hamburg and decided to abandon his musical career for painting.

1887- Studied painting at the Hamburg School of Arts and
1891 Crafts and at the Berlin Academy.

1892-1893 Visited Paris. Worked at Académie Colarossi.

1893- Lived in Berlin. Active collaboration as designer and
1906 illustrator with periodicals such as *Ulk* and *Lustige Blätter*.

1906- Returned to Paris for two years. Comic drawings for *Le*
1907 *Témoin* and *The Chicago Sunday Tribune*.

1908 Lived at Berlin-Zehlendorf.

1911 Another visit to Paris where he met Delaunay and saw the Cubists' work.

1913 Invited by Franz Marc to exhibit at the First German Autumn Salon.

1919- Taught drawing and the graphic arts at the Weimar
1924 Bauhaus. Founded the group of the "Blue Four" with Klee, Kandinsky, Jawlensky.

1925-1933 Lived and worked at the Dessau Bauhaus.

1931 Important retrospective exhibition at the Berlin National Gallery. After 1933 these works were shown at the Exhibitions of Degenerate Art.

1936 Returned to the United States and taught at holiday courses at Mills College, California. Returned to Berlin via Sweden in the autumn.

1937 Returned for good to the United States. Settled in New York City. Summer in Falls Village, Connecticut.

1939 Mural paintings at the Pavilions of Marine Transport and Fine Arts at the World's Fair, New York.

1944 Retrospective at the Museum of Modern Art, New York.

1946-1948 Summer at Stockbridge, Mass.

1949-1950 Exhibition at Jeanne Bucher Gallery, Paris.

1950 2nd Prize at Pittsburgh International Exhibition.

1956 Dies in New York, January 13.
(Information supplied by Miss Hannah Muller, Museum of Modern Art, New York.)

BIBLIOGRAPHY

P. Halke, *Kunstwelt*, Berlin 1912. — P. Westheim, *Das Kunstblatt*, Weimar, March 1917. — L. Coellen, *Das Kunstblatt*, Potsdam, May 1919. — R. Probst, *Neue Blätter für Kunst und Dichtung*, Dresden 1919. — W. Wolfradt *Junge Kunst*, vol. 47, Leipzig 1924. — W. Grohmann, *Deutsche Kunst und Dekoration*, Darmstadt, March 1930. — A. Ewald, *Der Querschnitt*, Berlin, December 1931. — L. Grote, *Museum der Gegenwart*, No. 2, Berlin 1931. — A. Schardt, *Das Kunstblatt*, Potsdam, July 1931. — J. Bier, *Die Kunst für Alle*, Munich 1932. — H. Klump, *Abstraktion in der Malerei: Kandinsky, Feininger, Klee*, Berlin 1932. — Museum of Modern Art, Catalogue, New York 1944. Bibliography by Hannah Muller.

FRIESZ, EMILE OTHON (1879-1949)

1879 Born February 6 at Le Havre of a family of shipwrights and sailors. His father's family came from Scandinavia and Holland (Friesz means "Frisian"), his mother from Normandy. Friesz's father was a sea-captain.

1885 Enters the Lycée where he soon strikes up a friendship with Raoul Dufy.

1891 Drawing is already his favorite pastime.

1895-1896 Learns the rudiments of painting at the Ecole des Beaux-Arts, Le Havre, under the supervision of Charles Lhullier, a follower of Ingres. In the same class is Raoul Dufy.

1897 Thanks to the good offices of Lhullier, he receives a grant of 1200 francs a year from the Municipality of Le Havre, enabling him to proceed to Paris.

1898 In October he enrolls at the Ecole des Beaux-Arts, Paris. Works at first in Bonnat's class (where Dufy joins him in 1900), then in Gustave Moreau's class, where he meets Matisse, Marquet, and Rouault.
At the Louvre, he "interprets" Veronese, Delacroix, Rubens, Corot.
At the Durand-Ruel Gallery, his eyes are opened to the Impressionists.

1900 First exhibition at the Salon des Artistes Français.

1901 Makes the acquaintance of Pissarro, and stays in the Creuse "Department," doing a good many landscapes; here he meets Guillaumin.

1903 Exhibits at Salon des Indépendants.

1904 Exhibits at Salon d'Automne, with Marquet, Matisse, Manguin, Puy, and others. Works at Cassis.

1905 Takes part in the Salon d'Automne, in the "Cage des Fauves."

1906 Visits Antwerp; then La Ciotat, accompanied by Braque.

1907 La Ciotat. Interest in arabesques and architectural composition. Druet becomes his exclusive buyer.

1908 Paints the *Cathedral of Rouen*, now at the Moscow Museum.

1909 Trip to Italy, via Munich; greatly impressed by Giotto.

1911 Trip to Portugal.

1912 Breaks off relations with Druet.

1913 Successful large-scale exhibition at Paul Cassirer's in Berlin.

1914 Appointed to professorships at the Académie Moderne, the Académie Scandinave and the Académie de la Grande Chaumière, Paris.

1915 Paints the famous portrait of Mme Othon Friesz.

1919 Stays in Provence and at Toulon.

1925 Awarded the Carnegie Foundation prize.

1935 *La Paix*: tapestry design for *Les Gobelins* (state factory for Gobelin tapestry).

1937 He and Dufy are commissioned to do decorations for the Palais de Chaillot: *La Seine*.

1938 Becomes a member of the Carnegie Foundation. Visits the United States.

1949 Dies in Paris, January 10.

BIBLIOGRAPHY

F. Fleuret, preface to catalogue (exhibition Galerie Druet), Paris, Nov. 1907. — A. Salmon, Paris 1920. — L. G. Cann, *The Arts*, New York, Nov. 1926. — F. Fleuret, C. Vildrac, A. Salmon, *Chroniques du Jour*, Paris 1928. — R. Brielle, Paris 1930. — F. Neugass, *Die Kunst*, Munich Sept. 1928. — M. Le Sieutre, Paris 1931. — F. Neugass, *L'Amour de l'Art*, Paris, July 1933. — M. Gauthier, Paris 1949.

GAUGUIN, PAUL (1848-1903)

1848 Born June 7; his father, Clovis Gauguin, was a journalist from Orléans employed on *Le National*, his mother, Aline Chazal, daughter of Flora Tristan, a famous propagandist and Saint-Simonian doctrinaire, of Peruvian ancestry.

1851 After the *coup d'Etat* the family sailed for Peru. His father died on the journey. Stayed four years at Lima.

1855 Returned to Orléans. Schooling at the Petit Séminaire.

1865 Entered the merchant-service, as a navigating cadet. Sailed from Le Havre to Rio several times on the *Luzzitano*.

1868 Served on the cruiser *Jérôme-Napoléon*.

1871 On leave, April 23. Gives up the sea, and by the good offices of his guardian Gustave Arosa enters Bertin's stockbroking business in the Rue Laffitte, where he makes friends with a colleague, Emile Schuffenecker. Does very well in business.

1873 Nov. 22, marries a Danish girl from a middleclass family, Mette Sophia Gad.

1874 Paints as an amateur. Builds up a collection of impressionist pictures (Manet, Cézanne, Pissarro, Renoir, Monet, Sisley).

1876 Has a picture, *Viroflay Landscape*, accepted at the Salon. Meets Pissarro.

1879 Stays with Pissarro at Pontoise during the holidays.

1880 Leaves his residence in Rue des Tourneaux, and rents a studio, 8, Rue Carcel. Takes part in the Fifth Impressionist Exhibition (7 paintings, 1 bust).

1881 Sixth Impressionist Exhibition. Huysmans describes his landscapes as "diluted Pissarro" but is loud in his praises of a nude study (now on loan at the Ny Carlsberg Glyptotek, Copenhagen).

1882 Seventh Impressionist Exhibition. Huysmans finds he "shows no progress."

1883 Crucial year. Gauguin throws up his post at Bertin's. "From now on I paint every day." Works with Pissarro at Osny.

1884 For economy's sake lives at Rouen from March to October. Early in November goes with his wife and children to Denmark. His exhibition there closed by order of the Academy.

1885 Jan. 14, in a letter to Schuffenecker expounds his theories about art. Quarrels with his wife's family. Fails to arrange for an exhibition and in June, leaving his wife, returns to Paris with his son Clovis. Extreme poverty. Works as a billsticker. Lives first in Impasse Frémin; moves Oct. 13 to Rue Cail. Ill in hospital.

1886 May 15-June 15. Eighth and Last Impressionist Exhibition. Fénéon says, "Monsieur Gauguin's tones are very near each other; hence the soft harmonies we find in his work."
June. Gauguin boards out his son at Antony and for the first time goes to Brittany, staying at the Pension Gloanec, Pont-Aven (Finistère). In November, returns to Paris; meets Van Gogh in Montmartre.

1887 Stays in Paris until April. April 10. With Charles Laval Gauguin embarks at Saint Nazaire for Panama, then Martinique, whence they return in December, prostrated by dysentery and fever. "I'm bringing back a dozen canvases, four with figures much superior to anything I did at Pont-Aven." (*Letters*, p. 116, 1946).
December. Back in Paris, Gauguin puts up with Schuffenecker, 29, rue Boulard.

1888 Second stay at Pont-Aven, until October. Fruitful meeting with Bernard, in August. Beginnings of Cloisonnism and Synthetism. *The Vision after the Sermon* (National Gallery of Scotland, Edinburgh). First one-man show at Boussod & Valadon's, by the good offices of Theo van Gogh, Vincent's brother.

October 20. Gauguin goes to Arles with a view to founding with Van Gogh the "Studio of the South." Funds are supplied to the two men by Theo; they reciprocally influence each other. They visit the Montpellier Museum. Gauguin makes his *Portrait of Vincent Painting Sunflowers* (on loan to Municipal Museum, Amsterdam). But the two men were very different and got on each other's nerves, with tragic results.

December 23. In a fit of madness Vincent cuts off his own ear. Gauguin hurries back to Paris, where he again stays with Schuffenecker until he secures a studio (25, avenue du Parc Montsouris).

1889 World's Fair. Gauguin enthusiastic over Japanese art. Exhibition of the Impressionist and Synthetist Group at the Café Volpini, Place du Champ-de-Mars. The public laugh it out of court, but the young Nabis—Sérusier, Maurice Denis, Bonnard—are much impressed.

April: return to Pont-Aven; Gauguin's third stay in Brittany, the longest and most decisive, broken by short stays in Paris at the beginning of 1890.

October. Irritated by the tourists and colony of artists infesting Pont-Aven, Gauguin moves to a small inn owned by Marie Henry (known as Marie Poupée) at Le Pouldu. Some of his cronies follow: Séguin, Filiger and, notably, the Dutchman Meyer de Haan. It is in the primitive setting of Le Pouldu, with its Breton "Calvaries," that Gauguin's personality takes definite form and he fully works out his new manner, at once simplifying and synthetic. The Visitors' Book at the inn shows that he stayed there from Oct. 2 to Nov. 7, 1890. *The Yellow Christ* (Albright Art Gallery, Buffalo), *Landscape at Le Pouldu* (Fierens Collection, Brussels).

1890 End December, returns to Paris. Homeless, he again stays with Schuffenecker, who is now living at No. 12, rue Durand-Claye; then in a hotel in the rue Delambre.

1891 Associates with the symbolist writers who meet once a week at the Café Voltaire. Etching of Mallarmé. Copies Manet's *Olympia*. Leads a poverty-stricken, Bohemian life in Montparnasse. Resolves to go to Tahiti. February 23. First sale of 30 pictures at the Drouot auction-rooms (catalogue prefaced by Mirbeau), to collect funds for his journey.

March 23. Farewell banquet in his honor at the Café Voltaire, presided over by Mallarmé. April 4. Sails for Tahiti.

June 8, lands at Papeete. Disappointed by the European colony at the capital, he acquires a hut amongst the natives in the Mataïeu region some 25 miles south of Papeete. *Ia Orana Maria*.

1892 Works hard despite ill-health. *Ta Matete* (Basel Museum). *Parau no te Varua Ino*.

1893 But no money is coming in and, at the end of his tether, a sick man, Gauguin is compelled to return to Europe. Tries again to organize an exhibition at Copenhagen. August 3. Arrives at Marseilles.

Trip to Orléans; inheritance from his uncle Isidore. In Paris, rents a studio, 4, rue Vercingétorix, where he lives with *Annah la Javanaise*, whose portrait he paints. Gives picturesque weekly parties at the studio.

November 4. Opening day of his exhibition at Durand-Ruel's, organized at Degas' suggestion (Preface by C. Morice). No financial success, it has much influence on Bonnard, Vuillard and the other Nabis.

1894 January. Travels to Bruges (Memling), then to Copenhagen (last meeting with his wife).

April-December. At Pont-Aven and Le Pouldu with Annah, who involves him in a brawl with drunken sailors in which he breaks his ankle.

December. Returns to Paris. Annah has vanished, after looting his studio.

1895 Disgusted with life in Paris, he decides to return to Tahiti.

February 18. Second auction-sale, catalogue prefaced by a letter from Strindberg. Sale a complete failure. July. Lands in Tahiti. Finds Papeete still more Europeanized and goes to the west coast, the Punoauia district, where he has a large and relatively palatial hut on native lines built for himself.

1896 October. His health is breaking up and he suffers horribly from his sense of being alone, an outcast. "I am so utterly discouraged and demoralized that I cannot conceive of anything worse in store for me."

However, in November, he is feeling better. "I am recovering and, thanks to this, have got through a lot of work."

1897 Death of his daughter Aline. Stops writing to his wife. In hospital. A year of masterpieces: *Nevermore* (Courtauld Institute, London). *Te Rerioa* (Id.), *Les Trois Tahitiens, Whence Come We?* (Boston Museum).

1898 Attempted suicide. Takes a job in the local Public Works office. *Le Cheval Blanc* (Louvre).

1899 In trouble with local authorities. Collaboration with the newspapers *Les Guêpes, L'Indépendant* and publishes satirical broadsheet: *Le Sourire, journal méchant*.

1900 April. "I am mustering all the energy that's left to me and, fond as I am of my house, I shall try to get rid of it and sell off everything with as little loss as possible. Then I shall move to one of the Marquesas, where living's cheap and easy."

August. "Am leaving for the Marquesas. At last!"

1901 November. Long letter to de Monfreid in which he describes his new home, which he calls *La Maison du Jouir* and the conditions under which he works. "Here poetry springs from the soil, unsummoned, and all one needs to body it forth is to let one's mind go dreaming as one paints."

1902 March. "Though my health is as bad as ever, I have started working steadily again; you can't imagine the peacefulness of my life, all alone amongst the leafage!" *Contes Barbares* (Folkwang Museum, Essen).

August. His heart is giving him trouble and eczema has broken out on his limbs, causing him intense suffering. He knows that he is mortally ill, and his one idea is to return to France for treatment. His friend de Monfreid dissuades him.

1903 March. In trouble with the Local Government, the Bishop, and the police (for championing the natives). Unjustly sentenced to three months' imprisonment and fine of 1000 francs (March 31). Unable to appeal, lacking funds for the journey to Tahiti.

April. Last letter to de Monfreid ends: "All these worries are *killing me*."

May 8. About 11 a.m. death of Gauguin.

BIBLIOGRAPHY

Noa-Noa, 1891-1893 (Paris 1924). — *Cahier pour Aline*, 1893. manuscript. — *Les Guêpes, Le Sourire, L'Indépendant de Tahiti*, 1899-1900, newspapers with articles by Gauguin. — *Racontars d'un rapin*, 1902, Geneva. — *Avant et Après*, 1902 (Paris 1923). — *Lettres à G.D. de Monfreid*, preceded by *Hommage à Gauguin*, by V. Ségalen, Paris 1919 and 1930. — *Lettres à A. Fontainas*, Paris 1921. — *Letters to A. Vollard and A. Fontainas*, ed. by J. Rewald, San Francisco 1943. — *Lettres à sa femme et à ses amis*, publ. by M. Malingue, Paris 1946. — *L'Ancien Culte Mahorie* (1892), facsimile, Paris 1951.

M. Guérin, *L'œuvre gravé de Paul Gauguin*, Paris 1927, 2 vols. — General Catalogue in preparation. — Centenary Exhibition at the Orangerie, Paris, July-Nov. 1949. Descriptive notices, with bibl. and unpublished documents by J. Leymarie, and Introduction by R. Huyghe.

J. de Rotonchamp, Paris 1906. New Ed. 1925. Basic. — See also C. Morice, Paris 1919. — W. Barth, Basel 1929. — A. Alexandre, Paris 1930. — R. Cogniat, Paris 1936. — Pola Gauguin, Paris 1938. — J. Rewald, Paris and London 1938. — E. Bernard, Lorient 1941. — A. de Witt, Milan 1946. — M. Malingue, Paris 1948. — René-Jean, Paris 1948. — J. Taralon, Paris 1949. — C. Estienne, Geneva 1953.

Important magazine articles: O. Mirbeau, *L'Echo de Paris*, Feb. 16, 1891. — G. A. Aurier, *Le Mercure de France*, March 1891. — *Revue encyclopédique*, April 1892. — E. Bernard, *Mercure de France*, June 1895; Dec. 1903; Dec. 1908. — A. Séguin, *L'Occident*, March, April, May 1903. — V. Ségalen, *Mercure de France*, June 1904. — M. Denis, *Mercure de France*, Jan. 1904. — *Occident*, May 1910. — M. Puy, *L'art décoratif*, April 1911. — G. de Chirico, *Convegno*, Milan, March 1920. — L. Venturi, *L'Arte*, March 1934. — C. Chassé, *L'Amour de l'Art*, April 1938. — A. M. Berryer, *Bull. des Musées d'Art et d'Histoire*, Brussels, January 1944. — D. Sutton, *Burlington Magazine*, April, Nov. 1949. — M. Raynal, Geneva 1949. — Special numbers of *Mercure de France*, Oct. 1903. — *L'Art et les Artistes*, Nov. 1925. — *Ver y Estimar*, Buenos-Aires, Nov. 1948.

GLEIZES, ALBERT (1881-1953)

1881 Born in Paris, December 8.

1901 Began to paint in an impressionist style.

1906 With Mercereau, Duhamel, Arcos, Vildrac, etc., founded the literary group "L'Abbaye de Créteil." Friendship with Gustave Kahn, René Ghil, Saint-Pol-Roux, Emile Verhaeren, and later with Apollinaire and Salmon.

1911 Exhibited at first general cubist exhibition at the Salon des Indépendants, in Room 41, and in Gallery 8 of the Salon d'Automne. Introduced to Picasso by Apollinaire.

1912 Exhibited at the "Section d'Or" of which he was a foundation member. With Metzinger published the first book on Cubism *Du Cubisme* (Ed. Figuière).

1913 Exhibited at the Armory Show, New York, and at the first German Autumn Salon.

1914 Called up at Toul. Painted *The Army Doctor*.

1915 Invalided out of army. Traveled to New York via Barcelona.

1919 Returned to Paris.

1920 Collaborated with Henri Barbusse's review *Clarté*.

1927 In the regions of Ardèche and Isère founded Moly-Sabata groups of peasants and artisans.

1937 Mural paintings. Showed at the exhibition of *Les Maîtres de l'art indépendant*, Petit Palais, Paris.

1939 Retired to Saint-Rémy in the South of France.

1941 Returns to Catholicism.

1947 Retrospective exhibition at Lyons.

1950 Exhibition of religious art at the Vatican, Rome. Illustrated Pascal's *Pensées* with engravings.

1953 Exhibition of Gleizes' pupils, in Art School, Paris. Died June 24, in Aix-en-Provence, after undergoing a surgical operation.

BIBLIOGRAPHY

G. Apollinaire, *Les Peintres cubistes*, Paris 1913. — G. Coquiot, *Les Indépendants*, Paris 1921. — M. Raynal, *Anthologie de la peinture en France de 1906 à nos jours*, Paris 1927. — A. Warnod, *Les berceaux de la jeune peinture*, Paris 1928. — *Amour de l'Art*, Paris 1933. Biography and bibliography. — A. H. Barr, *Cubism and Abstract Art*, New York, Museum of Modern Art 1936. — J. Chevalier, *Le dénouement traditionnel du cubisme*, *Confluences*, Paris 1942. — Dom Angelico Surchamp, with a contribution by the artist, *Destinée du Cubisme*, Lyons 1947.

GRIS, JUAN (1887-1927)

1887 Born José Victoriano Gonzalez, at Madrid, March 23. Son of Gregorio Gonzalez, Castilian, and Isabelle Perez, Andalusian.

1902 At the School of Arts and Crafts, Madrid.

1904 Influenced by "Jugendstil" which he encountered in the German magazines *Jugend* and *Simplicissimus*. Adopted pseudonym of Juan Gris.
Produces drawings for *Madrid Comico, Blanco y Negro* and other illustrated magazines. Works with the academic painter Carbonero; meets Kars, Geiger.

1906 Left for Paris. Lived at the *Bateau-lavoir* where Picasso had already settled in. Met Apollinaire, Max Jacob, André Salmon. Did drawings for *L'Assiette au Beurre, Le Charivari, Le Cri de Paris*.

1907 Friendship with Maurice Raynal. Kahnweiler met Gris while visiting Picasso.

1910- Started painting seriously. Sold some of first canvases
1911 to Clovis Sagot.

1912 Exhibited for the first time at Salon des Indépendants and then at the Section d'Or. *Homage to Picasso;* first *papiers collés*. Contract with Kahnweiler for all his work.

1913 Visit to Céret with Picasso and sculptor Manolo. Thickened his colors with sand and ashes.

1914 Summer at Collioure. Friendship with Matisse.

1915 Illustrations for Reverdy's *Poèmes en Prose*.

1916 Beginning of colored architectural period.

1917 Contract with Léonce Rosenberg.

1919 Started series of Harlequins and Pierrots.

1920 Exhibited at the Rosenberg Gallery. Visit to Bandol. Illustrations for *Ne coupez pas, Mademoiselle* by Max Jacob. At the Salon des Indépendants took part in last united cubist manifestation.

1921 Beginnings of *Open Windows* series (lithographs). Fall and winter at Céret. Met Diaghilev in Monte-Carlo. Return to Paris.

1922 Diaghilev commissioned decors for ballet *The Shepherdess's Temptation*. Settled at Boulogne-sur-Seine.

1923 For Diaghilev: decors for ballet *La Fête Merveilleuse* at Versailles; Gounod's opera *The Dove*; Chabrier's comic-opera *L'Education Manquée*.

1924 Exhibition at Kahnweiler Gallery, rue d'Astorg. Lived at Beausoleil. Exhibited in Berlin, at Flechtheim's. Lectured at the Sorbonne on *The Possibilities of Painting*, a definition of his deductive method. Illustrations for *Le Casseur d'Assiettes* by Salacrou.

1925 Illustrations for *Le Mouchoir de Nuages* by Tzara. Another exhibition at the Flechtheim Gallery, Berlin.

1926 Does illustrations for *Denise*, by Radiguet.

1927 11th May, died of uremia, Paris.

BIBLIOGRAPHY

G. Apollinaire, *Les Peintres cubistes*, Paris 1913. — M. Raynal, Paris 1920. — Id., *Esprit nouveau*, No. 5, Paris 1921. — H. Kahnweiler (publ. under pseudonym: Daniel Henry), in *Junge Kunst*. 55, Leipzig 1926. — C. Zervos, *Cahiers d'Art*, No. 10, Paris 1926. — H. Kahnweiler, *Der Querschnitt*, Berlin 1927. — G. Stein, *Transition*, No. 4, Paris 1927. — E. Tériade, *Cahiers d'Art* No. 5/6, Paris 1928. — W. George, Paris 1931. — *Cahiers d'Art* No. 5/6, Paris 1933. Issue devoted to J. G. Articles by D. Henry, J. Gris, Apollinaire, Raynal, Ozenfant, Zervos, et al. — A. H. Barr, *Cubism and Abstract Art*, New York 1936. — H. Kahnweiler, Paris 1946. With comprehensive documentation (bibliography, etc.).

GROMAIRE, MARCEL (1892)

1892 Born July 24 at Noyelles-sur-Sambre, in Northern France. His mother was Flemish.

1900- Paris. High school, then law studies, which he abandoned
1910 before their termination, feeling painting to be his true vocation. "Free student" in several art-schools in Montparnasse. Met the pupils of Matisse whose studio had just closed down; met also Matisse himself.

1914 Called up for military service. Wounded in the Battle of the Somme (1916).

1920 Somber, severely architectural paintings with a strongly marked Expressionist accent. Subjects drawn from the lives of peasants and workers. Backgrounds always in French and Belgian Flanders. The chief influences affecting his art: Romanesque-Gothic, French and Flemish Primitives, Rembrandt, Brueghel, and, amongst the moderns, Seurat and Cézanne.

1925 Painted *War*, an intensely emotive picture, and exhibited it the same year at Salon des Indépendants.

1933 Retrospective Exhibition at the Basel Kunsthalle.

1937 Decorated façades of the Pavillons de Sèvres at the Paris World's Fair.

1939 With Lurçat and Dubreuil sponsored a movement for the revival of the art of tapestry. Large Gobelins and Aubusson tapestries.

1947 Exhibition at Galerie Louis Carré, Paris.

1948 For centenary of the abolition of slavery executed a decoration in the French Union Assembly Hall.

1949 Exhibition at Louis Carré Gallery, New York.

1952 2nd Prize, Pittsburgh International Exhibition.

1955 Lives, works and teaches in Paris.
(Information supplied by the artist.)

BIBLIOGRAPHY

J. Cassou, Paris 1925. — M. Raynal, *Anthologie de la peinture en France de 1906 à nos jours*, Paris 1927. — W. George, Paris. 1928. — G. Pillement, Paris 1929. — G. Bazin, *L'Amour de l'Art*, Paris 1934. Bio-bibliographical note. — P. Fierens, *Les tendances expressionnistes de la génération de 90*, in *L'Amour de l'Art*, Paris 1934. — C. J. Delbo, *Interviews et opinions: M.G.*, *Arts de France*, No. 3, Paris 1946. — F. Gromaire, Paris 1949. — G. Besson *(Collection des Maîtres)*. Paris n.d.

JAWLENSKY, ALEXEI VON (1864-1941)

1864 Born March 26 in the Tver province of Russia (near Moscow). Military school in Moscow.

1889 Attends Art Academy, St Petersburg. Influenced by Ilya Repine.

1896 Moves to Munich and enrolls in Anton Azbe's art school, where he meets Kandinsky.
Becomes acquainted with Matisse and with Hodler; studies their works.

1903 First exhibition with the Munich Secession.

1905 Paints in Brittany (Carantec) and Provence.

1909 One of the founders of the New Association of Artists, Munich.

1911 Stays at Prerow (North Sea): portraits and landscapes.

1912 Meets Nolde and Klee.

1914 On the outbreak of war, takes refuge at St Prex (Switzerland).

1917- Paints his series of mystical portraits, figures of Christ.
1921 Stays in Zurich, then at Ascona.

1920 Retrospective exhibition at Gurlitt Gallery, Berlin.

1921 Settles at Wiesbaden (Germany).

1924 He, Feininger, Kandinsky and Klee found the group known as *Die Blauen Vier* (The Blue Four), whose largest exhibition takes place in 1929 at the Möller Gallery, Berlin.

1929-
1930 Portraits influenced by Cubism. His last works are reminiscent of Russian icons.

1941 Dies March 15 at Wiesbaden, after a protracted illness.

BIBLIOGRAPHY

W. A. Lutz, *Der Cicerone*, 1921. — R. Reiche, *Das Feuer*, Weimar 1921. — W. Grohmann, *Cahiers d'Art*, 1934. — W. Moufang, catalogue of exhibition at Ralfs Gallery, Braunschweig 1948. — In preparation, monograph by W. Moufang, Heidelberg.

KANDINSKY, Wassily (1866-1944)

1866 Born in Moscow, December 4.

1869 Rome and Florence. At 18 studied political economy, law and statistics at Moscow.

1889 May 28 to July 3, went as lawyer and ethnologist on a field-expedition, organized by "The Society of Natural Sciences," to the region of Vologda with the object of studying the legal code of the peasants and the pagan religion of the Syryenians. Impressed by popular Russian art. In autumn visited Paris for the first time.

1896 Broke off his career as a scientist. December: went to Munich to study painting.

1897-1898 At Anton Azbe's school where he met Jawlensky.

1900 Under Franz Stuck at the Munich Academy.

1901 Foundation of *Die Phalanx* group.

1902 Opened his own school of painting and drawing at 6 Hohenzollernstrasse, Munich. President of the "Phalanx" group.

1903 Visited Tunis and Kairwan.

1904 Traveled to Holland. Exhibited for the first time at Salon d'Automne, Paris.

1905 Traveled in Italy (Rapallo).

1906 In the spring settled for a year at Sèvres, near Paris.

1907 Visits to Berlin and Dresden. Sent several woodcuts to the exhibition of graphic arts organized by *Die Brücke* at Dresden. Returned to Munich.

1908 First steps towards abstract painting: *Landscape with a Tower*.

1909 In January founded and presided the "New Munich Artists' Association" with Jawlensky.

1910 First works completely free from nature-imitation. Wrote *Über das Geistige in der Kunst*, published in 1912 by Piper. Met Franz Marc with whom he became friends.

1911 Met Macke and Paul Klee. Visited by Arp. December 18: opening of the "First exhibition of the Directors of the Blue Rider." Throughout the year worked with Marc on the book *Der Blaue Reiter*.

1912 March to April: Second Blue Rider Exhibition (in black and white) at Goltz Gallery.
Exhibited with *Der Moderne Bund* at the Kunsthaus, Zurich. First retrospective exhibition at the Sturm Gallery, Berlin.

1913 *Klänge* published by Piper. Exhibited at First German Autumn Salon and at the Sturm Gallery, Berlin, which published an album *Kandinsky 1901-1913*.

1914 On the outbreak of war retired from August to October to Goldach near Rorschach, Switzerland. Returned to Russia.

1918 Made member of the Arts Section at the Commissariat for Popular Culture. Taught at the Moscow Academy of Fine Arts.

1919 Director of the "Museum of Pictorial Culture." Met Pevsner and Gabo.

1921 Founded the "Academy of Arts and Sciences of All the Russias" and elected vice-president.
From 1918 to 1921 founded 22 museums in Russia. In December returned to Germany.

1922 In Berlin. Exhibition at the Goldschmidt and Wallerstein Gallery. In June elected professor at the Weimar Bauhaus.

1924 Created the "Blue Four" group with Klee, Feininger and Jawlensky.

1925 With the Bauhaus at Dessau.

1926 *Punkt und Linie zu Fläche* (Bauhausbuch No. 9). Exhibitions for his 60th birthday.

1928 Decors for Moussorgsky's "Pictures at an Exhibition" at the Friedrich-Theater, Dessau.

1929 Visited Belgium where he met Ensor. First one-man show in Paris at Galerie Zak.

1931 In Egypt, Palestine, Syria, Turkey, Greece, Italy, France. Frescos for the Music Room in the International Exhibition of Architecture, Berlin.

1932 *Freies Bauhaus*, Berlin. Traveled to Jugoslavia.

1933 December, moved to Neuilly-sur-Seine, near Paris.

1934 Friendship with Arp, Pevsner, Thomas von Hartmann, Delaunay, Jeanne Bucher.

1936 Visited Italy: Genoa, Florence, Pisa and the Adriatic coast.

1937 Traveled to Switzerland. In Germany 57 works, labeled degenerate, were confiscated.

1940 During German occupation stayed two months in the Pyrenees.

1944 Died 13th December.
(Information supplied by Mrs Kandinsky.)

BIBLIOGRAPHY

H. Zehder, Dresden 1920. — W. Grohmann, Leipzig 1924. — Id., Paris 1930. — *Sélection No. 14*, devoted to K., Antwerp 1933. — "Kandinsky-Memorial," New York 1945. — "Kandinsky, Painting," New York 1945. — M. Arland, Paris 1947. — H. Debrunner, Zurich 1947. — M. Bill, "10 Farbenlichtdrucke...," Basel 1949. — M. Seuphor, *L'art abstrait*, Paris 1949. — *Art d'aujourd'hui* No. 6, issue devoted to K., texts by C. Estienne, C. Giedion-Welcker, R. v. Gindertael, Paris 1950. — C. Estienne, Paris 1950. — C. Giedion-Welcker, *Werk* No. 4, Winterthur 1950. — Collective book, directed by Max Bill, Paris 1951.

KIRCHNER, Ernst Ludwig (1880-1938)

1880 Born May 6 at Aschaffenburg, where his father was an engineer.

1901 Studies architecture at the Technical Institute in Dresden. Painting on the side.

1904 Meets Erich Heckel, architecture student.
Collaboration with Heckel and Bleyl. Studies the theories of color expounded by Goethe, Helmholtz, Newton and Rood.
Paintings in the pointillist style (influenced by Neo-Impressionist Exhibition of the "Phalanx", Munich, 1904).
Stimulated by Japanese prints.
Fascinated by the Negro art and carvings by the Palau islanders in the Ethnological Museum, Dresden.

1905 Through Heckel, meeting with the architecture student Karl Schmidt-Rottluff. Together they form the art group styled "Die Brücke" (The Bridge). Kirchner gets his degree in architecture and now devotes himself entirely to painting. First lithographs.

1906 Meeting with Cuno Amiet, Axel Gallén, Nolde, Pechstein. Works with Pechstein during the summer near Dresden. Draws up the program of Die Brücke. First and second exhibitions of Die Brücke at Dresden-Löbtau.

1910 The Die Brücke album of 1910 is his work.

1911 Moves in the spring to Berlin. *Der Sturm* publishes illustrations by Kirchner. He and Pechstein found the MUIM Institute *(Moderner Unterricht in Malerei)* in Berlin-Wilmersdorf. Not a single pupil enrolls.

1912 Kirchner and Heckel do frescos for the Chapel in the International Exhibition of the Sonderbund at Cologne. Under the influence of city life, Kirchner's style evolves towards psychological expressionism.
Takes part in the second Blue Rider Exhibition at the Goltz Gallery in Munich; also in the Blue Rider Exhibition at *Der Sturm* Gallery in Berlin.

1913 His friends reject the *Chronik der Brücke* as being too subjective. Only a few copies printed. Break-up of the group.

1915-
1916 Military training at Halle. Found to be physically and mentally unfit for service, Kirchner is released and sent to a sanatorium at Königstein, in the Taunus.
Paints his first murals, for the staircase of the sanatorium. Lives in dread of being called up again. Narcotics fail to calm his nerves.

1917 Goes to Davos on May 8, where he sets to work once more. With surprising quickness he adapts his technique to renderings of the countryfolk and Swiss mountains.

1918 With the Armistice, Kirchner's physical recovery is complete.

1922 From 1922 to 1938, the weaver Lise Gujer works with Kirchner, making carpets from his designs.

1923 Exhibition in the Basel Kunsthalle.

1924 Publication of the book *Umbra Vitae* by Georg Heym, with illustrations by Kirchner.

1925- The Basel painters Camenisch, Albert Müller and
1926 Hermann Scherer work under Kirchner's guidance. Together they form the "Red-Blue" group.

1929- Meeting with René Crevel.

1933 Commissioned to decorate the Folkwang Museum at Essen. The German government prevents Kirchner from carrying out the order.

1937 In Germany 639 of his works are confiscated as "degenerate." 32 of them are shown in the so-called "Degenerate Art" Exhibition in Munich.

1938 Suffering from a steadily worsening intestinal disease and in despair over the political and intellectual developments in Germany, Kirchner committed suicide at Davos-Frauenkirch in Switzerland on June 15.

BIBLIOGRAPHY

G. Schiefler, Berlin 1920. — Id., Berlin 1926. — W. Grohmann, Dresden 1925. — Id., Munich 1926. — R. Schapiro, *E. L. Kirchner*, in the *Thieme-Becker Allgemeines Lexikon der Bildenden Künstler*, vol. 20, Leipzig 1927. With bibliography.
Kirchner's views on art and outlook on life are set forth in some twenty articles he published in the course of his career, some under his own name, some with the pseudonym Louis de Marsalle.

KLEE, Paul (1879-1940)

1879 Born at Münchenbuchsee, near Bern, December 18, of a German father and a Swiss mother.

1898 Completed his schooling in Bern. In October left for Munich. Studied at Knirr's school.

1900 Studied at the Munich academy with Franz Stuck.

1901 In October traveled to Italy.

1903-1904 Series of grotesque etchings.

1905 Short stay in Paris.

1906 Married. Settled in Munich. First etchings exhibited with the "Secession" group, Munich.

1908 Influences of Cézanne, Van Gogh and Ensor.

1909 Much impressed by von Marées' exhibition at the "Secession" group, Munich.

1910 The designer and illustrator Alfred Kubin visited and encouraged him. In October: 55 works (drawings, watercolors, etchings, etc.) were exhibited at the Kunsthaus, Zurich, and later at Bern and Basel.

1911 First one-man show at the Thannhauser Gallery, Munich. Met Macke, Marc, Jawlensky, Münter, Werefkin, Kandinsky. At first exhibition of the Blue Rider group saw Delaunay's work for the first time.

1912 Exhibited at Second Blue Rider Exhibition at Munich. Visited Paris and met Picasso, Uhde, Delaunay, Le Fauconnier, Apollinaire. Strong cubist influence. Translated Delaunay's article *Sur la Lumière* which appeared in *Der Sturm*, January 1913.

1914 With other painters founded the "New Secession" at Munich. In the summer traveled to Tunisia with Macke and Louis Moillet.

1916- Served in different branches of the German army, first
1918 in the Infantry and later behind the lines. In 1918 *Der Sturm* published an illustrated monograph on Klee.

1920 May-June: retrospective exhibition at the Goltz Gallery, Munich (362 works). Collaborated in the book *Schöpferische Konfession*. Thanks to W. Gropius, elected professor at the Weimar Bauhaus.

1923 One-man show at the Kronprinz Palace, Berlin.

1924 First exhibition of Klee at "Société Anonyme," New York. Creation of the "Blue Four" group—Kandinsky, Feininger, Jawlensky, Klee.

1925 Publication of *Pedagogical Sketch-Book*. Second large-scale exhibition at the Goltz Gallery, Munich. Exhibited at the first general Surrealist exhibition at the Galerie Pierre, Paris. At the Dessau Bauhaus.

1926 First one-man show at Galerie Vavin-Raspail, Paris.

1929 Visited Egypt for purposes of study.

1930 Exhibition at Museum of Modern Art, New York.

1931 Taught at the Academy of Fine Arts, Düsseldorf. Traveled to Sicily.

1933 Returned to Bern at the end of the year.

1935 Retrospective exhibition in Bern, Basel, Lucerne.

1937 102 of Klee's works confiscated in Munich. 17 works exhibited at the Exhibition of Degenerate Art, Munich.

1940 Died at Muralto-Locarno, Switzerland, June 29.

BIBLIOGRAPHY

Sturmbilderbücher, III, Berlin 1918. — *Der Ararat*, Munich 1920. Issue devoted to K., with catalogue of the exhibition at Goltz Gallery, Munich 1920. — H. von Wedderkop (*Junge Kunst*. 13), Leipzig 1920. — L. Zahn, Potsdam 1920. — W. Hausenstein, *Kairuan...*, Munich 1921. — L. Scheewe in: *Thieme-Becker*, vol. 20, Leipzig 1927. With bibliography. — W. Grohmann, Ed. Cahiers d'Art, Paris 1929. With contributions by Aragon, Crevel, Eluard, Lurçat, Tzara, etc. — R. Crevel, Paris 1930. — *Bauhaus*, issue devoted to K., Dessau 1931. — W. Grohmann, *K.-Handzeichnungen 1921-1930*, Berlin 1934. — R. Bernoulli, Bern 1940. — Museum of Modern Art, New York, articles by A. H. Barr, J. and L. Feininger, J. J. Sweeney, New York 1945. With bibliography by H. B. Muller. — K. Nierendorf, New York 1945. — J. T. Soby, New York 1945. — *Cahiers d'Art*, Paris 1945-1946. Contributions by Bousquet, Duthuit, Grohmann, Tzara, Zervos. — *Du* (review), No. 10, devoted to K., Zurich 1948. — P. Eluard, *Voir*, Geneva 1948. —C. Giedion-Welcker, *Werk* No. 3, Winterthur 1948. — H. Read, London 1948. — J. Cassou, *L'Architecture d'Aujourd'hui*, Paris 1949. — D. Cooper (Penguin Books), London 1949. — Klee-Gesellschaft Bern. *Dokumente und Bilder aus den Jahren 1896-1930*, 1st part, Bern 1949. — W. Grohmann, New York 1954 (the most complete study).

KOKOSCHKA, Oskar (1886)

1886 Born March 1 at Pöchlarn-on-the-Danube (Austria).

1904- Student at the Vienna School of Arts and Crafts.
1908 Friendship with Egon Schiele, his schoolmate.

1907 First oil paintings: *The Trance Player* and the *Portrait of Frau Hirsch*. First poetic writings: the dramas *Sphinx and Straw Man* and *Woman's Hope*. These works rank high in the literature of Expressionism.

1908 The first Vienna Kunstschau exhibits Kokoschka's work for the first time: color illustrations from his book *The Dreaming Children* and the life-size drawings *Bearers of Dreams*. The works exhibited rouse the ire of the official critics, with the result that Kokoschka is expelled from the Art School. He now meets the well-known architect Adolf Loos, who becomes his friend and guide. Through Loos he meets the poets Peter Altenberg and Karl Kraus, whose magazine *Die Fackel* lends its support to the young painter.

1909 Takes part in the second Kunstschau. At the exhibition's open-air theater the plays *Sphinx and Straw Man* and *Woman's Hope* are performed and give rise to violent protests.

1910 Trip to Berlin.

1911 25 pictures and several drawings in the Hagenbund Exhibition in Vienna. Official criticism once again sharply challenges Kokoschka's work, culminating in the remark of the heir to the Austrian throne: "The fellow deserves to have every bone in his body broken."

1912- H. Walden organizes Kokoschka's second one-man exhi-
1914 bition in the *Sturm* Gallery. Friendship with Alma Mahler. On the outbreak of war, serves in the Dragoons.

1915- Wounded on the Eastern Front, he is sent to a hospital
1916 in Vienna, then returned to the front.

1917 Swiss première of his play *Sphinx and Straw Man* at the Dada Gallery in Zurich on April 14, and exhibition of his work.
Moves in a circle of young poets and actors who forgather in the "White Stag" Café, Dresden. Paints at this time the great portrait compositions *Exiles* and *Friends* (1917-1918).

1918 Writes the play *Orpheus and Eurydice*.

1919 Performances of *Job* and *The Burning Bush* in Max Reinhardt's Kammerspiele in Berlin with scenery by Kokoschka. Appointment to professorship at the Academy of Art, Dresden.

1924 Gives up his teaching post. A stay at Blonay, near Vevey (Switzerland). Landscapes. Death of his father. Return to Vienna. Portrait of the composer Arnold Schönberg. Visits Bordeaux, Biarritz, Avignon, Aigues-Mortes, Marseilles, Toledo, Madrid, Lisbon, Amsterdam. Landscapes.

1926 First stay in London. Paintings: *Waterloo Bridge* and *The Mandrill*.

1927 Exhibitions at Cassirer's, in Berlin, and in Zurich.

1928- Tunisia, Italy, Istanbul, Jerusalem, Ireland, Egypt,
1930 Algeria, Italy.

1931 Exhibition at Georges Petit's in Paris. Contract with Cassirer canceled. Returns to Vienna.

1937 First retrospective in Vienna. In Germany 417 of his works are confiscated as "degenerate." 16 works shown in the "Degenerate Art" Exhibition in Munich.

1938 Following the events at Munich, he leaves for London.

1940 After a stay in Cornwall, returns to London during the darkest days of the Battle of Britain. In articles and allegorical pictures he expresses his horror at what the war is making of the world, and man's degradation. *Alice in Wonderland* (1942), *What We Are Fighting For* (1943). Lives and works in London.

1947 Trip to Switzerland. Big Kokoschka Exhibition at the Basel Kunsthalle, continued at the Zurich Kunsthaus. Exhibitions in Amsterdam in 1947, at the Venice Biennale of 1948, and in the United States (Boston, New York, St. Louis and San Francisco).

1950 Executes a decoration for Count Seilern in London.

1952 Leaves England, settles in Switzerland.

1955 Lives and works at Villeneuve, on Lake Geneva.

BIBLIOGRAPHY

P. Westheim, Potsdam 1919 (2nd edition, revised and enlarged, 1925). — G. Biermann, *Junge Kunst*, No. 52, Leipzig 1929. — H. Heilmaier, Paris 1929. — Kokoschka, with 126 plates, Berlin 1935. — M. Masciotta, Florence 1942. — H. Platschek, Buenos-Aires 1946. — E. Hoffmann, foreword by H. Read, London 1947 (most important book thus far written on Kokoschka, with catalogue of his works, 1907 to 1945, and nearly complete bibliography).

LA FRESNAYE, ROGER DE (1885-1925)

1885 Born at Le Mans, France, July 11.

1903 At Académie Julian where he met Lotiron, Segonzac, Luc-Albert Moreau, Boussingault.

1908 Spent a few months with Maurice Denis and Sérusier at the Académie Ranson. Up to 1909 his painting was much influenced by Denis.

1910- Traveled in Germany and Italy.

1911 Landscapes at *La Ferté-sous-Jouarre*. With Apollinaire, Gleizes, Léger and Metzinger, takes part in the Sunday gatherings at Jacques Villon's studio at Puteaux where they found the *Section d'Or*.

1912 Landscapes at Meulan. Exhibits at Salon d'Automne *La Partie de cartes* and in Salon des Indépendants *L'Artillerie*. Begins sculpture.

1912-1913 Exhibited with the *Section d'Or*.

1913 Influenced by Braque and Picasso.

1913-1914 Series of still lifes. Seeks for a new classicism.

1914 Went through the war in the Infantry.

1917 Series of cubist drawings and watercolors.

1918 Invalided out of army with pneumonia. After the war lived at Hauteville (Ain), then at Grasse.

1925 Died of tuberculosis at Grasse, November 27.

BIBLIOGRAPHY

Roger Allard, Paris 1922. — A. Warnod, *Les berceaux de la jeune peinture*, Paris 1925. — W. George, *Dessins et gouaches 1919-1925 de R. de la F.*, Paris 1928. — M. Raynal, *De La F. à Fernand Léger*, Plans No. 1, Paris 1931. — *L'Amour de l'Art*, Paris 1933. Bio-bibliographical note by G. Bazin. — E. Nebelthau, Paris 1935. — R. Cogniat and W. George, *Œuvre complète*, Paris 1950.

LÉGER, FERNAND (1881-1955)

1881 Born at Argentan, Normandy, France, February 4.

1897 Apprenticed to an architect in Caen, Brittany.

1900-1902 At Paris. Architect's draftsman.

1902-1903 Military service at Versailles in the engineer corps.

1903- Studied at the Ecole des Beaux-Arts as an independent

1904 pupil in Gérome's studio, and later under G. Ferrier. Also worked at the Louvre and the Académie Julian. Earned his living by retouching photographs.

1905- Settled in *La Ruche*, Montparnasse, where he met

1907 Archipenko. Influenced by the Impressionists and Neo-Impressionists, chiefly by Signac and Cross. Throughout winter of 1905-1906 worked in Corsica. 1905-1907: influenced by Fauves, above all by Matisse.

1907- Influenced by Cézanne. Met Apollinaire, Max Jacob,

1908 Raynal, Reverdy, Salmon.

1908-1910 Friendship with Henri Rousseau.

1910 Exhibited at Independants: *Nudes in the Forest*. Met Kahnweiler through Apollinaire, and in Kahnweiler's Gallery Picasso and Braque.

1911- Joined in the meetings in Jacques Villon's studio, where

1912 the Section d'Or was founded. 1911: exhibited at the Salon des Indépendants (room 41) with Delaunay, Gleizes, Le Fauconnier, Marie Laurencin and Metzinger. Corresponded with Marinetti.

1913 Exhibited 15 works at *Erster deutscher Herbstsalon* at the Sturm Gallery, Berlin. *14th of July*.

1914- Called up in the Transport Corps. Drawings of soldiers

1916 at the front, and large war machines whose mechanical aspects were to have a great influence on his work in the following years. *Game of Cards* (1916-1917). Gassed near Verdun and invalided out of the army.

1917- Mechanical and dynamic period. Painted: *The Man and*

1919 *the Wheel, Red Disk, The Town* (1919).

1920 Met Le Corbusier.

1921- Decors for Swedish Ballet: 1921, *Skating Rink*, music

1922 by Honegger; 1922: *The Creation of the World*, music by Milhaud.

1923- Created the film *Ballet mécanique* with D. Murphy.

1924 Traveled in Italy (Ravenna and Venice) with Léonce Rosenberg. Founded his own art school. Relations with painters of the "Stijl" group, van Doesburg and Mondrian, and with the purists Jeanneret and Ozenfant.

1925- Mural paintings for the "Palace of the French Embassy"

1930 at the International Exhibition of Decorative Arts, Paris.

1931 First voyage to the United States. Greatly impressed by New York life and architecture, as the artist reported in *Cahiers d'Art*, No. 9/10, 1931.

1933 Traveled to Greece.

1937 Decor for *David Triumphant*, Serge Lifar ballet performed at the Paris Opera. Mural painting *Le Transport des Forces* at the "Palais de la Découverte" in the Paris World's Fair.

1938 Traveled to the United States to work with the architect Harrison on the decoration of Nelson Rockefeller's apartment.

1939 Decors for *Naissance d'une Cité*, play by Jean-Richard Bloch with music by Honegger and Milhaud given at the Vélodrome d'Hiver, Paris.

1940 December, arrived in America. Painted acrobats and bicyclists.

1945 December: returned to France.

1946 Mosaic for the façade of the Church at Assy (Savoy).

1948 Thomas Bouchard made film *Léger in America*.

1949 Large retrospective exhibition at the Musée d'Art Moderne, Paris.

1950 Decors and costumes for *Bolivar*, opera by Milhaud, given at the Paris Opera (700 costumes, 12 decors for moving scenery).

1951 Ceramic work. Stained glass windows for a church at Audincourt.

1952 Decors and costumes for J. Charret's ballet, created at Amboise for the 500th anniversary of Leonardo da Vinci. Lives, works and teaches in Paris.

1955 Dies at Gif-sur-Yvette, near Paris, August 17.

BIBLIOGRAPHY

G. Apollinaire, *Les Peintres cubistes*, Paris 1913. — D. H. Kahnweiler, *Der Cicerone*, T. 12, No. 19, Leipzig 1920. — M. Raynal, *Vingt tableaux*, 1st series, Paris 1920. — Id., *Anthologie de la peinture en France*, with remarks by the artist, Paris 1927. In English: *Modern French Painters*, New York 1928. — E. Tériade, Paris 1928. — M. Raynal, *De La Fresnaye à F.L.*, Plans, No. 1, Paris 1931. — *Cahiers d'Art*, Nos. 3/4, Paris 1933. Articles by G. Apollinaire, B. Cendrars, Le Corbusier, I. Ehrenburg, M. Raynal, A. Salmon, J. J. Sweeney, C. Zervos. — C. Zervos, *Cahiers d'Art*, No. 1/4, Paris 1934. — Montreal 1945. Articles by M. A. Cousturier, M. Cagnon, S. Giedion, S. Kootz, F. L. — S. Giedion, *Magazine of Arts*, Washington, December 1945. — P. Eluard, *Voir*, Geneva 1948. — D. Cooper, Geneva 1949. Comprehensive bibliography by H.B. Muller.

MAGRITTE, RENÉ (1898)

1898 Born at Lessines, Belgium, November 21. Classical studies at the Atheneum, Charleroi.

1916 Works for two years under Van Damme-Sylva, Combaz and Montald at the Brussels Academy of Fine Arts, but is a rather desultory student.

1920 First exhibition at the "Centre d'Art" Gallery, Brussels.

1925 Throwing in his lot wholeheartedly with the Surrealists, he took part in its most significant demonstrations and spread tidings of the movement in Belgium, together with Paul Nougé, Scutenaire and several others.

1928 Begins a two years' stay in Paris, marked by his exhibition at the Goemans Gallery. After returning to Brussels he contributes to the reviews *La Révolution Surréaliste*, *Le Surréalisme au service de la Révolution*, *Minotaure*, etc. Painting now in a rather severe style, he describes objects minutely and aims at creating effects of surprise. Exhibits regularly in the United States and Europe.

1940 A change comes over his art, and in a freer style he paints works "full of light and warmth" (Dotremont): *Alice in Wonderland*. After the war he strikes a certain balance between these two manners.

1948 Exhibitions in New York and Paris.

1955 Lives and works in Brussels.

BIBLIOGRAPHY

P. Nougé, Brussels 1943. — André Breton, *Le Surréalisme et la Peinture*, New York 1944. — L. Scutenaire, Brussels 1947. — Paul Fierens, *L'Art en Belgique*, Brussels 1947. — E.L.T. Mesens, *Peintres belges contemporains*, Brussels 1947. — L. Scutenaire, Brussels 1948.

MARC, Franz (1880-1916)

1880 Born at Munich, February 8. Studied theology and later philology.

1900 Studied art at the Munich Academy under Wilhelm Dietz and G. Hackl.

1902 In the autumn, traveled to Italy, with his brother Paul.

1903- Six months' visit to France, Paris and Brittany.
1904 First contacts with Impressionism. Admired Japanese color prints.

1905 Met the animal painter Jean B. Niestlé, who exercised a decisive influence on Marc, and Fräulein Schnür, a painter, who belonged to the Jugendstil group "Die Scholle." Marc was influenced by this group for a certain time (drawings in the *Stella Peregrina* folio).

1905- First attempts at sculpture: *Group of Sheep* (in wax). In
1906 the spring of 1906 visited Greece (Mount Athos).

1907 Second stay in Paris. Saw paintings by Van Gogh and Gauguin. Towards the end of the summer sketched in the Berlin Zoo.

1908 The Spring: first painting on the theme of *Horses of Lenggries*: four life-size horses. Developed this theme until 1914.

1909 December: visited the first exhibition of the "New Association of Munich Artists."

1910 January 6: first meeting with August Macke. February: first exhibition at the Brackl Gallery. Met Kandinsky. In search of absolute color he painted several pointillist pictures.

1911 Period of great activity: *Three Red Horses*, *Blue Horses*. With Kandinsky prepared almanach of *Der Blaue Reiter*. Member of the "New Association of Munich Artists." December 2: Marc, Kandinsky, Münter and Kubin resigned from the Association. December 18: Opening of the "First Exhibition of the Directors of the Blue Rider."

1912 Journalistic work. In March and April, second exhibition (in black and white) of the Blue Rider group at the Goltz Gallery, Munich. March 12: Opening of the Blue Rider exhibition at *Der Sturm* Gallery, Berlin. In September and October, short visit to Paris with his wife and August Macke. October 1: first meeting with Delaunay with whom he had corresponded. Influenced by the Futurists whose exhibition he had seen in Berlin, and by Delaunay. Admiration for Rousseau. *Der Blaue Reiter* published by Piper, Munich.

1913 Active work on the organization of the first German Autumn Salon at the Sturm Gallery, Berlin. *Large Yellow Horses* (painted between 1912 and 1914). *Deer in the Forest*, *Abstract Forms I, II*. *Tyrol*, his last picture, remained unfinished.

1914 Volunteered for the German Army.

1915 Notebook of abstract sketches *(Feldskizzenbuch)* was his last work.

1916 Killed at Verdun, March 4.

BIBLIOGRAPHY

T. Däubler, *Die Neue Rundschau*, Berlin 1916. — P. Colin, *L'Art libre*, No. 6, Brussels, 1922. — G. Pauli (Kunsthalle, Hamburg, *Kleine Führer*, 20), Hamburg 1922. — W. Przygode, *Sechzehn farbige Handzeichnungen*, Potsdam 1923. — E. Weiss, Phil. Dissertation, Frankfurt a. M. 1933. — W. Kandinsky, *Cahiers d'Art*, No. 8/10, Paris 1936. — A. J. Schardt, Berlin 1936. With catalogue of works and bibliography. — H. Büneman, Munich 1948. — H. Demisch, Berlin 1948. — R. Probst, 10 colorplates with introduction by R. P. (Meisterwerke), Munich 1948. — G. Schmidt, *F. Marc und August Macke im Kreis ihrer Zeitgenossen*, Basel 1948. Limited edition. — M. Seuphor, *L'art abstrait, ses origines, ses premiers maîtres*, Paris 1949.

MARIN, John (1870-1953)

1870 Born at Rutherford, New Jersey, December 23. Worked four years in an architect's office.

1893 Opened his own office as an architect.

1899- Decided to become a painter. At the School of Fine
1901 Arts, Philadelphia with T. P. Anschutz.

1901- At the Art Students' League, New York, with Frank
1903 V. Dumond.

1905 In Paris. At different schools and academies. Studied etching and made engravings after European monuments which bring out their architectural side. Impressed by Charles Méryon's engravings.

1909 The photographer Eduard Steichen organized the first exhibition of Marin's works at the Stieglitz Gallery. New York (25 watercolors).

1910 Another one-man show at the Stieglitz Gallery. 10 watercolors at the Salon d'Automne, Paris. Traveled to Austria.

1913 Exhibited watercolors of the Woolworth Building at the Armory Show.

1920 Exhibition at the Daniel Gallery, New York.

1929-1930 Visit to Mexico.

1936 Retrospective exhibition at the Museum of Modern Art, New York.

1950 Exhibited at the Biennale, Venice.

1953 Dies on October 1 at Cape Split, Maine, aged 82. *(Information supplied by Miss Hannah Muller, Museum of Modern Art, New York.)*

BIBLIOGRAPHY

C. Saunier, *Art décoratif*, Paris, January 1908. — J. Eglington *Arts and Decoration*, New York, August 1924. — *America and Alfred Stieglitz, a Collective Portrait*, Garden City, New York 1934. — E. M. Benson, Washington 1935. — L. Mozley, *Yankee Artist, Bulletin of the Museum of Modern Art*, No. 1, New York 1936. — J. Mellquist, *Tricolor*, New York, May 1945. — M. Helm, with preface by J. Marin, Boston 1948. — H. Riegner, *Werk*, No. 8, Winterthur, 1948. — J. T. Soby, *Contemporary Painters*, Museum of Modern Art, New York 1948. — Marin, in *Current Biography*, New York 1949. — R. Flint, New York n. d. (American Arts Portfolios). Text with 6 color plates.

MARQUET, Albert (1875-1947)

1875 Born March 27 at Bordeaux, where he first goes to school.

1890 Comes to Paris. Attends the Ecole des Arts Décoratifs, where he meets Matisse; forms a lifelong friendship with him.

1897 Moves on to the Ecole des Beaux-Arts, under Cormon, Aimé Morot, then Gustave Moreau; he finds again Matisse and meets Rouault, Manguin, Camoin.

1898 First landscapes in the Fauve manner. Paints with Matisse in the mornings in the Luxembourg Gardens, in the afternoons at Arcueil.

1901 Exhibits at the Salon des Indépendants yearly from 1901 to 1910.

1902 Exhibits at the Berthe Weill Gallery.

1903 Exhibits at Salon d'Automne.

1904 Paints André Rouveyre's portrait.

1906 Visits the Normandy coast with Dufy (Fécamp, Le Havre, Trouville, etc.).

1907 First one-man show at Druet's. Landscapes at Le Havre and St.-Jean-de-Luz.

1908-1909 Stays in Naples and Hamburg.

1910 Begins to travel more widely.

1911 Paints landscapes at Honfleur, Tangier, Conflans.

1912 Visits numerous seaports: Le Havre, Naples, Hamburg, Rotterdam, Rouen, Tangier, Sète, Bordeaux, Dunkerque. Trip to Norway.

1913 Travels to Morocco with Matisse and Camoin. Landscapes at La Varenne, Tangier.

1914 Stays in Rotterdam and Collioure.

1915 Settles at Marseilles.

1916- Stays in Marseilles with George Besson and in Nice with
1919 Matisse.

1920 Paints in La Rochelle and Algiers.

1923 Marries the writer Marcelle Marty and, until 1935, frequents stays in North Africa. Landscapes at Sidi-Bou-Saïd.
1925 Works more in watercolors than in oils.
Norwegian landscapes.
1928 Paints landscapes in Egypt.
1933 Trip to Rumania.
1934 Journey to U.S.S.R. (Moscow, Tiflis).
1936-1937 Stays in Switzerland.
1938 Winter in Stockholm.
1940 Leaves the banks of the Seine and settles at Algiers for the duration of the war where he is in touch with Saint-Exupéry and André Gide.
1940-1945 Works with his wife in Algiers.
1945 Returns to Paris.
1946 Illustrates *Parisian Rhapsody* by Jean Cassou.
1947 Dies on June 14.

BIBLIOGRAPHY

F. Fosca, Paris 1908. — C. L. Philippe, *Grande Revue*, 1908. — G. Besson, Paris 1920, 1927, 1929, 1948. — M. Mermillon, Paris 1928. — C. Terrasse, Paris 1928. — C. Sterling and G. Bazin, in *Histoire de l'art contemporain*, by René Huyghe, Paris 1935. — C. Roger-Marx, *Gazette des Beaux-Arts*, Paris, March 1939. — F. Schmalenbach, Basel 1941. — G. Besson and A. Rouveyre, *Drawings, Le Point*, Paris 1943. — J. W. Lane, *Gazette des Beaux-Arts*, Paris-New York, May-June 1947. — F. Jourdain, *Drawings*, Paris 1948. — *Carnet de voyage, Venise*, Paris. — M. Marquet, Paris 1951. — *Les voyages de Marquet*, drawings, Paris 1953.

MASSON, André (1896)

1896 Born at Balagny (Oise), France, January 4.
Studied at Brussels; then under Baudoin at Ecole des Beaux-Arts, Paris.
1914 Spring in Italy.
1918 Worked at Céret. 1919: settled in Paris.
1922- Cubist period. Pronounced influence of Gris. 1924: first
1924 exhibition organized by Kahnweiler at Galerie Simon, Paris. Still-lifes, landscapes.
1924 Illustrated *Soleil bas* by Limbourg.
1924- Met Antonin Artaud, Breton, Miro, Max Ernst and others.
1929 Joined the Surrealists. Exhibited at first general surrealist exhibition at Galerie Pierre, Paris. The works of Blake, the Marquis de Sade, and later of Kafka, Nietzsche and Chinese poetry and philosophy made lasting impressions on his mind.
Subjects: Metamorphoses, Dreams, Eroticism.
1925 Illustrated *Simulacre* by Leiris.
1928 Illustrated *Justine* by the Marquis de Sade.
1929-1932 Traveled to Germany and Holland.
1933 Exhibition with Miro at Pierre Matisse Gallery, New York.
1934- Stayed at Tossa, Catalonia. *Massacres; Don Quixote;*
1936 *Bull-Fighting.*
1936 Illustrated *Sacrifices* by Georges Bataille.
1937 Returned to France. Second surrealist period.
1938 Illustrated *Glossaire, j'y serre mes glosses*, by Leiris.
1939 Finished *Emblematical View of Toledo* (1933-1939).
1942-1945 In the United States. Graphic work.
1946 Back in France. Returned to impressionist formulas. Published *Bestiaire* (Animals) (12 lithographs and drawings). Decors for *Morts sans Sépulture* by J. P. Sartre (Théâtre Antoine), and *Hamlet* (Théâtre Marigny), produced by J. L. Barrault.
1947 Settled in Aix-en-Provence.
1949 Illustrated *The Conquerors* by André Malraux (33 etchings, Albert Skira).
1950 Large exhibition (94 works) with his friend Alberto Giacometti at the Kunsthalle, Basel.
1951 Exhibition at the Galerie Leiris, Paris.
1955 Lives and works at Le Tholonet, near Aix.

BIBLIOGRAPHY

A. Breton, *Le Surréalisme et la peinture*, Paris 1928. 2nd edition, New York 1945. — *Cahiers du Sud*, Marseilles, February 1929. Issue devoted to A. Masson. Contributions by J. Baron, J. Bousquet, et al. — P. Pia, Paris 1930. — C. Zervos, *Cahiers d'Art*, No. 6/7, Paris 1932. — A. H. Barr, *Fantastic Art, Dada, Surrealism*, Museum of Modern Art, New York 1936. — J. Levy, *Surrealism*, New York 1936. — Texts by J. L. Barrault, G. Bataille, Breton, Desnos, Eluard, Jouve, Leiris, Limbourg, Péret, Paris 1940. — M. Leiris and G. Limbourg, Geneva 1947.

MATISSE, Henri (1869-1954)

1869 Born December 31 at Le Cateau (in the North of France). His father was a grain-merchant at Bohain. His mother was artistic and used to spend her leisure painting china. At 12, he entered the Saint-Quentin Lycée and did well at classics; he was, however, an indifferent pupil and his attention was always wandering. It was his father's wish that he should study law.
1890 Goes to Paris to carry on his law studies, but prefers spending his time in the Louvre. Back at home with his parents, convalescing from an illness, he happens to read Goupil's *How to Paint*. His first picture is a *Still Life with Books*.
1891 His father puts him to work in a solicitor's office; at the same time, on the sly, Matisse enrolls in the Ecole Quentin de la Tour, where he works in the morning, before going to the office. In the end, his parents consent to his devoting himself wholly to painting.
1892 Matisse returns to Paris and enrolls at the Académie Julian. He works under Bouguereau and Ferrier, members of the Institute, and studies especially Chardin and Goya.
1893 Ecole des Beaux-Arts, in Gustave Moreau's class. This teacher gives him much kindly advice and help. He meets Rouault, Marquet, Piot, Camoin, Manguin. At the Louvre he copies the Masters.
1896 Exhibits for the first time at Salon de la Société Nationale, showing four pictures. During this period, Matisse still uses dark tonalities of academic art. It is not long, however, before he discovers Daumier, Degas, Lautrec, the Japanese and—most important!—the Seine. He and Marquet set up a studio together at 19, quai Saint-Michel. Begins his copy of Chardin's *The Ray*.
Stays in Brittany (Belle-Ile) with the painter Very, pupil of Bonnat; does land- and seascapes. He utilizes to the full the lessons of Impressionism, but soon moves beyond them.
Matisse now goes alone to Beurec-Cap-Sizun (Finistère), where he paints a *Church* and *Woman with a Pig*.
1897 Takes to using brighter colors. Paints *La Desserte ;* meets Camille Pissarro.
Exhibits five pictures at the Société Nationale.
1898 Matisse "discovers" Provence. Great admiration for Renoir and Cézanne. Stays in Corsica during the winter. Returns to Paris, with the intention of re-entering Moreau's class. His old teacher has passed away, however, succeeded by Cormon. Matisse studies a short time under Cormon, then enters Carrière's class, applying himself to the study of the human figure. Meets Derain, Laprade, Puy. When Carrière closes down his studio, he works at Jean Biette's, rue Dutot. Does a large male nude, painted wholly in blue.
Begins to have a hard time of it financially, finding few buyers for his pictures. He and Marquet get work doing decorations for the 1900 World's Fair.
Matisse now uses pure color *(Nature Morte Orangée)*. Exhibits *La Desserte* at Salon de la Société Nationale. He and Marquet spend the mornings painting at the Luxembourg, the afternoons at Arcueil. Buys Cézanne's picture *Les Baigneuses* at Vollard's.
1900 Turns his attention to problems of sculpture, working in a municipal studio, rue Etienne-Marcel.
1901 At the Van Gogh Exhibition in Bernheim-Jeune's Gallery, Derain introduces Vlaminck to Matisse. Matisse visits the two painters at Chatou, to have a look at their pictures.
1902 Exhibits at Berthe Weill's, rue Victor-Massé, alongside Marquet, Manguin, Camoin.
1903 Salon d'Automne is founded by Rambosson, Desvallières, Rouault, Piot. Director is Frantz Jourdain; Matisse, Marquet and Bonnard are the "shock-troops."
1904 First exhibition at Ambroise Vollard's (preface by Roger Marx). Sells his picture *Phlox* to Olivier Saincère. Has a brief fling at Pointillism, soon gives it up, all idea of "system" being repellent to him. The landscapes painted during the winter at Collioure and Saint-Tropez are done in broad tracts of flat color.
1905 It is at this year's Salon d'Automne, grouping a large number of works by Matisse, Vlaminck, Derain, Manguin and Rouault, that Vauxcelles' famous remark baptizes the young painters with the name "Fauves." Matisse exhibits *Luxe, Calme et Volupté*.

1906 Matisse gives up his studio at 19, quai Saint-Michel, moving to the former Couvent des Oiseaux in the rue de Sèvres, where he opens an art-school. Purrmann and Bruce are among the early pupils. Paints *Le Bonheur de Vivre*, an early revelation of his commanding personality. Severe criticism is hurled at the Fauves, particularly at Matisse, who is looked upon as the ringleader. Matisse moves his art-school to the former Couvent du Sacré-Cœur, boulevard des Invalides. More and more pupils flock to him.

Makes the acquaintance of Picasso at Gertrude Stein's. Shows Picasso a negro statuette he has picked up at Père Sauvage's shop, in the rue de Rennes. Beginning of a lifelong friendship between the two painters.

1907 Exhibits at Cassirer's in Berlin. Paints his remarkable *Blue Nude* (Souvenir of Biskra).

1908 In the *Grande Revue* he publishes his *Notes d'un Peintre*, an epoch-making article destined to have a considerable effect on European art.

Returns to the theme of *La Desserte*, painted in 1897, and makes two new versions: *Red Harmony* and *Blue Harmony*.

1909 Paints *Poissons Rouges et Statue de Terre Rose.*

1910 First Retrospective Exhibition at Bernheim-Jeune's. Sends in *La Danse* and *Musique* to the Salon d'Automne.

1911- Moves to Issy-les-Moulineaux. Makes two trips to
1913 Morocco, accompanied the second time by Camoin and the Canadian painter Morice. The African landscape gives Matisse a taste for the bare and formally patterned. He rejects the casual for what is permanent. He returns from Morocco with several pictures now reckoned among his masterpieces.

He now takes up sculpture. Interested in recent developments of Cubism.

1915- Paints several of his best works in these years: *The*
1916 *Piano Lesson, Young Girl Bathing, Moroccans in Prayer, Still Life with Colocynths.* In these pictures he combines elimination of all but essentials with a geometric calligraphy. Exhibition at Montross Gallery, New York.

1917 Moves to Nice, where he gets to know Renoir. Paints his famous *Interior with a Violin* (now in the Copenhagen Museum). This, he says, is "one of my most beautiful pictures."

1918 A certain realism reappears in his work. Paints the series of *Odalisques*. Moving away from both Fauve and Cubist methods, he harks back to Delacroix. Now sees Morocco from a more orientalizing angle.

1919 *The White Plumes* (Minneapolis Institute of Art). Large exhibition at Bernheim's.

1920 Visits Etretat. Sets for the ballet *Le Chant du Rossignol* (Stravinsky-Diaghilev). First monograph by Marcel Sembat.

1927 His *Le Compotier* is awarded first prize at the Pittsburgh International Exhibition. In 1930 he is invited to be a member of the jury.

1930 Retrospective Exhibition in Berlin.

1931 After a series of journeys—in Italy, Spain, Germany, England, Russia—Matisse sets out for the South Seas. Stays three months at Tahiti where he is fascinated by the utter novelty of everything he sees, and stores up innumerable impressions, haunted by memories of Gauguin. On the return journey, he stops in the United States, where Dr Barnes commissions him to decorate the largest hall in his museum at Merion (Pa.). Matisse undertakes the task. Through an error in measurement, he has to do the decoration twice (for an area of 52 square yards), only finishing in 1933. The first version is bought by the city of Paris.

This period is marked by a change in Matisse's work, a second flowering, so to speak. His conceptions of art have reached their most advanced stage. The supreme visions of his creative genius now are bodied forth in terms of a geometric compositional scheme giving them their fullest significance. Retrospective Exhibition at the Georges Petit Gallery, Paris, and at the Museum of Modern Art, New York.

1932 Illustrations for Mallarmé's *Poésies* (Skira).

1936 From now on, Matisse draws on the accumulated knowledge of long years of work to revive certain tendencies of his "Fauve period"; the resulting works are among the most serene and significant of his career. Retrospective Matisse exhibitions are put on in Paris, New York, Stockholm.

1939 Retires to the Var Valley (Vence). Drawn to illustration and typography, he illustrates several books whose entire format is his creation.

1943 After successfully undergoing a very dangerous operation, he branches out in several new directions. As a corollary to his usage of flat color, he now assembles compositions consisting of pieces of colored paper cut out with scissors. Begins preliminary studies for his illustrations of Ronsard's *Amours.*

1944 Large-scale Matisse Exhibition at Salon d'Automne. Does illustrations for Montherlant's *Pasiphaé.*

1945 Exhibition at Victoria and Albert Museum, London.

1947 Matisse Exhibition at Palais des Papes, Avignon. Illustrations for Baudelaire's *Fleurs du Mal.*

1948 Large-scale exhibition of his pictures, drawings and sculpture at Museum of Art, Philadelphia (271 items). Exhibits large colored papers at the Salon de Mai, Paris.

1949 Exhibition at the Kunstmuseum, Lucerne. At Vence, he undertakes the decoration of a Dominican chapel whose lay-out is designed by him. Matisse intends it to be at once a résumé and a solution of the problems engrossing him throughout his career.

1952 Matisse Museum is founded at Le Cateau.

1954 Dies at Nice, November 3.

BIBLIOGRAPHY

M. Sembat, Paris 1920. — H. Purrmann, Berlin 1922. — F. Fels, Paris 1929. — A. H. Barr, catalogue, Museum of Modern Art, New York 1931. — G. Scheiwiller, Milan 1933. — P. Courthion, Paris 1934. — R. Escholier, Paris 1937. — A. Romm, Moscow 1937. — P. Fierens, Bergamo 1938. — I. Grunewald, Stockholm 1944. — L. Swane, Stockholm 1944. — L. Aragon, catalogue, Philadelphia Exhibition, 1948. — A. H. Barr, New York 1951 (the most complete study). — G. Diehl, Paris 1954.

MIRO, JOAN (1893)

1893 Born at Montroig, near Barcelona, April 20.

1907 At the School of Fine Arts, Barcelona.

1912 At the Academy Gali, Barcelona.

1915 Worked independently at Barcelona and Montroig.

1918 February 16 to March 3: first exhibition at Dalmau's Gallery, Barcelona. Influenced by Van Gogh and Fauvism. *The Chauffeur.*

1919 March: first visit to Paris. Met Picasso.

1920 Series of *Still Lifes*. Cubist influence.

1921 April 29 to May 14: Exhibition at Galerie La Licorne, Paris. Catalogue by Maurice Raynal.

1922 Finished *The Farm* after nine months' work.

1925 Exhibition at Galerie Pierre, Paris. With Max Ernst executed costumes and decor for *Roméo et Juliette* (Russian Ballet). Exhibited at first Surrealist exhibition at Galerie Pierre. Greatly impressed by Klee.

1928 Journey to Holland. Admired Vermeer.

1930 Figured in *Exhibition of Collages* at Goemans', Paris. Catalogue prefaced by Aragon.

1931- Costumes and decor for *Jeux d'Enfants* (Ballets Russes
1932 de Monte-Carlo).

1934 A special number of *Cahiers d'Art* is devoted to him.

1937 A large mural painting in Spanish Pavilion of the Paris World's Fair.

1940 After German invasion of France, returns with his family to Barcelona.

1942 Decorates pottery fired by Artigas the ceramist.

1947 First journey to America. Mural in the Terrace Plaza Hotel, Cincinnati.

1948 Returns to Europe. Lives and works in Barcelona with frequent trips to Paris.

1950 Illustrates Tristan Tzara's *Parler seul* with 75 lithographs in color.

1953 Exhibition at Maeght Gallery, Paris.

1954 First prize for engraving at the Venice Biennale.

BIBLIOGRAPHY

A. Breton, *Le Surréalisme et la Peinture*, Paris 1928. 2nd edition, New York 1945. — S. Dali, *L'Amic de les Arts*, Sitges, June 1928. — D. Gascoyne, *A Short Survey of Surrealism*, London 1935. — A. H. Barr, *Fantastic Art, Dada, Surrealism*, Museum of Modern Art, New York 1936. — J. Levy, *Surrealism*, New York 1941. — J. J. Sweeney, Museum of Modern Art, New York 1941. With bibliography. — C. Greenberg, New York 1948. — A. Cirici-Pellicer, Barcelona 1949. — I. E. Cirlot, Barcelona 1949.

MODIGLIANI, AMEDEO (1884-1920)

1884 Born at Leghorn, Italy, July 12.
His father was a banker; his mother, born in Marseilles, was said to be a descendant of Spinoza.

1898 Seriously ill, left school.
First painting lessons with local landscape painter Micheli.

1900 Relapse. Convalescence in South Italy, then in Rome, Venice and Florence, where he studied in the museums and the academies.

1906 Influenced by Lautrec, Steinlen.
Settled in Paris. Studio in Montmartre.

1908 Exhibited for the first time 6 pictures at Salon des Indépendants. Led a hand-to-mouth existence and found a solace in drink and drugs. *Woman's Head; The Sad Nude.*

1909 Met Constantin Brancusi, who encouraged him to try sculpture. Brief stay at Leghorn. Greatly impressed by large Cézanne exhibition at Bernheim-Jeune's. Under Cézanne's influence painted *The Beggar, The Violoncellist* which he showed with five other canvases at the Salon des Indépendants, in 1910.

1913 Settled in Montparnasse. Frequented Café de la Rotonde. Friendship with Kisling, Soutine.

1914- Love affair with English poetess Beatrice Hastings.
1916 The connoisseur and (later) picture-dealer Zborowski becomes interested in him and tries to sell his pictures.

1915 Paul Guillaume buys some of his pictures. Exhibition in a private studio 6, rue Huyghens.

1917 For several months worked for the dealer Chéron in the rue de La Boétie. Was paid 40 francs and a bottle of brandy per picture. Met Jeanne Hébuterne who remained devoted to him until his death.

1917-1919: Period of intensive work: large reclining nudes and portraits.

1918 First one-man show at the Galerie Berthe Weill, rue Laffitte. Show closed after a few days by the police on the grounds of the alleged indecency of the nudes. Obliged by bad health to spend winter at Nice and Cagnes.

1919 Returned to Paris. Birth of his daughter. Taken to hospital gravely ill.

1920 January 25: died of tuberculosis. His friends Kisling and Salmon made a collection and a splendid funeral procession accompanied him to Père Lachaise cemetery. Jeanne Hébuterne threw herself from a fifth floor window a few hours after Modigliani's death.

BIBLIOGRAPHY

A. Salmon, Paris 1926. — G. Scheiwiller, Milan 1927. With bibliography. — M. Schwarz, Paris 1927. — M. Dale, New York 1929. — A. Pfannstiel, Paris 1929. With catalogue of works and bibliography. — L. Vitali, *Disegni, Arte Moderna Italiana 15*, Milano 1929. — G. Scheiwiller, Milan 1930. Contributions by Braque, Carco, Carrà, Chirico, Cocteau, Derain, Kisling, Lipchitz, Salmon, Severini, Soutine, Zborowski et al. — A. Basler, Paris 1931. — R. Franchi, Florence 1944. — *Note e ricordi*, Genoa, 1945. 6 reproductions. Contributions by W. George, Latourette, Venturi. — M. Raynal, Geneva 1951. French and English editions. — J. Cocteau, Paris 1952. — P. Descargues, Paris 1952.

MONDRIAN, PIET (1872-1944)

1872 Born at Amersfoort, near Amsterdam, March 7. Received first painting lessons from his uncle, the painter Frits Mondrian.

1892-1894 At the Rijksakademie, Amsterdam.

1895- Painted naturalistic pictures at Amsterdam, Brabant
1907 and for one summer at Ruurlo. From 1900 strongly influenced by painters Toorop and Sluyters. Landscapes and still lifes.

1908- At Domburg where Toorop also worked (1908): greatly
1910 impressed by Matisse. In search of new methods, turned to pure color.

1910- First visit to Paris: admired Van Dongen, Matisse
1912 and other Fauves. Under influence of Delaunay, Survage, Léger, Picasso, turned to Cubism. Predominance of grey in his work.

1914 July: returned to Holland. *Pier* and *Ocean.* Increasingly avoided use of curves in favor of horizontals and verticals. First neo-plastic works.

1917 Founded review *De Stijl* with van Doesburg; worked on it till 1925.

1918 Returned to Paris.

1920 Outlined his theories in *Le Néo-Plasticisme* published by Léonce Rosenberg, Paris.

1925 *Die Neue Gestaltung* (New Representation) (Bauhausbücher, No. 5).

1939- Went to London. Arrived New York October 3.
1940 *New York City*; the *Boogie-Woogie* series. His last work *Victory Boogie-Woogie* remains unfinished.

1944 February 1: Died of pneumonia at Murray Hill Hospital, New York.

BIBLIOGRAPHY

G. Apollinaire, *A travers le Salon des Indépendants, Montjoie* Paris 1913. — F. M. Huebner, *Die neue Malerei in Holland*, Leipzig 1921. — H. Kröller-Müller, *Die Entwicklung der modernen Malerei*, Leipzig 1925. — W. Grohman in: *Thieme-Becker*, vol. 25, Leipzig 1931. — A. H. Barr, *Cubism and Abstract Art*, New York 1936. — C. Giedion-Welcker, *Werk*. No. 4, Winterthur 1944. — Amsterdam Stedelijk Museum, Catalogue of retrospective exhibition, 1946. With contributions by C. van Eesteren, Oud, M. Seuphor. — J. J. Sweeney, New York 1948. — M. Seuphor, *L'art abstrait, ses origines, ses premiers maîtres*, Paris 1949.

MORANDI, GIORGIO (1890)

1890 Born July 20 at Bologna, Italy, where he has lived all his life. Has never visited Paris.

1909 Studies at Academy of Fine Arts, Bologna. Does painting and engraving; his engraved work is considerable.

1914 Influenced by Cézanne and Cubism. Devotes himself almost exclusively to the still life, and particularly to still lifes of bottles and vases on a table, a subject whose expressive values he thoroughly explores.

1917- Metaphysical Period. Approaches art from a less literary
1920 angle than Chirico and Carrà, with whom he takes part in the "Valori Plastici" exhibitions. Exhibits in Germany.

1920 Reverts to a more forthright, colorful art: landscapes, still lifes.

1925 Shows at the "Novecento" Exhibition, Milan.

1939 One-man show in Rome.

1945 One-man show in Rome.

1946 One-man show in Milan.

1948 Grand Prize of Italian Painting at the Venice Biennale. Exhibition of his engraved work in Rome.

1949 Exhibition of prints in Brussels.

1950 Takes part in the Modern Italian Art Exhibition, Musée d'Art Moderne, Paris.

1955 Lives in Bologna and teaches at the Academy of Fine Arts.

BIBLIOGRAPHY

A. Soffici, *L'Italiano*, 1932. — C. E. Oppo, *L'Italia letteraria*, 1932. — G. Scheiwiller, *L'Art Italien Moderne*, Paris 1930. — C. Brandi, Florence 1942. — C. Gnudi, Florence 1946. — F. Arcangeli, Milan 1950.

MUNCH, EDVARD (1863-1944)

1863 Born December 12 at Löyten, Norway. His father, Christian Munch, was a doctor.

1881- School of Arts and Crafts in Oslo. Painting lessons from
1884 Christian Krohg.

1885 First visit to Paris; stays three weeks.

1886 Joins the group styled "The Bohemians of Christiana," whose leading figure is the poet Hans Jäger.

1889 First stay at Aasgaardstrand in the summer; landscape painting. First one-man exhibition at Oslo. A government grant enables him to spend the winter in Paris.

1890 Four months in Léon Bonnat's class. Sees Japanese woodcuts, pictures by Pissarro, Seurat, Toulouse-Lautrec and, at Theo Van Gogh's gallery, Gauguin and Vincent Van Gogh. First trip to Germany.

1891 Journey to France, the Riviera, Italy. Paints in the pointillist style, influenced by Neo-Impressionism.

1892 First part of the *Frieze of Life* exhibited at Oslo. Invited to take part in the Exhibition of the Berlin Artists' Association, Munch comes to Berlin with 55 pictures. Exhibition opens November 5 in the Architektenhaus. Controversy over Munch's work leads to the decision to shut down the exhibition. As a reprisal, Munch puts on a one-man show at a gallery on the Friedrichstrasse. For him the scandal is a godsend. His name, bandied about in the newspapers, is soon on everyone's lips.

1894 First etchings. First book on Munch, by Przybyszewsky.

1895   First issue of *Pan*, with illustrated matter contributed by Munch, Signac, Toulouse-Lautrec, Vallotton, and others.

First lithographs printed by A. Clot in Paris, who also prints Toulouse-Lautrec.

1896   First woodcuts. In Paris he frequents the circle of Mallarmé and *Le Mercure de France*. Sets for Ibsen's *Peer Gynt* at the Théâtre de l'Œuvre. Exhibition at the "Art Nouveau" Gallery.

1897   His *Frieze of Life* exhibited at Salon des Indépendants. Works in the spirit of the Pont-Aven school.

1898-
1901   Travels in Germany. A period of rankling unease and economic troubles. Begins the series of life-size male portraits: *The Frenchman, Albert Kollmann*, etc.

1902   He meets the Lübeck oculist, Max Linde, who becomes his friend and patron. Commissioned to do portraits, as well as a second *Frieze of Life*. Album of etchings and lithographs *Aus dem Hause Linde* (From the Linde House). At the Berlin Secession Exhibition, Munch shows 28 pictures, 22 of them from his first *Frieze of Life*.

1903-
1904   Works on the second *Frieze of Life* for Linde. Completed, these pictures are not accepted, and are sold singly.

1906   Stays with Count Kessler at Weimar. Portrait of Kessler. Portrait of Nietzsche after photographs. Sets for Max Reinhardt's production of Ibsen's *Ghosts*. Reinhardt commissions him to do a third *Frieze of Life* for the foyer of the Berlin Kammerspiele.

1908-
1909   The state of his nerves brings him to Dr Jacobsen's sanatorium in Copenhagen. At Kragerö on the Oslo Fjord he does preliminary work on the murals for the University of Oslo. Change in his style: color is brighter, contour less important for him as a structural element.

1911-1913   Purchases a home near Hvitsen, on the Oslo Fjord.

1915   Completes his murals for the University of Oslo. Chief pictures: *History, Alma Mater, Sun Rising over the Fjord*.

1916   Purchases a home a Ekely, near Oslo. Now owns four houses, with 43 studios.

1920-
1922   Travels to Berlin, Paris, Italy. Large-scale exhibition in Zurich. Murals for the workers' dining-hall at the Freia Chocolate Factory, Oslo.

1937   Has many pictures in the Norwegian Pavilion at the Paris World's Fair. Three pictures and eight prints in Berlin, 82 works in the rest of Germany, confiscated as "degenerate."

1940   Norway occupied by the Germans, April 9. Munch refuses to join an "Honorary Art Council" then being formed by the Quisling Government.

1944   Dies of a heart-attack on January 23.

BIBLIOGRAPHY

S. Przybyszewsky, F. Servaes, W. Pastor, J. Meier-Graefe, Berlin 1894. — H. Esswein (Modern Illustrators, No. 7), Munich 1905. — G. Schiefler, Dresden 1907. — C. Glaser, Berlin 1917. 2nd edition, 1922. — G. Schiefler, Dresden 1923. — Id., *Das graphische Werk, 1906-1926*, Berlin 1928. — C. Glaser, in: *Thieme-Becker, Allgemeines Lexikon der bildenden Künstler*, vol. 25, Leipzig 1931. With bibliography. — P. Gauguin, Oslo 1933. 2nd edition, 1946. — J. Thiis, Oslo 1933. German edition, Berlin 1934. — R. Stenersen, Stockholm 1944. German edition, Zurich 1949. — P. Gauguin, *Litografier*, Trondheim 1946. — Id., *Tresnitt og Etsninger*, Trondheim 1946. With woodcuts and etchings. — J. P. Hodin, Stockholm 1928. With detailed documentation and bibliography. — O. Sarvig, Copenhagen 1948.

NOLDE, Emil (1867)

1867   Born August 7 at Nolde, on the Danish frontier. Came of old peasant stock (the family name is Hansen).

1884-
1888   Student at Sauermann's Wood-Carving School, Flensburg. Works as a wood-carver at Munich and Karlsruhe.

1889   Student at the Applied Arts School, Karlsruhe.

1892   Teacher at the Trade and Industry Museum, St. Gall.

1896   Nolde's first large picture, *The Mountain Giants*, is rejected for the Annual Exhibition in Munich.

1899   Studies under Adolf Hölzel at Dachau. First visit to Paris. Enrolls at Académie Julian. Copies Titian in the Louvre.

1901-
1903   Stays in Berlin, Copenhagen, Flensburg, and on Alsen Island. Marriage with Ada Vilstrup.

1904-
1905   Assumes the name Emil Nolde. His impressionist pictures of flowers and gardens announce a new style in his work. In Berlin he does the *Phantasien* etchings.

1906   Following an exhibition at the Arnold Gallery, Dresden, in which he took part, Nolde is invited to join *Die*

Brücke: "In tribute to the storm of your color." He becomes a member of *Die Brücke*. Does his first woodcuts. He and Schmidt-Rottluff paint together on Alsen Island. Begins his series of grotesque and religious pictures.

1907   Takes part in the Die Brücke Exhibition at Dresden-Löbtau, and in a show at the Richter Gallery. Quits the group. First lithographs.

1909   After a serious illness, he paints his first great religious picture, *The Last Supper*. The pictures of *The Last Supper* and *Pentecost* mark the transition from superficial aesthetic feeling to deep, spiritual emotion. Paints luminous land- and seascapes on Alsen Island, where he leads a secluded life.

1910   Hamburg: etchings of the harbor. Berlin: sketches at the cafés, dance-halls, theaters. At the instance of Liebermann, the jury of the Berlin Secession rejects *Pentecost*. Work of 26 other artists rejected, among them the painters of *Die Brücke* and the New Association of Artists in Munich. They organize the Exhibition of Artists Rejected for the Berlin Secession at the Macht Gallery, and unite to form the New Secession. On December 10, in an open letter to the magazine *Kunst und Künstler* Nolde attacks Liebermann's dominating position in the Berlin Secession.

1911   Trip to Belgium and Holland. Van Gogh's pictures leave a strong impression on him. Meeting with Ensor. Paints grotesque still lifes with masks.

1912   Period of great productivity: *Triptych of Santa Maria Egyptiaca, Resurrection, Soldier with his Wife*, and the big, nine-fold altarpiece *The Life of Christ*. Meeting with Macke and Lehmbruck. At an exhibition in the New Art Salon, Munich, he meets Jawlensky.

Takes part in the Blue Rider Exhibition at the Goltz Gallery, Munich.

1913   Accompanies the Külz-Leber South Sea expedition, traveling across Russia, China, Japan, to the South Seas.

1914   War breaks out during his return journey. His South Sea pictures are confiscated at Suez.

1915-
1921   Winters in Berlin, summers at Alsen.

1921   Visits Paris and England in February, 1921.

1927   Jubilee Exhibition in Dresden. 60th birthday tribute with written contributions by Klee, Schiefler, Westheim and others.

1931   Publishes *Das Eigene Leben*, the autobiography of his early years, and in 1934 the sequel, *Jahre der Kämpfe*, covering his life up to 1914.

1937   1052 works by Nolde confiscated in Germany as "degenerate." 26 paintings—including the nine-part *Life of Christ*—, 4 watercolors and 9 prints figure in the "Degenerate Art" Exhibition at Munich in the summer.

1941   Forbidden to paint by the Nazi authorities. During the war his Berlin studio destroyed by air-raids.

1946   Appointed to a professorship in Schleswig-Holstein. Now has his home at Seebüll, near the Danish frontier.

1952   The "Die Brücke" painters at the Biennale, Venice. Prize for his engraved work.

BIBLIOGRAPHY

G. Schiefler, *Das graphische Werk bis 1910*, Berlin 1911. — M. Sauerlandt, Munich 1921. — *Festschrift für Emil Nolde zum 60. Geburtstag*, with contributions by Paul Klee, Sauerlandt, Schiefler and others, and the catalogue of the Dresden exhibition, Dresden 1927. — G. Schiefler, *Das graphische Werk 1910-1925*, Berlin 1927. — P. F. Schmidt, in *Junge Kunst*, No. 53, Leipzig 1929. — W. Grohmann, in *Thieme Becker, Allgemeines Lexikon der bildenden Künstler*, vol. 25, Leipzig 1931: with bibliography. — W. Haftmann, *Holzschnitte*, Bremen 1947. — Id., *Radierungen*, Bremen 1948.

PERMEKE, Constant (1886-1952)

1886   Born July 31 at Antwerp.

Studied at the Academies of Bruges and Ghent. At the latter made the acquaintance of Van den Berghe, Albert Servaes and Leon de Smet.

Pupil of Delvin.

1909   Settled down at Laethem-Saint-Martin, where he joined the local group of painters including Servaes, Van den Berghe, Gustave and Leon de Smet.

1912-
1914   Works at Ostend. Impressionist landscapes and portraits. Under Servaes' influence tended towards Expressionism. Badly wounded in the defense of Antwerp and evacuated to England.

1916   Demobilized, he worked at Chardstock (Devonshire) until the end of the war. His output here included landscapes and large-scale compositions. *The Stranger.*

1918- Back in Belgium, resided at Antwerp, then at Ostend.

1925   Seascapes, pictures of sailors, harbor scenes, large drawings. Set up house at Jabbeke, a village near Bruges. Painted landscapes, studies of peasants, interiors. He now came to be regarded as the leading figure among the Flemish Expressionists.

1929   The picture *Maternity* bears this date.

1936   First plastic works.

1940-1945 He now painted chiefly nudes.

1947   Retrospective exhibition at Museum of Modern Art, Paris.

1952   Dies at Ostend, January 6.

BIBLIOGRAPHY

A. de Ridder, *La jeune peinture belge ; de l'impressionnisme à l'expressionnisme*, Brussels 1928. — *Cahiers de Belgique*, Brussels, February 1930. — P. Fierens, Paris 1930. — P. Lambotte, *Histoire de la peinture et de la sculpture en Belgique, 1830-1930*. Brussels 1930. — A. Stubbe, Brussels 1930. — *Thieme-Becker*, vol. 26, Leipzig 1932. With bibliography. — G. Marlier, *L'Expressionnisme flamand*, *L'Amour de l'Art*, Paris 1934. With bio-bibliographical note. — L. and O. Haesaerts, *Le mouvement expressionniste*, Ghent 1935. — E. de Seyn, *Dictionnaire biographique*, Brussels 1935. — P. Haesaerts, Amsterdam and Antwerp 1938. — W. Koninckx, Antwerp 1938. — P. Haesaerts, Brussels 1939. — Id., *L'Ecole de Laethem-St.-Martin*, Brussels 1945. Contains: *Dictionary (bio-bibliographical) of artists and writers living at Laethem-St.-Martin after 1880*. Important documentation. — Id., *L'apport belge à la peinture contemporaine*, *Arts de France*, No. 5, Paris 1946. — E. Langui, Antwerp 1947. — R. Avermaete, *Arts de France*, No. 19/20, Paris 1948. — E. Langui, in: *Peintres belges contemporains*, Brussels 1948.

PICABIA, Francis (1878-1953)

1878   Born in Paris, January 22. Studied at the Ecole des Beaux-Arts and the Ecole des Arts décoratifs. Pupil of Cormon.

1903-1908 Painted impressionist pictures in the style of Sisley.

1909   Influenced by the Cubists.

1911- With Apollinaire, Gleizes, La Fresnaye, Léger and

1912   Metzinger, he took part in the Sunday gatherings at Jacques Villon's studio at Puteaux where they founded the *Section d'Or*.

1912- Orphic period. February to April: first journey to United

1913   States. Figured in the "Armory Show," New York. Stieglitz exhibited Picabia's watercolors at his "291" Gallery.

1915   Second visit to the United States. Worked with Duchamp and collaborated with the review "291."

1916   Towards the end of 1916 stayed at Barcelona. Published the first number of the review "391" (25th January 1917). Returned to the United States where he published other numbers of this review with Marcel Duchamp.

1918   Stayed in Lausanne (Switzerland). Published the book *Poèmes et dessins de la fille née sans mère*. February: contacted the Dada group in Zurich.

1919   February: Published number 8 of "391" at Zurich. Returned to Paris and published other numbers of "391." Took part in Dada manifestations in Paris. Exhibition at Galerie Au Sans Pareil, Paris.

1920   Published the review *Cannibale* (2 numbers).

1921   With Breton moved away from orthodox Dadaism.

1924   Scenario and designs for *Relâche* (Swedish Ballet Company). Collaborated with various surrealist reviews and showed at their exibitions.

1926   Return to figurative art. Transparent paintings.

1930   First retrospective exhibition at the Rosenberg Gallery (Paintings from 1900 to 1930).

1940-1945 Spent the war in the South of France.

1945   Back in Paris. Returned to abstract painting.

1949   Large exhibition at the Galerie Drouin, Paris. The catalogue, entitled *491*, contained articles by Breton, Bott, Cocteau, Desnos and others.

1953   Dies in Paris, November 30.

BIBLIOGRAPHY

G. Apollinaire, *Les peintres cubistes*, Paris 1913. — M. de la Hire, Paris 1920. — A. Breton, Barcelona 1922. — P. de Massot, *De Mallarmé à '391'*, St-Raphaël 1922. — A. Breton, *Les pas perdus*, Paris 1924. — M. Raynal, *Anthologie de la peinture en France de 1906 à nos jours*, Paris 1927. — A. Breton, *Le Surréalisme et la peinture*, Paris 1928. 2nd Ed. 1945. — G. Isarlow, *Orbes*, No. 2, Paris 1929. — V. du Mas, *Orbes*, No. 3, Paris 1932. — D. Gascoyne, *A Short Survey of Surrealism*, London 1935. — A. H. Barr, *Cubism and Abstract Art*, New York 1936. — Id., *Fantastic Art, Dada, Surrealism*, Museum of Modern Art, New York 1936. — A. Breton, *Anthologie de l'humour noir*, Paris 1940. — M. Seuphor, *L'art abstrait, ses origines, ses premiers maîtres*, Paris 1949.

PICASSO, Pablo (1881)

1881   Born at Malaga, Andalusia, Spain, October 25. His father, José Ruiz Blasco, who came from the Basque country, was a practicing art master. His mother, Maria Picasso, came of a Genoese family. The Genoa Museum owned a work by a painter named Picasso (late 18th century).

1891   The family first settled at La Coruña in Galicia where Picasso made his first drawings; then in 1895 they moved to Barcelona.

1896- Rented his first studio in 1896. 1897: first exhibition

1900   in Barcelona when he was 16, and the first article on his work in *La Vanguardia*. Short visit to Madrid.

1900   First illustrations published by the review *Joventut*. First visit to Paris (October-December) during the World's Fair. Sold three sketches to Berthe Weill.

1901   Stayed in Madrid where he launched and illustrated a short-lived review *Arte Joven* (Young Art). From now on his pictures were signed simply "Picasso" instead of Pablo Ruiz Picasso. Second visit to Paris (May-January 1902). Studied the Impressionists. First Paris exhibition at Vollard's gallery. Met and became friends with Max Jacob. Beginning of "blue" period.

1902   In Barcelona. Autumn: third visit to Paris.

1903   In Barcelona. Influenced by Greco's Mannerism.

1904   Settled in Paris, 13, rue Ravignan at the *Bateau-lavoir* where he remained five years.

1905   Met Apollinaire. Frequented the circus and its performers. Beginning of the "pink" period. Traveled to Holland. The dealer Stchoukin bought more than 50 paintings before 1914 (now in Moscow and Leningrad). Sixteen etchings of clowns, published in 1913 by Vollard. Spent the summer at Gosol near Andorra.

1906   Met Matisse. Portrait of Gertrude Stein which for the first time showed the influence of ancient Iberian sculpture. Began *Les Demoiselles d'Avignon* (which recalls a street of the same name in Barcelona with a brothel).

1907   Finished *Les Demoiselles d'Avignon*. Two strongly colored and distorted women's heads recall certain Ivory Coast masks. "Negro" period. Apollinaire introduced him to Braque. The dealer, Kahnweiler, who had just opened a gallery, rue Vignon, made a contract for all his work.

1908   Organized a banquet in honor of the Douanier Rousseau. Paintings influenced by Cézanne.

1909   Summer at Horta del Ebro. Beginning of "analytical" Cubism. Exhibited in Munich (Thannhauser Gallery).

1910   Summer at Cadaquès (Spain) with Derain.

1911   Summer at Céret (Pyrenees) with Braque.

1912   Summer at Sorgues (Vaucluse) with Braque. Beginnings of "synthetic" Cubism which he developed along with other styles, until 1923. First "papiers collés."

1913   Summer at Céret with Gris. Visited by Tatlin.

1914   Cubism in bright flat color.

1915   Naturalistic portraits of Max Jacob, Vollard, etc.

1917   Jean Cocteau persuaded him to accept Diaghilev's offer to go to Rome to do decors and costumes for *Parade* (music by Satie, choreography by Massine). In the program, Apollinaire spoke of "Sur-réalisme."

1918   Paul Rosenberg became his principal dealer. Married the ballerina Olga Koklova.

1919   Traveled to London and to St. Raphael.

1920   Beginning of neo-classical period. Large nudes. Gigantic heads of women.

1921   Decors for ballet *Cuadro Flamenco*. Painted two versions of *Three Musicians*.

1923   Painted at the same time in a cubist manner with curved forms and rich colors and in a discreet and charming neo-classical style *(Harlequin)*.

1925- Dynamic figures with anatomical deformations and dis-

1927   tortions. Influenced by Surrealism.

1928   Summer at Dinard: period of the same name.

1929- Sculptural style. Period of "metamorphoses" or monsters

1931   by the sea.

1931 For Albert Skira illustrated Ovid's *Metamorphoses* in 30 "classical" etchings.

1932 Series of sleeping women. Large retrospective exhibition at Galerie Petit, Paris.

1934 Travels in Spain. Series of *Bull Fights*.

1935 Took to writing surrealist poetry. Jaime Sabartès became his private secretary.

1936 Traveling exhibition went to Barcelona, Bilbao, Madrid. July: outbreak of the Spanish civil war. Picasso supported the Republicans; accepted position of Director of the Prado, and later helped to safeguard its pictures.

1937 Engraved *Songe et mensonge de Franco* (with text) and painted *Guernica*. Engraved 31 plates in extremely naturalistic style, originally meant to illustrate Jules Renard's *Histoires Naturelles* but published in 1942 with texts by Buffon.

1938 Series of expressionist heads with double faces.

1939-
1945 Spent first year of the war at Royan, then returned to Paris. Picasso was left in peace by the occupation authorities, but his desire to continue working independently became symbolic. Statue cast in bronze *Shepherd Holding a Lamb*. After the Liberation and for the first time in his life he showed at the Salon d'Automne with about 80 works.

1946 Summer at Golfe-Juan. Resuscitated the art of ceramics at Vallauris. Presented several of his most important works to the Antibes Museum.

1947-
1950 Devoted himself mainly to lithography, in which he invented new processes which he often applied to naturalistic subjects (doves, toads, women's portraits, etc.).

1953 Completes *War* and *Peace*. Retrospective exhibitions in Rome, Milan and Lyons.

1954 Summer at Collioure and Perpignan.

1955 After spending the winter in Paris, Picasso settles into his new villa at Cannes.

BIBLIOGRAPHY

G. Apollinaire, *Les peintres cubistes*, Paris 1913. — A. J. Eddy, *Cubists and Post-Impressionism*, Chicago 1914. 2nd ed., 1919. — J. Cocteau, Paris 1919. — M. Raynal, Paris, Ed. L'Effort Moderne 1921. — Id., Paris, Ed. Crès, 1922. German ed.: Munich 1921. — W. George, Rome 1924. — P. Reverdy, Paris 1924. — M. Jacob, *Cahiers d'Art*, Paris 1927. — O. Schürer, Leipzig 1927. — W. Uhde, Paris 1928. In English: New York 1929. — E. d'Ors, Paris 1930. In English: New York 1930. — *Cahiers d'Art*, No. 3/5, Paris 1932. Special number with articles by Apollinaire, Cocteau, Einstein, Grohmann, Hugnet, Salmon, Stravinsky, Sweeney, Zervos, etc. — W. Grohmann, in: *Thieme-Becker*, vol. 27, Leipzig 1932. With bibliography. — C. Zervos. Vol. I (1895-1906), vol. II, in two parts (1906-1912 and 1912-1917), Paris. Ed. Cahiers d'Art, 1932-1942. — B. Geiser, illustrated catalogue of P.'s engravings and lithographs, 1899-1931, Bern 1933. — F. Olivier, *P. et ses amis*, Paris 1933. — *Cahiers d'Art*, No. 7/10, 1935. Special number on works from 1930-1935, with articles by Breton, Dali, Eluard, Man Ray, Miro, Zervos, etc. — J. T. Soby, New York 1935. — A. H. Barr, *Cubism and Abstract Art*, Museum of Modern Art, New York 1936. — *Cahiers d'Art*, No. 4/5, 1937. Special number on *Guernica*... — J. Cassou, Paris 1937. French, English, German text. — J. Sabartès, Milan 1937. — *Cahiers d'Art*, No. 3/10, 1938. Special number with an article by Zervos and a poem by Eluard. — G. Stein, Paris 1938. English ed.: London and New York 1939. — *Cahiers d'Art*, 1940-1944, Special number. — *Cinquanta disegni 1905-1938*, with articles by Carrà, Severini, etc., Novara 1943. — R. Desnos, *Seize peintures, 1930-1943*, Paris 1943. — E. Prampolini, Rome 1943. — P. Eluard, Geneva 1944. — E. McCausland, New York 1944. — L. Carré, Paris 1945. — C. Giedion-Welcker, *Werk*, No. 4, Winterthur 1945. — C. Palencia, Mexico City 1945. — S. Solmi, Milan 1945. With bibliography. — A. M. Barr, *Fifty Years of his Art*, Museum of Modern Art, New York 1946. With comprehensive bibliography by D. Simmons. — *Guernica*, New York 1946. With texts by G. Duthuit, P. Eluard, H. Read, J. J. Sweeney, C. Zervos, etc. — W. Liebermann, *The Ballet*, New York 1946. — J. Sabartès, *Portraits et souvenirs*, Paris 1946. — W. Erben, Heidelberg 1947. — E. Szittya, Paris 1947. — *Cahiers d'Art*, 1948. Special number on ceramics. — P. Eluard, photos by M. Sima, Paris 1948. — Id., *Voir*, Geneva 1948. — B. Geiser, *Lithographs 1945-1948*, New York 1948. — J. Sabartès, New York 1948. — T. Tzara, Geneva, 1948. — *Verve*, No. 18/19, text by P. and J. Sabartès, Paris 1948. — J. Bouret, Paris 1949. — H. Kahnweiler, *Les sculptures*, Paris 1949. — A. Leclerc, Paris 1949. — F. Mourlot, *P. lithographie, 1919-1947*, complete catalogue, Monte-Carlo 1949. — S. and C. Ramié, *Céramiques*, Geneva 1949. In English, Geneva 1951. — G. Walther, Stuttgart 1949. — C. Zervos, *Dessins*, Paris 1949. — A. Cirici-Pellicer, Geneva 1950. — J. Lassaigne, Paris 1950. — M. Raynal, Geneva 1953. — J. Sabartès and W. Boeck, Paris 1955.

REDON, ODILON (1840-1916)

1840 Born at Bordeaux, April 20. His father, an explorer and "squatter," had married a Creole lady (of French descent) of New Orleans. A delicate child, he was brought up in the country, in charge of a nurse, on the family estate at Peyrelabade.

1847 First visit to Paris, where his aunt takes him to the museums.

1855 Resolves to become a painter. Lessons from the watercolor painter Gobin. A meeting with Clavaud the botanist has a decisive influence; Clavaud interests the boy in biology, makes known to him Delacroix's art and *avant-garde* literature: Baudelaire, Flaubert, Poe. He is very fond of music; also of country walks.

1857 Studies architecture at Bordeaux. Sits for the entrance examination of the Ecole des Beaux-Arts in Paris, but fails. He returns to Bordeaux, and devotes himself to sculpture.

1858 At Paris, in Gérome's studio.

1863 At Bordeaux becomes intimate with the romantic etcher Bresdin who is to have much influence on him; "discovers" Rembrandt; first steps in etching.

1867 His first contribution to the Salon, an etching named *Landscape*.

1868 Art-critic of the newspaper *La Gironde* (May-July); articles on Fromentin, Courbet, Jongkind.

1870 Though exempted from military service, enlists as a volunteer. After 1870 lives in Paris, in the Montparnasse district. Growing admiration for Delacroix, whom he has already copied at the Bordeaux Museum. Makes acquaintance of Corot, and Fantin-Latour; works constantly with the last-named at the Louvre and learns from him lithography. Travels to Holland to see the Rembrandts.

1877 Summer at Barbizon.

1879 Publishes album of 10 lithographs, entitled (significantly) *Dans le Rêve*.

1880 May 1, marries Camille Fargue, a Creole from the Ile de Bourbon, who is to be for him, as he puts it, "the lodestar of his life."

1881-
1882 First exhibitions at *La Vie Moderne* and the office of the newspaper *Le Gaulois*. His work noticed by Huysmans and Hennequin.

1884 Exhibits at the first Salon des Indépendants, and presides at the gatherings preliminary to founding the *Société des Indépendants*.

1883-
1889 During this period—in which his first son, Jean, dies, and his younger son, Ari, is born—Redon does exclusively black-and-white lithography. Still little appreciated in France, has a better reception in Belgium and Holland.

1889 Takes part in exhibition of engraver-painters at Durand-Ruel's. Meets Mellerio, his biographer-to-be.

1891 Symbolist banquet in honor of Jean Moréas. Redon now frequents writers, amongst them Jammes, Gide, Valéry, and especially Mallarmé, with whom he becomes very friendly. Frankly admits the "literary" tendency of his art. "Painting is human beauty," he says, "with the prestige of thought superadded."

1899 Exhibition at Durand-Ruel's; *Hommage à Odilon Redon* (Bernard, d'Espagnat, Cross, Signac, Luce, van Rysselberghe, Ibels, Sérusier, André, Vuillard, Vallotton, Denis). Redon now leaves the Left Bank and settles in the Avenue de Wagram. Gradually gives up black-and-white (save for a short return to it in 1914) and goes back to painting, especially in pastel; his color has now an almost incredible intensity. Flowers, portraits of women and children, and religious subjects are his favorite themes.

1909 Buys a small house at Bièvres. Lives a retired, studious and meditative life, propitious to the extreme originality of his visionary inspiration. "I have been led to this self-imposed isolation by the absolute impossibility of practicing any other kind of art than that which I have always practiced." Nearly every winter he makes a stay at Cannes or at the Abbaye de Fontfroide (near Montpellier) with his friend Fayet, the collector, whose library he decorates.

1916 Dies, July 6, in Paris. Buried in the little graveyard at Bièvres.

BIBLIOGRAPHY

Like Delacroix, and likewise a brilliant writer, Redon kept up a fascinating Journal: *A soi-même* (1867-1915), Paris 1922. Introd. by J. Morland. — Also wrote articles in *La Gironde* (May-July 1868) and the Preface to the Bresdin Retrospective Exhibition at the 1908 Salon d'Automne. Some of his correspondence has been published: a letter to E. Picard, *L'Art Moderne*, Brussels, August 25, 1894. — *Lettres d'Odilon Redon*, Paris 1923. — *Lettres à E. Bernard*, Brussels 1942.

E. Hennequin, *Revue Art et Litt.*, March 4, 1882. — A. Salmon, *Art décoratif*, January 1913. — A. Mellerio, Paris 1913. New ed. Paris 1923. Catalogue of black-and-white work. — J. Drouin, *Mercure de France*, July 1914. — A. Mellerio, *Gazette des B.A.*, Aug. Sept. 1920. — W. Pach, *The Connoisseur*, Oct. 1920. — C. Roger-Marx, Paris 1925. — C. Fegdal, Paris 1929. — Illustrations for *La Tentation de Saint Antoine*, by G. Flaubert, Paris 1935 (Les Amis de Redon). Paris 1937 (A. Vollard). — M. and A. Leblond, Paris 1941.

ROUAULT, GEORGES (1871)

1871 Born May 27 in a Paris cellar during the bombardment of the city in the troubled days of the "Commune." His father, a cabinet-maker, hailed from Brittany; his mother was Parisian. His maternal grandfather, Champdavoine, was extremely fond of Manet, Courbet and Daumier, engravings of whose works he showed to his young grandson. Attends a Protestant primary school.

1885 Apprenticed to a stained-glass maker named Hirsch. Restores old stained-glass windows. Out of loyalty to his employer, he turns down a chance to work with Albert Besnard on the windows of the Ecole de Pharmacie. Evening classes at the Ecole des Arts Décoratifs.

1891 Ecole des Beaux-Arts, in Elie Delaunay's class. This teacher dies soon afterwards; succeeded by Gustave Moreau.

1892 With a series of religious subjects he wins first prize at the Ecole.

1893 First important picture: *Samson tournant sa meule*. Fails to get the Prix de Rome. Meets Matisse in Moreau's class.

1894 Awarded the Chenavard Prize for *L'Enfant Jésus parmi les Docteurs*, but the decision of the judges is annulled.

1895 Awarded instead the Fortin d'Ivry Prize, in addition to an award at the Salon. Competes for the Prix de Rome with *Le Christ mort pleuré par les Saintes Femmes*, but fails once again. Acting on the advice of Gustave Moreau he leaves the Ecole.

1898 Death of Moreau. Rouault is appointed Curator of the Gustave Moreau Museum, at 2400 francs a year, not enough to support those dependent on him. He is in constant pecuniary difficulties. Passes through a spiritual crisis; breaks with Academicism. Back from a convalescent stay in Savoy, he is filled with antipathy for his "dark" manner.

1902 Present at the first meetings preparatory to founding the Salon d'Automne. Works out new techniques for the new trends in his art. Ill again, he convalesces at Evian (Savoy). Shows an interest in the movement which later becomes Fauvism.

1903 Religious conception of the world. Becomes acquainted with Huysmans, who wants to form a group of Catholic artists and persuades Rouault to visit the Abbaye de Ligugé, in Poitou. Meets Léon Bloy, whose influence is strong for a time *(La Femme Pauvre)*. A series of pictures of prostitutes, performers at fairs and circuses. He stresses the dark side of life by violent contrasts of tones and colors evocative of night.
Takes part in the first Salon d'Automne, with Matisse and Marquet.

1904 Salon d'Automne: eight pictures, 32 watercolors and pastels, all in his new style.

1905 Salon d'Automne: exhibits three important works—not, however, in the Fauve gallery.

1906 First *Odalisque*. From 1906 on, he exhibits at Berthe Weill's.

1907 The *Clowns*. Pictures more varied in tone. At the instance of Vollard, paints ceramics and glazed earthenware (fired by Metthey). Stays at Bruges.

1908 Marries Marthe le Sidaner. Begins his series of *Judges* and *Tribunals*.

1909 First one-man show at Druet's.

1911 Social themes: peasants, workers, family life. Portraits.

1913 Returns to religious subjects.

1916 Now his sole agent, Vollard advises him to concentrate on illustration. He fits out a studio in his own home, to enable Rouault to complete some hundreds of unfinished works. Turns whole-heartedly to the illustration of books. Paints few pictures between 1917 and 1927.

1917 Works on the illustrations for Jarry's *Ubu Roi*, followed by Vollard's *Réincarnations du Père Ubu*, and *Le Miserere*. Illustrations for *Les Fleurs du Mal* remain unfinished.

1924 Receives the "Légion d'Honneur" for his services as Curator of the Gustave Moreau Museum.

1928 Resumes a number of unfinished works, restyling them according to his new ideas.

1929 Sets and costumes for a ballet by Diaghilev: *The Prodigal Son*, music by Prokofiev.

1930 Stays in Switzerland, in the Valais. His colors become more intense and varied. Etchings in color: *Le Cirque de l'Etoile Filante*, *La Passion*. Illustrations for *Le Cirque*, by Suarès, not yet published.

1932 After 1932 Rouault ceases to date his works.

1937 Exhibition of some of his most important works at Salon des Indépendants (Petit Palais). Does tapestries under the supervision of Mme Cuttoli.

1939 Death of Ambroise Vollard.

1940 Devotes himself almost entirely to religious painting.

1946 Exhibition with Braque at the Tate Gallery, in London.

1947 Involved in a law-suit with the Vollard heirs. The court decides in Rouault's favor, that pictures unsigned and unsold by him remain his property.

1948 In the presence of the bailiff, Rouault burns the 314 pictures restored to him by decision of the court. Makes his first journey to Italy.

1948 Makes stained-glass windows for the village church at Assy (Haute-Savoie).

1949 Trip to Belgium and Holland.

1952 Retrospective Exhibition at the Musée d'Art Moderne, in Paris.

BIBLIOGRAPHY

M. Puy, Paris 1921. — G. Charensol, Paris 1926. — R. Cogniat, Paris 1930. — W. Grohmann, New York and Munich 1930. — R. Ito, Tokyo 1936. — Special number of *Le Point*, with contributions by Rouault, L. Lehmann, J. de Laprade and G. Besson, Lanzac, 1943. — A. Jewell, New York and Paris 1945-1947. — R. Marx and G. Geffroy were the first to acclaim Rouault's work in the Salons of 1895 and 1901; A. Alexandre, L. Vauxcelles and Thiébault-Sisson, with reference to the Salons d'Automne of 1903 and 1908. — The basic work is Lionello Venturi's *Georges Rouault*, New York 1940; re-issued Paris 1948.

ROUSSEAU, HENRI (called Le Douanier) (1844-1910)

1844 Born at Laval (Mayenne), France, May 21.

1864- Although exempted as a student he went into the army.
1868 No documents and no evidence—except from the painter himself—remain to prove that he took part in the Mexican campaign although this once was commonly believed. In any case the official records of the campaign have been destroyed.

1869 Married his first wife, Clémence Boitard, who bore him nine children (eight died in infancy). Went to live in Paris; worked first as lawyer's clerk and then as minor Customs official.

1880 First signed canvases.

1884- Copied old masters in the Louvre. Exhibited for first
1885 time two canvases at Salon des Indépendants which had
1886 been founded a year before. Except for 1890 and 1900 he exhibited there regularly until 1910.
Left the Customs and lived on a small pension and occasional music lessons.

1889 Wrote a comedy in three acts and ten scenes: *A Visit to the Exhibition of 1889*.

1890 *Myself, Portrait-landscape*. Met Gauguin, Redon, Seurat, Pissarro and the critic Gustave Coquiot.

1891 In *Storm in the Jungle* he used exotic scenery for the first time, inspired by visits to the Jardin des Plantes (Botanical and Zoological Gardens).

1895 *War*: a large and striking canvas which was lost and rediscovered after the second world war when it was bought by the Louvre. Painted Jarry's portrait at whose suggestion he collaborated in *L'Ymagier*.

1898 Offered *The Sleeping Gipsy* for a small sum to the Municipality of Laval which refused it.

1899 Married for second time to Rosalie-Joséphine Nourry who died four years later. Wrote with Mme Barkowski a drama in five acts: *A Russian Orphan's Vengeance* and submitted it to the Comédie-Française.

1906 Met Delaunay, Vlaminck, Picasso, Max Jacob, Raynal, Salmon, Apollinaire.

1907 Friendship with young American painter Max Weber and the German critic W. Uhde who wrote the first monograph on Rousseau and bought some canvases.

1908 Picasso held a banquet in his honor at the Bateau-lavoir.

1909 *The Poet inspired by his Muse.* In January arrested and convicted for complicity in an affair concerning bad checks in which he was unwittingly involved. The jury suspended sentence largely on account of the "naïveté" of his paintings.

1910 *The Dream.* At New York Max Weber organized the first American exhibition of Rousseau's work for the "291" Gallery. Ill-fated love affair with a widow, "Madame Léonie." Caught pneumonia following an unwise excursion and died at the Necker Hospital, Paris, 2nd October.
Buried in the Bagneux cemetery. His ashes were taken to Laval where an epitaph written by Apollinaire was engraved on his tomb.

BIBLIOGRAPHY

W. Uhde, Paris 1911. German edition: 1914. — *Les Soirées de Paris*, No. 20 devoted to H.R. le Douanier, Paris 1913. With contributions by Apollinaire, M. Raynal, etc. — T. Däubler, *Valori Plastici*, No. 9, Rome 1920. — R. Delaunay, *L'Amour de l'Art*, No. 7, Paris 1920. — H. Kolle, *(Junge Kunst. 27)*, Leipzig 1922. — E. Szittya, *Malerschicksale*, Hamburg 1925. — A. Basler, Paris 1927. — P. Soupault. Paris 1927. With autobiographical notes and letters. — C. Zervos, Paris 1927. — W. Grohmann, in: *Thieme-Becker*, vol. 29, Leipzig 1935. With bibliography. — R.H. Wilenski, *Modern French Painters*, New York 1940. With comprehensive article on R.'s life and work. Bibliography. — M. Weber, *Art News*, Febr. 1942. — R. Grey, preface by A. Salmon, Paris 1943. — D. Cooper, *Burlington Magazine*, London, July 1944. — P. Courthion, Geneva 1944. With bibliography. — Paris, Musée d'Art Moderne. Catalogue of exhibition commemorating 100th anniversary of H.R.'s birth. With articles by G. Apollinaire, P. Eluard, M. Gauthier, A. Jakovsky, et al. (Paris 1944). — D.C. Rich, Museum of Modern Art, New York 1946. With bibliography by B. Karpel. — M. Raynal, Geneva 1949. — M. Gauthier, Paris 1950. — Delaunay, *Lettres françaises*, 1952. Film: directed by Lo Duca (1950).

SCHMIDT-ROTTLUFF, KARL (1884)

1884 Born December 1 at Rottluff, near Chemnitz, Saxony.

1905 After obtaining his school-leaving certificate, he moves to Dresden. Begins studying architecture. Meeting with Kirchner, through Heckel. Collaboration with Heckel, Kirchner, Bleyl. Formation of Die Brücke (The Bridge).

1906 Stays on the island of Alsen. Meeting with Nolde. First and second exhibitions of Die Brücke at Dresden-Löbtau.

1909 The Die Brücke album of 1909 is his work.

1910 Takes part in the New Secession exhibitions in Berlin (1910-1912). Exhibition of Die Brücke at Arnold Gallery, Dresden.

1911 Hamburg. Exhibits at Commeter Gallery. Summer in Norway. Moves in the autumn to Berlin. Collaborates on the magazine *Der Sturm*. Meeting with Otto Müller and Lyonel Feininger. Increasing massiveness of form. Pronounced tendencies towards abstraction.

1912 Hamburg. Takes part in the Sonderbund Exhibition in Cologne and in that of Der Blaue Reiter in Goltz Gallery, Munich. First Berlin exhibition of Die Brücke at Gurlitt Gallery.

1913 Hamburg. Break-up of the Die Brücke group.

1914 Berlin. Collaboration on the magazine *Die Aktion*.

1915- Service on the Eastern Front from May 1915 until the
1919 end of the war. Exhibits at Goltz Gallery, Munich. Series of woodcuts on religious themes during 1918. Returns in 1919 to Berlin, where he now makes his home.

1923 Trip to Italy with the sculptor Kolbe.

1924 Stays in Paris with Kolbe.

1931 Appointed to the Academy of Fine Arts in Berlin.

1933 Expelled from the Academy.

1935 Exhibition at K. Buchholz Gallery, Berlin.

1936 Exhibition at the Westerman Gallery, New York.

1937 In Germany 608 works by Schmidt-Rottluff are confiscated as "degenerate." 51 of them figure in the "Degenerate Art" Exhibition at Munich.

1941 Forbidden to paint. Under police surveillance.

1946 Appointed to a professorship at the Institute of Plastic Arts in Berlin, where he now lives.

1948 Exhibition at the Kunsthalle, Bern (P. Modersohn and the Die Brücke painters).

1950 Die Brücke Exhibition at the Biennale, Venice.

BIBLIOGRAPHY

R. Schapiro, Darmstadt 1920. — W. R. Valentiner, in *Junge Kunst.* 16, Leipzig 1920. — V. Firksen, in *Kleine Führer der Kunsthalle.* 21, Hamburg 1921. — W. Niemeyer, *Kündung*, Hamburg 1921. — R. Schapiro, Berlin 1924. With descriptive catalogue. — W. Grohmann, in *Thieme-Becker, Allgemeines Lexikon der bildenden Künstler*, vol. 30, Leipzig 1936. With abundant documentation. — *Katalog der Ausstellung des städtischen Kunstsammlung Chemnitz*, with articles by A. Behne, W. Grohmann, C. G. Heise, O. Jäger, W. R. Valentiner and others, Chemnitz 1946.

SÉRUSIER, PAUL (1863-1927)

1863 Born at Paris. His father was manager of the Houbigant perfumery. He did very well at school (Ecole Fénelon and Lycée Fontanes). Bachelor of Letters and of Science.

1888 Exhibits his *Breton Weaver's Workroom* at the Salon. Student-in-charge at the Académie Julian. After beginning with academic realism and somber tones he now makes the acquaintance of Gauguin at Pont-Aven and, on his advice, paints a *"Bois d'Amour,"* which he calls his "talisman" and proudly shows on his return to his fellow-students at Julian's: Bonnard, Vuillard, Roussel, Denis and Ranson.

1889 At his instance they form a group, the Nabis. Their meeting-place is a little restaurant in the Passage Brady; their discussions turn chiefly on philosophy and religion.

1889- Stays at Le Pouldu in Brittany with Gauguin, Filiger,
1890 Meyer de Haan.

1891 Sérusier meets Verkade under whose influence he takes up theosophy.

1892 At Pont-Aven with Verkade, Ballin, Rassetti (the ceramist) and Ranson; then at Huelgoat.

1893 Collaborates in the Théâtre de l'Œuvre now founded by Lugné-Poe. Spends winter in Paris (studio, rue de Hauteville) and the summer at Châteauneuf-du-Faou in Brittany.

1895 Travels in Italy with Maurice Denis: Giotto, Sienese art, Fra Angelico.

1897 After the unhappy ending of a love-affair travels in Central Europe. Meets again Jan Verkade, now a monk at the Beuron Monastery.

1899 Second stay at Beuron; meets Père Didier, founder of the School of Religious Art, based on the theory of the "holy proportions."

1903 His mother dies. Another stay with Maurice Denis at Beuron. Buys a house at Châteauneuf-du-Faou.

1904 Travels in Italy with Maurice Denis: Rome, Monte Cassino; interviews with Père Didier; Naples and Pompeii.

1907 Goes to Munich; meets Verkade again.

1908 With Denis teaches at the Académie Ranson (R. de La Fresnaye and Goerg amongst his pupils). Hieratic and mathematical painting.

1912 Marries one of his pupils. Honeymoon at Florence.

1914- Lives a retired life in Brittany; more and more interested
1927 in Celtic mediaeval tapestry. Decorates his house and Châteauneuf Church. Stays at Kermouster with Henry Joly; at Perros-Guirec with Maurice Denis.
Dies of a stroke at Morlaix and is buried in Breton soil, his "true home, since he was spiritually born there."

BIBLIOGRAPHY

P. Sérusier published: *A.B.C. de la peinture*, inspired by the aesthetics of Père Didier, whose pamphlet, *Les Saintes Mesures* he had translated in 1905. Paris 1921 (republished 1942).
M. Denis, *L'Occident*, Dec. 1908. — J. Dupont, *Art Sacré*, Jan. 1937. — E. de Thubert, *Art et Décoration*, 1932. — M. Denis, *Sérusier, sa vie, son œuvre*, Paris 1943.

SEURAT, Georges (1859-1891)

1859 Born Dec. 2, in Paris, rue de Bondy. Son of a bailiff in La Villette. Schooling until 16. An obedient, earnest, rather reserved lad.

1875 At the Municipal School of Design near the church of St Vincent-de-Paul, presided over by a sculptor, Justin Lequien, who had won a *Prix de Rome*. Became close friend of a fellow-student, Aman-Jean.

1877 Haunts museums and libraries. Copies Holbein, Ingres, Poussin, Raphael. Much enthusiasm for the writings of the Goncourt brothers.

1878 With Aman-Jean enters Ecole des Beaux-Arts, where their master is Henri Lehmann, who imparts to them the principles, now rather insipid, of Ingres. Studies Chevreul's treatise on *The Harmony and Contrast of Colors* and C. Blanc's *Grammar of Painting and Drawing*.

1879 Nov. Leaves the studio he has been sharing with Aman-Jean in rue de l'Arbalète and does his term of military service at Brest in a line regiment. First contact with the sea. Does many sketches.

1880 Nov. Returns to Paris. Lives at No. 19, rue de Chabrol.

1881- Devotes himself to drawing and also to studying Dela-
1887 croix's color technique. In 1882 paints his first pictures with small separate touches and also large sweeping strokes giving the effect of broken gleams.

1883 His *Portrait of Aman-Jean* (Stephen C. Clark Coll., New York), a Conté crayon life-size drawing, is accepted at the Salon and praised by Roger Marx, as being "an excellent study in chiaroscuro." Seurat now paints his first big picture based on the contrast of colors, *Une Baignade à Asnières* (Tate Gallery, London); he uses the divisionist technique but in a free manner, resembling that of Impressionism. For this picture he made a number of sketches from nature, jotted down on the little panels of his painter's box, which he called "croquetons"— this method he adopted for all his later compositions.

1884 Rejected at the official Salon, *Une Baignade* was shown at the first Salon des Indépendants (May 15-July 1), along with contributions by Redon, Angrand, Dubois-Pillet, Cross and Signac. These artists now got to know each other and decided to found a *Société des Artistes Indépendants* and have another exhibition in December. The group meetings took place every Monday at Signac's studio and in the evening at the Café d'Orient or the Café Marengo. Seurat was especially friendly with Angrand and Signac.

1885 Prompted by Signac who had much fondness for all things maritime, he goes in the summer to the little seaport of Grandcamp, near Le Havre, and makes his first seascapes. Through Signac, too, he comes to know Pissarro, who now joins the ranks of the "Divisionists." Paints his *Sunday Afternoon on the Island of La Grande Jatte* (Art Institute, Chicago)—a sort of "manifesto" of the new technique, for which he made elaborate preparations in no less than 38 painted studies and 23 drawings. Many months went to its making, his mornings being spent on the Island itself, while in the afternoons he worked in his studio.

1886 Thanks to Pissarro's insistence, Seurat and Signac appear at the 8th and Last Impressionist Exhibition (May 15-June 15). Monet, Renoir, Sisley, hostile, stand out. Degas insists on the omission of the word "impressionist" on the poster. Seurat sends in 6 landscapes, 3 drawings and his *Grande Jatte*, which rouses a storm of protests. With the exception of Verhaeren and Félix Fénéon most artists and connoisseurs are disgusted with this picture.

1887 Feb. Goes to Brussels for the opening of the "XX" exhibition, to which Octave Maus has invited him. Has sent 6 Honfleur landscapes and the *Grande Jatte* which is the subject of heated discussion.

1888 Fourth Salon des Indépendants. 8 drawings and 2 new compositions, his masterpieces: *Parade de Cirque* (Stephen C. Clark Collection, New York) and *Les Poseuses* (Barnes Foundation, Merion). Pointillist technique, contrasts of tones and colors, attempt to bring even the frame into harmony with the lay-out. Spends summer at Port-en-Bessin, a small seaport near Bayeux. Reads scientific works on optics: N. O. Rood, David Sutter, C. Henry.

1889 Leaves Paris in the spring and goes to Le Crotoy, a seaside resort in Picardy, where he paints nine seascapes

which lead Angrand to remark: "He is the first to render the emotion the sea inspires on calm days." Exhibits with the "XX" at Brussels and the Indépendants in Paris, drawings and paintings made at Port-en-Bessin and Le Crotoy. Pissarro breaks with Divisionism.

1890 Stays at Gravelines, exhibits at the Indépendants, *Le Chahut* (Rijksmuseum Kröller-Müller, Otterlo), based on linear contrasts (it was bought by Gustave Kahn), and *Jeune Femme se poudrant* (Courtauld Coll., National Gallery, London), in consequence of which such terms as "static" and "lifeless" come to be applied more and more to his work. Seurat made a complete mystery of his private life and it was only after his death that his friends discovered that the *Jeune Femme* of the picture was his mistress, Madeleine Knobloch. His studio this year is at No. 39, Passage de l'Elysée-des-Beaux-Arts.

1891 Feb. Present at the famous "Symbolist Banquet" presided over by Mallarmé, and attended by Gide, France, Renard, Barrès, Gauguin, Mirbeau, Redon, de Régnier. March. Helps with the installation of the Exposition des Indépendants, whose opening day is March 10. At it he shows 4 views of the *Cheval de Gravelines* and his last, unfinished work, *Le Cirque* (Louvre). A sore throat followed by an access of fever obliges him to take to his bed. He died in his mother's house, on the Boulevard de Magenta, on March 29.

BIBLIOGRAPHY

Hitherto unpublished notes on Delacroix, by Seurat, *Bull. de la Vie Artistique*, April 1922. — Extracts from Seurat's letters have been published by R. Rey, *La Renaissance du Sentiment Classique*, Paris 1931 (letter to Beaubourg, dated Aug. 20, 1890, gives a full exposé of his theories). — O. Maus, *Trente Années de Lutte pour l'Art*, Brussels 1926. — J. Rewald, New York 1943, 1946. Paris 1947.

Until his death in 1944, F. Fénéon was working on a catalogue of Seurat's works, a studio-inventory of which he had made with Luce and Signac. "The list included some 170 small paint-box panels, 420 drawings, 6 sketch-books and some sixty canvases (figures, seascapes, landscapes), five of which were several square yards in size and might be reckoned as masterpieces."

J. Christophe, Paris 1890. — A. Salmon, Brussels 1921. — L. Cousturier, Paris 1921. — A. Lhote, Rome 1922 and Paris 1947. — W. Pach, New York 1923. — G. Coquiot, Paris 1924. — G. Kahn, Paris 1926 (2 vol. with reproductions). — W. George, Paris 1928. — C. Roger-Marx, Paris 1931. — D. C. Rich, Chicago 1935 *(La Grande Jatte)*. — J. Rewald, New York 1943 and Paris 1947 (Indispensable, based on Fénéon's records). — J. de Laprade, Monaco 1945. — D. Cooper, London 1946 *(La Baignade)*. — H. Bertram, Copenhagen 1946. — G. Seligman, New York 1947 (Illustrations).

SEVERINI, Gino (1883)

1883 Born at Cortona, Italy, April 7.

1901 In Rome: met Boccioni and later Balla.

1906 In Paris: friendship with Modigliani and Max Jacob, Suzanne Valadon, Utrillo, Braque, Dufy.

1910 Signed *Manifesto of the Futurist Painters*. First important works: *Pan-Pan at Monico, Memory of a Voyage*. Met Picasso.

1912 Exhibited in Futurist Exhibitions at Paris, London, Berlin, etc. Introduced his Italian friends to the Parisian painters and writers.

1913 Marries Paul Fort's daughter.

1914 *Lady on a Balcony; The Lancers.*

1915- Cubist period, and series of still lifes with musical ins-
1921 truments. 1917: Exhibition at Stieglitz Gallery, New York. Seeks a new classical form through the calculation of proportions. 1918-1920: studied mathematics. 1921: published *Du Cubisme au Classicisme*.

1922 Series of Harlequins.

1924- Murals and mosaics commissioned by public institutions
1935 and churches. (Several of these decorations are in Switzerland.) The Reception Room of Palazzo della Triennale, Milan (1933). Decorative panels for Léonce Rosenberg's house (1929). Prize for painting at 2nd Quadriennale, Rome (1935).

1950 Exhibited at the Biennale, Venice (First Prize). Lives and works at Meudon, near Paris. *(Information supplied by the artist.)*

BIBLIOGRAPHY

A. Behne, *Der Sturm*, No. 172/173, Berlin 1913. — U. Boccioni, *I futuristi plagiati in Francia, Lacerba*, Florence 1913. — P. A. Birot, *Sic*, Paris 1916. — A. Salmon, *L'Art vivant*, Paris 1920. — C. Fegdal, *Ateliers d'artistes*, vol. I, Paris 1925. — R. Landau, *Das unbestechliche Minos*, Hamburg 1925. — A. Warnod, *Les berceaux de la jeune peinture*, Paris 1925. — M. Raynal, *Anthologie de la peinture en France de 1906 à nos jours*, Paris 1927. — C. Carrà, *Artisti d'oggi, L'Ambrosiano*, Milan, Nov. 6, 1930. — P. Courthion, (Arte Moderna Italiana. 17). Milan 1930. New ed. 1941, 1945. With extensive bibliography. — J. Maritain, Paris 1930. — O. Freundlich, *A bis Z*, Cologne 1931. — J. Cassou, Paris 1933. — M. Besson, *L'Illustrazione vaticana*, Rome, March 1935. — A. H. Barr, *Cubism and Abstract Art*, Museum of Modern Art, New York 1936. — P. Fierens, Paris 1936. — L. Servolini, in: *Thieme-Becker, Allgem. Lexikon der bildenden Künstler*, vol. 30, Leipzig 1936. With bibliography. — P. M. Bardi, *Stile*, Milan 1942. — G. Severini, *Tutta la vita di un pittore*, Milan 1946. Autobiography.

SIGNAC, PAUL (1863-1935)

1863 Born in Paris, Nov. 11. His father kept a saddlery shop in the Rue Vivienne. The family lived in Montmartre (Rue Frochot).

1880 His parents wish him to become an architect, but a visit to the Monet Exhibition in the premises of *La Vie Moderne* "settles his career." He writes to Monet, who gives him advice, and Guillaumin, who has seen him painting on the Seine bank, also encourages him to persevere.

1884 Shows his *Pont d'Austerlitz* at the first Salon des Indépendants. Meets Cross and Seurat with whom he strikes up a friendship—a decisive factor in his career. Gives up the impressionist palette and decides to paint solely with the colors of the spectrum, employing Seurat's scientific Pointillism. Visits Chevreul in the Gobelins. Has an exuberant, forthright temperament, revels in controversy and bold innovations. Every Monday his friends forgather in his studio and hold debate far into the night. He becomes the theoretician of the group. Lives near Seurat in Montmartre.

1885 Shares studio in Rue de Steinkerque with Henri Rivière. Sub-editor of periodical *Le Chat Noir*.

1886 First experience of the South, at Collioure.

1888 Invited to show in Salon of the "XX" Group at Brussels. Became a member of it in 1891.

1889 Visits Van Gogh at Arles. Friendly with C. Henry, the physicist.

1892 As much a sailor as a painter; always cruising off the coast, from Brittany to the Mediterranean. Sailed in no les than 32 yachts at one time or another. In summer 1892, sailing South "discovers" Saint-Tropez and installs a small house there, *La Hune*, to which he returns yearly. His technique changes, he gives up the "point" for a square mosaic-like spot and aims at violent color harmonies.

1899 Publication of his technical treatise *D'Eugène Delacroix au Néo-Impressionnisme*. Travels abroad : Holland 1896, 1898, 1906; Italy 1904, 1905, 1907, 1908; Constantinople, 1907.

1935 Dies in Paris. Had been President of the Salon des Indépendants since 1898.

BIBLIOGRAPHY

Signac published a series of articles in: *Le Cri du Peuple*, March 1888. — *Art et Critique*, Feb. 1890. — Study of *Jongkind*, Paris 1927. — *D'Eugène Delacroix au Néo-Impressionnisme*, Paris 1899. — Preface to the Exhibition *Seurat et ses amis*, Paris 1933-1934. — *Les besoins individuels et la peinture*, Encyclopédie française, vol. XVI, Ch. 2, Paris 1935. — *Fragments du Journal de Signac, Arts de France*, Jan. 1947. — Extracts from unpublished letters, published by J. Rewald, *Seurat*, Paris 1947.
F. Fénéon, Paris 1890. — L. Cousturier, Paris 1922. — G. Besson, Paris 1934. — C. Roger-Marx, Paris 1924. — J. Guenne, *L'Art vivant*, March 1925. — J. de Laprade, *L'Art vivant*, 1935. — L. Deshairs, *Art et décoration*, 1923. — G. Besson, *Arts de France*, Jan. 1946.

SOUTINE, CHAÏM (1894-1943)

1894 Born at Smilovitchi, near Minsk, Lithuania, the tenth of eleven children. His father, a tailor, wished him to take up the same trade. The family lived in the ghetto in great poverty. While still a youngster, Soutine ran away from home. Already at Minsk, he showed an interest in painting.

1910 Enrolls at the School of Fine Arts, Vilna, earning his living as assistant to a photographer.

1913 Through the kindness of a doctor, whose acquaintance he has made, Soutine is enabled to go to Paris. He attends the Ecole des Beaux-Arts, in Cormon's class.
Lives at *La Ruche* (The Hive), the well-known community house in the rue de Dantzig, near the Vaugirard slaughterhouse. Makes friends with the butchers and slaughterers, who lend him quarters of meat from time to time, to serve him as models.
Strikes up friendships with many artists and writers living at *La Ruche*: Chagall, Laurens, Lipchitz, Kremegne, Blaise Cendrars, Fernand Léger, and others.
Down and out, in despair he tries to hang himself. His compatriot, the painter Kremegne, prevents this.
He meets Modigliani and they become fast friends. Through Modigliani, he gets to know the art dealer Zborowski, who buys his first pictures.

1919 On Zborowski's advice, he moves to Céret.

1920 Profoundly affected by Modigliani's death.

1922 Returns to Paris, bringing back with him more than 200 pictures.

1923 January 1: Dr Barnes, who is getting together his famous collection, buys about a hundred pictures by Soutine.

1925 Stays at Cagnes.

1926 Paris. Still lifes with quarters of meat, dead animals.

1927 Does many portraits, including a series of choirboys.

1929 Stays at Chatelguyon. Meets M. and Mme Castaing, with whom he lives in the Château de Lèves, near Chartres. The affection and tranquillity he finds here are reflected in the growing calmness of his pictures. Nevertheless, his art remains at bottom one of profound despair.
He interpreted works by his favorite painters: Courbet, *Les Demoiselles de la Seine*, Rembrandt, *Woman Bathing*, Corot, *Chartres Cathedral*.
He is obsessed by a craving for solitude. No longer to be seen at Montmartre, he also refuses to take part in exhibitions.

1943 A refugee at Champigny-sur Vende, in Touraine. Rushed to Paris for an emergency operation for perforated intestine. Operation unsuccessful, and Soutine dies on August 9.

BIBLIOGRAPHY

M. Raynal, *Anthologie de la peinture en France*, Paris 1927. New York 1928. — E. Faure, Paris 1928. — W. George, in *Le Triangle*, 1928. — Basler and Kunstler, *La peinture indépendante en France*, Paris 1929. — Drieu la Rochelle, in *Formes*, 1930. — R. Escholier, *La peinture française au XXe siècle*, Paris 1937. — R. H. Wilenski, *Modern French Painters*, London 1944. — R. Cogniat, Paris 1945. — B. Dorival, *Les Etapes de la peinture française contemporaine*, Paris 1948. — M. Zahar, *Panorama des arts*, Paris 1948. — J. T. Soby, *Contemporary Painters*, New York 1948. — M. Raynal, *Peintres du XXe siècle*, Geneva 1948. — R. Huyghe, *Les contemporains*, Paris 1949. — M. Wheeler, New York 1950. — R. Cogniat, Geneva 1952.

TAMAYO, RUFINO (1899)

1899 Born at Oaxaca, Mexico. Zapotec Indians, his parents settled in Mexico City when he was a boy and made a living as fruit-vendors.

1917 Enrolls in San Carlos Academy (the official Art School of Mexico City), but does not stay there long. Sees books, reviews, newspapers from Paris, and a few paintings, through which he discovers Impressionism and Cubism, notably Picasso and Braque. Period of exalted ambition. Mixes with the poets of the "Contemporanos" group who are devotees of "pure poetry." Haunts the Archaeological Museum where he becomes thoroughly familiar with ancient Mexican art.

1926 Simultaneous exhibitions in New York and Mexico City.

1933 Mural decoration for the National Conservatory of Music, Mexico City. Named to official posts, first as supervisor of instruction in plastic art in schools, then as professor of painting at the National School of Fine Arts.

1938 Settles in New York. Spends his summers in Mexico.

1943 Mural decoration for the Smith College Library, Northampton, Mass.

1948 Retrospective exhibition ("20 Years of Painting") at the Instituto Nacional de Bellas Artes, Mexico City.

1950 Makes a trip to Europe. Takes part in the Venice Biennale and exhibits at the Galerie Beaux-Arts, Paris.

1951 Retrospective at the Palais des Beaux-Arts, Brussels.

1952 Takes part in the Exhibition of Mexican Art at the Musée d'Art Moderne, Paris.
Exhibits at the Kunsthalle, Bern.

1955 2nd Prize, Pittsburgh International Exhibition.

BIBLIOGRAPHY

Robert Goldwater, New York 1937. — Raymond Cogniat, Paris 1951. — See also: *La Nube y el reloj*, Mexico City 1940. — *Modern Mexican Painters*, New York 1941. — *20 años de su labor*, catalogue of the exhibition "20 Years of Painting," Mexico City 1948. — *Modern Mexican Art*, 1949. — *Drawings by Tamayo*, Mexico City 1950.

TANGUY, YVES (1900-1955)

1900 Born in Paris, January 5, of Breton parents: his father was a naval officer. Studied in Paris. Short service in the merchant navy (traveled to England, Portugal, Spain, Africa and South America).

1922 Returned to Paris. Two years of indecision. Discovered Chirico's painting one day by accident (in Paul Guillaume's window). Without ever having thought of handling a brush, he at once started painting.

1925 Towards the end of the year met the Surrealists and joined them. First works reproduced in *La Révolution Surréaliste*. Exhibited at all the surrealist exhibitions in France and abroad.

1939 November 1, arrived in New York.

1940 August: in Reno, San Francisco, Los Angeles.

1942 In Canada and Washington. Settled at Woodbury, Conn.

1948 Became an American citizen.
Lives and works at Woodbury, Conn., U.S.A.

1952 Exhibition at Renou Gallery, in Paris.

1955 Dies at Waterbury, Conn., January 15.

BIBLIOGRAPHY

A. Breton, *Le Surréalisme et la peinture*, Paris 1928. 2nd ed. New York 1945. — D. Gascoyne, *A Short Survey of Surrealism*, London 1935. — A. H. Barr, *Fantastic Art, Dada, Surrealism*, New York 1936. — J. Levy, *Surrealism*, New York 1936. — *View*, 2nd series, No. 2, New York 1942. Issue devoted to T. — C. Zervos, *Histoire de l'Art contemporain*, Paris 1938. — R. Huyghe, *Les Contemporains*, Paris 1939. — J. T. Soby, *The Early Chirico*, New York 1941. — P. Guggenheim, *Art of this Century*, New York 1942. — *Cahiers d'Art*, Paris 1945-1946. — R. Huyghe, *La peinture actuelle*, Paris 1945. — R. Renne and C. Serbanne, *View*, New York 1945. — A. Breton, New York 1946. — J. J. Sweeney, *Eleven European Artists in America*, New York 1946. — J. T. Soby, *Magazine of Art*, Washington 1949.

TOULOUSE-LAUTREC, HENRI DE (1864-1901)

1864 Born November 24, at Albi. Son of Alphonse de Toulouse-Lautrec-Monfa and Adèle Tapié de Celeyran. A direct descendant of the famous Counts of Toulouse, ennobled under Charlemagne. Precocious talent for drawing.

1872 Comes to Paris with his family. Brilliant studies at Lycée Fontanes (Lycée Condorcet of today), completed by private tuition under the guidance of his mother, a highly cultured woman, who played a great part in his life. A delicate lad. Treatment at Amélie-les-Bains. A schoolfellow at the Lycée, Maurice Joyant, is his bosom friend; later, his biographer.

1878- In two successive accidents, at Albi in 1878, and some
1879 months later during a "cure" at Barèges, he breaks both thighs. This infirmity prevents his leading the normal life of a country gentleman, and throws him back on painting. Seeing in art a possible compensation for his physical deformity, his parents encourage him.

1880- His first teachers are René Princeteau, a painter of
1881 military and sporting scenes, then Lewis Brown and Bastien-Lepage. His first pictures, *Artilleur sellant un Cheval* (Albi Museum), *Le Mail-Coach à Nice* (Petit-Palais, Paris) show his brilliant craftsmanship, his extraordinary virtuosity in drawing, and his taste for "modern" subjects.

1881- Despite his success, Lautrec decides to recommence his
1883 art education from the beginning and after passing his baccalauréat at Toulouse in 1881, he enters, in 1882, Bonnat's studio (Bonnat finds his drawing "atrocious"!); then, Cormon's studio.

1884- Is influenced by Willette, Forain; makes a parody of
1885 *Bois-Sacré* (Puvis de Chavannes), discovers and admires the art of Manet, of Berthe Morisot and above all that of Degas, who liberates him from his academic prepossessions and leads him towards naturalistic themes.

1886- During one of his rare attendances at Cormon's studio
1888 he meets Van Gogh who has just come to Paris. He rents a studio at the corner of Rue Tourlaque and Rue Caulaincourt, where he remains till 1897. Lives in the heart of Montmartre, whose nocturnal activities supply him with subjects till 1893. Frequents *Le Mirliton*, Bruant's famous "Cabaret artistique," and *Le Moulin de la Galette*, where he becomes friendly with the floor dancers, Grille d'Egout, La Goulue, Jane Avril.

1889 His first exhibition at the Indépendants.

1891 Draws his first poster for the Moulin Rouge, and at once proves himself a master of this form of art. The elliptical technique of the poster, with its clean-cut, flat planes, reacts on his painting.

1893 On Joyant's initiative, exhibits with Charles Maurin at the Goupil Gallery. Invites Degas, who looks at the pictures in silence and, on leaving, says: "Well, Lautrec, I can see you're one of our trade!"

1894 Arsène Alexandre launches *Le Rire* and invites the collaboration of Lautrec, who is already drawing for *L'Echo de Paris*, *L'Escarmouche*, and *Le Figaro Illustré*. Visits Brussels. The Boulevards and Champs-Elysées become his new sector of observation.
Publishes an album, *Yvette Guilbert* (16 lithographs).

1895 Decorates the *La Goulue's Booth* (Louvre). Makes a trip to London where he meets Oscar Wilde, Beardsley, Arthur Symons, Conder. Discovers Whistler; detests the Pre-Raphaelites; in National Gallery admires the Primitives, Giotto, Uccello, Piero della Francesca.

1896 Trip to Holland with Maxime Dethomas; in Spain and Portugal with Maurice Guibert.

1897 Moves from Rue Tourlaque to a new studio in Avenue Frochot. Gives up poster painting and concentrates on color lithography, which both calls for subtler treatment and gives him more scope. Frequent stays at Villeneuve-sur-Yonne, with his friends the Natansons, founders of *La Revue Blanche*. Other subjects now appear in his works: brothels, the circus and sporting events, nudes, medical scenes, pictures of animals, interiors, numerous portraits.

1898 Goes to London during his exhibition at the Goupil Gallery. His health is seriously impaired by his insatiable appetite for night-life and heavy drinking.
Illustrations for *Au pied du Sinaï* by Clemenceau.

1899 Confined from February to May in the Saint-James clinic at Neuilly where attempts are made to break him of his disastrous habits. It is here that he paints his admirable series, *Le Cirque*. Released as a result of a press campaign launched by his friends, he breaks his stays in Paris with trips to Arcachon, Bordeaux, Le Havre and Malromé.
Illustrations for *Histoires naturelles* by Jules Renard (22 lithographs).

1901 Starts drinking again and his health deteriorates rapidly. A paralytic stroke immobilizes him at Taussat, where he is under treatment. Foreseeing the end, he asks to be taken to his mother, and he dies at the Château de Malromé on Sept. 9th, aged 37, like Van Gogh, after a very different but no less feverishly agitated life. His mother collected all the works in his studio and presented them to the town of Albi; they are housed in the Toulouse-Lautrec Museum, which was inaugurated on July 30, 1922, in the episcopal palace of La Berbie.

BIBLIOGRAPHY

The basic work (biography and catalogue) is that of Maurice Joyant, 2 vols. Paris 1927. — See also: L. Delteil, *Le peintre-graveur illustré* (vol. X and XI), Paris 1920. — E. Julien, *Catalogue of Albi Museum*, Albi 1939.
The chief monographs are: H. Esswein, *Moderne Illustratoren*, Munich 1904. — G. Coquiot, Paris 1913. — T. Duret, Paris 1920. — P. de Lapparent, Paris 1927; New York 1928. — F. Fosca, Paris 1928. — G. Jedlicka, Berlin 1929. — P. Mac Orlan, Paris 1934. — Schaub-Koch, Paris 1935. — G. Mack, New York 1938. — G. de la Tourette, Paris 1939. — E. Julien, *Les Dessins*, Monaco 1942. — W. Rotzler, *Affiches*, Paris 1946. — H. Delaroche-Vernet Henraux, Paris 1948. — G. Schmidt, Basel 1948. — F. Jourdain, Lausanne 1948; Paris 1951. — Art Institute of Chicago, 1949. — M. G. Dortu, Paris 1950. —

T. Natanson, Geneva 1951. — F. Jourdain and J. Adhémar, Paris 1952. — J. Lassaigne, Geneva 1953.

Among articles from reviews: T. Natanson, *La Revue Blanche*, Febr. 16, 1893. — Id., *Labyrinthe*, June 1, 1946. — A. Salmon, *L'Art vivant*, Sept. 15, 1931. — *L'Amour de l'Art*, Special No., April 1931. — H. Focillon, *Gazette des B. A.*, June 1931. — A. d'Eugny, *L'Amour de l'Art*, 1946, p. 188-195. — L. Venturi, *Les Arts plastiques*, Brussels 1947, p. 3-14.

UTRILLO, Maurice (1883-1955)

1883   Born at Paris, December 26. His mother was the painter Suzanne Valadon.

1891   Adopted by Miguel Utrillo, Spanish art-critic.

1893   Lives at Montmagny near Paris where his mother had a house. Studied at Lycée Rollin.

1899   Clerk-job in a bank.

1900   Sainte-Anne Asylum. To calm his nerves, his mother urged him to paint as a distraction.

1902   Beginning of his painting at Montmagny.

1903   Lived with his mother in Montmartre, 2, then 12 rue Cortot. Influenced by Pissarro, Sisley. From 1905 onwards, signed his canvases: Maurice Utrillo V. Sells pictures to Anzoli and Clovis Sagot for a few francs.

1908-   Period in which white predominated in his work. Exhibited for the first time at Salon d'Automne.
1910

1910   Francis Jourdain and Elie Faure interested in his painting.

1912   Interned in an establishment at Sannois.

1913   First one-man show at Eugène Blot's, rue Richepanse (31 pictures). Preface by Louis Lourmel (Libaude).

1917   In and out of hospital. Obtained some money through the dealer Zborowski, friend of Modigliani.

1918   Under treatment again, in Picpus Asylum.

1919   Exhibition at Galerie Lepoutre, 23, rue de la Boétie.

1921   In an asylum, at Ivry, place de la Mairie.
Exhibition with Suzanne Valadon at Berthe Weill's. First monograph by Francis Carco.

1924-   Settled with his mother and her friend André Utter in the rue Junot, Montmartre.
1926

1927   Employs a brighter, more varied palette. Period of great productivity.

1930   Awarded Legion of Honor decoration.

1936   Married Madame Pauwels (Lucie Valore).

1938   Suzanne Valadon died.

1948   Retrospective exhibition at the Salon d'Automne.

1953   Retrospective exhibition at Galerie Pétridès, Paris. Lived at Le Vésinet.

1955   Dies on November 5 at Dax (Landes), aged 71.

BIBLIOGRAPHY

F. Carco, 27 repr. of paintings and sketches, Paris 1921. — Id., Paris 1921. — M. Raynal, Paris 1924. — A. Basler, Paris 1925. — G. Coquiot, Paris 1925. — R. Rey, Paris 1925. — A. Tabarant, Paris 1926. — C. J. Gros, Paris 1927. — F. Carco, Paris 1928. — G. Charensol, Paris 1929. — F. Fels (Albums d'art Druet. 22), Paris 1930. — A. Basler, Paris 1931. — S. Miayata, Tokyo 1933. (Text in Japanese). — M. Gauthier, Paris 1944. — P. Courthion, Bern 1947. — C. J. Gros, Lausanne 1947. — F. Jourdan, Paris 1948. — G. Ribemont-Dessaignes, Geneva 1948.

VALLOTTON, Félix (1865-1925)

1865   Born December 28 in Lausanne (Switzerland). Attends evening drawing-classes, and is passionately fond of reading and music.

1882   Paris. He is 17. After a brief stay at the Académie Julian, passes rapidly through the Ecole des Beaux-Arts (Jules Lefèbvre's studio). Frequent visits to the Louvre, admires Courbet.

1885   Exhibits in the Salon. *Portrait de M. Ursenbach*.
In the 1886 Salon, *Portrait de Mme X*. Copies Dürer, Leonardo, Antonello da Messina.

1887   At the Salon, *M. Jasinsky* (Helsinki Museum), a portrait of a Polish engraver, shocks public opinion. Some say: "Deliberate revolt against the School"; others hail it as a masterpiece. Works with a picture restorer. Also in 1887, *Portrait de mes Parents* (Lausanne Museum).

1889   Travels to Vienna, Venice. Makes friends with Charles Cottet, and Charles Maurin, inventor of a new lithographic process, "le crachis"; also friendly with Toulouse-Lautrec and the milliner Hélène Chatenay.

1890-   Specializes in black-and-white, for material reasons.
1900   Woodcuts.

1890-1895   Art critic for the *Gazette de Lausanne*.

1891   Stops showing at the Salon after contributing for 7 years. Exhibits for the first time at the Salon des Indépendants. From 1891 to 1894, and from 1901 to 1909, collaborates in *La Revue Blanche*. Artists' and writers' portraits (T. Natanson, Mirbeau).

1893   Exhibits his "Masks" at the Indépendants. In October exhibits at Le Barc de Boutteville's with Roussel, Vuillard, Bonnard, Denis, Ranson, Ibels and Sérusier.

1894   Second group exhibition in the Paris office of *La Dépêche de Toulouse*.

1896   Illustrations for *La Maîtresse* by Jules Renard (26 drawings) and for the *Livre des Masques* by Remy de Gourmont (30 drawings).

1898   Illustrations for the second *Livre des Masques* by Remy de Gourmont.

1899   With Thadée Natanson at Cannes. In Paris, lives in the Rue de Milan.

1900   June 3. Vallotton acquires French nationality. Exhibits at Zurich.

1902   A number of *L'Assiette au Beurre* ("Crimes et Châtiments") meets with great success.

1903   Exhibits at Salon d'Automne; lives in Paris, Rue des Belles-Feuilles.

1904   Hébrard, the founder, casts four of Vallotton's statues: *Femme qui marche, Femme à l'amphore, Femme à la chemise, Maternité*. Abandons small-scale works for big compositions.

1906-   Period of Nudes: *L'Enlèvement d'Europe, La Baigneuse*
1910   *au Rocher*.

1908   Breaks his sojourns at Honfleur with annual visits to Lausanne and to his friends and admirers, the Hahnlosers, at Winterthur.

1913   Travels in Russia, Italy, Germany.

1921-1922   Stays at Cagnes. Landscapes.

1925   Dies in Paris, on December 28. His last work: a picture of the Bois de Boulogne under snow.

BIBLIOGRAPHY

Vallotton contributed to the *Gazette de Lausanne* and wrote several books, amongst which his *Journal*, a play: *L'Homme fort*, Paris 1907, and an autobiographical novel: *La Vie meurtrière*, Lausanne 1930 (preface by A. Thérive).

Vallotton himself compiled his *Livre de Raison*, a descriptive list of 1379 pictures.

J. Meier-Graefe, Paris, Berlin 1898. — A. Thérive, *L'Amour de l'Art*, 1921. — C. Fegdal, Paris 1931. — L. Godefroy, Paris 1936. — H. Hahnloser-Bühler, Paris 1936 (basic work). — F. Jourdain, Geneva 1953.

VAN DOESBURG, Theo (1883-1931)

(Pseudonym of C. E. M. Küpper)

1883   Born at Utrecht, Holland, August 30.

1899   First paintings.

1908   First exhibition at The Hague.

1913   Published first book of poems: *Volle Maan* (Full Moon).

1916   First collaboration with architects Wils and Oud.

1917   October: with Mondrian and others founded review *De Stijl* (Style) which ceased publication only on his death (1931) after 87 numbers.

1918   Contacts with Italian group "Valori Plastici" (Plastic Values) and with German and Russian artists of same tendencies.

1920-   Traveled in Italy, Belgium, France, Germany to propa-
1921   gate *De Stijl*. Visited Berlin at invitation of Hans Richter and Viking Eggeling. January 1921 at the Bauhaus, Weimar. Met Mies van der Rohe and Le Corbusier.

1922-   Under pseudonym J. K. Bonset started Dadaist review
1923   *Mecano*. In Paris. Exhibition of Painting and Architecture by "Stijl" Group, Galerie Léonce Rosenberg.

1924   Lectured on *Stijl* in Vienna, Prague, Brno. Beginnings of *Elementarism*.

1926-   Reconstructed Restaurant *L'Aubette* at Strasbourg, with
1928   Arp and Sophie Täuber according to the principles of *Stijl*. 1926: *Manifesto of Elementarism* in *Stijl* No. 75/76.

1930   Lectured on European architecture at Madrid and Barcelona. Published periodical *Art Concret* with Hélion, Carlsund, Tutundjan.

1931   March 7, died at Davos, Switzerland.
(Information supplied by Mrs van Doesburg.)

BIBLIOGRAPHY

F. M. Huebner, *Die Neue Malerei in Holland*, Leipzig 1921.
— H. Arp and El Lissitzky, *Die Kunstismen*, Erlenbach-Zurich 1925. — W. Gropius, *Internationale Architektur*, (Bauhausbücher 1), Munich 1925. — J. Tschichold, *Die Neue Typographie*, Berlin 1928. — L. Moholy-Nagy, *Von Material zu Architektur* (Bauhausbücher 14), Munich 1929. — F. Kiesler, *Contemporary Art*, New York 1930. — P. Citroën, *Palet*, Amsterdam 1931. — S. Giedion, *Cahiers d'Art* No. 4, Paris 1931. — J. J. Sweeney, *Plastic Redirections in 20th Century Painting*, Chicago 1934. — A. H. Barr, *Cubism and Abstract Art*, New York 1936. — S. Giedion, *Space, Time and Architecture*, Cambridge 1941. — S. Janis, *Abstract and Surrealist Art in America*, New York 1944. — A. Dorner, *The Way beyond Art*, Chicago 1947. — L. Moholy-Nagy, *Vision in Motion*, Chicago 1947. — M. Seuphor, *L'art abstrait, ses origines, ses premiers maîtres*, Paris 1949.

VAN GOGH, VINCENT (1853-1890)

1853 March 30, birth of Vincent Willem Van Gogh at the parsonage of Groot Zundert, a small village in Dutch Brabant, south of Breda, near the Belgian frontier. Eldest son of Pastor Theodorus, who came of an ancient, much respected Calvinist family, amongst whom we find clergymen, sailors, businessmen and patrons of art. Three of Vincent's uncles were art-dealers. His mother, Anna Cornelia Carbentus, was daughter of a Court bookbinder at The Hague.

1857 May 1. Birth of Theo, Vincent's favorite brother.

1865- Studies at a Provily boarding-school, then at the neigh-
1869 boring town of Zevenbergen.

1869 July 30. Employed at the Goupil art-gallery at The Hague, then in Brussels.

1872 Begins exchanging letters with Theo.

1873 June 18. Transferred to the London branch while Theo enters the Brussels office.

1874 October, in Paris; December, returns to London.

1875. May. Transferred to headquarters of the Goupil Gallery in Paris. Quarrels with the Goupil staff and with customers. His obsession with the Bible begins.

1876 March. Loses his post in Paris. Returns to England, and is a schoolmaster at Ramsgate, then at Isleworth. December, comes home to Etten for Christmas.

1877 Jan. 21-Apr. 30. Clerk in a bookshop at Dordrecht. May 9, goes to Amsterdam to study for admission to the theological college.

1878 July 22, fails to pass the examination, and abandons his studies. Home again. In August begins a three-months' course at an evangelical training-college in Brussels. On Nov. 15 sent on a mission as lay-preacher to the miners in the Borinage.

1879 Jan. Temporary pastor at Wasmes, in the heart of the black country. July, relieved of his duties. Complete destitution, equally complete despair.

1880 Summer. During these anxious months, the darkest of his life, he glimpses his artistic vocation. Writes to his brother Theo the long, emotional letter in which he announces his decision. Lives at Cuesmes, near Mons.

1880- Brussels. Lodges at a small hotel, 72 Bd du Midi. Meets
1881 and makes friends with the painter Ridder van Rappard (1858-1892), with whom he corresponds for five years. Private lessons in anatomy and perspective. First monetary aid from Theo, who is now working for Goupil in Paris.

1881 Etten (Apr.-Dec.). With his parents. Conflicts with his father about his artistic career. Ill-fated love-affair, with his cousin "K."

1882- The Hague (Dec. 1881-Sept. 1883). Asks advice of his
1883 cousin the painter Mauve, who, sensing his genius, helps him in his work, gives him lodging, but with whom he quarrels almost at once. In his first paintings the tones are somber, the impasto very thick. Takes walks to Scheveningen, Woorburg, Leidschendau. Watercolors, lithographs; studies of peasants, fishermen, seascapes, landscapes.

1883 Drenthe (Sept., Nov.). Stays at Hoogeveen, in a land of moors and peat-bogs. Studies of heath-land, thatched cottages, hamlets, peasants at work.

1883 Dec. Returns to his parents' house at Nuenen, where his father has been appointed pastor. Sets up his studio in the vicarage barn. Works hard, reads Dickens, Carlyle, Beecher-Stowe.

1885 March 27. Sudden death of his father. Still lifes, peasants, weavers, studies of heads. *The Potato Eaters* (April-May

1885); *Head of a Peasant Woman*, Nov. 23. Starts for Antwerp. Studio at 194, Rue des Images. "Discovers" Rubens and Japanese prints. Enters the Academy and works under Sieber and Verlat, whose conformist outlook gets on his nerves.

1886 February. Starts for Paris. Theo welcomes him enthusiastically and puts him up, first in the Rue Laval (now Rue Victor-Massé), then at 54 Rue Lepic. Enters Cormon's studio where he meets Toulouse-Lautrec. Frequents the Louvre but is also influenced by the Impressionists. Often visits Père Tanguy's shop and the Cabaret du Tambourin. Meets Pissarro, Degas, Seurat, Signac and Gauguin. Adopts the pointillist technique for a time.

1887 April. Makes friends with Emile Bernard. June, works with Bernard at Asnières. His palette gradually grows brighter and his style is completely changing. More than 200 pictures date from this Paris period: self-portraits, still lifes, views of Montmartre, studies of the outskirts of Paris, interiors.

1888 Feb. 20, leaves suddenly for Arles, on Lautrec's advice. "It's in the South that the studio of the future must set up."
Feb. Puts up at the Restaurant Carrel, in Rue Cavalerie.
April. Spring landscapes: *Orchard in Bloom*. May: Settles in a small house, 2, Rue Lamartine, "a yellow house with a tiny white studio." June. Stays a week at Saintes-Maries-de-la-Mer. Enraptured by this first sight of the Mediterranean. *Boats on the Shore*. July. Drawings of La Crau, near Montmajour. August. Becomes very friendly with the household of the local postman, Roulin; makes portraits of him. *The Sunflowers*. Sept. Nightscapes. *Outdoor Café at Night*. Oct. 20. Arrival of Gauguin, who has a great influence on him. Two months of life in common, during which the tension grows between these two men of fiercely opposed natures. Dec. 24. The crisis. Van Gogh attempts to kill Gauguin, then cuts off his own ear. Gauguin hurries back to Paris. Theo arrives. Two weeks' confinement in hospital.

1889 Jan. 7. Vincent returns to his house. *Self-Portrait with the Cut Ear. Still Life with Onions. La Berceuse*. Feb. Hallucinations. He is again put into confinement, until the end of March. March. Signac visits him. 200 pictures are painted during this period, the most important and prolific of his career.
May 9. At his own request, Vincent is admitted to the asylum at Saint-Rémy, a small town near Arles. Dr Rey takes care of him.

1890 Jan. First article dealing with his work: Albert Aurier's enthusiastic appreciation, in the *Mercure de France*.
March. One of Vincent's pictures. *La Vigne Rouge* is sold for 400 francs at the exhibition of "Les XX" in Brussels; it is the only picture sold during his lifetime.
May 16. Comes to Paris, visits Theo.
150 pictures painted during this period of feverishly intensive productivity: amongst them *Cypresses, Harvest, The Hospital Yard*, self-portraits, portraits of the asylum staff. About thirty copies from Millet, Delacroix, Daumier, Rembrandt, Doré.
May 21. Arrives at Auvers. Becomes the patient and friend of Dr Gachet, whose portrait he paints.
July 1. Spends some days in Paris: at Theo's meets Lautrec, Albert Aurier. Returns to Auvers and paints "three huge canvases, three far-flung wheatfields, under lowering skies"; also, on July 14 *La Mairie d'Auvers*. July 27. In the evening, when in the open country, shoots himself.
July 29. Dies, aged 37, with faithful Theo at his side. His last words were: "There'll never be an end to human misery."

1891 Jan. 25. Theo dies. The brothers lie side by side in the cemetery of Auvers.

BIBLIOGRAPHY

His correspondence remains our main source of information on Van Gogh's life and work, and his letters are amongst the most moving ever penned. *Brieven aan zijn broeder* (letters to Theo), complete Dutch edit. with Preface by J. Van Gogh-Bonger, 3 vols., Amsterdam 1914. 2nd édit. 1923-1924. English ed., London 1927 and 1929. — *Selected Letters*, A. H. Barr, New York 1935. French ed., selected by G. Philippart, Paris 1937 and 1947. — *Lettres à Emile Bernard*, Paris 1911. — *Briefe an E. Bernard und Paul Gauguin*, Basel 1921. — *Brieven aan A. G. A. Ridder Van Rappard*, 1881-1885, Amsterdam

1937. — *Letters to Emile Bernard*, edited, translated, with a foreword by D. Lord, London 1938. — H. Thannhauser, *Van Gogh and John Russell, An unpublished Correspondence*, *Burlington Magazine*, Sept. 1938. — See also: *Les Lettres de Théo à Vincent*, Amsterdam 1932. — Mr. V.W. Van Gogh is preparing in Amsterdam a complete edition of Van Gogh's letters.

J. B. de la Faille, *L'Œuvre de Van Gogh*. Catalogue raisonné. 4 vols. Paris and Brussels, 1928. — W. Vanbeselaere, *De Hollandsche period in het werk van V. Van Gogh*, Antwerp, Amsterdam 1937. — A. M. Hammacher, *Rijksmuseum Kröller-Müller, Catalogue van 264 werken*, Otterlo 1949.

G. A. Aurier, *Mercure de France*, January 1892. — J. Meier-Graefe, Munich 1910. — W. Hausenstein, Berlin 1914. — E. Bernard, Amsterdam 1915. — Havelaar, Amsterdam 1915. — T. Duret, Paris 1916. — L. Piérard, Paris 1924. — Sternheim, Berlin 1924. — P. Colin, Paris 1925. — B. Stockvis, Amsterdam 1926. — J. B. de la Faille, Paris 1927. — V. Cleerdin, Te's Hertogenbosch 1929. — A. Bertram, London and New York 1929. — G. Knuttel, Stockholm 1932. — J. Meier-Graefe, New York 1933. — C. Terrasse, Paris 1935. — W. Pach, New York 1936. — L. Vitali, Milan 1936. — W. Uhde, Vienna and Paris 1936. — R. Huyghe, Paris 1936. — M. Florisoone, Paris 1937. — C. Nordenfalk, Stockholm 1943. — A. Artaud, Paris 1947. — P. Courthion, Geneva 1947. — A. Rüdlinger, Bern 1947. — A. Hammacher, Amsterdam 1948. — M. Shapiro, New York 1950. — J. Combe, Paris 1951. — Jean Leymarie, Paris 1952. — Charles Estienne, Geneva 1953.

VILLON, JACQUES (1875)

(Pseudonym of Gaston Duchamp)

1875 Born July 31 at Damville (Eure), France. A brother of the sculptor Raymond Duchamp-Villon and the painters Marcel and Suzanne Duchamp.

1894 Worked in Cormon's studio. Up to 1910 did drawings for *L'Assiette au Beurre*, *Gil Blas*, *Le Rire* and *Le Courrier Français*.

1904 Member of the Salon d'Automne; member of the committee till 1911.

1905 First exhibition with Duchamp-Villon at Rouen.

1911 Joined cubist group. Series of engravings for the publisher Clovis Sagot. In his studio at Puteaux, Léger, Picabia, La Fresnaye, Metzinger and Gleizes met on Sundays and founded the *Section d'Or*. Exhibited at the first exhibition of the *Section d'Or* at the Galerie de la Boétie.

1914 In army, up to the end of war.

1919- First abstract period. Exhibition at the *Société Anonyme*
1922 at New York.

1921- To earn his living made color etchings of works by mo-
1930 dern artists, published by Bernheim-Jeune.

1930 Gave up engraving to devote himself to his painting.

1931-1933 New abstract period.

1935 Journey to the United States.

1939 Exhibited at the first *Salon des Réalités Nouvelles* (Galerie Charpentier, Paris).

1940 Took refuge in South of France (Eure and Tarn).

1949 Awarded the First Prize for engraving at the International Exhibition at Lugano.

1950 A pavilion at the Venice Biennale devoted entirely to his work. First Carnegie Prize.

1955 Lives and works at Puteaux, near Paris.
(Information supplied by Galerie Louis Carré, Paris.)

BIBLIOGRAPHY

J. D. Maublanc, *Le bon plaisir*, December 1930. — *Abstraction, création, art non figuratif*, Paris 1932, 1933. — *L'Amour de l'Art*, Paris 1933. Bio-bibliographical article by G. Bazin. — A. H. Barr, *Cubism and Abstract Art*, Museum of Modern Art, New York 1936. — B. Dorival, *Les Etapes de la peinture française contemporaine*, vols. 2, 3, Paris 1944, 1946. — René-Jean, Lyons 1945. — P. Eluard and René-Jean, Paris 1948. — J. Auberty and C. Perusseaux, *Catalogue de son œuvre gravé*, Paris 1950. Complete catalogue.

VLAMINCK, MAURICE (1876)

1876 Born April 4 in Paris. His father was Belgian; his mother came of a Protestant family in Lorraine: both were accomplished musicians.

1879 The family settles at Le Vésinet.

1894 Vlaminck gets married; many children were to be the issue of this marriage.

1895 Becomes a cycling enthusiast; his athletic abilities gain him a certain amount of success. Takes drawing lessons from an obscure member (Robichon) of the Salon des Artistes Français. Studies with Henri Rigal, visiting the Island of Chatou in his company. Much attracted by the impressionist pictures exhibited by the Paris art-dealers.

1896 Military service.

1899- Discharged, he earns a living giving music lessons. For
1900 two months, near the end of the World's Fair, he is a "gipsy" bandsman at the Restaurant des Cadets de Gascogne. He next finds a job as violinist at the Théâtre du Château d'Eau.

Meeting with Derain. They fit up a studio in an abandoned house on the Island of Chatou, where they work together. Levasseur, owner of the place, lets it to them for ten francs a month. Vlaminck wrote: "The building creaked in all its limbs and seemed always on the verge of lurching over into the Seine. The beams and joists holding up the floor sagged underfoot. It was winter and we imported a small stove. But there was no fuel. Armed with a saw and a hatchet, we turned our attention to the chairs and tables stored in an adjoining room, feeding them piece by piece into the stove. Needless to say, the owner was kept in the dark as to the fate of his furniture."

Makes the acquaintance of Claude Monet at Durand-Ruel's.

1901 With Derain, he visits the Van Gogh Exhibition at Bernheim's. Enraptured with what he sees.

Derain introduces him to Matisse. Vlaminck paints his *Little Girl with a Doll*, which is shown at Salon des Indépendants—his first appearance there.

1901- Writes his first novel, *Grains au Vent*, the title which
1902 his publisher substituted for its original name *D'un Lit dans l'Autre*. For this book Derain does thirty-odd sketches; Félicien Champsaur writes the preface. Two other novels follow later: *Tout Pour Ça* and *Ame de Mannequin*.

1905 Joins the group of artists of the "Bateau-Lavoir" at the Café Azon, Montmartre. Here he meets Van Dongen, Picasso, Max Jacob, Guillaume Apollinaire, and others. Encouraged by Matisse, Vlaminck and Derain exhibit for the first time at the Salon des Indépendants. Each of them sells a picture for 100 francs to an art-lover and patron from Le Havre who is known to loathe modern painting. The story goes that he visited the exhibition with the avowed intention of buying the ugliest canvases he could find, with a view to making a present of them to his son-in-law.

Exhibition at Berthe Weill's, and at Salon d'Automne in the famous "Cage des Fauves."

1906 Ambroise Vollard buys up all the pictures in Vlaminck's studio.

1908 Vlaminck abandons pure color; his palette grows darker. He now comes under the influence of Cézanne.

1914 During the war, he works in the Loucheur Factory.

1918 Sees much of Zborowski, André Salmon and Francis Carco.

1919 Large-scale Exhibition at Druet's.

1920 Settles at Auvers-sur-Oise.

1925 Moves to Rueil-la-Gadelière, where he still lives.

BIBLIOGRAPHY

D. H. Kahnweiler, Leipzig 1920. — F. Fels, Paris 1928. — G. Bazin, *L'Amour de l'Art*, Paris, June 1933. — W. Gaunt, New York 1939. — W. Grohmann, Leipzig 1940. — K. G. Perls, New York 1941. — M. Gauthier, Paris 1949. — R. Queneau, Geneva 1949. — M. Genevoix, Paris 1954.

VUILLARD, EDOUARD (1868-1940)

1868 Born Nov. 11 at Cuiseaux (Saône-et-Loire). Son of a former officer and tax-collector, who dies in 1883. His father is 27 years older than his mother, Marie Michaud, who survives him for forty-five years, dying after devoting her whole life to her son Edouard, who is the youngest of the family, which includes Marie (the eldest child) and Alexandre who becomes a pupil at the Ecole Polytechnique.

1877 The family settles in Paris. Edouard begins his studies at the Marist School (Ecole Rocroy).

1883 Death of the artist's father. Edouard continues his studies at the Lycée Fontanes (now Lycée Condorcet). He makes friends with K. X. Roussel, his future brother-in-law. The family lives in the Rue Daunou, where Mme Vuillard, to supplement her income, opens a corset factory.

1886   His devotion for Roussel makes him give up studying for the Ecole de Saint-Cyr, and turns his thoughts to painting. Both friends work in various studios; first at Maillard's where they meet Cottet. Through Lugné-Poe, a former pupil of the Lycée and future director of the Théâtre de l'Œuvre, they make the acquaintance of Maurice Denis.

1888   Académie Julian. Our young painters meet Bonnard, who, with Vuillard and Roussel, is working under Bouguereau and Robert Fleury.

1889   Sérusier, student-in-charge at Julian's, and Denis prevail upon Ranson, Piot, Ibels, then Bonnard and finally Vuillard to form an association called the "Nabis." At the Ecole des Beaux-Arts Vuillard works in Gérome's studio, but leaves it before long. Paints *La Femme endormie* (1890). Opposed to academic art and also to Impressionism. Simplified forms, broken tones. Painting on cardboard; influenced by Japanese art.

1891   First exhibition in the offices of *La Revue Blanche*, which the Natanson brothers have just launched. Vuillard, Bonnard, Denis and Lugné-Poe, stage-manager of the Théâtre Libre, share a studio at 28, Rue Pigalle.

1892   Exhibition at Le Barc de Boutteville's. Vuillard meets Verlaine and Mallarmé. Roger Marx the critic and Jos. Hessel the dealer are their first admirers and patrons.

1893   K. X. Roussel marries Marie Vuillard. Foundation of the Théâtre de l'Œuvre by Lugné-Poe. According to him, it is Vuillard who is most interested in the theater; he is also the best general adviser, is good at finding titles and takes an active part in the rehearsal and staging of the first play performed: Ibsen's *Rosmersholm*.

1894   First great decorative composition (in 9 panels): *Jardin des Tuileries* (Musée d'Art Moderne, Paris).

1896-   Decorative works for Dr Vaquez (Petit-Palais, Paris),
1899   for the novelist Claude Anet, for Princess Bibesco. Vuillard now lives in the Rue Truffaut. His art has reached its climax. Stays at the Natansons' in Villeneuve-sur-Yonne.

1900   At Romanel with Vallotton. Paints Vallotton's portrait.
1900-   *Paysages de Paris*. Simplification, bareness, gravity. Still
1910   paints on cardboard.

1908   Moves to Rue de Calais, facing Place Vintimille. Leaves this house only in 1927, when he finds a new studio in Square Vintimille. Teaches for a while in Ranson's Academy with Roussel and Denis.

1903-   Summer holidays in Normandy and Brittany with the
1914   Hessels and their friends.

1913   Goes to London and, with Bonnard, to Holland.

1914   Vuillard is mobilized for a time as a signaler in the Army Reserve.

1917-1924   Stays at Clos Cézanne, Vaucresson.

1918   Vuillard's 50th birthday falls on Armistice day, Nov. 11, and his friends celebrate both together.

1924-1940   Stays at Château des Clayes (Seine-et-Oise).

1930   Travels in Spain with Prince Bibesco.

1930-   Many commissions, society portraits: *La Parisienne,*
1937   1930, *Mme L. Marchand*, 1931, *Mme de Noailles*, 1932, *Comtesse de Polignac*, 1932, *Simone Berriau*, 1934, *Mme Henraux*, 1937, *Elvire Popesco*, 1937, *Dr Viau*, 1937.

1937   Decorates the Palais de Chaillot. Elected member of the Institute.

1939   Decorates the Palace of the League of Nations, Geneva.

1940   Dies in La Baule on June 21.

BIBLIOGRAPHY

T. Leclerc, *Art et décoration*, 1920. — F. Fosca, *L'Amour de l'Art*, 1920. — R. Coolus, *Art vivant*, 1938. — A. Lhote, *N.R.F.*, March 1941. — B. Dorival, *Revue des Beaux-Arts de France* 1942. — J. Salomon, Paris 1945. — C. Roger-Marx, Paris 1945. — A. Chastel, Paris 1946. — C. Roger-Marx, *L'œuvre gravé*, Paris 1948. — J. Mercanton, Geneva 1949. — Vuillard's unpublished notebooks will be opened only in 1980.

Selected Bibliography

GENERAL

J. Meier-Graefe, *Entwicklungsgeschichte der modernen Kunst,* Stuttgart 1904. New edition, Munich 1927. In English: *The Development of Modern Art,* New York 1908. — A. Fontainas, *Histoire de la peinture française au XIX⁰ siècle,* Paris 1906. New edition 1922. — Thieme-Becker, *Allgemeines Lexikon der bildenden Künstler,* 35 vols., Leipzig 1907-1942. — G. Coquiot, *Cubistes, futuristes, passéistes.* Paris 1914. New edition 1923. — A. J. Eddy, *Cubists and Post-Impressionism,* Chicago 1914. New edition 1919. Extensive bibliography. — W. H. Wright, *Modern Painting,* London and New York 1915. — H. Walden, *Einblick in Kunst: Expressionismus, Futurismus, Kubismus,* Berlin 1917. — G. Coquiot, *Les Indépendants, 1884-1920,* Paris 1920. — *Jahrbuch der jungen Kunst,* 5 vols., edited by G. Biermann, Leipzig 1920-1924. — A. Salmon, *L'Art vivant,* Paris 1920. — E. Faure, *Histoire de l'art,* vol. IV: *L'Art moderne,* Paris 1921. American edition, New York 1924. — C. Bell, *Since Cézanne,* New York 1923. — B. Manguard, *Tradición, resurgimento y evolución del arte mexicano,* Mexico City 1923. — H. Hildebrandt, *Die Kunst des 19. und 20. Jahrhunderts,* Potsdam 1924. — W. Pach, *The Masters of Modern Art,* New York 1924. — F. Fels, *Propos d'artistes,* Paris 1925. — R. Hamann, *Die deutsche Malerei vom Rokoko bis zum Expressionismus,* Leipzig 1925. — El Lissitzky and Hans Arp, *Die Kunstismen, 1914-1924,* Erlenbach-Zurich 1925. Texts in French, German, English. — A. Warnod, *Les berceaux de la jeune peinture,* Paris 1925. — R. Fry, *Transformations,* London 1926. — H. Kröller-Müller, *Die Entwicklung der modernen Malerei,* Leipzig 1926. — C. Einstein, *Die Kunst des 20. Jahrhunderts,* Berlin 1926. 3rd edition 1931. — F. Rutter, *Evolution in Modern Art,* London 1926. — F. J. Mather, *Modern Painting,* New York 1927. — P. Courthion, *Panorama de la peinture française contemporaine,* Paris 1927. — M. Raynal, *Anthologie de la peinture en France de 1906 à nos jours,* Paris 1927. In English: *Modern French Painters,* New York 1928. — K. Woermann, *Geschichte der Kunst aller Zeiten und Völker,* 6 vols., Leipzig 1927. Vol. 6: *Die Kunst... von 1750 bis zur Gegenwart.* With extensive bibliography. — H. Focillon, *La peinture aux XIX⁰ et XX⁰ siècles,* Paris 1928. — A. Ozenfant, *Art,* Paris 1928. In German: *Leben und Gestaltung,* Potsdam 1930. In English: *Foundations of Modern Art,* New York 1931. — A. Basler and C. Kunstler, *La peinture indépendante en France,* 2 vols., Paris 1929. — W. Uhde, *Picasso et la tradition française,* Paris 1929. In English, New York 1929. — E. Joseph, *Dictionnaire biographique des artistes contemporains, 1910-1930,* 3 vols., Paris 1930-1934. — *Dictionnaire Bénézit,* 8 vols., Paris 1948-1955. — E. Waldmann, *La peinture allemande contemporaine,* Paris 1930. — R. Rey, *La peinture française à la fin du XIX⁰ siècle,* Paris 1931. — V. Costantini, *Pittura contemporanea,* Milan 1931. — L. Justi, *Von Corinth bis Klee,* Berlin 1931. — A. H. Barr, *German Painting and Sculpture,* New York 1931. — H. Sérouva, *Initiation à la peinture d'aujourd'hui,* Paris 1931. — B. Weill, *Pan dans l'œil,* Paris 1932. — *Histoire de l'art contemporain,* in *L'Amour de l'Art,* Paris 1933-1934. Extensive bio-bibliographical notices by G. Bazin. — H. Read, *Art Now,* London 1933. — G. Castelfranco, *La pittura moderna,* Florence 1934. — J. J. Sweeney, *Plastic Redirections in 20th Century Painting,* Chicago 1934. — T. W. Earp, *The Modern Movements in Painting,* London 1935. — *Histoire de l'art contemporain: la peinture,* edited by R. Huyghe assisted by G. Bazin, Paris 1935. Extensive bio-bibliographical notices. — R. Escholier, *La peinture française, XX⁰ siècle,* Paris 1937. — J. Fernandez, *El arte moderno en Mexico,* Mexico City 1937. — W. Uhde, *Von Bismarck bis Picasso: Erinnerungen und Bekenntnisse,* Zurich 1938. — C. Zervos, *Histoire de l'art contemporain,* Paris 1938. — J. Klein, *Modern Masters,* New York 1938. — C. Terrasse, *La peinture française au XX⁰ siècle,* Paris 1939. In English: *French Painting in the 20th Century,* New York 1939. With bibliography. — R. Huyghe, *Les contemporains,* Paris 1939 (notices by G. Bazin) New edition, 1949. — E. H. Ramsden, *An Introduction to Modern Art,* London 1940. — Catalogue of the exhibition *20 Centuries of Mexican Art,* Museum of Modern Art, New York 1940. — M. Georges-Michel, *Peintres et sculpteurs que j'ai connus,* New York 1942. — P. Guggenheim, *Art of this Century,* New York 1942. — B. Dorival, *Les étapes de la peinture française contemporaine,* 3 vols., Paris 1943-1946. Extensive bibliography.

— M. Georges-Michel, *Les grandes époques de la peinture moderne,* New York and Paris 1944. — S. Cheney, *The Story of Modern Art,* New York 1945. — R. H. Wilenski, *Modern French Painters,* London 1945. With extensive documentation. — A. Henze, *Fibel der modernen Malerei,* Baden-Baden 1946. — J. Lassaigne, *Panorama des arts,* Paris 1946, 1947. — A. Lhote, *Ecrits sur la peinture,* Brussels 1946. — J. Lassaigne, *100 chefs-d'œuvre de l'Ecole de Paris,* Paris 1947. — M. Raynal, *Peintres du XX⁰ siècle,* Geneva 1947. — L. Venturi, *Pittura contemporanea,* Milan 1947. — M. Davidson, *An Approach to Modern Painting,* New York 1948. — P. Eluard, *Voir,* Geneva 1948. — A. Malraux, *Psychology of Art,* 3 vols., Geneva 1948-1950. — A. Hulftegger, *Evolution de la peinture en Allemagne et dans l'Europe centrale des origines à nos jours,* Paris 1949. With bibliography. — L. Venturi, *Pour comprendre la peinture: de Giotto à Chagall,* Paris 1950. — Catalogue of the Mexican Art Exhibition, Musée d'Art Moderne, Paris 1952. — *Premier bilan de l'art actuel,* Paris 1953. — A. Malraux, *The Voices of Silence,* New York 1953.

DIVISIONISM

F. Fénéon, *Les impressionnistes en 1886,* Paris 1886. — P. Signac, *D'Eugène Delacroix au Néo-Impressionnisme,* Paris 1899. — G. Coquiot, *Les Indépendants,* Paris 1921. — E. Verhaeren, *Sensations,* Paris 1927. — Catalogue of the exhibition *Seurat et ses amis,* Paris 1933. — P. Signac, *Le Néo-Impressionnisme,* in *Gazette des Beaux-Arts,* Paris 1934. — J. Rewald, *Seurat,* New York 1946. — J. Rewald, F. Fénéon, in *Gazette des Beaux-Arts,* Paris 1947-1948.

GAUGUIN AND THE PONT-AVEN GROUP

A. Aurier, *Œuvres posthumes,* Paris 1893. — E. Bernard, *Notes sur l'Ecole dite de Pont-Aven,* in *Mercure de France,* December 1903. — C. L. Hind, *The Post-Impressionists,* London 1911. — C. Chassé, *Gauguin et le groupe de Pont-Aven,* Paris 1921. — Catalogue of the exhibition *Gauguin, l'Ecole de Pont-Aven et l'Académie Julian,* Paris 1934. — J. Rewald, *Gauguin,* New York 1938. — E. Bernard, *Souvenirs inédits sur l'artiste Paul Gauguin et ses compagnons,* Lorient 1941.

SYMBOLISM AND THE NABIS

A. Aurier, *Le Symbolisme en peinture,* in *Mercure de France,* Paris 1891. — A. Mellerio, *Le Mouvement idéaliste en peinture,* Paris 1896. — R. Barré, *Le symbolisme,* Paris 1911. — M. Denis, *Théories,* Paris 1913. — A. Segard, *Les décorateurs,* Paris 1913. — M. Denis, *L'Epoque du Symbolisme,* in *Gazette des Beaux-Arts,* Paris 1934. — H. Hahnloser-Bühler, *F. Vallotton et ses amis,* Paris 1936. — A. Armstrong-Wallis, *The Symbolist Painters of 1890,* in *Marsyas,* 1941. — J. Robert Goldwater, *Symbolist Art and Theater,* in *Magazine of Art,* 1946. — C. Roger-Marx, *Vuillard et son temps,* Paris 1945. — C. Chassé, *Le mouvement symboliste,* Paris 1948. — Many magazine articles in *La Revue Blanche, La Plume, Le Mercure de France, La Revue Artistique,* by A. Aurier, T. Natanson, Roger Marx, G. Geffroy and others. — Catalogue of the exhibition *Carrière et le symbolisme,* Musée de l'Orangerie, Paris 1949.

FAUVISM

Books: G. Coquiot, *Les Indépendants,* Paris 1920. — G. Diehl, *Les Fauves,* Paris 1943. — G. Duthuit, *Les Fauves (Braque, Derain, Van Dongen, Dufy, Friesz, Manguin, Marquet, Matisse, Puy, Vlaminck),* Geneva 1949; New York 1950.

Articles and Prefaces: A. Gide, *Promenade au Salon d'Automne,* in *Gazette des Beaux-Arts,* Paris 1905. — *Le Salon d'Automne,* in *L'Illustration,* Paris, November 4, 1905. Reproduced in *Cahiers d'Art,* No. 5-6, 1931. — L. Vauxcelles, *Salon des Fauves,* in *L'Illustration,* Paris 1905. — L. Vauxcelles, *Salon des Indépendants,* in *Gil Blas,* Paris 1906. — A. Ozenfant, *Les Fauves 1900-1907,* in *L'Esprit Nouveau,* Paris 1922. — G. Rouault, *Gustave Moreau,* in *L'Art et les Artistes,* Paris 1926. — A. Salmon, *Les Fauves et le Fauvisme,* in *L'Art Vivant,* Paris 1927. — W. George, *Le mouvement fauve,* in *L'Art Vivant,* Paris 1927. — V. Costantini, *La pittura dei "Fauves,"* in *La Fiera Letteraria,* Milan 1928. — G. Duthuit, *Le Fauvisme,* in *Cahiers d'Art,* Paris 1929, 1930, 1931. — P. Fierens, *Le Fauvisme,* in *Cahiers de Belgique,* Brussels 1931. — R. Huyghe, *Le Fauvisme,* in *L'Amour de l'Art,* Paris 1933. — R. Cogniat, *Du Fauvisme à l'après-guerre*, in *L'Amour de l'Art*, Paris 1934. — J. Baschet, *Au temps des Fauves*, in *L'Illustration*, Paris 1935. — G. Diehl, *Le Fauvisme*, in *Beaux-Arts*, Paris 1942. — M. Feurring, *Henri Matisse und die Fauvisten*, in *Prisma*, Munich 1946.

EXPRESSIONISM

General: P. Fechter, *Der Expressionismus*, Munich 1914. — H. Bahr, *Expressionismus*, Munich 1916. — H. Walden, *Einblick in Kunst, Expressionismus, Futurismus, Kubismus*, Berlin 1917. — H. Walden, *Expressionismus, die Kunstwende*, Berlin 1918. — H. Hildebrandt, *Der Expressionismus in der Malerei*, Stuttgart 1919. — *Schöpferische Konfession*, Berlin 1920 (with contributions by Beckmann, Hölzer, Hoetger, Klee, Marc, Pechstein and others). — E. von Sydow, *Die deutsche expressionistische Kultur und Malerei*, Berlin 1920. — R. Hamann, *Die deutsche Malerei vom Rokoko bis zum Expressionismus*, Leipzig 1925. — W. Willrich, *Säuberung des Kunsttempels*, Berlin 1937 (Nazi pamphlet attacking modern art). — P. Thoene, *Modern German Art*, preface by H. Read, London 1938. — F. Schmalenbach, *Grundlinien des Frühexpressionismus*, in *Kunsthistorische Studien*, Basel 1941. — G. F. Hartlaub, *Die Graphik des Expressionismus in Deutschland*, Calw 1947. — C. Lorck, *Expressionismus*, Lübeck 1947. — P. O. Rave, *Kunstdiktatur im 3. Reich*, Hamburg 1949 (contains invaluable information regarding the fate of expressionist painters and works of art under the National-Socialist government).

A SELECT LIST OF MAGAZINES BEARING ON THE EXPRESSIONIST MOVEMENT

Zeitschrift für bildende Kunst, Leipzig 1866-1932, with appendix: *Kunstchronik* (contains, from 1907 on, regular reports on Expressionist exhibitions as well as many articles on Expressionism). — *Deutsche Kunst und Dekoration*, Darmstadt 1897-1932. — *Die Kunst*, Munich 1899-1937. — *Kunst und Künstler*, Berlin 1903-1933. — *Der Cicerone*, Leipzig 1909-1930. — *Der Sturm*, Berlin 1910-1932. — *Die Aktion*, Berlin 1911-1933 (most important years: 1911-1919). — *Der Anbruch*, Berlin, J. B. Neumann, 1917-1922. — *Das Kunstblatt*, Weimar-Potsdam-Berlin 1917-1932. — *Neue Blätter für Kunst und Kultur*, Dresden 1918-1920. — *Der Ararat*, Bulletin issued by the Goltz Gallery, Munich 1919-1921. — *Genius*, Munich 1919-1921. — *Jahrbuch der jungen Kunst*, Leipzig 1920-1924. — *Der Querschnitt*, Berlin 1921-1936. — *L'Amour de l'Art*, Paris 1934. — *Das Wort*, Moscow 1936-1939.

DIE BRÜCKE

E. L. Kirchner, *Chronik K(ünstler) G(emeinschaft) Brücke*, 1913, with woodcuts by Heckel, Kirchner, Müller, Schmidt-Rottluff (privately printed; reprinted in catalogue of the exhibition *Paula Modersohn und die Maler der Brücke*, with contributions by A. Rüdlinger and W. F. Arntz, Kunsthalle, Bern 1948; extensive bibliography). — P. F. Schmidt, *Blütezeit der Dresdener "Brücke,"* in *Aussaat*, Lorch 1947.

NEW ASSOCIATION OF MUNICH ARTISTS (Neue Künstler-Vereinigung München)

O. Fischer, *Das neue Bild, Veröffentlichung der Neuen Künstler-Vereinigung*, Munich 1912 (containing a narrative account of the group, studies of the artists, and a critique of the defection of Kandinsky, Marc, Kubin, and Münter). — Catalogue of the exhibition *Der Blaue Reiter*, Munich, September-October 1949 (with an historical study by Ludwig Grote of art life in Munich from 1900 to the advent of the Blue Rider; well documented).

ABSTRACT ART

Der Sturm, edited by H. Walden, Berlin 1910-1932. — W. Kandinsky, *Über das Geistige in der Kunst*, Munich 1912. English edition: *The Art of Spiritual Harmony*, London 1914. American edition: *Concerning the Spiritual in Art* (Documents of Modern Art 5), New York 1947. French edition: *Du spirituel dans l'art*, Paris 1949. — *De Stijl*, edited by T. van Doesburg, Leyden and Paris 1917-1932. — *Ma-buch neuer Künstler*, edited by L. Kassàk and L. Moholy-Nagy, Vienna 1922. — T. van Doesburg, *Grundbegriffe der neuen gestaltenden Kunst*, Bauhausbücher 6, Munich 1925. — W. Kandinsky, *Abstrakte Kunst*, in *Der Cicerone*, No. 13, Leipzig 1925. — P. Mondrian, *Die neue Gestaltung, Neo-plastizismus, Nieuwe Beelding*, Bauhausbücher 5, Munich 1925. — W. Kandinsky, *Punkt und Linie zu Fläche*, Bauhausbücher 9, Munich 1926. — K. Malevitch, *Die*

gegenstandslose Welt, Bauhausbücher 11, Munich 1927. — *Cahiers d'Art*, Paris 1931. Inquiry into abstract art. Articles by Mondrian (No. 1), Léger (No. 3), W. Baumeister, (No. 4), Kandinsky, A. Dörner, Arp (No. 7-8). — H. Klump, *Abstraktion in der Malerei: Kandinsky, Feininger, Klee*, Berlin 1932. — *Abstraction-Création*, Paris 1932-1936. — A. H. Barr, *Cubism and Abstract Art*, New York 1936. — *Abstract Art*, Proceedings of a Congress devoted to the abstract in painting, photography and architecture, held at the University of Witwatersrand, Johannesburg 1937. — *Plastique*, 1937-1939. — Gabo and Nicholson, *Circle*, International Survey of Constructive Art, London 1938. — W. Kandinsky, *L'Art concret*, in *XXᵉ siècle*, No. 1, Paris 1938. — *Abstrakt-Konkret*, Bulletin of Galerie des Eaux-Vives, 12 Nos., Zurich 1944-1945. — S. Janis, *Abstract and Surrealist Art in America*, New York 1944. — *American Abstract Artists*, New York 1946. — P. Mondrian, *Plastic Art and Pure Plastic Art, 1937, and Other Essays, 1941-1943*, New York 1947. — O. Domnick, *Die schöpferischen Kräfte in der abstrakten Malerei*, Bergen 1947. — G. Kepes, *Language of Vision*, introduction by S. Giedion, Chicago 1947. — L. Moholy-Nagy, *The New Vision, from Material to Architecture* and *Abstract of an Artist*, New York 1947. — *Réalités Nouvelles*, Yearbook, Paris 1947, 1953. — *Pour ou contre l'art abstrait*, in *Cahier des Amis de l'Art*, Paris 1947. — M. Seuphor, *L'Art abstrait, ses origines, ses premiers maîtres*, Paris 1949. — M. Shapiro, *Nature of Abstract Art*, reprinted from *Marxist Quarterly*, vol. I, No. 1, n.d. — *L'Art d'Aujourd'hui*, Paris 1949-1953. — Catalogue of the De Stijl Exhibition, Amsterdam 1951.

THE BAUHAUS

Programm des Staatlichen Bauhauses in Weimar, 1919. First announcement of the Bauhaus with preface by W. Gropius. — *Staatliches Bauhaus*, Weimar, 1919-1923, Weimar-Munich 1923. — Bauhaus publications (Bauhausbücher), A. Langen Verlag, Munich: (1) W. Gropius, *Internationale Architektur*, 1925. (2) P. Klee, *Pädagogisches Skizzenbuch*, 1925. (3) A. Meyer, *Ein Versuchshaus des Bauhauses in Weimar*, 1925. (4) O. Schlemmer, *Die Bühne im Bauhaus*, 1925. (5) P. Mondrian, *Die neue Gestaltung, Neoplastizismus, Nieuwe Beelding*, 1925. (6) T. van Doesburg, *Grundbegriffe der neuen gestaltenden Kunst*, 1925. (7) W. Gropius, *Neue Arbeiten der Bauhauswerkstätten*, 1925. (8) L. Moholy-Nagy, *Malerei, Photographie, Film*, 1925. (9) W. Kandinsky, *Punkt und Linie zu Fläche*, 1926. (10) J.J.P. Oud, *Holländische Architektur*, 1926. (11) K. Malevitch, *Die gegenstandslose Welt: Begründung und Erklärung des russischen Suprematismus*, 1927. (12) W. Gropius, *Bauhausbauten Dessau*, 1930. (13) A. Gleizes, *Kubismus*, 1928. (14) L. Moholy-Nagy, *Von Material zu Architektur*, 1929. In English: *The New Vision, from Material to Architecture*, New York, 1931. — *Bauhaus Zeitschrift für Gestaltung*, Dessau, 1926-1929, 1931. — *Offset, Buch- und Werbekunst*, no. 7, Leipzig 1926, issue devoted to the Bauhaus. — W. Grohmann, *Une Ecole d'art moderne, le "Bauhaus," Académie d'une plastique nouvelle*, in *Cahiers d'Art*, no. 5, Paris 1930. — W. Gropius, *The New Architecture and the Bauhaus*, New York 1936. — *Bauhaus, 1919-28*, by H. Bayer, W. and I. Gropius, New York 1928. — *Die Maler am Bauhaus*, catalogue of the exhibition in Haus der Kunst, Munich, May-June 1950. — Catalogue of the Moholy-Nagy Exhibition, Paris 1952.

THE BLUE RIDER

Catalogue of *Erste Ausstellung der Redaktion Der Blaue Reiter* (1911-1912), Thannhauser Gallery, Munich. — Catalogue of *Zweite Ausstellung der Redaktion Der Blaue Reiter (schwarzweiss)*, Goltz Gallery, Munich, March-April 1912. (315 works in black-and-white). — W. Kandinsky, *Über das Geistige in der Kunst*, Munich 1912. — W. Kandinsky and F. Marc, *Der Blaue Reiter*, Munich 1912, 2nd edition, 1914. — F. Marc, *Briefe, Aufzeichnungen, Aphorismen*, 2 vols., Berlin 1920. — W. Kandinsky, *Der Blaue Reiter*, in *Das Kunstblatt*, no. 2, Potsdam 1931. Letter from Kandinsky to P. Westheim on the origin and development of the Blue Rider group. — W. Reich, *Der Blaue Reiter und die Musik*, in *Schweizerische Musikzeitung*, no. 8-9, Zurich 1945. — W. Haftmann, *Der Blaue Reiter*, in *Frankfurter Hefte*, no. 11, Frankfort 1949. — Catalogue of the exhibition *Der Blaue Reiter, der Weg von 1908-1914*, Haus der Kunst, Munich, September-October 1949. — J. A. Thwaites, *Le Blaue Reiter et le développement de l'art abstrait*, in *Art d'Aujourd'hui*, no. 3, Paris 1949. — K. Lankheit, *Zur Geschichte des Blauen Reiters*, in *Der Cicerone*, no. 3, Cologne 1949. — Catalogue of the exhibition *Der Blaue Reiter*, Kunsthalle, Basel, 1950.

CUBISM

V. Crastre, *Naissance du cubisme* (Céret 1910), Paris n.d. — A. Gleizes and J. Metzinger, *Du Cubisme*, Paris 1912. — G. Apollinaire, *Les peintres cubistes*, Paris 1913. In English: New York 1944. New edition: Geneva 1950. — A. J. Eddy, *Cubists and Post-Impressionism*, Chicago 1914, 2nd edition, 1919, with bibliography. — G. Coquiot, *Cubistes, futuristes, passéistes*, Paris 1914. 2nd edition, 1923. — A. Soffici, *Cubismo e futurismo*, Florence 1914. — M. Raynal, *Quelques intentions du cubisme*, Paris 1916. — H. Kahnweiler, *Der Weg zum Kubismus*, Munich 1920. Published under the pseudonym of Daniel Henry. American edition: *The Rise of Cubism*, New York 1949. — A. Gleizes, *Du cubisme et des moyens de le comprendre*, Paris 1920. — L. Rosenberg, *Cubisme et tradition*, Paris 1920. — P. E. Küppers, *Der Kubismus*, Leipzig 1920. — A. Gleizes, *Kubismus*, Bauhausbücher 13, Munich 1928. — G. Janneau, *L'Art cubiste*, Paris 1929. — C. Pavolini, *Cubismo, futurismo, espressionismo*, Bologna 1929. — *Les Expositions de Beaux-Arts et de la Gazette des Beaux-Arts, Les Créateurs du Cubisme*, Paris 1935. Catalogue with preface by M. Raynal and texts by R. Cogniat. — A. H. Barr, *Cubism and Abstract Art*, Museum of Modern Art, New York 1936. — E. Bonfante and J. Ravenna, *Arte Cubista*, Venice 1945. — A.H. Barr, *Picasso, 50 Years of his Art*, New York 1946. — *The Cubist Spirit in its Time*, Tate Gallery, London 1947. — Catalogue of the exhibition *Le Cubisme*, Musée d'Art Moderne, Paris 1953.

DADA AND SURREALISM

Cabaret Voltaire, literary and artistic digest edited by Hugo Ball, Zurich 1916. Contributions by Apollinaire, Arp, Ball, Cendrars, Hülsenbeck, Kandinsky, Marinetti, Picasso, Tzara, and others. — *Dada*, edited by T. Tzara, Nos. 1 to 4-5, Zurich 1917-1919; No. 6 (Bulletin Dada) and No. 7 (Dadaphone), Paris 1920. — J. Vaché, *Lettres de guerre*, introduction by A. Breton, Paris 1919. New edition with four prefaces by Breton, Paris 1949. — *Littérature*, 1st series edited by Aragon, Breton, Soupault 1919-1921; 2nd series edited by Breton, 1922-1924. 33 numbers, Paris 1919-1924. — R. Hülsenbeck, *Dada siegt! Eine Bilanz des Dadaismus*, Berlin 1920. — R. Hülsenbeck, *En avant dada: die Geschichte des Dadaismus*, in *Die Silbengäule*, No. 50-51, Hanover 1920. — *Le Cannibale*, edited by F. Picabia, 2 numbers, Paris 1920. — *Dada Almanach*, edited by R. Hülsenbeck, Berlin 1920. With contributions by Arp, Ball, Picabia, Ribemont-Dessaignes, Soupault, and others. — P. Massot, *De Mallarmé à 391*, Saint-Raphaël 1922. — A. Schinz, *Dadaïsme, poignée de documents sur un mouvement d'égarement de l'esprit humain après la Grande Guerre* (Smith College Studies in Modern Languages, vol. V, No. 1), Northampton, Mass. 1923. — A. Breton, *Les pas perdus*, Paris 1924. With important articles on Dada. — A. Breton, *Manifeste du Surréalisme; Poisson soluble*, Paris 1924. — T. Tzara, *7 manifestes dada*, Paris 1924. — *La Révolution surréaliste*, Nos. 1-12, Paris 1924-1929. — H. Ball, *Die Flucht aus der Zeit*, Munich 1927. — A. Breton, *Le Surréalisme et la peinture*, Paris 1928. 2nd edition, New York 1945. — *Le Surréalisme au service de la révolution*, Nos. 1-6, Paris 1930-1933. — L. Aragon, *La peinture au défi*, Paris 1930. — A. Breton, *Second manifeste du surréalisme*, Paris 1930. — G. Ribemont-Dessaignes, *Histoire de Dada*, in *La Nouvelle Revue Française*, June-July, Paris 1931. — G. Hugnet, *L'esprit dada dans la peinture*, in *Cahiers d'Art*, 1932 (Nos. 1-2, 6-7, 8-10), 1934 (Nos. 1-4), 1936 (Nos. 8-10), Paris. — *Minotaure*, Nos. 1-13, edited by A. Skira and E. Tériade, Paris 1933-1939. — G. Mangeot, *Histoire du Surréalisme*, Brussels 1934. — *Documents 34*, Brussels 1934. Special number: *Interventions surréalistes*. — A. Breton, *Qu'est-ce que le surréalisme?*, Brussels 1934. — G. Hugnet, *Petite anthologie poétique du surréalisme*, Paris 1934. With an important preface. — A. Breton, *Position politique du surréalisme*, Paris 1935. — J. Topass, *La pensée en révolte, essai sur le surréalisme*, Brussels 1935. — D. Gascoyne, *A Short Survey of Surrealism*, London 1935. — J. T. Soby, *After Picasso*, New York 1935. — A. H. Barr, *Fantastic Art, Dada, Surrealism*, New York 1936. — *Cahiers d'Art*, 1935 (No. 5-6), 1936 (No. 1-2), Paris. Special numbers devoted to Surrealism. — G. Hugnet, *Dada* and *In the Light of Surrealism*, in A. H. Barr's *Fantastic Art, Dada, Surrealism*, New York 1936. — J. Levy, *Surrealism*, New York 1936. — *Surrealism*, edited and with a long introduction by H. Read, London 1936. — G. Buffet-Picabia, *On demande: Pourquoi 391? Qu'est-ce que 391?* in *Plastique*, No. 2, Paris 1937. — G. Buffet, *Arthur Cravan and American Dada*, in *Transition*,

No. 27, Paris 1938. — *Dictionnaire abrégé du surréalisme*, Paris 1938. — G. Lemaître, *From Cubism to Surrealism in French Literature*, Cambridge 1941. Extensive bibliography. — W. Kern, *Zurich 1914-1918*, in *Werk*, No. 5, Zurich 1943. — S. Janis, *Abstract and Surrealist Art in America*, New York 1944. — C. Bo, *Bilancio del surrealismo*, Padua 1944. Extensive bibliography. — A. Breton, *Situation du surréalisme entre les deux guerres*, Paris 1945. Lecture given to French students at Yale University, December 10, 1942. — E. Gengenbach, *Surréalisme et christianisme*, Paris 1945. — M. Nadeau, *Histoire du surréalisme*, Paris 1945. — A. Breton and M. Duchamp, *Le Surréalisme en 1947*, catalogue of the International Surrealist Exhibition, Galerie Maeght, Paris 1947. — C. Giedion-Welcker, *Poètes à l'écart*, Bern 1947. — *Néon*, Paris 1947. — H. Arp, *On My Way, Poetry and Essays 1912-47*, Documents of Modern Art 6, New York 1948. — H. Arp, *Dadaland, Zürcher Erinnerungen aus der Zeit des ersten Weltkrieges*, in *Atlantis*, Zurich 1948. Special number. — R. Vailland, *Le Surréalisme contre la révolution*, Problèmes, Paris 1948. — H. Matarasso, *Surréalisme; poésie et art contemporains*, Paris 1949. — G. Buffet-Picabia, *Dada*, in *Art d'Aujourd'hui*, No. 7-8, Paris 1950. — G. Hugnet, *Le Surréalisme*, in *Art d'Aujourd'hui*, No. 7-8, Paris 1950. — D. Wyss, *Der Surrealismus: Eine Einführung und Deutung surrealistischer Literatur und Malerei*, Heidelberg 1950. — Special number of *La Nef*, Paris 1951.

FUTURISM

F. T. Marinetti, *Le futurisme: théories et mouvement*, Paris 1910. — *Les futuristes italiens*, catalogue of the first Futurist Exhibition, Galerie Bernheim-Jeune, Paris 1912. — U. Boccioni, *Pittura, Scultura futuriste: dinamismo plastico*, Milan 1914. — A. Soffici, *Cubismo e futurismo*, Florence 1914. — C. Carrà, *Guerra pittura*, Milan 1919. — Fillia, *Pittura futurista, realizzazioni, affermazioni, polemiche*, Turin 1919. — F. Flora, *Dal romanticismo al futurismo*, Milan 1925. — C. Pavolini, *Cubismo, futurismo, espressionismo*, Bologna 1926. — F. Cangiullo, *Le serate futuriste*, Naples 1930. — F. T. Marinetti, *Il futurismo*, in *Enciclopedia italiana...*, vol. 16, Milan 1932. — F. T. Marinetti, *Manifesti del futurismo*, 4 vols., Milan 1932. — Fillia, *Il futurismo*, Milan 1932. — V. Costantini, *Pittura italiana contemporanea*, Milan 1934. — G. Severini, *L'Italie et le futurisme*, in *L'Amour de l'Art*, Paris 1934. — N. Moscardelli, *Il trentennale del futurismo*, in *Il libro italiano nel mondo*, Rome 1940. — Tato, *Raccontato da Tato, 20 anni di futurismo*, Milan 1941. — R. T. Clough, *Looking Back at Futurism*, New York 1942. — J. T. Soby and A. H. Barr, *20th-Century Italian Art*, New York 1949. — *Cahiers d'Art*, Paris 1950. Special number.

METAPHYSICAL PAINTING

G. de Chirico, *Sull'arte metafisica*, in *Valori Plastici*, No. 4-5, Rome 1919. — C. Carrà, *Pittura metafisica*, Florence 1919. — F. Roh, *Nach-Expressionismus, Magischer Realismus, Probleme der neueren europäischen Malerei*, Leipzig 1925. — A. H. Barr, *Fantastic Art, Dada, Surrealism*, New York 1936. — V. Costantini, *La peinture italienne après le futurisme*, in *L'Amour de l'Art*, Paris 1934. — C. Zervos, *La poésie de l'énigme*, in his *Histoire de l'art contemporain*, Paris 1938. — R. Carrieri, *La pittura metafisica di de Chirico*, in *Tempo*, Rome, November 9, 1939. — U. Apollonio, *Pittura metafisica di de Chirico*, in *Popolo di Trieste*, Trieste, January 3, 1940. — M. Masciotta, *La pittura metafisica*, in *Letteratura*, No. 3, Florence 1941. — E. Vietta, *Metaphysische Malerei*, in *Das XX. Jahrhundert*, Jena, February 1941. — S. Branzi, *La pittura metafisica*, in *Camene*, Catane, July 1948. — A. Dell'Aqua, *La peinture métaphysique*, in *Cahiers d'Art*, Paris 1950.

PURISM

A. Ozenfant and C. E. Jeanneret (Le Corbusier), *Après le Cubisme*, Paris 1918. — M. Raynal, *Le purisme et la logique*, in *Valori Plastici*, No. 3, Rome 1919. — L. Vauxcelles, *L'Ecole puriste*, in *Excelsior*, Paris, January 14, 1919. — *L'Esprit Nouveau*, edited by Ozenfant and Jeanneret, Paris 1920-1925. — A. Ozenfant and C. E. Jeanneret, *Le Purisme*, in *L'Esprit Nouveau*, No. 4, Paris 1921. — A. Ozenfant, *Le Purisme*, in *Cahiers d'Art*, No. 4-5, Paris 1927. — W. George, *From Purism to Magic Realism*, in *Formes*, No. 16, Paris 1931. — R. Cogniat, *Le Purisme*, in *L'Amour de l'Art*, Paris 1933. — Le Corbusier, *Purisme*, in *Art d'Aujourd'hui*, No. 7-8, Paris 1950.

General Index

331

The Colorplates

337

Contents

Chapter-headings marked with a star refer to folding pages.

339

THIS NEW AND REVISED EDITION
OF "MODERN PAINTING"
WAS PRINTED BY THE

COLOR STUDIO

AT IMPRIMERIES RÉUNIES S. A., LAUSANNE
FOR SKIRA INC., PUBLISHERS, NEW YORK, N.Y.
FINISHED THE FIRST DAY OF APRIL
NINETEEN HUNDRED AND FIFTY-SIX